Anthropological Papers
Museum of Anthropology, University of Michigan
Number 96

The Last *Pescadores*
of Chimalhuacán, Mexico

An Archaeological Ethnography

Jeffrey R. Parsons

Ann Arbor, Michigan
2006

Printed in the United States of America
ISBN 0-915703-62-9

Cover design by Katherine Clahassey

The University of Michigan Museum of Anthropology currently publishes three monograph series: Anthropological Papers, Memoirs, and Technical Reports, as well as an electronic series in CD-ROM form. For a complete catalog, write to Museum of Anthropology Publications, 4009 Museums Building, Ann Arbor, MI 48109-1079.

Library of Congress Cataloging-in-Publication Data

Parsons, Jeffrey R.
  The last pescadores of Chimalhuacán, Mexico : an archaeological ethnography / Jeffrey R. Parsons.
        p. cm. -- (Anthropological papers / Museum of Anthropology, University of Michigan ; no. 96)
  Includes bibliographical references and index.
  ISBN-13: 978-0-915703-62-3 (alk. paper)
  ISBN-10: 0-915703-62-9 (alk. paper)
 1. Indians of Mexico--Fishing--Mexico--Santa María Chimalhuacán. 2. Indians of Mexico--Ethnobotany--Mexico--Santa María Chimalhuacán. 3. Indians of Mexico--Food--Mexico--Santa María Chimalhuacán. 4. Fish remains (Archaeology)--Mexico--Santa María Chimalhuacán. 5. Plant remains (Archaeology)--Mexico--Santa María Chimalhuacán. 6. Wetland ecology--Mexico--Santa María Chimalhuacán. 7. Aquatic plants--Mexico--Santa María Chimalhuacán. 8. Aquaculture--Mexico--Santa María Chimalhuacán. 9. Santa María Chimalhuacán (Mexico)--Social life and customs. 10. Santa María Chimalhuacán (Mexico)--Antiquities. I. Title.
F1219.1.S227P37 2006
972'.01--dc22

                                2006024758

The paper used in this publication meets the requirements of the ANSI Standard Z39.48-1984 (Permanence of Paper)

Dedicated to the memories of my mother,
Elisabeth Oldenburg Parsons
1911-2005

and my colleague,
Alba Guadalupe Mastache
1942-2004

Contents

Tables

Figures

Plates

Preface

When I first came to the Valley of Mexico to do archaeological fieldwork in 1961, I found myself surrounded by a viable, living economy that emphasized subsistence agriculture and traditional craft production. Over the next decade, in the course of our surveys and excavations, I saw people walking behind horse- and ox-drawn plows working the soil, the use of hand tools for hoeing and weeding crops, and the extraction of maguey sap and its subsequent fermentation to make pulque. When I looked a little closer into some communities it was easy enough to observe chinampa farmers at work in the southern Valley, the manufacture of mold-made pottery at villages near Teotihuacan, the continuing use of backyard sweat baths (*temascales*) in settlements southeast of Chalco, and an archaic form of saltmaking at Nexquipayac on the northeastern shore of Lake Texcoco. Eventually I stumbled across some collectors of edible aquatic insects along the south shore of Lake Texcoco.

I quickly realized that the living people I saw engaged in these activities were the biological and cultural descendants of the prehistoric populations who had produced and discarded the archaeological remains I was helping to investigate. This realization helped make the potsherds, stone tool fragments, and ruins of ancient domestic and public architecture that I encountered in such abundance much more meaningful to me. In his study of modern (mid-1950s) traditional agriculture, William Sanders (1957) had already demonstrated the importance of studying the present in order to better understand the past in this region. Although I did not immediately imitate Sanders' example of using ethnography to assist in interpreting the archaeological record, my interest in this kind of endeavor gradually increased as the years went by. However, because the archaeological research I was involved in was so interesting and so demanding of my time and energy, I did not turn to ethnography until the mid-1980s.

By that time, things had changed a lot in the Valley of Mexico. Mexico City and its suburbs had expanded tremendously. Agricultural production had become increasingly mechanized and commercialized. Many artisans had abandoned their traditional crafts in the face of overwhelming competition from cheap, industrialized foods, textiles, plastics, and metals. Entire landscapes had been swallowed up by massive new industrial, residential, commercial agricultural, and highway and mass-transit construction. Entire lifeways had changed in response to these and other forces. Increasingly, rural villages became suburban bedroom communities inhabited by people whose livelihoods were derived not from work in the surrounding fields or in local workshops, but in distant urban factories and offices and shops to which they commuted daily from their homes.

By the 1980s I had come to understand that what I had observed in the Valley of Mexico during the 1960s were the "last gasps" of traditional lifeways deeply rooted in the precolumbian past. I realized that even the few surviving remnants of these lifeways would soon vanish from the scene, and that future archaeologists working in central Mexico would not have the opportunity that Sanders and I had had of observing at their work the living descendants of the prehistoric people we were studying. This realization motivated me to undertake three ethnographic studies between 1983 and 1992 of activities I had observed in a much more general way in earlier years: maguey utilization in the area around Ixmiquilpan, Hidalgo, just northeast of the Valley of Mexico (in 1983-1986) (Parsons and Parsons 1990); saltmaking at Nexquipayac, on the northeastern shore of Lake Texcoco (in 1988) (Parsons 2001); and aquatic-insect collection at Chimalhuacán, in the southeastern corner of Lake Texcoco (in 1992) (this monograph).

Originally I envisioned this monograph as a descriptive account of what I observed at Chimalhuacán in 1992, and its historical antecedents and environmental contexts (approximately what is now contained in Chapters 2, 3, 4, and 5 of this monograph). However, as I began to work up my fieldnotes and to pursue some promising library research—paleoenvironmental, geomorphological, historical, and ethnographic—I came to realize that the vestiges of the aquatic economy I observed at Chimalhuacán in 1992, and the historically described uses of aquatic resources in the Valley of Mexico, were very similar to activities in other parts of the world that I had begun to read more about. I also discovered that geomorphological and biological studies in wetland environments in other regions contained a rich store of information that was potentially relevant to the less-well-studied Valley of Mexico, whose natural environment had been so radically transformed prior to the modern era.

One thing led to another, and the short, descriptive monograph that I had first envisioned expanded significantly over the past decade. Chapter 5, my original contribution, became a relatively short section in the middle of a much longer study of broadly comparative scope. In this monograph I devote considerable attention to the details of production, processing, and consumption of aquatic resources in traditional aquatic economies in other parts of the world. My principal rationale for including so much comparative detail is because many readers of this work will probably have only limited familiarity with how aquatic resources have been traditionally utilized in wetlands in other parts of the world—just as I did when I embarked on this study. Too often, I suspect, the use of ethnographic analogy in archaeological investigation tends to focus too narrowly on a single region. In trying to develop credible and compelling archaeological implications of the ethnographic work I did at Chimalhuacán, I have felt obliged to go as far afield in time and space as the available information enabled me.

Acknowledgments

Many people have assisted me in the course of this study, many more than I can now hope to acknowledge or even, I fear, to remember. However, I will do my best, and to those I may have forgotten, please forgive me: you know who you are. William Sanders introduced me to the Valley of Mexico some forty-five years ago, and inspired virtually all of my subsequent archaeological and ethnographic studies there. His pioneering study of traditional modern agriculture was the principal model for my own ethnographic studies, and he has continued to encourage me in these undertakings. For forty years my wife, Mary Hrones Parsons, has been my principal research associate in the field, in the laboratory, and in the library. Her support and expertise have been essential to this study, and to many previous ones. My 1992 field study was funded in large part by the University of Michigan Museum of Anthropology. My fieldwork was very significantly aided by Mari Carmen Serra Puche, then Director of the Museo Nacional de Antropología in Mexico City, who arranged a loan to me of a Museum pick-up truck for use as a field vehicle. Mari Carmen had also accompanied me on two earlier visits to Chimalhuacán, and encouraged me to continue and expand my investigation there.

Carmen Aguilera informed me about her early work with fishermen in Lake Zumpango, and gave me several articles and photographs. Peter Attema provided me with several useful references to the work of himself and others in and around the Pontine marshes of southern Italy. Elizabeth Brumfiel generously read and critiqued an earlier version of this monograph. Edward Calnek provided me with important insights about the Pantitlán shrine, and with leads to relevant ethnohistoric sources. In 1963 Thomas Charlton and I worked together in archaeological surveys around the northeastern shores of ex-Lake Texcoco, where, for the first time, I encountered the living remnants of the traditional aquatic lifeways that came to interest me so much in later years. Sergio and the late Karen Chavez, and John Janusek a few years later, alerted me to several important references on the Titicaca Basin. Charles Cleland, John Halsey, and John O'Shea gave me the benefit of their knowledge about chert gunflints of the early historic period in North America—this became potentially relevant as we discovered, during our 2003 survey of central Lake Texcoco, many chert artifacts that may have been eighteenth-century gunflints.

Robert Cobean and Kenneth Hirth provided me with useful information about chert sources in central Mexico, and Bob Cobean has advised me for many years on Postclassic ceramic chronology—knowledge that I relied on heavily during our 2003 survey of central Lake Texcoco. Bernice (Sunday) Eiselt and Richard Ford provided me with several important references on traditional aquatic economy in the U.S. Great Basin. Kent Flannery identified several insect and bird species on the basis of my photographs. Charles Frederick has provided me with several unpublished reports of his geoarchaeological studies in Lake Xaltocán and Lake Chalco. Augustin Holl provided me with a number of important references to aquatic resource use in West Africa. Thomas Moore arranged for identifications by Richard C. Froeschner (whom I have never met, but to whom I am very grateful) of the insect specimens I brought back from Chimalhuacán.

Robert Kelly provided me with several key references and photographs from his research in the U.S. Great Basin. Catherine Liot introduced me to her study area around Lake Sayula, Jalisco, a few years ago, and continued to encourage my own lacustrine research during her visit to our fieldwork locality in central Lake Texcoco during 2003. Luis Morett collaborated with me as co-field director of our Lake Texcoco archaeological survey in 2003, and the assistance of his staff and students at the Museo Nacional de Agricultura, Universidad Autónoma de Chapingo, was instrumental in our lakebed fieldwork. The 2003 fieldwork was funded by the National Geographic Society and the University of Michigan. Deborah Nichols and the late Guadalupe Mastache have encouraged my lakebed work for many years. Helen Pollard provided me with a number of important references and reprints about the archaeology and geoarchaeology of Lake Pátzcuaro, Michoacán. Janet Richards gave me a number of useful references to aspects of aquatic resource use in the Nile Valley.

I have learned a great deal about atlatls and their uses from John Speth. John Staller made me aware of an important paper on landscape domestication that he co-authored, and provided me with some important references on the use of fish poisons in South America. Yoko Sugiura has provided me with several opportunities to visit her study area in the marshlands near Toluca, west of the Valley of Mexico, and for many years she has actively encouraged my lacustrine studies in the Valley of Mexico. Eduardo Williams has given me a great deal of information about the use of aquatic resources in and around Lake Cuitzeo, Michoacán. Henry Wright provided me with several very useful references on the Marsh Arabs.

I am very grateful to Kay Clahassey for her invaluable assistance in the preparation of illustrations for this monograph, and to Sally Mitani and Jill Rheinheimer for their diligence in editing the manuscript. I thank Anne Murray, Curator of Archives and Documentation at the Museum of Ethnography, Stockholm, Sweden, for her assistance in arranging for me to use several 1930s photographs from that Museum's archives. I also thank Imrgard W. Johnson for her help in obtaining several photographs of Lake Texcoco taken by Bodil Christensen in the 1930s. Charlene Stachnik and other staff members of the University of Michigan's fine research library were very helpful in procuring many essential volumes, some of them quite obscure.

Our 2003 archaeological survey in central Lake Texcoco was made possible and greatly facilitated by the cooperation of the Dirección de Arqueología, Instituto Nacional de Antropología e História, and by Ing. Alberto Luck, Director of the Proyecto Lago de Texcoco, Gerencia Regional de Aguas del Valle de México, who provided us with the necessary permits and authorizations.

Finally, I am tremendously indebted to Porfirio Peralta and his large and amiable family, my informants at Chimalhuacán in 1992. Porfirio is, in fact, the "last pescador" of Chimalhuacán. Without his cooperation and good will, my study and this monograph could never have happened.

Jeffrey R. Parsons
August, 2006

Introduction

Ancient people were attracted to wet areas not because they wanted to live in the wet, but because of the wealth in plants and animals (wildfowl, fish, eels, mammals, reeds, withes, and plant foods), the ease of travel and transport (in the absence of roads), and in some cases because of the isolation and defense offered by certain wetlands.
[*Coles 1998:7*]

[F]our centuries of scholarship have not sufficed to bring limnological knowledge of the Valley of Mexico up to the stage attained by the Aztecs and used by them in their daily lives.
[*Deevey 1957:228*]

Half a century ago, Edward Deevey clearly recognized the fundamental, and even unique, economic and sociocultural importance of lacustrine landscapes in Middle America. He also realized that western scholarship in general neither appreciated nor understood the full significance of wetland resources in this part of the world during precolumbian times. Deevey's prescient insights may have been founded on his realization that prehispanic Middle America, alone among the world's major hearths of ancient complex society, lacked domestic herbivores (like llamas and alpacas in Andean South America, and sheep, goats, and cattle in much of the Old World). In other regions, these domesticated animals formed the basis of pastoral and agro-pastoral economies fully complementary to those based on agriculture and horticulture, and provided (among other things) a rich store of high quality animal proteins.

The neglect by western scholarship noted by Deevey may have culminated in the influential assertions by Michael Harner (1977) and Marvin Harris (1978, 1979) that the agriculturally based diet of the large, urbanized populations of late prehispanic central Mexico was so lacking in protein that they resorted to mass cannibalism to supply this critical nutritional deficiency. This assertion was vigorously opposed by other scholars, such as Bernard Ortiz de Montellano who argued that

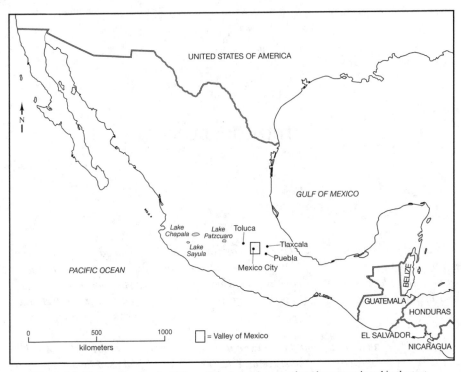

Figure 1.1. Mexico, showing the Valley of Mexico and some other places mentioned in the text.

the Aztecs . . . lived in a resource-rich environment and exploited a superb variety of foods, which even in small amounts would have remedied all the shortcomings of a corn diet. . . . the Basin of Mexico was not populated near the limits of its carrying capacity and . . . the Aztecs were neither malnourished nor suffering from protein or vitamin deficiencies. [Ortiz de Montellano 1990:119]

Ortiz de Montellano's conclusion (originally developed in Ortiz de Montellano 1978) parallels ideas expressed by Price (1978), and is based largely on the well-documented utilization of protein-rich aquatic resources from the huge wetlands in the central Valley of Mexico (Fig. 1.1). I agree that Harner and Harris seriously underestimated the role of these aquatic resources in supplying high quality protein and other nutrients. However, I believe Harris correctly emphasized the fact that prehispanic Mesoamerica was the only one of the "populous ancient states" that lacked domestic herbivores (Harris 1979:335). As noted above, in Andean America and in much of the Old World, pastoral economies complemented agriculture and supplied large, urbanized populations with substantial quantities of animal protein in the form of meat, cheese, or milk, in addition to fiber, hides, fertilizer, fuel, and transport. Following the lead of others, it seems to me that a full answer to the protein deficiency question raised by Harner and Harris is to be found in a fuller understanding of the very aquatic resources that they dismissed as irrelevant.

Western Bias and the Unique Aspects of Ancient Mesoamerica

As Deevey forewarned long ago, Harner, Harris, and many other western scholars have continued to incompletely understand the role of aquatic resources in the traditional economies of Middle America and, especially, in the most highly urbanized areas of Mesoamerica. Western scholars like Harner and Harris saw that aquatic resources were of secondary, or even tertiary, importance in the ancient Old World civilizations most familiar to them, all of whom had a major pastoral component. This was especially true for all aquatic flora and for all aquatic fauna apart from waterfowl and fish. Edible resources like algae and aquatic insects, with enormous productive and nutritional potential, were simply dismissed as irrelevant, or ignored altogether. For ancient Old World civilizations, this may not have been an altogether unreasonable point of view. However, such reasoning seems unsound when applied to ancient Mesoamerica, where a pastoral component was absent.

Horn (1984) and Coles (1998) have suggested, correctly I think, that part of this neglect of wetland resources by western scholars derives from an inherent and deeply embedded bias in Western culture against marshes and swamps as places full of disease, foul odors, pestilence, and sinister forces. In modern times such prejudice has taken the form of concerted efforts to drain wetlands and convert them into agricultural land. Some of this prejudice has apparently derived from the role of marshes in harboring mosquitoes, the vectors of endemic malaria—an undeniable and very serious problem in many wetlands in modern and ancient times. In this regard, too, Deevey's insights about the unique character of Middle American wetlands seem right on the mark: malaria was absent in the New World prior to its introduction from Europe and Africa after the early sixteenth century (Dunn 1965; Newman 1976).

Some of these issues had been anticipated by the Mexican anthropologist Eduardo Dávalos (1954) who argued that many Western scholars were biased in their characterization of the prehispanic Mesoamerican diet:

> *[English translation]* Classified as agriculturalists who lacked large domestic animals of the type that provided abundant meat and milk, [ancient Mesoamericans] have been considered an underfed people who, because of the supposed lack of protein in their diet, resorted to cannibalism. [Dávalos 1954:103]

Dávalos went on to discuss the abundant historic documentation of the great variety and nutritional value of the traditional prehispanic diet in the Valley of Mexico, with particular attention to nonagricultural aquatic resources. He also noted the documented prohibitions of the consumption of human flesh in Aztec society, and the restriction of this activity to a few important priests on major ritual occasions. A few years earlier, Muller (1952) had called attention to some of these same data. Muller's and Dávalos' prescient observations were largely ignored until decades later when some other scholars began to seriously consider the importance of nonagricultural resources in the Valley of Mexico (e.g., Farrar 1966; Furst 1978; Moreno 1969; Rojas 1985; Santley and Rose 1979). By the late 1980s, after reading Rojas' (1985) comprehensive discussion of the historically documented "harvesting" of aquatic resources in the former wetlands of the Valley of Mexico, I realized the need for additional archaeological and ethnographic study.

Agriculture, Pastoralism, and Wild Resources: Ethnographic and Archaeological Perspectives

Most scholars, myself included, who have studied food production in ancient Meso-america have focused primarily on seed-based agriculture. This is true even for several out-standing studies of the role of wetlands in ancient economies (e.g., Armillas 1971; Harrison 1978; Puleston 1978; Siemens 1998; Sluyter 1994). Discussions of prehispanic carrying capacity in the Valley of Mexico have rarely, if ever, considered the potential contribution of aquatic resources (e.g., Evans 1980; Evans and Gould 1982; Gorenflo 1996; Gorenflo and Gale 1986; Hassig 1981, 1986; Ivanhoe 1978; Offner 1980; Parsons 1976; Sanders et al. 1979; Whitmore and Williams 1998; Williams 1989). One textbook on Mesoamerican prehistory even stated that "in the highland valleys [of Mesoamerica] the surest way of producing a surplus was to plant maize everywhere" (Blanton et al. 1981:174). This ten-dency to downplay the variability and diversity in prehispanic Mesoamerican subsistence has been critiqued over the past quarter century by some Mexican anthropologists, both archaeologists and ethnographers, who have studied traditional adaptations to wetlands (Albores 1995:41-52; Serra 1980, 1988; Sugiura 1998; Sugiura and Serra 1983).

While there is a huge literature on Mesoamerican agriculture (much of it synthesized recently by Whitmore and Turner 2002), other aspects of the Mesoamerican food quest have not been ignored. For example, ethnobotanists and geographers have long been interested in the dietary contribution of wild plants (e.g., Bye 1981; Messer 1972; Wilken 1970), and entomologists have addressed the role of edible insects in the traditional Me-soamerican diet (Hitchcock 1962; Ramos-Elorduy 1999; Ramos-Elorduy and Pino 1996). These nonagricultural foods, together with some cultivated cacti (maguey [*Agave* sp.] and nopal [*Opuntia* sp.]) (Parsons and Parsons 1990) and trees (e.g., *ramon* [*Brosimum alicastrum*]) (Puleston 1968, 1978), have often been recognized as important, especially in terms of their nutritional input and as emergency foods. However, the economic im-portance of these wild aquatic resources and cultivated trees and cacti has usually been regarded (however implicitly) as secondary relative to that of the cultivated annual seed crops. This has also been true for Egypt's Nile Valley where scenes of fishing and fowling are abundant in murals on the walls of ancient tombs (e.g., Figs. 1.2 and 1.3).

Interest in "wild" resources as supplements, or even as complements, to ancient ag-ricultural and agro-pastoral production has developed in other parts of the world over the past several decades. Many researchers have drawn attention to the significance of wild resources in societies that are usually regarded as agricultural or agro-pastoral: (1) archaeologists including O'Shea (1989), working in interior North America; Robb and Van Hove (2003), working in Italy; Sutton (1974), Muzzolini (1993), and Erlandson (2001), working across north-central Africa; and J.D. Clark (1971), Wetterstrom (1993), and Murray (2000:636), working in the Nile Valley; (2) paleo-ethnobotanists including Korstanje (2001), working in northwest Argentina; (3) entomologists with a broadly

Figure 1.2. Netting waterfowl in the Nile Valley (from Darby et al. 1977:1:267).

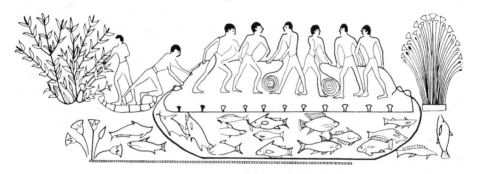

Figure 1.3. Netting fish in the Nile Valley (from Darby et al. 1977:1:345).

comparative perspective on insects as human food (e.g., Bodenheimer 1951; Boyd 1968, 1974; Boyd and McGinty 1981); and (4) ethnographers who have published accounts (often in journals primarily devoted to archaeology) of the importance of insects and aquatic resources in traditional economies in many parts of the world (e.g., Allen 1974; Posey 1978).

Wild resources can buffer periods of scarcity or uncertainty in agricultural and pastoral production, and they often stand out as essential components of local economies; access to them can enter into considerations of territoriality, pioneering expansion into unoccupied terrain, and intergroup exchange. Some archaeologists working in southeast Asia have called attention to the continuum that often exists in that region between hunting and gathering economies and agricultural economies, and the ease with which specific societies can oscillate between the two modes of production, even over relatively short time periods (e.g., Griffin 1981; Peterson 1981).

A common theme in many of these studies is the primary importance of aquatic environments as sources of edible wild plants and animals. Marshes, lakes, estuaries, rivers and riverine deltas are all richly stocked with abundant and dependable fauna and flora that can be effectively procured with traditional technologies. Carl Sauer (1962, and in many earlier publications) had long emphasized the importance of aquatic resources in the economy of early humans. Sutton's (1974) intriguing concept of the "aqualithic" era of early cultural development across north-central Africa; Erlandson's (2001) recent broadly comparative discussion of the aquatic foundation of ancient human economies; recent archaeological studies of ancient wetland adaptations around Lake Chad in north-central Africa (Breunig et al. 1996; Gronenborn 1998); Attema's (1993, 1996) investigations in and around the Pontine Marshes of southern Italy, in which he demonstrated the long-neglected economic importance of these marshlands in pre-Roman times; and a variety of studies in wetlands along the British coast (Fulford et al. 1997) represent extensions of Sauer's original insights in Old World settings. Similarly, New World archaeologists working in Andean South America (e.g., Moseley 1975), in North America (e.g., Bernick 1998; Purdy 2001), and in Mesoamerica (e.g., Blake et al. 1992; Niederberger 1979; Serra 1988) have emphasized the primary role of wetland resources—and in the case of Andean South America and Mesoamerica, it has become increasingly evident that these resources probably provided a significant component of the economic foundation of the earliest complex societies in these regions. Hayden (1990) has developed a similar line of reasoning from a worldwide comparative perspective.

However, most of this considerable interest in aquatic and other "wild" resources has been directed most effectively at relatively small, comparatively uncentralized, pre-state societies in the ancient world. Harris' most essential question has still not been fully addressed, especially not by archaeologists: how did the largest, most highly urbanized Mesoamerican societies, whose economies lacked a pastoral component, manage to provide their large, dense populations with enough protein? This monograph, building on the earlier efforts of others, extends and amplifies our understanding of the role of aquatic resources in ancient Mesoamerica.

Wetland Ecology

The biology of aquatic wildlife is, of course, closely linked to the ecology of the organic food chain in wetlands (e.g., Odum 1975; Orme 1990; Williams 1990). Ecologists have noted the truly impressive "net primary productivity" of marshlands:

> The biological yield of wetlands is enormous. They are amongst the most productive eco-systems in the world, rivaled only by some tropical rainforests and the most intensively cultivated areas of land, such as prime corn fields in the Midwest of the U.S. . . . Varia-tions of net primary productivity within different wetland types are not known globally, but Richardson (1979) has calculated the relative productivity of some North American wetlands on the basis of tonnes per hectare per year, all of which exceed grasslands . . . by a factor of 2-5 [Table 1.1].
>
> Many wetland plants . . . are perennials and are nearly all leaf with little or no woody or thickened tissues. Therefore they are constant and efficient converters of solar energy (photosynthesis) to fix carbon and create biomass. In addition, their root systems are specially adapted to take up inorganic nutrients and incorporate them into organic forms. Moreover, repeated flooding and/or tidal flux provides constant new supplies of nutrients and circulates others. [Williams 1990:22]

Table 1.1. Productivity of North American wetlands.

Type	Tonnes/hectare/year
cattail marshes	27.4
reed marshes	21.0
freshwater tidal	16.2
swamp forests	10.5
sedge-dominated marshes	10.4
bogs, fens, muskegs	9.1
grasslands	5.1

(After Richardson 1979)

It is important to realize that much of the natural productivity of wetland plants cannot be directly appropriated by humans or by other higher-level animal consumers. Humans appropriate this productivity by harvesting the plants and animals that, in turn, feed directly upon the decayed remains of lower-order plants and animals in wetland settings:

> The greatest food value [for humans and other higher-order animals] of wetlands comes from the death of the plants to form detritus on which heterotrophic organisms such as larvae, fungi, bacteria, and protozoa thrive. This forms the basis for the aquatic food web of high-yielding animals and fish such as salmon, crabs, shrimps, and worms. . . . Thus, the wetland can be regarded as "farmlands of the aquatic environment" . . . where large volumes of food are produced. . . .
>
> Although the relationship between wetlands, net primary productivity and abundant invertebrate life, and hence fish and animal life, is beyond doubt, the mechanisms of the food chain are imperfectly understood. *First*, the process of decomposition on which the productivity depends, and how it relates to the food chain, is not fully known, and rates of decomposition will vary with a host of local physical factors, including salinity, flow, and . . . temperature. *Secondly*, the efficiency of the wider food chain depends on the export or flushing of the nutrients from the wetlands to other areas (e.g., estuaries or further out to sea) on the assumption that detritus is the main source of nutrients. . . . the pathways whereby the nutrients are incorporated into food chains is not well established. It is done either by the grazing of living plants or by the consumption of dead material by lower-level hetero-trophs, which in turn become the indirect source of wetland-derived nutrients to higher-level consumers. [Williams 1990:23-24]

E.P. Odum characterizes freshwater marshes, where the oceanic tidal forces that circulate nutrients in coastal marshlands are absent, as

> [n]aturally fertile ecosystems. Tidal action, of course, is absent, but *periodic fluctuation in water levels resulting from seasonal and annual rainfall variations often accomplishes the same thing in terms of maintaining long-range stability and fertility* [emphasis added]. Fires during dry periods consume accumulated organic matter thereby deepening the water-holding basins and aiding subsequent aerobic decomposition and release of soluble nutrients, thus increasing the rate of production. In fact, if such events as drawdown and fire do not occur, the buildup of sediments and peat (undecayed organic matter) tends to lead to the invasion of terrestrial woody vegetation. . . .
>
> In addition . . . marshes are valuable in maintaining water tables in adjacent ecosystems. [Odum 1975:183-84]

Referring to Asian aquaculture, Odum provides insight into the managed productivity of fish in wetland settings:

> *Since shallow bodies of water can be as productive as an equal area of land* [emphasis added], aquaculture can be a useful supplement to agriculture, especially for the production of high-protein food. Aquaculture is a highly developed art and science in oriental countries where large yields of algae, fish, and shellfish are obtained from managed but semi-natural bodies of fresh and salt water. The approach to fish culture . . . is greatly influenced by population density. Where man is crowded and hungry, ponds are managed for their yields of herbivores, such as carp; yields of 1000-5000 lbs/acre/year [1140-5680 kg/hectare/year] can be obtained (more if supplemental food is added). Where man is not crowded or hungry, sport fish are what is desired; since these fish are usually carnivores produced at the end of long food chains, the yields are much less, 100-500 lbs/acre/year [114-568 kg/hectare/year]. [Odum 1975:183]

The Scope and Objectives of This Monograph

In this monograph I have three interrelated objectives, similar to those of my earlier study of saltmaking at nearby Nexquipayac (Parsons 2001):

(1) To describe the last gasps of the aquatic economy in the Valley of Mexico as I observed them during the summer months of 1992 at the ex-village (now a Mexico City suburb) of Chimalhuacán in the remnants of southeastern Lake Texcoco. This economy has literally vanished before my eyes during the decades in which I have worked in the Valley of Mexico, and it deserves to be recorded in fuller detail before it vanishes altogether over the next few years.

(2) To consider my ethnographic observations at Chimalhuacán in the broader context of relevant geomorphological, historical, ethnographic, and archaeological documentation available from the Valley of Mexico and from several other parts of the world. I am convinced that such a broadly comparative perspective can help explain how aquatic resources were procured, processed, and consumed over the long sweep of prehistoric time in the Valley of Mexico.

(3) To develop realistic expectations, on the basis of these data, about those components of the archaeological record that should prove useful in future studies of the ancient aquatic economy in the Valley of Mexico and across the wetlands of central Mexico, and perhaps in other regions as well. This effort necessarily includes an appreciation of both the possibilities and the limitations of archaeology to address the central issues of how prehistoric peoples utilized the wetlands at their disposal.

My emphasis throughout is on the saline lakes in the Valley of Mexico, particularly on Lake Texcoco, by far the largest expanse of open water and marshland in the region, and the only major sector of this wetland zone where agricultural production was not significant in later prehispanic and modern times, although Ávila (1991) has shown that chinampa agriculture was developed in late prehispanic times along the southwestern lake shore where in-flowing streams provided localized concentrations of freshwater.

In thinking about the economic significance of wetlands in densely inhabited regions like the Valley of Mexico, I have been impressed by some of the ideas advanced in "landscape domestication," as it has been recently articulated by several scholars (e.g., Terrell et al. 2003). Some of these ideas about the archaeology of landscapes have been around for many years. Pedro Armillas (1971), working in the southern Valley of Mexico, called attention to all components of a productive landscape, not just the strictly agricultural. Armillas, in turn, noted the fundamental pioneering of the concept of landscape archaeology by British archaeologists and geographers going back to the 1930s. This reasoning requires that any study of plant and animal domestication must consider not only those well-studied plants like maize and wheat, and those well-studied animals like llamas and sheep, but also those "wild" plants and animals that were managed and exploited in closer concert with nature. From such a conceptual foundation, a legitimate question might be: to what extent did the Aztecs and their ancestors in the Valley of Mexico "domesticate" their wetlands to render their aquatic resources more dependable and productive in a setting where pastoralism was lacking?

This monograph responds to the challenge posed long ago by Edward Deevey in his prescient critique of western scholarship relating to the study of the prehispanic aquatic economies in Middle America. We have been too focused for too long on a single dimension—seed-crop agriculture—of precolumbian production in this region. As a consequence, we may have misled both ourselves and those who depend on our findings about complementary dimensions of this production. I trust this study will help correct this imbalance, and will link the present to the past.

The Organization of This Monograph

The remainder of this monograph is organized into seven chapters. Chapter 2 describes the wetlands in the Valley of Mexico, utilizing historical and geomorphological information from that region, with insights from relevant studies of marshland ecology in comparable environments that have been more fully studied by geologists, biologists, and ecologists in the U.S. Great Basin and in the African Chad Basin. This comparative perspective seems essential because the radical and accelerating transformation of the former wetlands in the Valley of Mexico over the past four centuries in the face of drainage and urban sprawl has meant fewer opportunities for modern scholars to study its earlier environment and ecology. This description provides a backdrop for my discussion in Chapter 3 of the historically documented utilization of aquatic resources in the Valley of Mexico from the sixteenth through the twentieth centuries. Here I include many direct quotes from the historical sources that should enable the reader to appreciate the full significance of the aquatic economy in the Valley of Mexico throughout the past five centuries.

Chapter 4 provides the identifications by modern botanists and zoologists of the specific species of plants and animals that were once exploited in the Valley of Mexico wetlands. In some cases, the precise identifications remain uncertain, but the efforts of modern scholars provide important insights into the characteristics, nutritional value, and behavior of the aquatic resources once so abundantly utilized in this region. Chapter 5 presents the results of my observations of the last vestiges of the traditional aquatic economy as they existed at Chimalhuacán in southeastern Lake Texcoco during August 1992. This is my only original substantive contribution to this monograph, and it provides, of course, much of the justification for the larger effort.

Chapter 6 provides a broad comparative perspective on traditional aquatic economies to amplify the basis for using historical and ethnographic information to develop analogues for prehistoric production, processing, and consumption of aquatic resources, and to assist in making predictions about the possible archaeological manifestations of these kinds of activities in the prehispanic Valley of Mexico. This leads directly to the development, in Chapter 7, of these archaeological implications in light of the known archaeological record. Chapter 8 summarizes the most important points of the monograph, and ends with suggestions for future research.

For Spanish-language quotes from sources prior to the nineteenth century, I have provided both the original text and an English translation. For more recent Spanish-language sources, I provide only an English translation of quotations. Unless otherwise noted, the English translations are my own.

Unless otherwise noted, the photographs in this monograph were taken by the author.

The Lacustrine and Marshland Environment in the Valley of Mexico

Gazing on such wonderful sights, we did not know what to say, or whether what appeared before us was real, for on one side, on the land, there were great cities, and in the lake ever so many more, and the lake itself was crowded with canoes, and in the Causeway were many bridges at intervals, and in front of us stood the great City of Mexico, and we—we did not even number four hundred soldiers! [Bernal Diaz del Castillo 1956:192]

The physical nature of the lacustrine environment in the Valley of Mexico has radically altered since Bernal Diaz del Castillo described what he saw in 1519. The term "lake" is actually somewhat misleading, since the area commonly denoted by this term comprises not only standing water but also large expanses of marshland. Seasonal variability in rainfall has always produced major changes in water levels over any given annual cycle. Long-term climatic changes could have affected water levels over cycles of several centuries duration. Drainage, deforestation, over-grazing, salinization, alkalinization, and various types of air and water pollution over the past 400 years have produced significant long-term changes in water levels and in aquatic fauna and flora. Changing economic, sociopolitical, and ideological forces during this same period have strongly affected human lifeways in the region. In this chapter I discuss some of these changes and their impacts on lacustrine and marshland environment and ecology.

The Changing Size of the Lakes and Marshes

The Valley of Mexico is a large internal-drainage basin that measures about 8000 square kilometers in surface area (ca. 110 km north-to-south by ca. 80 km east-to-west). It is one of several internal-drainage basins that occur within the central Mexican volcanic axis (Figs. 2.1-2.3). Lacking natural external drainage, the Valley of Mexico forms a great natural saucer, rimmed by higher ground that surrounds a central depression.

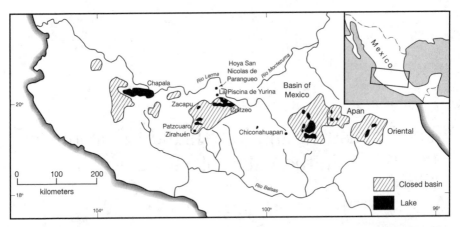

Figure 2.1. Internal-drainage basins within the central Mexican volcanic axis (adapted from Metcalfe et al. 1989:121).

Artificial drainage begun in the early seventeenth century was not completed for over 300 years (Garay 1888; Gurría 1978; Maudsley 1916; Ramírez 1976). Rainfall on the surrounding slopes and plains drained into the lowest part of the basin to form a series of interconnected shallow lakes and marshes: from north to south, Lake Zumpango, Lake Xaltocán, Lake San Cristobal, Lake Texcoco, Lake Xochimilco, and Lake Chalco (Figs. 2.2 and 2.3).[1] Of these, Lake Texcoco, with its bed at slightly below 2235 m asl, was the lowest. The bed of Lake Zumpango was some 6 m elevated, while the floors of Lakes San Cristobal and Xaltocán were about 3.5 m higher; to the south, the bottoms of Lakes Chalco and Xochimilco were about 3 m above the bed of Lake Texcoco (Beltran 1958:14-15). Lake Texcoco, at the bottom of the drainage gradient, was saline; Lakes Zumpango, Xaltocán, and San Cristobal were fresh to brackish, while Lakes Chalco and Xochimilco were freshwater, in part due to the abundance of springs along their southern margins. Although the waters of Lake Texcoco are commonly thought of as saline, there were many freshwater inputs into the lake: from its entire perimeter, many streams and small rivers flowed directly into the lake (Figs. 2.2 and 2.3). At such junctures, overall salinity was considerably reduced, especially during the annual rainy season, and there would have been some localized movement of water as freshwater currents flowed into the main lake system.

The climate of the Valley of Mexico features a highly seasonal distribution of rainfall and temperature. The fundamental division is between a four-month rainy season (June through September) and an eight-month dry season (October through May). Roughly 80% of the average annual rainfall of 600-800 mm falls during the rainy-season months, and cloud cover is significantly greater during this period as well. The oldest rainfall data I have found are from A.D. 1855-1875: during that period the average annual rainfall was 603 mm, with a low of 355 mm in 1860 and a high of 924 mm in 1865 (Reyes 1878);

---

[1]In the sixteenth-century sources, western Lake Texcoco is commonly referred to as "Lake Mexico."

Figure 2.2. The Valley of Mexico, showing place names mentioned in the text.

Figure 2.3. The Valley of Mexico as a hydrographic unit (adapted from Lorenzo 1988:257, Fig. 93).

the measuring station location is unknown. Generally speaking, rainfall increases from lower to higher elevation and from north to south within the region. There is little variation in average *maximum* daily or monthly temperatures (ca. 22-28°C) over the entire annual cycle. However, the average *minimum* temperatures are decidedly lower from November through March (ca. 1-4°C) than during the rest of the year (ca. 6-9°C) (Parsons 1971:6-7). This seasonal variability has influenced the nature of aquatic resources available over the annual cycle.

Hernán Cortés, the leader of the invading Spanish forces, described the lacustrine setting of the Aztec capital and its environs based on his observations in 1519 and 1520 (Cortés' letter, his second to the Spanish king, was dated Oct. 30, 1520, about six months before his final conquest of the Aztec military forces, and following many months of maneuvering by the Spanish forces and their Tlaxcalan allies in and around Lake Texcoco):

[E]n el dicho llano hay dos lagunas [he was speaking only of what we now call Lakes Chalco-Xochimilco and Texcoco] que casi lo ocupan todo, porque tienen canoas en torno más de cincuenta leguas. Y la una de estas dos lagunas es de agua dulce, y la otra, que es mayor, es de agua salada. Divídelas por una parte una cuadrillera pequeña de cerros muy altos que están en medio de esta llanura, y al cabo se van a juntar las dichas lagunas en un estrecho de llano que entre estos cerros y las sierras altas se hace. El cual estrecho tendrá un tiro de ballesta, y por entre una laguna y la otra, y las ciudades y otras poblaciones que están en las dichas lagunas, contratan las unas con las otras en sus canoas por el agua, sin haber necesidad de ir por la tierra. Y porque esta laguna salada grande crece y mengua por sus mareas según hace la mar todas las crecientes, corre el agua de ella a la otra dulce tan recio como si fuese caudaloso río, y por consiguiente a las menguantes va la dulce a la salada. [Cortés 1963:71-72]

[English translation] [T]he plain is almost filled up by two lakes whose perimeter measures about 50 leagues [ca. 210 km]. One of these lakes is of freshwater, while the water of the other, which is larger, is salty. These lakes are divided by a small range of high hills which are in the middle of the plain, and the two lakes join at a narrows between these hills and the high sierras [to the west]. This narrows is about a cannon-shot wide, and people can travel in boats between the lakes and between the different lake settlements without the need to go by land. And because the large salty lake expands and contracts like the sea according to the tides, the water flows from the salty into the sweetwater lake as swiftly as if it were a strong river, and when the salt lake contracts the freshwater flows into it.

Based on his study of sixteenth-century documentary sources, Gardiner (1956:59) estimated that at the time of initial Spanish contact in 1519 the entire lake surface (Lake Texcoco plus the northern and southern lakes) covered some 442 square miles (ca. 1132 km^2), about 20% of the entire Valley of Mexico basin area below the encircling mountain slopes and ridges. A surface area of about 1000 km^2 is commonly used by modern authors (e.g., García Sanchez 1998:37). Rzedowski (1957:21), following Flores (1918), suggests that a reasonable estimate of Lake Texcoco's size in "modern" times can be derived by measuring the area contained within the 2240 m asl contour line: approximately 270 km^2. Alcocer and Williams (1993:859) estimate that in 1990 the maximum surface area of Lake Texcoco varied between 82 and 116 km^2, depending on the annual rainfall. They note that in 1608 (at the time of the initial report on lake drainage [Garay 1888:26-27]) the area of Lake Texcoco was about 410 km^2, a figure that probably approximates fairly well the sixteenth-century lake extent.

The Lakes in Prehispanic Times: Geomorphological and Paleoclimatological Studies

It is more difficult to estimate the lake areas farther back in prehispanic time, although Bradbury's (1989:75) study of diatoms indicates that the historic lake levels were established roughly 5000 years ago, following an interval of widespread volcanic ash eruption (also Bradbury 2000; Caballero et al. 1999; Lozano-García and Xelhuantzi-López 1997; Niederberger 1976:253; Watts and Bradbury 1982:56). While still far from definitive, several more recent studies across central and western Mexico of ancient lacustrine deposits, pollen, ostracods, diatoms, and oxygen isotope ratios have all pointed to a relatively more arid period beginning after about 1000 A.D. and extending well into the eighteenth century (Berres 2000; Bridgewater et al. 1999; Caballero and Ortega 1998; Davies et al. 2004; Lozano-García et al. 1993; Lozano-García and Ortega-Guerrero 1993, 1994, 1997; Metcalfe et al. 1989, 2000; O'Hara et al. 1994), although some investigators have concluded that the fourteenth through seventeenth centuries were relatively wetter (O'Hara and Metcalfe 1997). These findings accord reasonably well with studies in North America and Europe that indicate a period of significant, long-term drought approximately A.D. 800-1350, and commonly referred to as the "Medieval Climatic Anomaly" (Jones et al. 1999). There is also some indication that episodes of intensive volcanism may have produced some changes in water levels that were independent of other climatic causes (Lozano-García and Ortega-Guerrero 1998).

Cordova (1997:485-86) provides somewhat more refined paleoclimatic data from several excavations he undertook in the bed of southeastern Lake Texcoco: these data indicate that the Terminal Formative (ca. 250 B.C.-A.D. 100) was a time of falling lake levels, with rising levels during the subsequent Classic and Epiclassic periods (ca. A.D. 100-900), and with falling levels again by A.D. 1100. Cordova's excavations also indicate that there has been very limited Holocene sedimentation in the central bed of Lake Texcoco (1997:415, 428). This finding has significant implications for the surficial archaeological record of the former lakebed (see Chap. 7).

Aside from external climatic forces, in the densely populated lake basins of central Mexico the anthropogenic component of landscape development and change must always be considered. Some have argued that the increased erosion associated with pre-columbian deforestation and agricultural intensification may have played a major role in changing lake levels (Davies et al. 2004; Metcalfe et al. 1989; O'Hara et al. 1993, 1994). As noted above, other studies suggest that "catastrophic geological events" (such as volcanic eruptions) probably played a significant role in these processes (Fisher et al. 2003; Israde-Alcántara et al. 2005; Lozano-García and Ortega-Guerrero 1998). The steep decline of native population, combined with extensive erosion and deforestation caused by introduced sheep pastoralism, resulted in serious environmental degradation after the mid-sixteenth century in highland central Mexico (Frederick 1995; Melville 1994).

At this point in our overall understanding, the available data imply that lake levels across central Mexico would have been somewhat higher during Middle and Late Formative, and Classic times, than they were in the Terminal Formative, Postclassic and early Colonial periods. The Epiclassic (ca. A.D. 650-900) would appear to have been an era transitional between relatively wetter and relatively drier conditions. Berres (2000) has recently suggested that lowered lake levels after A.D. 1100 could have produced an expansion of marshlands, and an expansion of insect collecting together with intensified fishing and waterfowl hunting, with more efficient seines and large nets replacing earlier reliance on spearing, hooks, lines, and small dip nets. Berres' reasoning, if valid, might also imply a comparable expansion and intensification of aquatic resource exploitation during the Terminal Formative more than a millennium earlier.

Lacustrine surface area in the Valley of Mexico is closely related to water depth. On the basis of historical sources, Rojas (1985:2) has estimated that throughout the later Prehispanic and Colonial periods, average water depth in the lake system oscillated 1-3 m, with a few deeper pockets where water was up to 5 m deep (northeastern Lake Chalco).

Table 2.1. Surface areas of lakes in the Valley of Mexico at the beginning of the nineteenth century.

Lake	Area in Square Leagues[a]	Square Kilometers
Chalco-Xochimilco	6.5	114.4
Texcoco	10.1	177.8
San Cristobal[b]	3.6	63.4
Zumpango	1.1	19.4
Total	21.3	375.0

(Adapted from Humboldt 1984:136)
[a]One Spanish league in Mexico equals 2.6 miles (4.19 km) (Haggard 1941:78).
[b]Includes Lake Xaltocán.

Table 2.2. Surface area and water depth in 1861.

Lake	Dry Season Area (km²)	Wet Season Area (km²)	Water Depth (m)
Chalco	104.5	114.2	2.40
Xochimilco	47.1	63.4	2.4-3.0
Texcoco	183.3	272.2	0.5
San Cristobal	11.0	11.0	0.6
Xaltocán	54.1	54.1	0.4
Zumpango	17.2	21.7	0.8
Total	417.2	536.6	

(Adapted from García Sanchez 1998:37)

Table 2.3. Lake measurements in 1866.

Lake	Area (km²)	Av. Depth (m)	Volume (m³)
Texcoco	239	1.80	429,372,000
San Cristobal-Xaltocán	121	0.39	47,360,430
Zumpango	26	0.55	14,478,200
Total	386		491,210,630

(Adapted from Niederberger 1987:1:88, 93)

The nineteenth-century sources considered below indicate the complicated interrelationships between water depth and surface area.

Estimates of Lake Area and Depth

At the beginning of the nineteenth century, Alexander von Humboldt (1984) estimated the lake areas in the Valley of Mexico (Table 2.1). A half century later, Poumaréde (1859:467) estimated that Lake Texcoco covered an area of about 225 km². According to a survey carried out by the Comisión del Valle de México in 1861 (Gonzalez 1902: IV, cited in García Sanchez 1998:37), the surface areas and water depths of the different lakes measured as indicated in Table 2.2. A survey by M. Iglesias in 1866, cited in Niederberger (1987:1:88, 93), revealed the area, depth, and volume measurements shown in Table 2.3.

I attribute the discrepancy between these various nineteenth-century figures to uncertainties of measurement and, perhaps, to seasonal variability at the times when measurements were made. These figures probably apply best to the full extent of the lakes during the annual rainy season. During the annual dry season, of course, the lakes would have been somewhat smaller and shallower, as Table 2.2 indicates. Orozco y Berra (1864:133) reported that in April 1862 (near the end of the dry season), the maximum water depth of Lake Texcoco was 0.50 m. Hay (1870:553) noted that between April 22 and Oct. 27, 1865 (from near the end of the dry season to the end of the rainy season), the water level in Lake Texcoco rose 1.54 m. Such annual fluctuations in water depth in this nearly level region imply a substantial seasonal expansion and contraction of the water-covered area on the lakebed. They also imply significant seasonal and inter-annual changes in the spatial distribution and availability of different kinds of aquatic plants and animals.

On the basis of sixteenth-century eyewitness accounts, Gardiner (1956:130-31) calculated that the brigantine vessels constructed by the Spaniards for their final assault on Aztec Tenochtitlán during April and May 1521 "probably drew between two and two and one-half feet [0.6-0.8 m] of water." This figure is suggestive of the minimal depth of the open-water sections of Lake Texcoco at that time of year during late prehispanic times. Gardiner (1956:125) also determined that in order for the Spanish to launch their boats from where they were constructed on the shoreline near Texcoco, it was necessary to excavate a canal a half league long (ca. 2.1 km), 12 ft wide and 12 ft deep (3.6 m) to reach water deep enough to float the vessels. The Spanish boats were launched April 28, 1521, near the end of the dry season, at a time when the water level would have been close to its annual low point. An early eighteenth-century drawing depicts how that 1521 naval engagement might have appeared (Fig. 2.4).

Some sense of the changing size and configuration of the lakes over time can be gained from eighteenth- and nineteenth-century maps (Figs. 2.5-2.9; see also Carballal and Flores 2004 and Aréchiga 2004). Figure 2.10 suggests the extent and configuration of the lacustrine environment at about A.D. 1500. A late nineteenth-century painting evokes much of the general lacustrine setting of that period (Fig. 2.11), as does a description written in approximately 1900:

> *[English translation]* Because the Valley of Mexico is so extensive—surrounded by high mountains, some forested, others with *barrancas*, and drained by streams fed by crystalline springs, and with lakes covered with floating vegetation and bordered by fertile fields, isolated hills, volcanic cones, ridges and sandy expanses—its physical aspect is varied and picturesque. When the traveler descends to the floor of the basin, coming from the heights of Ajusco or the Sierra de las Cruces [mountain ranges on the southern and southwestern borders of the Valley of Mexico], he contemplates and admires a panorama whose beauty rivals that of the most renowned places on earth. But, to enjoy this spectacular beauty it is enough to climb one of the small hills near the capital city [Mexico City]. If, on a clear day in June, one ascends the Cerro de Gachupines, near the end of the Tepeyac ridge [on the northwestern shore of Lake Texcoco], the view that meets the eye equals that offered by the Bay of Naples. . . . From that height one takes in the full expanse of the Valley. Just below is a band of arid terrain, and then Lake Texcoco fills the adjoining landscape, its tranquil waters appearing golden in the light of the setting sun, and farther off across the distant plains of the Chalco and Texcoco valleys, with intermixed greens and yellows of the cultivated fields and the dark expanses of the woodlands, there stands out against the clear blue sky the imposing Sierra Nevada, with the peaks of Tlaloc and Telapón [two major peaks on the eastern border of the Valley of Mexico], and then the silhouettes of the snow-capped peaks of Ixtaccihuatl and Popocatépetl with their enveloping clouds bathed in multiple colors. [Ramírez 1902:697]

Figure 2.4. Eighteenth-century drawing depicting 1521 naval battle in Lake Texcoco (Solis 1704:572).

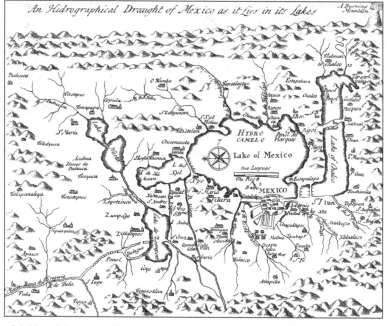

Figure 2.5. Map of the Valley of Mexico in 1726 (Herrera 1726:3:194-95, Pl. 104). North is to the left.

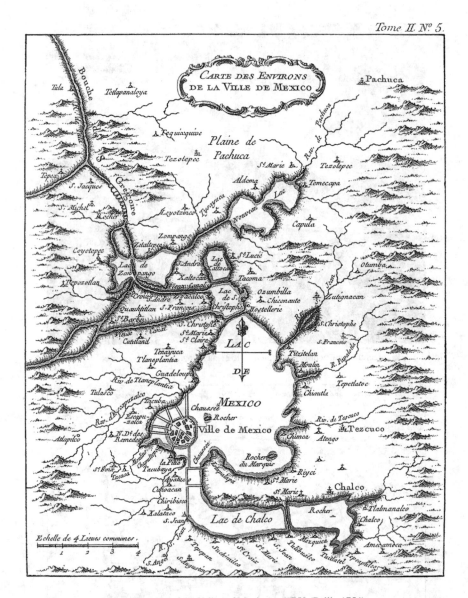

Figure 2.6. Map of the Valley of Mexico ca. 1750 (Bellin 1754).

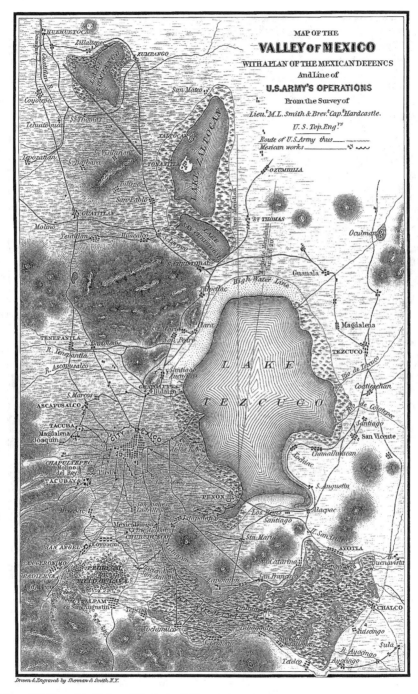

Figure 2.7. Map of the Valley of Mexico in 1847, made by U.S. military engineers (Mayer 1850:1:381).

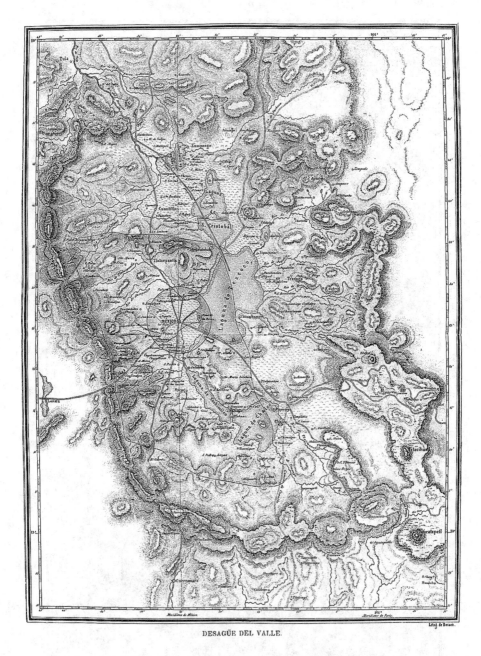

DESAGÜE DEL VALLE.

Figure 2.8. Map of the Valley of Mexico in 1858 (Garcia y Cubas 1858).

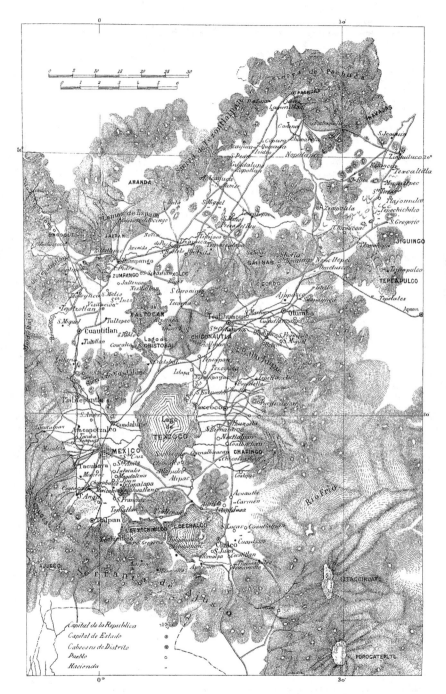

Figure 2.9. Map of the Valley of Mexico ca. 1900 (Ramírez 1902:697, Lamina XL).

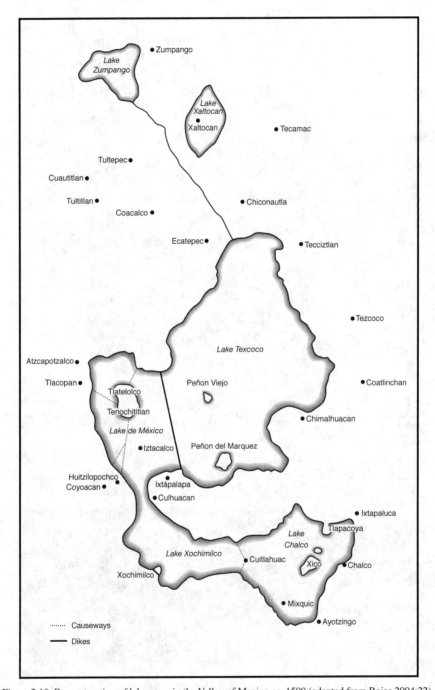

Figure 2.10. Reconstruction of lake areas in the Valley of Mexico ca. 1500 (adapted from Rojas 2004:22).

Figure 2.11. Facing east-southeast across México City and the southern third of Lake Texcoco in 1894. Painting by José María Velasquez: "Valle de México desde Las Lomas de Tacubaya" (Pellicer 1970:125).

Chimalhuacán

In sum, available information indicates that by the mid-nineteenth century, the area of Lake Texcoco had been reduced to approximately half its sixteenth-century extent. By the middle of the twentieth century, its area had been halved again, with another halving (or more) by the century's end. Over the past quarter of a century, enveloping smog has largely obscured the memorable views that José Ramírez so enjoyed a century ago, and that had so impressed even the battle-hardened Spanish *conquistadores*, Hernán Cortés and Bernal Díaz del Castillo, in 1519. During this same period, an urban sprawl, with few equals anywhere else in the world, has filled much of the landscape that had captivated earlier observers (Pick and Butler 2000). Today, the last few dozen square kilometers of the lake in its "natural" (though polluted) state are on the verge of final and complete disappearance. However, as recently as September 1951 (late in the rainy season), there was still sufficient water in southern Lake Texcoco to require the rescue by canoe of 37 passengers from an airplane that made a forced landing there (*New York Times* 1951).

It is important to emphasize that in this setting what is commonly referred to as "lake" actually comprised substantial areas of marsh and swamp, as well as open water, with significant seasonal contraction and expansion of water-covered zones during annual dry and rainy seasons, respectively. Longer term variability in water levels remains to be better defined by paleo-environmental studies.

Documented Changes in Salinity and Alkalinity during the Eighteenth and Nineteenth Centuries

Gibson (1964:306) noted that as lake drainage proceeded during the Colonial period, the historical sources reveal that

[s]ub-surface alkaline waters continued to rise in drained areas and with their evaporation soils became impregnated with salts. . . . wherever the water receded, the alkali proportionately advanced. Salinization was evident on the eastern shore of Lake Texcoco in the sixteenth century, where *lagunillas* [ponds] had formed, where soils were alkalized, and where sterile years for crops were common. . . . the draining of the lakes, far from creating new agricultural land, rendered existing agricultural land [along the lakeshore] less serviceable.

Writing about the character of the lakebed environment in the 1780s, Alzate (1831) observed that

[English translation] The mineral alkali, or *tequesquite*, is taking possession of these lands. . . . In the 1789 edition of *Gacetas de México*, I noted that Mexico City is very dry, and that the surrounding land contains an abundance of mineral alkali; the alkali increases at the ground surface as the lakewaters seasonally dry up, producing a very caustic salt. . . . The old historians tell us that the *barrio* of Tlatelolco [northwestern Lake Texcoco] was formerly very pleasant; today it presents a landscape in which not a load of grass can be gathered during the entire rainy season. In the parroquia of San Sebastian is a district known as Zacatlán, that is, grass land; today not a plant grows there, because as the water has receded it has been replaced by alkali. The plains that formerly provided food for the fine Mexican cattle, don't we now see them almost lacking in vegetation? Is not the alkali day by day destroying the fertility of the farms to the south of Mexico City? [Alzate 1831:2:52]

Referring to other parts of Lake Texcoco in the late eighteenth century, Alzate noted that

[English translation] travelling northeastward from Mexico City one passes the saltlands that formerly were the lakebed, but that today are all dried up. On the hillslopes are found several farms: why don't their owners, who never forget to plant whatever small piece of elevated land they possess, use the dried up lakebed for anything? It is because practice has taught them that it is useless, that seeds won't grow there. . . . The nitrous waters, although not useful for irrigation or for drinking, do humidify the air; along the shores grow plants that are somewhat useful; however, when they dry up they increase the dust and harm the health, because caustic alkali is absorbed by breathing and through the body's absorbent pores. . . .

The indians from the town of Ixtapalapa, to the south of Mexico City, have a great plain that formerly provided pasture for their livestock; the waters have diminished, and today it is all dried up, with not a single plant to be seen. . . . [Alzate 1831:2:122-23]

Writing at the beginning of the nineteenth century, Alexander von Humboldt (1984) offered his understanding of the nature and causes of changes in lacustrine ecology in the Valley of Mexico since the sixteenth century:

[English translation] [T]he abundance and circulation of the waters have visibly diminished over the entire valley. Because of widespread deforestation, Lake Texcoco now receives much less water by infiltration than it did in the sixteenth century. . . .

But the most important cause for the shrinkage of Lake Texcoco is the famous Huehuetoca drainage canal. . . . This cut has not only reduced the size of Lakes Zumpango and San Cristobal, but has also prevented the flow of their waters into Lake Texcoco during the rainy season.

In effect, the lake water and vegetation have diminished with the same rapidity that the quantity of tequesquite (carbonate of soda) has increased. . . . The fertility of the plain, always of great concern in the southern part of the valley, is no longer as great as it was when Mexico City was in the middle of the lake. . . .

The present limits of Lake Texcoco are not well determined because the soil is clayey and the land is so flat that in a distance of a mile there is no more than 20 cm difference in elevation. When the east wind blows strongly, the lake waters retreat toward the western lake shore, and sometimes spaces up to 600 meters wide are left dry. Perhaps it was the periodic action of such winds that gave Cortés [see quote above] the idea that these movements were regular tides, whose existence has never been confirmed by any later observations.

The water of Lake Texcoco usually is no more than three to five meters deep, and in some places it is less than one meter. Because of this, the commerce of the inhabitants of Texcoco declines considerably during the dry months of January and February, since the shallow water then makes it difficult to travel from there to Mexico City by boat. This inconvenience does not occur in Lake Xochimilco, as boat navigation from Chalco, Mixquic, and Tlahuac is never interrupted.

Of the five lakes in the Valley of Mexico, the water of Lake Texcoco is most highly charged with muriate and carbonate of soda [i.e., Tequesquite]. Lake Xochimilco has the purest and cleanest water. The quantity of hydrogen sulfide released from all the lake surfaces, and which the lead acetate test shows in particular abundance in Lakes Texcoco and Chalco, undoubtedly contributes in certain situations to the valley's unhealthy air. Nevertheless, it is worthy of note that around the shores of these same lakes, whose surfaces are partly covered with reeds and other aquatic plants, intermittent fevers are very rare. [Humboldt 1984:117-18]

Orozco y Berra (1864) offered a vivid mid-nineteenth-century description of Lake Texcoco during the dry season:

> *[English translation]* The dried-up lakebed presents a desolate and dead aspect that saddens the heart. There are vast plains where scarcely is to be found a spindly plant, hard and glassy, known by the Mexicans as *tequixquicacatl*, little liked by the livestock; verdolaga plants [*Portulaca oleracea*] grow in some places, as do other plants suited to salty lands, such as triantemas, gratiolas, *atriplex*, chenopods, and saltsosas; in winter time on the rest of the ground surface appears a crust of efflorscent white or yellow salts, offensive to the eyes blinded by the suns rays, that produces an impression of anguish and depression. [Orozco y Berra 1864:145]

The historical sources clearly depict a steadily shrinking lake, with accelerating reduction in the area covered by lake and marsh after the late nineteenth century. These references suggest that by no later than the late eighteenth century, the large-scale drainage projects initiated in the early seventeenth century had produced a significant increase in the salinity and alkalinity of the lakebed environment. It is unclear what negative impact this may have had upon the abundance, distribution, and availability of aquatic fauna and flora relative to prehispanic times. This impact may have been significant.

The published studies of Mexican lake systems provide only limited insight into the precise nature of the aquatic environment in the Valley of Mexico prior to the mid-twentieth century, especially in terms of the expectable variability and availability of aquatic plant resources over time and space according to seasonal and long-term variation in water levels. To help remedy this problem, I turn to the comparatively more thoroughly studied U.S. Great Basin and the Lake Chad region in north-central Africa.

Insights from Studies of Marshland Ecology in the U.S. Great Basin

In her discussion of indigenous lifeways in and around the extensive marshes of the Great Basin in the western U.S., Fowler (1992:44-46) uses studies of marshland ecology in that region that seem to have general applicability to the Valley of Mexico. Although the U.S. Great Basin is situated in a temperate latitude (ca. 40° north latitude), and is characterized by a much more arid environment, many of its plant and animal species and general geochemical conditions appear to be similar to the marshlands of central Mexico. Citing Weller (1981), Fowler notes the complex interrelationships between water depth, salinity and alkalinity, and biology:

> Species diversity [both plant and animal], as well as total numbers of forms, is at its highest and the marsh at its richest when water is neither too deep nor too shallow. Deep water allows little in the way of fringing elements, such as hardstem bulrush and cattail. . . . This, in turn, discourages utilization for feeding and/or nesting by waterfowl that are waders, shore feeders, or dabblers.
>
> Shallow water, on the other hand, may be fringed with alkali bulrush, an important plant food for some [waterfowl species], but contains few cattails and tules that are important for nesting and feeding for other species, such as diving ducks. A number of submergents, such

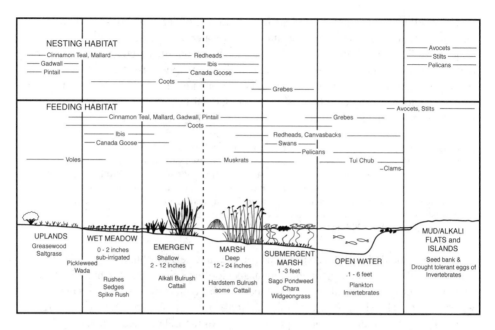

Figure 2.12. Habitats and water depth, Stillwater Marsh, Nevada, U.S. (adapted from Raymond and Parks 1990:39, Fig. 4).

as sago pondweed (*Potomogeton pectinatus*) and duckweed (*Lemma* sp.), also important foods for waterfowl, will not be found if the water is too shallow. Thus, to be at its best, a marsh should have areas of open water, roughly 50% to 75%, but broken up into small ponds. These will then be fringed with hardstem bulrush, a plant that does well next to open and deeper water. Closer to shore will be cattails; next to them in drier areas will be alkali bulrush [Fig. 2.12].

With these conditions met, along with provision of some upland feeding zones, species diversity will be at its highest and numbers of biotic forms at maximum density. Individual marshy areas will vary in terms of this ideal mix, but if the overall system approximates it, the marshes are highly productive.

. . . An additional feature of desert marshes that are terminal for water inflow . . . is the role of increasing alkalinity in the distribution of plants and animals. As fresh water progresses through the system, it picks up increasing amounts of alkali and other elements from the surrounding desert soils. As the water reaches the endpoint, and as evaporation increases, it concentrates these materials in solution so that only species that can tolerate high levels of these materials can survive. Thus, toward the end of the system [in the Valley of Mexico this would be most particularly central Lake Texcoco], sometimes without regard for water depth, if emergents are present they will likely be alkali bulrush. The other emergents, as well as most submergents, disappear. This influences the feeding and nesting habits of waterfowl, which affects the presence of certain mammals such as carnivores. Thus, from the point where water enters a system . . . to where it exits for total evaporation, species composition and numbers can change drastically. . . . [Weller 1981:65]

Using ethnographic and historical information, Fowler (1992:45-46) discovered significant changes in species composition at Stillwater Marsh, Nevada, over the period 1900-1952. The underlying causes of these changes remain uncertain: some are almost certainly anthropogenic, whereas others may be linked to long-term "natural" changes in precipitation, evaporation rates, and so on. Fowler's findings are suggestive of the kinds of decades-long ecological changes and successional cycles that may have occurred throughout prehispanic and historic periods in the Valley of Mexico.

[H]ardstem bulrush was roughly twice as common in 1900 as in 1952; [while] . . . cattails were roughly 2/3 less extensive; and . . . alkali bulrush was about 1/3 more common. . . . These conditions seem to suggest the presence of more open water in 1900. This would have encouraged submergent vegetation and increased numbers of diving ducks, such as American Coot and Canvasback, that favored Cattail-eater foods. More acreage of alkali bulrush would have favored shore feeders such as Great Blue Heron, American Bittern, and others. . . . [Fowler 1992:46]

Raymond and Parks (1990) consider the complex interrelationships and spatial configurations of different aquatic plant and animal species that exist within the huge Stillwater Marsh according to seasonal and inter-annual variability in temperature, water depth and water salinity. The short-term dynamic quality of this marsh ecosystem seems highly relevant to understanding the prehispanic ecology of the Lake Texcoco marshlands:

Under natural conditions Stillwater Marsh is a complex and fluctuating ecosystem. Silt lunette dunes, punctuating the flat expanse of water, create over 200 islands and a mainland shore of 225 miles [360 km]. In the spring, the Carson [system of freshwater streams] delivers freshets from melting mountain snow. Water spreads over playas and shallow ponds. Emergents including cattail (*Typha* spp.), hardstem bulrush (*Scirpus acutus*), and alkali bulrush (*Scirpus maritimus*) rejuvenate. The nesting season [for waterfowl] begins in early March for geese, and continues through June for some ducks and ibis. In summer 100-degree temperatures partially evaporate downstream ponds and increase water salinity. *Tui chub* [fish] spawn and thousands of ducks and coots molt. Autumn slows the 4 to 5 foot [1.2-1.5 m] annual evaporation rate. Submergent vegetation like sago pondweed (*Potomageton pectinatus*), widgeon grass (*Ruppia maritma*) and *Chara* sp. matures in the deeper ponds, while the seeds of bulrush ripen in the drying ponds. These and other plants provide fuel to over a quarter of a million waterfowl which stop at the marsh in the fall on their way south along the Pacific flyway. By December most birds have left for points further south, but some remain longer, including as many as 5000 tundra swans.

Water depth and salinity influence the assemblage of flora and fauna in Stillwater Marsh. Upstream ponds support vastly different vegetation than downstream ponds. The upstream ponds contain fresher water and do not evaporate completely. The downstream ponds hold saltier water, the result of evaporation, leaching, and flushing of upstream playas. Water depth crosscuts water salinity, providing a complex mosaic of habitats. Two feet [0.6 m] of water in a downstream salty pond supports different plants and animals than two inches [0.05 m] in the same pond, and different plants and animals than two feet of water in a fresh upstream pond. Stillwater Marsh, in a few miles, contains more environmental diversity than scores of miles in the pinyon-juniper zone on the adjacent Stillwater Range.

Marsh productivity and diversity is maintained by fluctuating water conditions. Fluctuating water budgets cause one plant or animal species in any one location to undergo boom and bust cycles. Partial drying of shallow ponds produces dense micro-vegetation. This becomes food for aquatic invertebrates, which in turn become food for waterbirds and fish. Drying of deeper ponds allows decomposition of bottom organic deposits and aeration of the ground. A release of nutrients feeds a new surge of vegetation and invertebrates when water returns seasonally, or in dozens of years when seeds germinate after dormancy. An increase in water . . . will wipe out emergent vegetation and seeds and nesting they offer. But *tui chub* [a fish species], annual plants and invertebrates explode, which attracts record numbers of pelicans and waterfowl. If a new water level is maintained for even a few years, plants and animals will adjust, so that habitats initially lost are replaced elsewhere in the basin. As the water budget increases and decreases, the marsh will expand and contract, while retaining the same habitat structure. . . . [Raymond and Parks 1990:35-37]

Insights from Environmental Studies in Lake Chad, North-Central Africa

Environmental (Carmouze and Lemoalle 1983; Grove 1970) and botanical (Iltis and Lemoalle 1983) studies of Lake Chad may help elucidate some of the general aspects of botanical and geomorphological variability over time and space in Lake Texcoco. At first glance, such an effort may not seem very useful. Obviously, Lake Chad and Lake Texcoco are thousands of miles apart, separated by the entire width of the Atlantic Ocean plus large expanses of the Middle American and African land masses. Botanically they are also quite distinct, with many different genera and species of aquatic plants. With a surface area of roughly 20,000 km^2, Lake Chad is far larger than Lake Texcoco, and its elevation above sea level is much lower (averaging slightly below 300 m asl). The Chad basin is somewhat drier—average annual rainfall ranges between 300 and 500 mm (Carmouze and Lemoalle 1983:49), about one-half to two-thirds that of the Valley of Mexico.

Nevertheless, there are some striking similarities in the physical and geomorphological characteristics of both regions. Both "lakes" are shallow bodies of water with substantial seasonal and inter-annual variation in water depth (Lake Chad has a mean water depth of 4 m, "and the seasonal and between-years variations in water level are, respectively, about 0.5 and 5 m" [Carmouze and Lemoalle 1983:27]). Both are situated in comparable latitudes (the Lake Chad basin lies between 12° and 14°20' north latitude; central Lake Texcoco is at 19°31' north latitude). Both are largely, or exclusively, internal drainage basins, with substantial expanses of saline water, whose salinity varies according to changing water level and proximity to in-coming freshwater drainage. Both are in semi-arid zones with markedly seasonal rainfall. Both have been characterized by significant loss of moisture in comparatively recent times. Both have substantial sectors of diverse aquatic vegetation, and both have large indigenous human populations who have exploited aquatic resources for millennia.

So, despite the obvious differences between the two lake basins, we might expect some general similarities in terms of the complex interrelationships between water, plants, animals, soils, and exploitation by human beings. These similarities may help us more clearly envision the ancient lacustrine environment of the central Valley of Mexico.

Iltis and Lemoalle (1983:125) note that there has been a significant recession of water in the Chad basin since the late 1960s. Their field studies in the 1970s revealed how this drying out of the landscape has affected the abundance and distributions of aquatic flora.

The four principal ecological factors that influence the existence, composition, and density of aquatic plants in Lake Chad are: (1) variation in water level; (2) nature and slope of the underlying ground surface; (3) force of the wind and exposure to it—wave action, for example, has a significant impact on the presence or absence of certain floating plant species; and (4) chemical composition of the water, primarily salt concentration that varies directly with distance from freshwater sources around the perimeter of the lake. Changes in these variables have produced some very notable changes in the distribution of aquatic flora in Lake Chad over a period of only 5-10 years. We might expect to see changes of comparable scope for aquatic plant communities of Lake Texcoco, over both the long- and short-term.

Iltis and Lemoalle (1983:129-33) distinguish five aquatic plant communities in Lake Chad, each of which may have had analogues in Lake Texcoco prior to the early twentieth century:

(1) *Aquatic meadows.* "Found especially in the deltaic zones [i.e., where freshwater enters the lake]. . . . The river waters flow through it by some well defined channels during recession and by filtering through the vegetation during high waters. *Vossia cuspidata* ['hippo grass'], which occurs in 1-3 m of water, is the most widespread species" (Iltis and Lemoalle 1983:129).

(2) *Reed islands.* "These are the vegetation islands established on the shallows and associated with *Cyperus papyrus* ['papyrus'] and *Phragmites australis* ['common reed'] as well as other less abundant species. The latter develop on a compost of rhizoides and roots forming a thick mat of 1-2 m under the water surface. The islands are anchored in the shallows whose form and size determines that of the reed island. These vegetation formations, which can be several hundred meters long, often include some clear gaps and some small closed ponds where some associations characteristic of sheltered waters develop" (Iltis and Lemoalle 1983:130).

(3) *Floating islands.* "Some floating islands detach from the reed islands or from the vegetation borders of the islands and archipelago peninsulas and float away as they are pushed by the wind. Consisting mostly of *Cyperus papyrus* . . . these islands are usually circular. . . . Their size varies from a few meters to several hundred meters. . . . [according to how they are pushed by the winds] these islands move back and forth, modifying the aspect of the reed islands and closing the channels of the archipelagos" (Iltis and Lemoalle 1983:131).

(4) *Vegetation borders of the islands of the archipelago.* "All the islands and peninsulas of the archipelago possess a vegetation fringe several meters wide and 3-4 m high. *Cyperus papyrus*, *Vassia cuspidata*, and especially *Phragmites australis* are the most abundant and largest species. . . . This vegetation barrier is interrupted in only a few places by narrow passages which allow local boats to land" (Iltis and Lemoalle 1983:132).

(5) *Submerged vegetation banks.* "These banks are very extensive in the shallow marshy zones situated to the east of the Shari delta [the main freshwater inlet], at the foot of the . . . rock hills. . . . the coast appears to be poorly delimited and is marked by vegetation. The wider channels are overgrown by beds of *Potamogeton schweinfurthii* ['pondweed'], *Vallisneria* sp. ['eel grass'], and *Ceratophyllum demersum* ['coon's tail'] alternating with submerged vegetation islands of *Vossia* and *Phragmites*" (Iltis and Lemoalle 1983:133).

A period of drought from 1972 through mid-1975 produced a spatial separation between the northern and southern segments of Lake Chad. From that point, vegetation developed independently in the two sectors, and there were very substantial changes in the distributions of each of the five plant communities noted above. In particular, marsh vegetation cover extended over about half the area that had formerly been open water, and there was a progressive impoverishment of aquatic flora in the drier northern sub-basin related directly to the water's increasing salt concentration. Carmouze and Lemoalle (1983:61) summarize the impact of fluctuating water level during the 1967-1975 drought period in the Chad Basin:

> The fluctuations of the water level are such that . . . profound changes in lacustrine zones must be expected both in time and apace. So, after a lake subsidence [i.e., lowering of water level], a region of open water can be turned into a region of reed islands, a region of archipelago, and a dry region within a few years. During 1973-1975, numerous shallows appeared in the northern open waters and became an archipelago before drying up in 1975. During the period of flood, the opposite situation can occur.

Iltis and Lemoalle (1983:141-42) summarize the complex geochemical processes involved as water level, water salinity, and plant composition changed over a period of a few years in Lake Chad:

> The influence of macrophytes on the water chemistry is both direct, by the transfer of salts from the water to the plant tissues and the sediments, and indirect, by modification of the physical conditions of the environment. . . . When the macrophytes were abundant [which occurred with the expansion of marsh vegetation after the 1972-1975 drought] . . . the indirect effects noted were (1) a dampening effect of water level oscillations and a diminution in the fetch of the wind; (2) a lowering of pH and of the dissolved oxygen with an increase of the CO_2 tension. These new environmental conditions limited the neoformation of clay which participates in the salinity regulation in the lake.
> One of the direct effects was the variation of ion concentrations, especially of potassium and chloride which were assimilated by plants during the growth periods in flooded environment and re-dissolved during submersions at the time of lacustrine floods. The phosphate concentrations . . . also became greater during these periods.
> . . . The salts accumulated in the plants initially originate from dried sediments on which they have developed considerably. Later on, the macrophytes remove salts from the sediments and the water in unknown proportions. Inversely, decomposition rapidly provides a considerable amount of dissolved elements while a smaller fraction remains trapped for a time in the organic matter of the sediments.

As in the U.S. Great Basin, these studies in Lake Chad imply that in the pre-modern Valley of Mexico we should expect a great deal of variability in the distribution and composition of aquatic plants, plant formations, and animals over time and space according to seasonal, inter-annual, and longer-term variability in water availability. Such variability has probably been particularly notable over the past 400 years as artificial drainage resulted in increasing desiccation of the lake basin in the Valley of Mexico. However, we might also expect some variation in the configuration, distribution, and availability of plant and animal communities within the wetland zone during earlier centuries in the

Plate 2.1. Fisherman's camp on natural reed island in Lake Chad (from Iltis and Lemoalle 1983:128, Photo 9).

face of (still poorly understood) shorter- and longer-term climate variability within both the Valley of Mexico and central Mexico as a whole.

Of particular interest are the potential implications for human occupation within the Mexican lakes on the natural "reed islands" and "floating islands" comprised of natural masses of buoyant aquatic vegetation that are so commonplace in Lake Chad (and in Lake Titicaca in Peru/Bolivia; see Chap. 6). Fishermen often establish their camps on these reed islands, residing there in insubstantial reed shelters for some periods of time (Grove 1970:436; Iltis and Lemoalle 1983:128, Photo 9) (Plate 2.1). These African fishermen use reed boats (Plate 2.2) and wood-reed floats (Plate 2.3) to move from their camps across open water from one fishing area to another. Their reed boats are remarkably similar to those described in other parts of Africa (Worthington 1933), in the U.S. Great Basin, and in the Titicaca Basin in South America (see Chap. 6).

Features comparable to the natural reed islands of Lake Chad and Lake Titicaca may well have existed in the Valley of Mexico where they could have provided convenient, dry-surfaced living spaces for temporary or permanent habitation. Such natural islands could have been expanded into larger, more permanent "artificial" islands through filling operations using masses of lakebed soil and plants piled up around and atop the natural features. Recent geoarchaeological investigations have shown that expansion of small natural islands probably occurred at Xaltocán in central Lake Xaltocán (Frederick et al. 2005), at El Tepalcate in southeastern Lake Texcoco (Cordova 1997:428), at Chalco on the eastern shore of Lake Chalco (O'Neill 1962), at Tlahuac in central Lake Chalco-Xochimilco (Armillas 1971), and around Tepetitlán in western Lake Texcoco (Carballal and Flores 1993).

Plate 2.2. Reed boat used by Lake Chad fisherman (from Iltis and Lemoalle 1983:137, Photo 11).

Plate 2.3. Wooden pole wrapped in reeds for use as an individual float for crossing open water on Lake Chad (from Iltis and Lemoalle 1983:129, Photo 10).

Summary and Conclusions

In the early sixteenth century, Lake Texcoco (including expanses of shallow, open water and reed-filled marshlands) covered an area of approximately 400 km² in the central Valley of Mexico. Available paleoclimatic data suggest that the periods of approximately 1000-300 B.C. and A.D. 200-900 were relatively more moist, with higher water levels and a larger lake surface area, than were the periods of about 300 B.C.-A.D. 200 and post-A.D. 1000. By the early twentieth century, large-scale drainage had been underway for three centuries, and the sixteenth-century lake area had been reduced by more than half. This drainage apparently resulted in a significant increase in the salinity and alkalinity of Lake Texcoco and the lakeshore environment, and this may have negatively affected the abundance and distribution of some aquatic resources relative to prehispanic conditions.

Botanical and geomorphological studies in the comparable aquatic environments in the North American Great Basin and African Chad Basin imply that it will eventually be necessary to disentangle in the Valley of Mexico a very complex series of dynamic spatial and temporal relationships between plants, animals, water, soils, and wind that we still understand very incompletely for Lake Texcoco. For example, the studies in North America and Africa suggest that it may be necessary to critically evaluate Berres' (2000) intriguing suggestion that decreased rainfall after approximately A.D. 1100 may have caused an expansion of marshland in the Valley of Mexico: while declining water levels at that time may well have caused the marshlands to expand into lacustrine areas formerly covered by open water, the marshlands probably would have retreated lakeward on their inland sides.

I think it is particularly important to consider the implications for ancient occupation of the lacustrine environment in the Valley of Mexico of the presence and shifting distribution of natural "islands" formed by masses of compacted buoyant aquatic plants that have been observed in Lake Chad (and also in Lake Titicaca and in the Tigris-Euphrates delta; see Chap. 6). These islands may well have had counterparts in Lake Texcoco that could have provided places for enduring lakebed occupation without any necessary regional desiccation or lowering of water level.

— 3 —

The Historically Documented Utilization of Aquatic Resources in the Valley of Mexico, A.D. 1500-1970

This chapter presents historical and ethnographic information from the sixteenth through the twentieth centuries. Several comparable studies have been published (e.g., Deevey 1957; García Sanchez 1998; Gibson 1964:339-43; Linne 1948; Moreno 1969; Muller 1952; Niederberger 1987:111-17; Ortiz de Montellano 1990; Rojas 1985; Sugiura 1998:79-87). Although some of these are quite comprehensive (especially García Sanchez 1998 and Rojas 1985), most are not well known outside Mexico. I will present the highlights of these important data, with particular attention to the primary sources and to those aspects of aquatic resource utilization that seem most amenable to future archaeological study.

The Sixteenth-Century Sources

The two definitive works are Fray Bernardo Sahagun's *Florentine Codex* and Francisco Hernández's *Historia Natural de Nueva España*; both are based on observations made during the middle and late sixteenth century (that is, one or two generations after initial Spanish contact). The detail and specificity of both sets of descriptions indicate the considerable importance attached to aquatic resources by the indigenous inhabitants of the Valley of Mexico.

I begin this section with the very modest mention of aquatic resources in the prehispanic tribute lists (primarily the *Códice Mendocino* as interpreted by Barlow 1949). Then I note the specific mentions and illustrations of aquatic products in the documents compiled by Lord Kingsborough under the title *Antiquities of Mexico*, and explicated in Spanish as *Antigüedades de México*, Vol. 1, by Agustin Yáñez and José Corona Nuñez (Corona 1964). After that, I refer to brief observations by two Spanish eyewitnesses of preconquest Tenochtitlán: Cortés (1963) and Diaz del Castillo (1908). I then consider the two major sources, Sahagun and Hernández, in more detail. It is not always easy to

Figure 3.1. Tribute from Quauhtitlan province: 4000 rush seats
and mats (Corona 1964:60-61,
Lamina XXVIII).

cross-reference the lists compiled by Sahagun and Hernández: some categories of plants and animals are mentioned by both writers, but others are not. I merely note the most obvious correspondences between the two lists. Finally, I note useful descriptions in other, less comprehensive sixteenth-century accounts.

The Extent of the Empire of the Culhua Mexica (Barlow 1949)

Aquatic products are scarce in the sixteenth-century tribute lists. Barlow (1949:42) lists only one tributary province, Quauhtitlan in the northwestern Valley of Mexico, from which significant quantities of such products derived annually: 4000 "rush mats [*petates*, or *esteras*] and seats"; these items comprised "a distinctive tribute of the province."

Antigüedades de México (Corona 1964)

The *Códice Mendocino* contains several illustrations of aquatic products and activities associated with their procurement. Lamina XXVIII shows the symbol for the 4000 rush seats and reed mats mentioned by Barlow (1949:42) as tribute from the Quauhtitlan province in the northwestern Valley of Mexico (Corona 1964:60-61) (Fig. 3.1). Several drawings show the use of reed mats in both domestic and administrative center settings. Lamina LXII (Corona 1964:128-29), for example, shows a man and woman seated on a reed mat in a kitchen where food is being prepared (Fig. 3.2). Lamina LXX (Corona 1964:144-45) shows reed mats as floor coverings in Moctezuma's palace (Fig. 3.3). There are numerous illustrations of important men seated in rush seats (e.g., Corona 1964:138-39, 142-43, 266) (Fig. 3.4).

Lamina LX shows a young boy learning how to use a wood-framed fishing net (Corona 1964:124-25), while Lamina LXI shows an older youth fishing from a canoe with a similar net (Corona 1964:126-27) (Fig. 3.5*a*). Another portion of Lamina LXI illustrates a youth carrying a load of rushes and transporting them in a canoe (Fig. 3.5*b*). In Lamina LXIV

Figure 3.2. Man and woman seated on a reed mat in their kitchen (Corona 1964:128-29, Lamina LXII).

a man transports building materials (probably adobes, or sod blocks) in a canoe (Corona 1964:132-33) (Fig. 3.6*a*). Similarly, Lamina LXV (Corona 1964:134-35) shows a man transporting a canoe-load of rocks for temple construction (Fig. 3.6*b*). These two latter drawings illustrate the importance of water-borne transport of heavy materials within the Valley of Mexico.

Cartas y Documentos (Cortés 1963)

Cortés (1963:72-73) provides some detail on wild fowl and fish products available in the large marketplace in Tenochtitlan-Tlatelolco:

Hay calle de caza donde venden todos los linajes de aves que hay en la tierra, asi como gallinas, perdices, codornices, lavancas, dorales, zarcelas, tortolas, palomas, pajaritos en cañuela, papagayos, búhares, águilas, halcones, gavilanes y cernicalas. . . .
    Venden pasteles de aves y empanados de pescados. Venden mucho pescado fresco y salado, crudo y guisado. Venden huevos de gallinas y de ánsares, y de todos las otras aves que he dicho, en gran cantidad; venden tortillas de huevos hechas.

[English translation] There is a street where all kinds of native fowl are sold, such as turkeys, partridges, quail, wild ducks, fly-catchers, widgens, turtle doves, doves, caged birds, parrots, owls, eagles, falcons, hawks and kestrels. . . .
    They sell pastries made from birds and fish. They sell much fish, fresh and salted, raw and cooked. They sell great quantities of turkey and goose eggs, as well as those of all the other types of birds I have mentioned; they sell prepared tortillas made from eggs.

The True History of the Conquest of New Spain (Diaz del Castillo 1908)

In describing the great market in Tenochtitlan-Tlatelolco in 1519, Diaz del Castillo (1908:73) noted the presence of

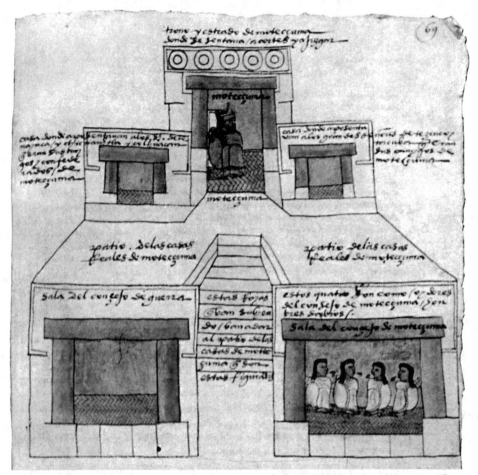

Figure 3.3. Moctezuma's palace, showing use of reed mats as floor coverings throughout the structure (Corona 1964:144-45, Lamina LXX).

fisherwomen and others who sell some cakes made from a sort of ooze which they get out of the great lake [Texcoco], which curdles, and from which they make a bread having a flavor something like cheese.

Deevey (1957:227-28) suggests that these cakes may not have been made of algae, as commonly believed, but rather of corixid eggs, *ahuauhtli*. The sources cited below indicate that both algae and insect eggs were prepared for consumption in similar fashion.

The Florentine Codex (Sahagun 1963)

Sahagun (1963:26-39, 62-65) describes numerous types of edible (or otherwise useful) aquatic fauna and flora in the Valley of Mexico. These include 5 types of fish, at least 38 types of waterfowl, 14 categories of "small animals which live in the water," and at least 18 categories of aquatic plants (Tables 3.1 and 3.2).

Figure 3.4. Important man seated on a rush seat (Corona 1964:142-43, Lamina LXIX).

a

Figure 3.5. *a*, youth fishing from canoe (Corona 1964:126-27, Lamina LXI); *b*, youth carrying load of reeds and transporting them in a canoe (Corona 1964:126-27, Lamina LXI).

b

Figure 3.6. *a*, man transporting load of adobe bricks or sod blocks in a canoe (Corona 1964:132-33, Lamina LXIV); *b*, man transporting load of rocks in a canoe (Corona 1964:134-35, Lamina LXV).

Table 3.1. Aquatic fauna described by Sahagun (1963).[a]

Category Names *Nahuatl name (common English name; scientific name)*	Sahagun's Descriptions
I. Fish (Sahagun 1963:62-65)	
amilotl (*Chirostoma humboldtianum*)	"Also its name is xouilin. It is called white amilotl [and] white xouilin. The amilotl is especially understood to be the white xouilin; amilotl is also especially understood to be the thick fish, the dark one. The one called amilotl they sell; they eat the especially fattened white amilotl. The amilotl, the xouilin have eggs. Their food is waterflies and those which are small insects, and tlalcuitlaxcolli, and mud. Pools are their homes; underwater caverns, caves, sink holes are their dwelling places. Amilotonti are small; they are white. Xouilton are small; they are dark." (p. 62)
cuitlapetotl (*Girardinichthys innominatus*) (noted by Hernández 1959b:402)	"It is a big-bellied fish, small and round, stiff-necked, like the topotli. Its head is bitter, dark." (p. 62)
michçaquan	"It means 'baby fish.' It is a small fish which goes in schools. It is a darter, an agile one. It is agile, it darts, it swims in schools. The yayauhqui michin or dark fish lives everywhere. The white fish is small; it breeds in saline water." (p. 62)
michteuhtli	"It means 'very small fish,' either white or dark. Especially it means 'small dried fish.' " (p. 62)
michpictli	"These are fish cooked on a griddle. They are [wrapped] in [maize] husks. Michtlacectli are small fish cooked on a griddle. Michtlaxquitl are xouilin, amilotl, xalmichin roasted, cooked on a griddle." (pp. 62-63)
michpili (fish eggs and very young fish) (see Fig. 3.7*a, b*)	"It is as if to say 'baby fish.' It is a very small fish, round, like an acauatl. It has legs; it is dark green—red when cooked. It is good tasting, savory, of good, pleasing odor. I catch michpili in a net…; I bake michpili; I cook michpili in an olla, I eat michpili. Michpili eggs or amilotl eggs are round, roundish, like amaranth…white, like maguey fiber; crunchable, crushable. They become round; they become like maguey fibers. They crush. They are amilotl eggs." (pp. 64-65)
II. Waterfowl (Sahagun 1963:26-39, 57-58)	
canauhtli (duck, Mexican duck, mallard)	"It lives on the water; it feeds on fish, water flies, worms, water snails….It is white-breasted;…of average size, not too large….It has a wide, black bill, quill feathers, wing feathers, neck feathers, downy feathers….The head [feathers] are dark green. The head is black. Its head feathers are resplendent, shimmering." (p. 26)
concanauhtli (goose; *Anser albifons*)	"It is ashen, large, squat. It is wide-billed, broad-billed, broad-footed, wide-footed….It is a dweller in the lagoon here, and here it raises its young, builds its nests, lays eggs, sits, hatches its young." (p. 26)
tlalalacatl (atlatlalacatl, or atototl) (white-footed goose; *Anser albifons*)	"Also they call it 'water bird.' It is large. The legs are chili-red. [The bill] is ashen; the back is rounded. It is good-tasting, savory. It has downy feathers; its down is used for capes. It has breast feathers." (p. 27)
tocujlcoiotl (brown crane; *Grus canadensis*)	"The bill is long, like a nail, dart-shaped; the head is chili-red, [the body] ashen, the neck long. It is tall, high, towering. The legs are stringy, very long, black, like stilts. It is edible, savory, of good taste." (p. 27)
xomotl (duck)	"It is crested, short-legged, squat. The feet are wide, black, dark, blackish. It is a water-dweller, a fish-eater." (p. 27)

Table 3.1 cont.

General comment on the above three categories	"The goose, the brown crane,...the Mexican duck are white-breasted. The mallard, the xomotl, the teçoloctli are sea-dwellers. They hatch on the seashore, on the sand, especially there to the west. And when frost comes, they come here to feed." (p. 27)
quachilton (American coot; *Fulica americana*) (noted by Hernández 1959b:324-25)	"It lives on the water; it belongs with the ducks. Its head is chili-red, its bill pointed. It lives, it is hatched only here, among the reeds." (p. 27)
vexocanauhtli, oactli (black-crowned night heron; *Nycticorax nycitcorax*)	"Its legs are long, dark green. Its bill is pointed, long and pointed, green....The head becomes chili-red; its legs become long, rope-like. Its legs are stringy." (p. 27)
açolin (Wilson snipe; *Capella gallinago*) (noted by Hernández 1959b:321)	"It is long-billed, long-legged. It is varicolored like a quail....Its home is in the water, among the reeds." (p. 28)
atzitzicujlotl (northern phalarope; *Lobipes lobatus*)	"It is round-backed. The bill is long and pointed, needle-like, pointed, very pointed, black. The legs are long, very long, stilt-like,...broom-like, slender. Its dwelling place is [the province of] Anahuac [the Valley of Mexico]. It is white-breasted...heavily fleshed, fat, greasy." (p. 28)
aztatl (teoaztatl) (snowy egret; *Leucophoyx thula*) (noted by Hernández 1959b:320)	"It is white, very white....The back is rounded, dry, old looking. It is long-necked, stringy, curved. The bill is pointed, long and pointed, black. The legs are very long, stringy, stilt-like, black. The tail is stubby." (p. 28)
axoquen (light blue heron; *Florida caerulea*)	"It resembles the brown crane [in color]: it is ashen, grey. It smells like fish, rotten fish, stinking fish." (p. 28)
atotolin (pelican; *Pelecanus* sp.)	"It is the ruler, the leader of all the water birds, the ducks. When the various birds come, this is when it comes; it brings them here at the time of the Feast of Santiago, in the month of July. And the head of this pelican is rather large, black. Its bill is yellow, round, a span long. Its breast, its back are all white; its tail is not long, only average. Its legs have no bones at all; its feet are at its body. They are about a span long, very wide. Its body is long, very thick. Its wings are not very large; its wing feathers are not very long. This pelican does not nest anywhere in the reeds; it always lives there in the middle of the water, and it is said that it is the heart of the lagoon because it lives in the middle." (p. 29)
acoiotl (water turkey; *Anhinga anhinga*)	"It comes after the pelican [as a waterfowl]. It is also the heart of the water; it also is the leader of the [water] birds. It also appears at the time that the water birds come, on the Feast Day of Santiago [July]. Its head is as large as the turkey hen's. The bill is pointed, black, quite cylindrical; the outer edge of the tip is yellow. Its breast is rather white. Its back, its wings are all ashen, blackish, like duck feathers. It is long-bodied. Its legs are thick, not long; they are at its rump, almost at its tail. Its feet are very wide, like our hands. It also is rare...." (p. 30)
acitli (western grebe; *Aechmophorus occidentalis*)	"It is also rare. Likewise, it comes when the various [water] birds come. Its head is quite small, black, with a pointed, chili-red bill. Its eyes are like fire. It is long-necked. Its body is small and straight, small and thick; its breast very white, its back black, its flight feathers white, its wing-bend tips black, its legs black: they are also somewhat towards its rump, like a duck's legs. It lives there in the lagoon and is caught in nets....This western grebe does not fly very high; sometimes the water folk only chase it in boats; they spear it. And when they chase it, when they harass it exceedingly, when they are about to spear it, then it ruffles up, cries out, summons the wind. The lagoon foams much, it breaks into waves. So before the eyes of the water folk it vanishes, it suddenly enters the depths of the water. Occasionally they hit their mark; [the bird] is successfully speared. Also it brings forth no young [here]; it also migrates." (p. 31)

Table 3.1 cont.

tenitztli (black skimmer; *Rynchops nigra*)	"It flies high always at night there over the lagoon. It is the same size as a dove. Its head is quite small, black. Its breast is somewhat white, somewhat dark. Its back is black; its wings quite small. Its body is all small and round, its tail small, and its legs are like a dove's. For this reason it is called 'obsidian bill': it has three bills in all. Its food enters in two places [though] there is only one throat by which it swallows it. It has also two tongues....The food of the black skimmer is water flies, flying ants which fly high." (p. 31)
quapetlaoac (wood ibis; *Mycteria americana*)	"It is a bald-head—big, tall, the same as the little blue heron. Its head is large, like that of our native turkey cock; its head is featherless, bald, bare to the back of its head. The sides of its head are chili-red, reaching to its neck. It is long-necked. Its bill is very thick as well as cylindrical, long, like a bow. Its breast is black. Its back, its wings are completely ashen, except that the wing-bends are very black. Its tail is short, black. This wood ibis also comes when [water] birds come. It is quite rare....Its food is fish and all which live in the mud. Its flesh is very good to the taste." (p. 32)
quatezcatl (purple gallinule; *Porphyrula martinica*)	"It likewise is rare. Also it comes when [the other water] birds come. It is of average size, like a dove. For this reason is it called 'mirror-head': on its head is something like a mirror, a round [patch] on the crown of its head....On the front of its head is a thin row of feathers, somewhat ashen. Its bill is quite small, cylindrical. Its breast, its back are completely light blue. All its feathers are a little white. Its legs are yellow. And when it swims, when it paddles with its feet in the water, it looks like an ember; it goes glowing, glistening." (p. 32)
tolcomoctli (American bittern; *Botaurus lentiginosus*)	"It is rather large, the same size as the Castillian chicken, the capon. Its head is dark yellow; its bill yellowish, small, and cylindrical, about a span in length. Its breast, its back, its tail, its wings are all dark yellow, slightly blackened; its legs, its shanks, are dark....This American bittern always lives here in the reeds; here it raises its young. It sits on only five, or four eggs." (p. 33)
acuitlachtli	"It is as small as a small dog. Its head, ears, muzzle, belly, back, front feet, hind feet, claws are just like [those of] the forest-dwelling wild beasts, except that its tail is a cubit long, but broad, like the tail of the alligator;....The water folk used to hunt the acuitlachti. Also they said that this acuitlachti was the heart of the lagoon. It lived there in Santa Cruz Quauhacalco, where there is a spring [whose water] comes to Santiago [Tlatelolco]. When the acuitlachti dwelt there, because of it the water overflowed foaming, and the fish welled up to the surface." (p. 33)
covixin (black-bellied plover; *Squatarola squatarola*)	"It is a waterfowl....It is quite small; it is a little larger than a dove. Its head is quite small; its bill is chili-red, back at the end, small and cylindrical. Its back, its wings, its tail are all like quail feathers; its breast alone is tawny. Its legs are chalky, very long.... This bird also rears no young here; it also comes and it also goes. It eats fish. Its flesh is edible." (p. 34)
icxixoxouhqui (American avocet; *Recurvirostra americana*) (noted by Hernández 1959b:336)	"It is a waterfowl. It is named icxixoxouhquj because its legs are green. Its bill is small and cylindrical, small and slender, black, curved upward. Its head is quite small, white; its tail is also white. Quite small are its wings; the upper surfaces are black, and the under surfaces quite white; its wing-bends have black placed on both surfaces....It raises its young here, two or four young, when the rains come. It is also edible. And it also leaves when [the other water] birds migrate." (p. 34)

Table 3.1 cont.

quetzalteçolocton (common teal; *Anas crecca*)	"It is a duck called quetzalteçolocton because its head is ornamented as if with quetzal feathers. On the crown of its head its feathers are yellow. Its bill is black, small, and wide. Its neck is yellow, its wings resplendent [green]. But otherwise its wings are all ashen. Its back, its tail are likewise ashen. Its breast is white, its legs ashen though a little chili-red, small, and wide. It does not rear its young here. Its flesh is edible." (p. 34)
metzcanauhtli (blue-winged teal; *Anas discors*)	"…on its face it is decorated with white feathers like the [crescent] moon. On the crown of its head its feathers are ashen; its breast, back, tail are all ashen, resembling a quail. Its wing feathers are of three kinds. The upper coverts are pale blue; those lying in second place white; those lying in third place green, resembling quetzal feathers. The tips of its wings are black; its axilla white; its legs yellow, small and wide. It does not rear its young here; it also migrates. Its flesh is edible." (p. 35)
quacoztli (canvasback; *Aythya valisineria*)	"It is a duck, called quacoztli because its head and its neck are tawny to its shoulder. It is as large as a female Peru [duck]. Its eyes are chili-red; its breast white; its back ashen, a little yellow; its tail likewise somewhat yellow, quite small. The feathers of its under wings are mingled white and ashen; its legs ashen tending to chili-red, small and wide. Of its down are made capes. It does not rear its young here, but also migrates. Its flesh is very savory." (p. 35)
hecatototl (hooded merganser; *Lophodytes cucullatus*) (noted by Hernández 1959b:329)	"It is called ecatototl because its black feathers adorn the face [in the manner of the wind god]. It is the size of a duck. Its head is quite small; it is crested. Its feathers are tawny, ashen, somewhat dark. Its breast is white interspersed with black. Its legs are black, small, and wide. It does not rear its young here; it also migrates. It is edible. Many of them come." (p. 35)
amanochoche (bufflehead; *Bucephala albeola*)	"It is called amanochoche because of its white feathers placed on both sides of its head. It is the size of a common teal. The crown of its head is ashen; its neck is also ashen. Its breast is white; its back black: its tail black with two white [feathers], one on one side, one on the other. Its wing-bends have white placed on both surfaces; its wings half white, half black, the tips black. Its legs are black. It also migrates; it does not rear its young here. Many come. They are edible." (pp. 35-36)
atapalcatl (ruddy duck; *Oxyura jamaicensis*)	"It is a duck. It comes here in the vanguard, before [other water] birds have come. It is named atapalcatl because if it is to rain on the next day, in the evening it begins, and all night [continues], to beat the water [with its wings]. Thus the water folk know that it will rain much when dawn breaks….its bill is light blue, small, wide. And near its head [the bill] is white. Its head is tawny; its wings, breast, back, tail are all tawny; only its belly is white [and] blackish. Its feet are black, wide, and small. It rears its young here; [it has] ten, fifteen, twenty young. Sometimes not all leave; some remain. They are edible." (p. 36)
tzitzioa (pintail; *Anas acuta*)	"It is a duck. It is named tzitziua because of the feathers growing from its rump; among its tail feathers are two very white ones, located one above the other. A third, a small [white] one, stands between them. Their points are curved; they turn upward. Its head is ashen; its neck, its throat white. Following down the back of its neck, it is ashen. Its breast is white, its tail ashen; its feet black, wide, and small. It does not rear its young here; it also migrates. Neither does it come singly; there are many. Their flesh is edible, good-tasting, savory, [and] not fishy." (p. 36)

Table 3.1 cont.

xalquani (baldpate; *Mareca americana*) (noted by Hernández 1959b:345)	"It is named xalquani because it always eats sand, though sometimes it eats atatapalacatl [water plants]. It is the size of a goose. [On] its head, its feathers are white on the crown; the sides of its head green, resplendent. Its neck is like a quail's; its back ashen; its breast white; its tail dark ashen, [but] on each side is placed a white [feather]. Its wings are silvery, not long; its wings glisten; the ends are white, the wing tips black. On both sides [of the bird] are placed tawny [feathers]. Its legs are black, short, and small. It does not rear its young here; it also comes, it also migrates. Many come. They are edible, savory." (pp. 36-37)
yacapitzaoac (nacaztzone) (eared grebe; *Colymbus nigricollis*)	"…its bill is small and pointed, something like a small nail, and it pierces one sharply. And it swims under water; it always feeds under water. And it is named nacaztzone because its feathers which are over its ears, inclined toward the back of its neck, are somewhat long, tawny. Those at the crown of its head are dark ashen, slightly white. Its eyes are like fire, chili-red. Its neck, its back are dark ashen; its breast somewhat white. Its tail is also dark ashen, quite small; its wings black; white [feathers] lie underneath. Its feet are like the claws of a turkey, [but] very flat. It does not rear its young here; it also migrates. Its food is its [own] feathers, only sometimes it eats fish. It is not fishy, its flesh is savory." (p. 37)
tzoniaiauhquj (unidentified species of duck)	"…its head is very black,…reaching to its neck. Its eyes are yellow; its neck, its breast very white; its back dark ashen. Its tail is quite small, also dark ashen; its belly black, [but two] white [feathers] are placed on both sides near its tail. Its feet are black and broad. It does not rear its young here; it just comes [and] goes. Many come. They eat what is in the water, [as well as] the sand from the rocks and water plant seeds. Good-tasting is their flesh; it is fat, like bacon." (p. 37)
colcanauhtli (mallard; *Anas platyrhynchos*)	"…its feathers are all like quail feathers. It is rather large, the same size as a Peru [duck]. White [feathers] are set only on the point of each wing-bend. Its bill is small and wide; its legs black, wide, small. It is an eater of atatapalcatl [water plant] and achichilacachtli [gibbous duckweed]. It also comes, it also migrates with the others. It does not rear its young here. Many come here. Good-tasting is their flesh." (p. 37)
chilcanauhtli (cinnamon teal; *Anas cyanoptera*) (noted by Hernández 1959b:326)	"…its head, breast, back, tail are all like tawny chili: likewise its eyes. Its wings are silvery, its flight feathers black, its wing tips also black. Only its axilla they are mingled silver and yellow. Its belly is black; its feet chili-red, somewhat wide. It eats fish. Also it does not rear its young here; it also goes, comes with the others. Many come. They are edible." (pp. 37-38)
achalalacatli (*Stroptoceryle alcyon*)	"It is a duck….It is the size of a teçolocton. But this bird does not live in the brackish lagoon; rather it lives in the fresh water. It frequents the crags. Also it does not settle upon the water but always goes to alight upon the tops of willows, on treetops. And when it wishes to feed, from there it descends, suddenly dives into the water, it takes what it hunts, perhaps a fish, perhaps a frog…. Its head is crested; ashen are its feathers. White ones are placed on the sides of its head. Its bill is black, small, pointed, cylindrical. It is rather long-necked; [black and] white mixed are its feathers. Its breast is white, its back dark grey, its tail small [and] dark grey. Its wing-bend tip is white on both surfaces. Its flight feathers, the flight feather tips are dark ashen. Its legs are black, its claws like those of the northern phalarope, wide and small. It always lives here; [there are] not very many; they are somewhat rare. It is not known where they rear their young. They are edible." (p. 38)

Table 3.1 cont.

iacapatlaoac (shoveler; *Spatula clypeata*)	"It is a duck....its bill is somewhat long and very wide at the end. It is the size of a goose. When it comes here, its feathers are still completely ashen: but when it lives here, it molts twice....Its head is a very resplendent black as far as its shoulders. Its eyes are yellow, its breast whitish, its back ashen. Its tail is white at the base, ashen at its ends. Its wings are silvery; its flight feathers green, glistening, black at the ends. Its wing tips are ashen; its belly shows tawny; its legs are chili-red. Also it does not rear its young here; it also migrates. It is edible. Many come here." (p. 38)
pipitztli (probably *Larus franklini*)	"It also lives in the water. Its head is black; its eyes are also black; white [feathers] are set on the eyelids [so that these] appear to be its eyes. It is somewhat long-necked. The throat and breast are white. Down the back of its neck, on its back, its tail, wings, wing tips, it is black. The tips of both wing-bends are white. Its legs are quite long, chili-red, slender. There is really not very much to its body, but it is quite tall. Some migrate, some remain and rear their young here. Four are its eggs; only on the ground, on dried mud, on the plain, or somewhere on the top of a clod it lays its eggs; not on grass nor feathers. It is edible." (p. 3)
acachichictli (western grebe; probably *Aechomophorus occidentalis*)	"It lives on the water....And it lives only among the canes, the reeds....Its head is quite small; its bill is pointed and small. All of its feathers are yellow, slightly ashen. Its legs are yellow, greenish. It always lives here; it rears its young here. Four are its eggs; like a dove's are its eggs. It is edible." (p. 39)
III. "small animals which live in the water" (Sahagun 1963:62-65)	
atepocatl (tadpole)	"It lives in fresh water, among the reeds, the algae, the ducks, the waterlillies....Its food is mud and very small water-living insects.... It is good-tasting, edible...." (p. 63)
cueiatl (frog; *Rana esculenta*, *Rana temporaria*)	"It is black, dark; it has hands, it has feet. It is big bellied. It can be skinned." (p. 63)
tecalatl (frog)	"This is a very large frog, the mature frog, the old female. It is good, it is edible. The eggs, the offspring of the frog...are very many—countless." (p. 63)
acacueyatl (frog)	"It is green, black-spotted, blotched black, speckled. It is long-legged, a jumper...." (p. 63)
çoquicueyatl (frog)	"It is black. When in water which is drying up, it does not go elsewhere; it just enters into the mud. Even if the earth cracks, it does not die; where it is, it is absorbing [moisture]. It is edible." (p. 63)
axolotl (larval salamander; *Amblystoma tigrinium* L., *Proteus mexicanus*, *Sideron humboldti*)	"Like the lizard, it has legs, it has a tail, a wide tail....It is...well fleshed, heavily fleshed, meaty...good, fine, edible, savory...." (p. 64)
acocilin, Acocili (probably tiny crabs; *Cambarellus montezumae*, according to Deevey 1957:228; perhaps a small shrimp).	"It is like the shrimp....It is edible; it can be toasted, it can be cooked. I toast, I cook, I sell acocilin." (p. 64)
aneneztli (maybe dragonfly larva, according to Deevey 1957:228) (see Fig. 3.8*a*)	"It is long and small, cylindrical, glistening. It has legs....It is edible. It is an insect which transforms itself. It turns itself into a cincocopi." (p. 64)
axaxayacatl or quatecomatl (insect; *Ephidra californica* T., or *Corixa* sp.) (see Fig. 3.8*b*) (noted by Hernández 1959b:390)	"It is small and round, small and wide....It has legs, it has wings....It is a water traveler, a flyer, a swimmer, a diver." (p. 64)

Table 3.1 cont.

amoyotl (insect) (see Fig. 3.8c)	"It is like a fly, small and round. It has legs, it has wings; it is dry. It goes on the surface of the water; it is a flyer. It buzzes, it sings." (p. 64)
ocuiliztac (probably larvae of the dytisoid beetle, according to Deevey 1957:228) (see Fig. 3.8d) (noted by Hernández 1959b:393)	"It is long, small and long, cylindrical, white....It darts; it is agile, agitated." (p. 64)
izcauitl (insect larva) (noted by Hernández 1959b:395)	"It is slender, small and slender, pointed at both ends. I gather izcauitl; I take izcauitl; I roast, I cook, I sell izcauitl." (p. 65)

[a]Scientific and common names have been provided by the volume's editors (C. Dibble and A. Anderson). Cross references to Hernández (1959b) are noted.

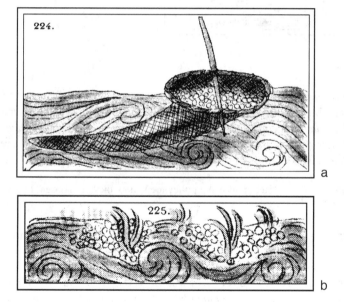

Figure 3.7. Sixteenth-century drawings of fish eggs. *a*, harvesting *Michpiltetei*, fish eggs, with a net (Sahagun 1963: Fig. 224); *b*, *Michpiltetei*, fish eggs, in their lacustrine context (Sahagun 1963: Fig. 225).

Figure 3.8. Sixteenth-century drawings of four different aquatic insect products. *a, Aneneztli*, probably dragonfly larvae (Sahagun 1963: Fig. 220); *b, Axaxayaxatl* and *ahuauhtli*, showing egg nurseries formed of reed bundles (Sahagun 1963: Fig. 221); *c, Amoyotl*, a lacustrine insect (Sahagun 1963: Fig. 222); *d, Ocuiliztac*, insect larvae (Sahagun 1963: Fig. 223).

Fauna

In addition to his specific comments about hunting *Acitli* waterfowl by spearing them from boats (Table 3.1; Fig. 3.9), Sahagun (1963:58) notes that several other species (*atlatlalacatl, teçoloctli, çoquicanauhtli, yacacintli, atzitzicujlotl, atapalcatl, atoncuepotli, atapalcatl, acoyotl, atotolin, xomotl, acacalotl, aztatl,* and *acujcujialotl*) are hunted in the following manner:

> These birds are thus hunted, thus caught: they are netted, they are noosed, they are caught by a cord about the feet, they are snared.

Sahagun (1963: Fig. 187) also illustrates the capture of waterfowl in large nets set on upright poles in shallow water (Fig. 3.10; see also Fig. 3.11 for another sixteenth-century illustration of this same activity).

Sahagun indicates that seven types of waterfowl rear their young within the Valley of Mexico: *Concanauhtli* (Goose), *Quachilton* (American Coot), *Tolcomoctli* (American Bittern), *Icxixoxouhqui* (American Avocet), *Atapalcatl* (Ruddy Duck), *Pipitzli* (probably Franklin's Gull), and *Acachichictli* (Western Grebe). Their eggs would have been available to human collectors. Sahagun (1969:3:147) also mentions the sale of duck (*pato*) and quail (*condornice*) eggs in marketplaces and notes that these were consumed in "tortillas" (omelettes) and "guisado de cazuela" (stews).

In his long listing of "foods which the lords ate," Sahagun (1979:37-40) includes a number of meals prepared from aquatic animals and plants:

Figure 3.9. Hunting waterfowl with pronged spear, in canoe (Sahagun 1963: Fig. 87).

birds with toasted maize; small birds; dried duck; duck stewed in a pot; the *atzitzicuilotl* bird stewed in a pot; . . . white fish with yellow chili; grey fish with red chili, tomatoes, and ground squash seeds; frog with green chilis; newt with yellow chili; tadpoles with green chilis; small fish with small chilis; . . . sardines with red chili, tomatoes, and ground squash seeds; large fish with the same; a sauce of unripened plums with white fish; . . .
. . . water-greens; . . . a water-edge plant called *acuitlacpalli*; . . . small tuna cactus fruit with fish eggs; . . . sauces with . . . lobster, small fish, large fish; . . .

Plants

Sahagun (1963:131-37) identified at least eighteen types of edible, artisanal, or medicinal plants that were *explicitly* aquatic (Table 3.2); nine of these plants were edible. Most, or all, appear to have been native to the Valley of Mexico.

Sahagun (1982:3:572-73) describes the work of a mat-maker:

El que es official de hacer esteras, tiene muchos juncias u hojas de palma, de que hace los petates, y para hacerlos primero extiende los juncos en algún lugar llano para asolearlos, y escoge los mejores, y pónelos en concierto; y de los petates que vende unos son lisos, pintados, y otros son hojas de palma.

[English translation] The mat maker uses different types of rushes or palm leaves, and in order to make the mats he lays out the reeds in some flat place in order to dry them in the sun, then he selects the best, and arranges them; and some of the mats he sells are smooth and painted, while others are made of palm leaves.

Sahagun (1963:257) also describes the use of "reed stem fibers" for tempering clay used for pottery making.

The Significance of Lake Texcoco in Prehispanic Cosmology

One of the principal functions of Tlaloc, a major Mesoamerican deity, was control over water (Broda 1971; Nicholson 1971). Bodies of water—springs, streams, rivers, and lakes—were closely identified with festivities, ceremonies, and rituals associated with Tlaloc and other lesser supernatural beings linked to water sources and rainfall. Sahagun described Tlaloc and his material accoutrements in the following manner:

Table 3.2. Edible or useful *explicitly* aquatic plants, native to the Valley of Mexico, described by Sahagun (1963).[a]

Sahagun's Type	Sahagun's Description
tecuitlatl, acuitlatl, açoquitl, amomoxtli (algae) (see Fig. 3.12*a*, *b, c, d*) (noted by Hernández 1959b:408-9)	"It is green. It coagulates. When the acoquitl wells up, spreads over the surface of the water, congeals there, the water folk take it there. They ball it together, throw it into the canoes, spread it upon the ashes. I am a tecuitlatl gatherer; I spread tecuitlatl; I pick up, I sell, I roast tecuitlatl." (Sahagun 1963:65)
atlepatli ("possibly *Ranunculus stoloniferus*") (Sahagun 1963: Fig. 454)	"It is a small herb which lies along the ground. It grows by the water, in the mud. It is deadly. He who eats of it dies of it; the animals which eat it die of it. It blisters, it burns wherever it is placed on the surface of our body. It is a remedy for skin sores. It burns one, it causes blisters. "I apply atlepatli to skin sores." (Sahagun 1963:131)
acuitlacpalli (Sahagun 1963: Fig. 466*a*)	"[Its leaves] are straight, broad. Its growing place is at the water's edge, in the water. It is cookable in an olla." (Sahagun 1963:135)
tziuinquilitl or atziuenquilitl (Sahagun 1963: Fig. 466*b*)	"Its habitat is in the water, at the water's edge. [Its leaves] are serrated, blue. It is cookable in an olla." (Sahagun 1963:135)
mamaxtla or mamaxtlaquilitl (*Iresine* sp.) (Sahagun 1963: Fig. 466*d*)	"It resembles the acuitlacpalli herb. Its habitat is in the water, at the water's edge. It is cookable in an olla; it is savory." (Sahagun 1963:135)
tzitzicazquilitl (*Jatropha urens*) (Sahagun 1963: Fig. 467*b*)	"It is prickly; it bites. Its growing place is in the water, at the water's edge. It can be cooked in an olla." (Sahagun 1963:135)
tzayanalquilitl (Sahagun 1963: Fig. 469*c*)	"Its growing place is in the water. Its branches are hollow, like reeds. It is called tzayanalquilitl for this reason: the center of [the stem] is split." (Sahagun 1963:135)
achochoquilitl (*Eupatorium deltoideum* Jacq.) (Sahagun 1963: Fig. 470*a*) (Hernández 1959a:113)	"It is light green, like turquoise. It causes one to belch. Its growing place is at the water's edge. "Auexocaquilitl is the same as Achochoquilitl." (Sahagun 1963:136)
uitzquilitl (*Circium mexicanum*) (Sahagun 1963: Fig. 472*a*)	"It is prickly, thorny, ashen; a rustler. It is stringy, fibrous. It has blossoms, it is blossoming. It grows at the water's edge." (Sahagun 1963:137).
chichicaquilitl (*Carraja mexicana, Sonchus siliatus, Mimulus glabratus*) (Sahagun 1963: Fig. 472*c*)	"It grows in the water, at the water's edge, in the reeds, on good lands, on cultivated lands. It is very tender. The roots are white. It is only a little bitter." (Sahagun 1963:137)
çacateztli ("probably *Panicum* sp.") (Sahagun 1963: Fig. 484) (see Fig. 3.13)	"[The root] is small and round like a maize kernel: small and cylindrical, white, fine-textured. It can be cooked in an olla; it is tasty, savory, pleasing, insipid,…small. Its foliage is straight, its blossom white like the izquixochitl. Its stalk is reed-like, cylindrical, hollow. It grows in the water; it is grubbed up in the mud." (Sahagun 1963:126-27) "The root is round and small. It can be cooked in an olla. It is fine-textured, savory, tasty." (Sahagun 1963:140)
acacapacquilitl (*Aganippea bellidiflora*) (Hernández 1959a:31)	"It grows in the water. It is hollow; it has stems, blossoms." (Sahagun 1963:195)
acaxilotl (Sahagun 1963: Fig. 446)	"It is cylindrical, cord-like, long, like the tolpatlactli. Its root can be eaten uncooked. It is cookable in an olla. It is quite fine-textured. It grows in the water." (Sahagun 1963:126)

Table 3.2 cont.

atzatzamolli (probably *Castalia gracilis*) (Sahagun 1963: Fig. 447c[?])	"Like volcanic rock, it is rough. It can be cooked in an olla. Its skin is gourd-like, tough, black. The center of this is what is edible; it is white, tamal-like. Its leaves are wide, round; it is called atlacueçonan. Its blossom is white; its name is atzatzamolxochitl. Its stalk is slender, hollow. It grows in water, forms a droplet, grows large, becomes like a volcanic rock, roughens, forms leaves [which] become broad. It opens on the surface of the water, it opens spreading on the surface of the water; it blossoms, it produces blossoms; it flowers." (Sahagun 1963:126) "Its root is [like that] of the atlacueçonan. It is pitted, rough, black; the center [of the root] can be cooked in an olla. [It is] like maize leached in wood ashes." (Sahagun 1963:140)
aitztolin (*Cyperus* sp.?) (Sahagun 1963: Fig. 582)	"It grows by the water, on the water's edge. Its green leaves are many, solid, like the reeds of Castile. Its leaves have a sharp edge; they are hard. Its blossom forms a stalk; it is tawny, small, straight and long. Two, three cluster together. It is edible. "And if I shall feel much hunger, I shall relieve it with this when I have nothing to eat. Also [with the blossoms] tortillas can be made; they can be cooked on a griddle. "Its root is small and round, black on the surface, white on its inside. And when it is ground, it is peeled; it becomes red. This is a little sweet. It is required by those whose urine is completely stopped, when he can no longer urinate [and] his stomach really distends. He drinks it during fasting, whenever he desires. Thereby [the urine] drops out; it removes the sand or whatever is clotted within the bladder. "It grows everywhere in the sweet water." (Sahagun 1963:171)
çacayaman, çacayamanqui (Sahagun 1963: Fig. 633)	"It is soft, fluffy. Its growing place is at the water's edge; in damp places. It lies shining; it is thick; it lies fluffed." (Sahagun 1963:193)
caltoli (*Cyperus* sp.)	"It is triangular, cylindrical, pointed at the end, long, pithy within. It is the real food of animals, especially of horses. Its roots are cord-like, asperous. The name of the asperous place is acuateuitzatl. It is edible, sweet. Its growing place is in the water." (Sahagun 1963:194)
xomali or xomalli (*Cyperus* sp.) (Sahagun 1963: Fig. 646) (Hernández 1959a:127)	[Author's note: Sahagun mentions no growing habitat, but because he indicates that it is a rush, I assume it is an aquatic plant.] "It is green, slender, thin—thin in all parts, stringy, compact—very compact, quite tawny. "I pull up rushes." (Sahagun 1963:195)
atetetzon (Sahagun 1963: Fig. 645)	"It is small and cylindrical, small and stubby. It grows in the water." (Sahagun 1963:195)

[a]Some scientific and common modern names have been provided by the volume's editors (C. Dibble and A. Anderson).

Tlaloc, the provider. To him was attributed the rain; for he created, brought down, showered down the rain and the hail. He caused the trees, the grasses, the maize to blossom, to sprout, to leaf out, to bloom, to grow. And also were attributed to him the drowning of people, the thunderbolts.

And he was thus arrayed: his face was covered with soot; his face was painted with liquid rubber; it was anointed with black; his face was [spotted] with [a paste of] amaranth seed dough. He had a sleeveless cloud-jacket of netted fabric; he had a sleeveless dew-jacket of netted fabric; he had a crown of heron feathers; he had a necklace of green stone jewels. He had foam sandals, and also bells. He had a green and white plaited reed banner. [Sahagun 1970:7]

Sahagun (1970, 1981) noted some of the most important activities associated with Tlaloc and other water spirits that were strongly oriented toward Lake Texcoco and that especially concerned those "water folk" who benefited from aquatic resources:

the god *Opochtli* . . . the god of the water folk; they worshipped him.

They said that he invented, he revealed, the net, the atlatl, the trident, the pole for propel-ling boats, the bird snare—these were his innovations, his inventions.

And when his feast day was celebrated the offerings became drink, food, wine, and the cane of maize plants, flowers, tobacco, incense, sweet-smelling herbs. These they spread before him, thus welcoming him. They shook their rattle-boards for him. They strewed popcorn for him which represented hailstones. And also his old men, his old women, the elders of the *calpulli*, made music for him. [Sahagun 1970:37]

The festival of another water deity, *Chalchiuhtlicue*, "the goddess of water," was celebrated by

those who sold water, as well as those who fished, and those who gained other livelihoods which there are in the water. These arranged her image and laid offerings before her, and revered her in the house called *calpulli*. [Sahagun 1981:39]

A more elaborate series of lakeshore/lakebed rituals were associated with the an-nual feast of *Etzalqualiztli*, another manifestation of Tlaloc. Pantitlán, a large whirlpool (*sumidero*) near Cerro Tepetzinco, a prominent hill in southwestern Lake Texcoco (Fig. 2.2), was of particular importance on this occasion:

Before the arrival of this feast, at the time it was celebrated, first the offering priests fasted for Tlaloc. For four days before their fasting began, first they gathered reeds there at Citlaltepec [north shore of Lake Zumpango]. For indeed at that place were formed very long reeds . . . very long, very high, and very white at the base; and rounded like a stone column.

And those who gathered them, at a place in the water called Temilco [or] Tepexicoztoc, they plucked them by their white ends.

And when they had gathered them, thereupon they arranged them, they tied them at the base in groups; they wrapped them up. . . .

Thereupon they used the tumplines . . . [to carry the reed bundles on their backs back to the Temple of Tlaloc, where they were made into mats and seats]. [Sahagun 1981:78-79]

After several days of ceremonial and ritual activities at the Temple of Tlaloc, the priests and their entourage went down to the lake edge:

Figure 3.10. Capturing waterfowl in large nets set on upright poles in shallow water (Sahagun 1963: Fig. 187).

Figure 3.11. Netting waterfowl and fish (adapted from sixteenth-century *Codice Azcatitlan* by Rojas 2004:27).

b   a

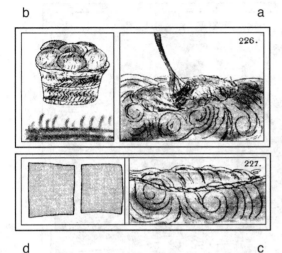

Figure 3.12. Sixteenth-century drawings of collecting and processing algae
(*tecuitlatl*), as re-interpreted by Ortega
(1972:163). *a*, collecting floating mass
of algae with a forked instrument (Sahagun 1963: Fig. 226*a*); *b*, processed
wafers of algae in a basket (Sahagun
1963: Fig. 226*b*); *c*, collecting algae on
a submerged thick rope (Sahagun 1963:
Fig. 227*a*); *d*, "bricks" of dried algae
(Sahagun 1963: Fig. 227*b*).

d   c

And when they went reaching the water's edge, the offering priests' bathing place, the mist
houses were at the cardinal points. Thereupon there was stretching out in each one [of the
mist houses], there was their seating themselves. . . .

    When this was done, then spoke the old man called the old precious stone priest; he said
    "[Behold] the place where the serpents are wrathful, the place where the water gnats
buzz, the place where the ruddy ducks take off, the place where the white reeds rustle,"

    When he had said this, thereupon there was plunging into the water, there was churning
the water, there was going beating it with their hands, there was going beating it with their
feet. . . . they mimicked all the birds.

    Some [of the priests] spoke like ducks; . . . Some mimicked gulls; . . . Some mimicked
jabirus; . . . Some spoke like white herons. Some spoke like little blue herons. Some spoke
like brown cranes.

    When they bathed, in the midst of things were poles. For four days it was done. And
when this was done, then there was ornamenting. Then there was returning; they went back
[to their homes]. [Sahagun 1981:81-82]

More ritual activities at the Tlaloc temple followed over the next few days—feasting,
burning incense, offerings (including human sacrifices), and dancing. Commoners also
undertook feasting and other forms of celebration at their homes and visited their neighbors
for additional feasting in honor of the occasion. The Tlaloc priests performed additional
rituals involving offerings at the edge of the lake. At one water-side locale, Totecco,

    the fire priest and still other fire priests from various places thereupon [sacrificially] burned
    the papers and the incense gods and the rubber gods. And the *yauhtli* [ground-up sea shells]
    they scattered in various directions; they spread it over the reed beds. [Sahagun 1981:85]

More ceremonies followed, involving feasting, fasting, incense burning, and offerings
(including "green stones") over the course of several more days. Novice priests who
participated in these activities at the main temples and *calmecacs* (formal schools where
elite young men were instructed in appropriate behavior and other forms of learning)

Figure 3.13. Sixteenth-century drawing of the *çacateztli* plant, illustrating how the plant's roots are cooked in an olla (Sahagun 1963: Fig. 484).

returned to their own homes and local *calmecacs*, where additional rituals were apparently performed (Sahagun 1981:87-88).

The concluding ceremony of the feast of *Etzalqualiztli* was carried out at Pantitlán:

> And when this [the ceremonies at temples on the mainland] was done ... thereupon the priests came down [to the water's edge]. They brought down all the offerings—the rubber-spattered sacrificial banners, and the maguey fiber capes painted with designs, ... and the green stones, and the quetzal feathers, and the incense pieces which looked like men. And they brought down the cloud vessel; it went filled with [human] hearts [from sacrificed victims].
>
> Then they took them directly to the water's edge, to a place called Tetemaçolco.
>
> And when they had gone to arrive, thereupon they loaded a boat; they filled a boat with all the offerings. And all of the offering priests embarked. Thereupon it was poled. . . . [Fig. 3.14].
>
> And when they went to arrive in mid-water, at a place called Pantitlán, there they brought the boat in. And when they had brought it in, thereupon trumpets were played. The fire priest arose in the prow of the boat. Then they gave him the cloud vessel, which went there filled with hearts. Thereupon he cast it in the midst of the water, before the stakes [which were in the water] [Fig. 3.15]. It immediately was swallowed ... [by the whirlpool].
>
> And then the water foamed, kept surging, roared, crackled continually, crackled as it surged. Bits of foam formed.
>
> Thereupon were hung out, were tied to the stakes, to the poles, the sacrificial banners. And they bound on green stones, but some of them they cast, scattered, strewed on the water.
>
> And when this was done, thereupon there was going forth. And when there was coming to go forth, when there was going forth there at the opening in the [barrier of] stakes, then [the fire priest] took up the incense ladle, on which he arranged four sacrificial banners. Thereupon he dedicated [the incense ladle with papers]; when he had dedicated them, he scattered them ... [on the water].
>
> And when he had cast them away, then they turned the boat about. Then there was the return; there was poling. Some went in the prow; others in the stern. [Sahagun 1981:89-90]

Figure 3.15. Priests depositing offerings at Pantitlán, southern Lake Texcoco (Sahagun 1970: Fig. 33).

Figure 3.14. Priests embarking in boats laden with offerings to be deposited at Pantitlán, southern Lake Texcoco (Sahagun 1981: Figs. 22-23).

The Pantitlán whirlpool and nearby Cerro Tepetzinco also were places where the bodies of human sacrifices were ritually deposited (Sahagun 1981:43).

This same ritual was described later in the sixteenth century by Fray Diego Duran (1971) (see below).

História Natural de Nueva España (Hernández 1959a, b)

Hernández describes seven categories of edible insects, including eggs, larvae, and adults. He also describes several types of waterfowl (Table 3.3) and useful aquatic plants. All these categories appear to have been native to the Valley of Mexico. For some items, he describes the techniques for harvesting these products and preparing them for human consumption.

Aquatic Insects

Axaxayácatl, axayácatl (Hernández 1959b:390; noted by Sahagun 1963:64)
Es el *axaxayácatl* una mosca pequeña y lacustre, cuya cara es de una blancura como de agua, de donde toma el nombre, y que en ciertas épocas se recoge con redes en el lago mexicano [western Lake Texcoco] tan copiosamente, que machacadas en gran cantidad y entremezclados se forman con ellas bolitas, las cuales se venden en los mercados durante todo el año; las cuecen los indios envueltos en hojas de espiga de maíz y en agua nitrada, y constituyen así un alimento bueno, abundante, y no desagradable; también alimentan con ellas innumerables especies de aves domésticas que, enjauladas, deleitan con su canto a quienes las oyen. Hay dos especies de estas moscas, unas mayores y otras menores. . . .

[English translation] The *axaxayácatl* is a small, lacustrine fly, whose face is white like the water, from which it takes its name, and which in certain seasons is collected with nets from the lake in such great quantities that great numbers of them are cut up and mixed together to form little balls, which are sold in the markets throughout the year; the indians cook them in salty water wrapped up in maize husks, and prepared in this way they comprise a good food, abundant and agreeable; also they use these to feed innumerable types of domestic caged birds, whose songs delight those who hear them. There are two species of these flies, one large and the other smaller. . . .

Ahuauhtli (Hernández 1959b:392)
Se saca del lago mexicano [western Lake Texcoco] en gran cantidad cierta substancia con sabor de pescado llamada *Ahuauhtli*, parecida a la semilla de adormidera, y que son huevos del *Axacayácatl.* . . . Se recoge echando en el lago, donde las aguas están más agitadas, cables del grueso del brazo o del muslo pero flojamente torcidos, y a las cuales, alborotado y removido, se adhiere; lo arrancan de allí los pescadores y lo guardan en grandes vasijas. Hacen de él tortillas muy parecidas a las de maíz, o las bolas que llaman tamales en la lengua nacional, o dividido en porciones la guardan envuelto en hojas de mazorca de maíz, para después, en su oportunidad, preparar con él alimentos cociéndolo o tostándolo.

[English translation by Ortiz de Montellano 1990:118] [A] great quantity of a certain substance called *ahuauhtli*, with a fishy taste, is taken from the Mexican lake [Lake Texcoco]. It looks like a poppy seed, and it is the eggs of the *axaxayácatl.* . . . It is gathered by throwing into the lake, where the waters are most turbulent, loosely twisted cables as thick as a man's arm or thigh. The [eggs] shaken and swirled, adhere to these, from which the fishermen remove them and store them in large vessels. They make tortillas [from it] similar to corn ones, or the balls they call tamales . . . or they save it, split into portions and wrapped in corn husks, toasting or cooking it at a later time. . . .

Ahuihuitla (Hernández 1959b:393)
Es una specie de insecto o de gusano con carapacho duro, del grueso de una pluma de ganso y tres pulgadas de ancho, de color leonado por encima y blanco por debajo, un tanto ancha y armada de tenazas. Es alimento bueno y agradable. . . .

[English translation] It is a species of insect or worm with a hard shell, as thick as a goose feather and three inches wide, of yellowish color above and white underneath, somewhat wide and armed with claws. It is a good and agreeable food. . . .

Ocuiliztac [probably larval stage of axaxayácatl] (Hernández 1959b:393)
Suelen llamar así los mexicanos a ciertos gusanillos que viven en la laguna de Tenochtitlán [northwestern Lake Texcoco], ... Cuando están crudos se ven negros, pero tostados en

Table 3.3. Hernández's (1959b) listing of waterfowl on Lake Texcoco. Cross listings with Sahagun (1963) are noted.

Category	Description [with English translations]
aztatl (white heron) (1959b:319-20) (noted by Sahagun 1963:28)	"Viven junto a la laguna mexicana." [They live next to Lake Texcoco.]
xoxouhqui hoactli (1959b:320)	"Es ave lacustre migratoria, visitante de la laguna mexicana." [A migratory lake bird, a visitor to Lake Texcoco.]
atapálcatl (1959b:320) (noted by Sahagun 1963:36)	"...semejante al ánade silvestre....Es...ave lacustre...visitante del lago mexicano...emigra en invierno al mismo lago con las demás aves palustres." [...similar to the wild duck....A lacustrine bird...a visitor to Lake Texcoco...it comes in winter to the same lake with the rest of the marsh birds.]
atótotl (1959b:320) (noted by Sahagun 1963:29)	"Es nativo del lago mexicano, y empolla en primavera entre los juncos y carrizas;....Se come asado o cocido, y proporciona un alimento no malo ni del todo insípido." [A native of Lake Texcoco, it breeds in the spring among the reeds and cane plants;....It is eaten roasted or baked, and provides a fairly good food.]
acacálotl (cormorant) (1959b:320-21)	"Es nativo de esta región, vive junto a los lagos y se alimenta de peces....Empolla en primavera, en sitios lacustres; suministra un alimento bueno...." [A native of this region, it lives around the lakes and feeds on fish....It breeds in the spring on the lake; it provides good food.]
azolin (cormorant) (1959b:321) (noted by Sahagun 1963:28)	"Habita en los lagos; suministra un alimento con resabio a pescado, pero no muy desagradable. Se nutre de gusanos, moscas y otros animalillos que se encuentran por el lago. Es oriundo del lago mismo." [It lives in the lakes; it provides a fish-flavored food that is not disagreeable. It feeds on worms, flies and other small creatures that are found in the lake. It is a native of the lake zone.]
azazahoactli (1959b:321)	"...vive junto a los corrientes de agua por necesidad de su nutrición....Se alimenta de peces; se domestica facilmente...se le ha de alimentar cuidadosamente con gusanillos y otros pequeños animales que se crían en los lagos....Es oriundo de esta región, y empolla en primavera entre los juncales." [...it lives next to the flowing waters because of its food needs....It feeds on fish; it is easily domesticated and should be carefully fed with worms and other small creatures from the lake....It is a native of this region, and breeds in the spring amongst the reed beds.]
amacozque (1959b:322)	"Es ave indígena, habitante del lago mexicano, y empolla en primavera. Su carne es comestible....Se alimenta de mosquitos, pececillos y gusanos del agua...." [It is a native bird, an inhabitant of Lake Texcoco, which breeds in the spring. Its meat is edible.... It feeds on small flies, little fish, and worms from the lake....]
atotolquíchil (1959b:322-23)	"Es originario de la región mexicana, y cría sus hijos entre los juncales y carrizales....Su carne es comestible y de alimento bueno y no desagradable." [It is a native of the Lake Texcoco region, and raises its young amongst the reed and cane beds....Its meat is edible and provides a good food.]
chichictli (1959b:323)	"Suele vivir cerca del lago mexicano o de la ciudad misma." [It usually lives near Lake Texcoco or near Mexico City itself.]
comáltecatl (1959b:324)	"...un ave lacustre que...en invierno, emigra de las frías regiones del septentrión a este suelo mexicano....Su carne es comestible pero con resabio de pescado." [...a lake bird which comes here in winter from the cold northern regions....Its meat is edible but has a strong fish flavor.]

Table 3.3 cont.

chochopitli (1959b:324)	"…es extranjero…que visita el lago mexicano….La calidad de su carne y sus propiedades alimenticas son las mismas del comáltecatl." […a foreign visitor to Lake Texcoco….The quality of its meat and its properties as a food are the same as those of the comáltecatl.]
quachilton (1959b:324-25) (noted by Sahagun 1963:27)	"Es tambien lacustre y visitante de la laguna mexicana; se nutre de peces, y constituye…un alimento no malo ni desagradable." [A lake bird and a visitor to Lake Texcoco; it feeds on fish and constitutes…a fairly good food.]
chilcanauhtli (1959b:326) (noted by Sahagun 1963:37-38)	"Es visitante del lago mexicano. Su carne es oscura y con resabio de pescado." [It is a visitor to Lake Texcoco. Its meat is dark and has a strong fish flavor.]
tequixquiacatzónatl (1959b:326)	"…vive junto a los lagos salados….uelan en grandes, inmensas bandadas, y devastan los sembrados en que se posan. Se come su carne." […it lives around the salt lakes….It flies in great flocks and devastates the crops in fields where it comes to rest. Its meat is eaten.]
ecatótotl (1959b:329) (noted by Sahagun 1963:35)	[an inhabitant of the lake area]
hoactli (1959b:330-31)	"Es ave del lago mexicano….Es visitante del lago mexicano y… oge las peces de que se alimenta. Empolla en los cañaverales…." [It is a bird of Lake Texcoco….It is a visitor to Lake Texcoco and seizes the fish upon which it feeds. It breeds in the cane beds….]
iztactzonyayauhqui (1959b:334)	"Se alimenta como los demás aves acuáticas, pues es visitante del lago mexicano." [It feeds like the other aquatic birds, and is a visitor to Lake Texcoco.]
yacatópil (1959b:335)	"Es visitante de esta región, y…se encuentra en el lago mexicano. Se alimenta de gusanos, y tiene el sabor y las propiedades alimenticias de los demás ánades silvestres…." [It is a visitor to this region, and…it is found in Lake Texcoco. It feeds on worms, and has the flavor and food properties of the other wild ducks.]
yacatexotli (1959b:335)	"…puede contarse entre los ánades acuáticos….Es…de la misma naturaleza que los ánades lacustres…." […it can be counted among the aquatic ducks…. It has the same characteristics as the lake ducks….]
ixixouhqui (1959b:336) (noted by Sahagun 1963:34)	"Se encuentra junto a los lagos de la provincia mexicana, a donde suele retirarse todos los años en determinado tiempo." [It is found around the lakes in the Mexican province, to which it is accustomed to return every year at the determined season.]
tempatláhoac (1959b:336-37)	"Es visitante del lago mexicano, y, lo mismo que las demás aves lacustres, comestible." [It is a visitor to Lake Texcoco, and, like the other lake birds, is edible.]
mozotótotl (1959b:337)	"Es…visitante del lago mexicano…." [It is…a visitor to Lake Texcoco….]
pepatzca (1959b:338)	"Es visitante del lago mexicano, y no es, como alimento, mejor ni más aceptable que las demás aves lacustres." [It is a visitor to Lake Texcoco, and, as a food, is neither better nor more acceptable than the other lake birds.]
pipixcan (1959b:338)	"Es visitante de los lagos mexicanos, pero no empolla allí; es comestible…es acuática…." [It is a visitor to Lake Texcoco, but it does not breed there; it is edible…it is aquatic….]
xalcuani (1959b:345) (noted by Sahagun 1963:36-37)	"Es visitante de esto lago, con resabio a pescado y nada grato como alimento." [It is a visitor to this lake, with a strong fishy flavor, and not especially desirable as food.]
xoxouhquihoactli (1959b:346)	"Es ave lacustre visitante del lago mexicano, en el que también se caza…." [It is a lake bird, a visitor to Lake Texcoco, where it is also hunted….]

Table 3.3 cont.

nepapantótotl (1959b:346)	"Es una especie de ánade silvestre frecuente en la laguna mexicana...." [It is a species of wild duck abundant in Lake Texcoco....]
opipixcan (1959b:353)	"Viva cerca de los lagos, y proporciona el mismo alimento que las demás variedades de ánades." [It lives around the lakes, and provides the same food as the other varieties of ducks.]
metzcanauhtli (1959b:354)	"Vive en la laguna de México, donde generalmente es presa de los cazadores mexicanos." [It lives in Lake Texcoco, where generally it is captured by Mexican hunters.]

platos o en los lamados *comalli*, se vuelven blancos al punto. Los comen los indios con sal. ... Todos los años, en determinada época, se ofrece una abundante y fácil captura de estos gusanos, principalmente cuando hay largas lluvias. ... no se hallan en las mesas de los ricos ... sino en las de quienes no tienen abundancia de alimentos mejores. ...

[English translation] The mexicans refer by this term to certain little worms that live in Lake Texcoco, ... When raw these are black, but once toasted in plates or on comales they promptly turn white. The indians eat them with salt. ... Every year, primarily during the rainy season, they occur in abundance and it is easy to capture them. ... they are not found on the tables of rich people ... but amongst those who do not have an abundance of better food. ...

Cocolin [probably the pupal stage of Ephydra hians Say., *according to Deevey 1957:226-27]* (Hernández 1959b:395)

Llaman los indios *cocolin*, o sea "cieno de olor fuerte," a cierta sustancia que produce el lago mexicano [western Lake Texcoco], que flota sobre el agua y es semejante al limo y de olor parecido también, de donde le viene el nombre. Lo venden los indios y lo emplean en sus comidas para saciar su gula de cualquier manera, pues exhala un olor fétido y es alimento dañino.

[English translation] The indians apply the term *cocolin*, meaning "mud with a strong odor," to a certain substance produced in Lake Texcoco, which floats on the surface of the water and is similar to mud and of a similar smell, from which comes the name. The indians sell it and eat it themselves in order to satisfy their appetites in any way they can, even though it has a fetid smell and is a poor food.

Izcahitli [probably the larval stage of Ephydra hians Say., *according to Deevey 1957:226-27]* (Hernández 1959b:395; noted by Sahagun 1963:65)

El *izcahuitli* es una masa de pequeñísmas lombrices que, capturadas con redes en el lago mexicano y guardadas en amplios recipientes, se venden en los mercados. ... Cocidas por los mercaderes adquieren un color neguzco, un olor como de huevos de pescados, y una consistencia como de miga de pan comprimida. Aumentan la leche a las mujeres que crían, por lo que algunos hacen con ellas tortillas que ponen a secar y guardan, aunque ni de este modo se conservan en buen estado por mucho tiempo. Cuando están a medio cocer dichas lombricillas, se les agregan pimiento y sal para darles mejor sabor. ...

[English translation] Izcahitli is a mass of small worms that, captured with nets in Lake Texcoco and stored in large vessels, are sold in the markets. ... When cooked by the sell-

ers they acquire a blackish color, an odor like fish eggs, and a consistency like compressed bread crumbs. They increase the quantity of milk in nursing mothers, for which purpose some make them into tortillas that they dry and store, although they do not preserve in a good state for very long in this manner. When these worms are half cooked, spices are added to improve their flavor. . . .

Waterfowl

Hernández (1959b:319-54) lists thirty different kinds of edible waterfowl that inhabited Lake Texcoco (the western part of which was sometimes referred to as "el lago mexicano") and its marshy shorelands during the sixteenth century (Table 3.3). Six of them are identified as rearing their young in the Valley of Mexico (*Atótotl, Acacálotl* [cormorant], *Azazahoactli, Amacozque, Atotolquíchil,* and *Hoactli*). These birds would have produced eggs in their nesting grounds.

Fish and Fish Eggs

Hernández (1959b:396) described the edible fish eggs that were abundant in Lake Texcoco.

Este producto lacustre y blanco formado de la multitud de peces que viven en el lago mexicano . . . y que en determinadas épocas del año se saca del mismo lago . . . parece ser una masa de pececillos no mayores que liendres que avanza por mitad del lago sin inclinarse a una u otra orilla, y en tan copiosa abundancia que ocupa un espacio de cinco o más codos. . . . los pescadores . . . los sacan en sus redes. . . . Se cuecen luego en vasijas de cobre o de barro, y agregando pimiento o chilli forman parte de las comidas. Constituyen, así preparados, un alimento bueno y agradable que comen con gusto no sólo los indios, sino con frequencia también los españoles aquí residentes.

[English translation] This white lacustrine product, formed by the multitude of fish that live in Lake Texcoco . . . and which at certain times of the year is taken from the same lake . . . appears like a mass of small fish, no bigger than tiny nits, that moves through the middle part of the lake without being carried to either shore, and is so abundant that it occupies a space of five or more cubits.[1] . . . the fishermen . . . catch it in their nets. . . . They then cook it in copper or clay vessels, and, together with added spices or chile, it forms part of their meals. Prepared in this way it is a good and agreeable food which both the indians and spaniards residing here eat with pleasure.

Although he does not describe lake fish in much detail, Hernández (1959b:402) briefly notes a distinctive fish native to the Valley of Mexico (the *Cuitlapétotl*), also mentioned by Sahagun (1963:62):

Es un pececillo del largo y grueso de un dedo, llamado así porque vive en aguas cenagosas . . . en los lagos mexicanos.

[English translation] It is a little fish the length and thickness of a finger, named thus because it lives in marshy waters . . . in the Mexican lakes.

---

[1]A cubit "is a measure of length equal to the distance from the elbow to the end of the middle finger" (Velázquez et al. 1993:169).

Aquatic Plants

Hernández described at least nine types of *explicitly* aquatic plants that appear to have been native to the Valley of Mexico. Many of these had medicinal uses, although three were described as edible. To some of the following descriptions I have added useful comments supplied by the anonymous editors of the 1942 edition of Hernández's work. These editors, in turn, relied heavily on the studies of Manuel Urbina (1904).

Tecuitlatl (algae) (Hernández 1959b:408-9; noted by Sahagun 1963:65)

Brota el *tecuitlatl*, que es muy parecido a limo, en algunos sitios del vaso del lago mexicano, y gana al punto la superficie de las aguas de donde se saca o barre con redes o se apila con palas. Una vez extraído y secado un poco al sol, le dan los indios forma de pequeñas tortas; se pone entonces otra vez al sol y sobre yerbas frescas hasta que se seca perfectamente, y se guarda luego como el queso por sólo un año. Se come cuando es necesario con maíz tostado o con las comunes tortillas de los indios. *Cada venero de este limo tiene su dueño particular* [emphasis added], a quien rinde a veces una ganancia de mil escudos de oro anuales. Tiene sabor de queso . . . pero menos agradable y con cierto olor a cieno; cuando reciente es azul o verde; ya viejo es color de limo. . . . comestible sólo en muy pequeña cantidad, y esto en vez de sal o condimento del maíz. En cuanto a las tortillas que hacen de él, son alimento malo y rústico. . . .

[English translation by Ortiz de Montellano 1990:104] Tecuitlatl, which resembles slime, sprouts in certain places in the Mexican basin and rises to the surface from which it is swept with nets or is removed with shovels. Once extracted and slightly sun dried, the Indians shape it into small loaves. It is again placed on fresh leaves until it is completely dry and then it keeps like cheese for only one year. It is eaten as necessary with roasted corn or with the common tortillas of the Indians. *Each source spring of this slime is owned privately* [emphasis added] and sometimes yields a profit of a thousand gold ducats yearly. It has a flavor like cheese . . . but less agreeable and with a muddy odor; when fresh it is blue or green; when old, it is the color of mud. . . . [It is] edible only in small quantities, and this instead of salt or as a condiment for maize. The tortillas made from this material are a poor and rustic food. . . .

Del Apancholoa o hierba que brota en las aguas (Hernández 1959a:11-12)

El *apancholoa* echa raíces muy semejantes a fibras, blancas, delgadas y algo cabelludas, de donde nacen tallos de cerca de cuatro palmas, delgados, cilíndricos, purpúreos y leñosos, con hojas ralas, oblongas y como de sauce, y flores purpúreos o blancas, alargadas y escasas, en casi toda la extensión de los tallos. Es de naturaleza fría, seca y astringente, por lo cual cura las quemaduras o las úlceros de la boca; el agua en que se hayan remojada por algún tiempo las raíces después de macharacarlas, coloda y tomada detiene el flujo de vientre, principalmente el de los niños, y evita el aborto. . . . presta además otros muchísimos auxilios propios de dicho temperamento. Nace en lugares campestres de regiones templadas, como la de *Tetzcoco*, . . . en terrenos húmedos o acuosos. . . .

[English translation] The *apancholoa* has roots very similar to fibers, white, thin, and somewhat hairlike, from which grow stems about four hands long, thin, cylindrical, purple colored and woody, with thin, oblong leaves like those of the willow, and with a few thin purple or white flowers along almost the entire length of the stems. It is by nature cold, dry, and astringent, and so cures burns or mouth ulcers; when drunk, the water in which the mashed roots have been soaked for some time prevents stomach flux, primarily in children, and prevents abortion. . . . it also provides many other benefits appropriate to its nature. It grows in rural places in temperate regions like Texcoco . . . in humid or watery terrain. . . .

According to the editors of the 1942 edition of Hernández's botanical work (Hernández 1942:1:34), the term "apancholoa" means "planta de las acequias en que brota el agua" [plant from along canals through which water flows]. It is identified as *Cuphea aequipetala* Cav., and described as a

> *[English translation]* herbaceous plant some 40 cm high, with thinly covered stems and lower leaves, the latter ovoid and pointed, flowers in solitary clusters, with a thick, veiled calyx and irregular corolla, violet colored.
>
> Commonly a decoction is used as a vulnerary or applied to wounds, contusions and tumors, also as a corroborant for births by bathing the back and hips with a solution of the freshly mashed plant after a steam bath. It is said to be "somewhat poisonous."

Del Atenxíhuitl, o hierba lacustre (Hernández 1959a:22)

Parece ser el *Atenxíhuitl* una especie extranjera de láber que echa ramas de sólo seis pulgadas de largo, purpúreas en su parte inferior y que nacen de raíces semejantes a fibras; tiene en la parte superior de las ramas hojas en grupos de tres, medianas, redondeadas, aserradas y semejantes a las de láber, a las que también son iguales en sabor, propiedades nutritivas y temperamento, que es caliente y seco. Se comen crudas o cocidas, provocan la orina y hacen desaparecer las obstrucciones. Nace en *Tetzcoco*, en lugares pantanosos.

> *[English translation]* The *Atenxíhuitl* appears to be a foreign species with branches less than six inches long, purple colored on its lower part and with roots similar to fibers; in the upper part of its branches it has leaves in groups of three, middle sized, rounded, serrated and similar to those of the *laber*, which it resembles in taste, nutritive properities and character, which is hot and dry. Eaten raw or cooked, it promotes urination and reduces internal obstructions. It grows in Texcoco in swampy places.

According to the editors of the 1942 edition of Hernández's botanical work (Hernández 1942:1:69-70), the term "atenxihuitl" means "yerba de la orilla del agua, o mejor yerba lacustre" [an herb from the water's edge, or, better, a lacustrine herb]. They identify it as *Ranunculus geoides* H.B.K., and characterize it as

> *[English translation]* perennial plants, stems with 1-3 veiled flowers, with trifid, silky-veiled leaves; incised-serrated lobes, with sub-trilobed mid-sections; hairy-veiled flower stalks; hairy-reflexive calices; 10 petals.

Del acacapaquílitl, o verdura que crepita en las aguas (Hernández 1959a:31)

Es el *acacapaquílitl* una hierba lacustre con raíces semejantes a cabellos, que salen por todas partes del conjunto mismo de los tallos; son éstos huecos, purpúreos, redondos, lisos y medianamente gruesos, con hojas ralas, largas, angostas y parecidas a las de caña, aunque menores, con muchas nervaduras longitudinales, y flores como manzanilla. Es de naturaleza fría y húmeda; se come, cruda o cocida, como hortaliza. Vive todo el año en la laguna mexicana, a menos que lo impida el invierno riguroso, y florece con las demás hierbas.

> *[English translation]* The *acacapaquílitl* is a lacustrine plant with roots similar to hairs, that protrude everywhere from the cluster of stalks; these are hollow, purplish, round, smooth and moderately thick, with long, narrow, thin leaves similar to those of cane although smaller, with many longitudinal nervatures, and chamomile-like leaves. It is by nature cold and damp;

it is eaten raw or cooked, like a garden plant. It lives year-round in Lake Texcoco, although its growth is impeded by unusually cold winters, and it flourishes with other plants.

The editors of the 1942 edition of Hernández's botanical work (Hernández 1942:1:97) identify the plant as probably either *Nasturitium palustre* D.C. or *Cardamine gambelli* S. Wats, and they add that

> *[English translation]* according to Dragendorff, the properties of *N. palustre* are: its roots for making drinks that purify the blood, its seeds as those of mustard, and the plant itself as a green vegetable.

Del acaquílitl, o verdura semejante a caña (Hernández 1959a:31-32)
Es hierba palustre, comestible, de raíces semejantes a cabellos, de tallo hueco y purpúreo, hojas como de sauce y flor parecida al crisantemo, pero con el centro purpúreo. Es de naturaleza caliente y seca, y de partes sutiles correspondientes al régimen de alimentación para adelgazar. Nace junto a las aguas estancadas o de corriente lenta, en lugares templados o un poco cálidos, y principalmente junto a la laguna mexicana.

[English translation] It is an edible marsh plant, with hair-like roots, a hollow, purplish stalk, with leaves like those of the willow and flowers similar to those of a chrysanthemum, but with a purplish center. It is by nature hot and dry, and with slender parts corresponding to a diet for losing weight. It grows near to ponds or to slow-moving water, in cool or slightly warm places, primarily next to Lake Texcoco.

According to the editors of the 1942 edition of Hernández's botanical work (Hernández 1942:1:98), the term "acaquilitl" means "quelite del carrizo" ["quelite" that grows in the reeds]. They identify it as *Bidens chrysanthemoides*, and note that it is "muy abundante en el Valle de México" [very abundant in the Valley of Mexico].

Del tepeácatl, o caña silvestre (Hernández 1959a:37)
No tiene el *tepeácatl* ningún uso, pero su forma es digna de verse. Echa raíz larga, delgada y fibrosa, un solo tallo, verde, y ramas con hojas alargadas, angostas y puntiagudas; además, en unas alas que tiene en la punta desprovista de hojas, florecillas blancas con rojo, pequeñas y redondas, en números de siete u ocho. Nace en regiones templadas o un poco frías, como son la *xochimilcense* y la *tetzcoquense*, en lugares húmedos y pantanosos.

[English translation] The *tepeácatl* is not useful for anything, but its form is worthy of study. It has a long, thin, fibrous root, a single green stalk, and branches with long, narrow, and sharp-pointed leaves; and at the leafless edge of which are seven or eight small, rounded red and white flowers. It grows in cool or slightly warm regions, such as the Xochimilcan and Texcocan, in wet and swampy places.

Del Atlatzonpillin, o hierba acuosa que cuelga de un cabello (Hernández 1959a:41)
Hay dos variedades de esta planta, una que por su color puede llamarse roja, y otra que por ser algo más clara puede llamarse blanca. Ambas echan raíz gruesa, rojiza y llena de fibras; tallos flexibles llenos de médula blanda, parecidos a los de higuera, cilíndricos, de cuatro codos de largo y del grueso del meñique; hojas de vid vinífera en la extensión de tallo, vellosas y ralas; flor roja y oblonga de donde nace el fruto, que está formado por tres cabezuelas

triangulares de un rojo coral, comestibles y llenas de semilla negra. Es de naturaleza fría en primer grado, húmeda y salivosa; y así, el agua en que se haya remojado por algún tiempo el polvo de la raíz o del tallo, tomada como agua de uso por los que padecen flujo de vientre o cualquier otra enfermedad que provenga de causa cálida, los cura rápidamente, y alivia la retención y el ardor de la orina así como las inflamaciones de los ojos. Es propio de clima templado o un poco cálido, como el mexicano y el *tetzcoquense*, y de las tierras húmedas y campestres. Brotan sus flores en agosto, y con ellas, así como con los frutos y hojas que caen, suele guardarse la raíz para usarse durante el año.

[English translation] There are two varieties of this plant, one of which for its color might be called red, and the other, clearer in color, which might be called white. Both have a thick, fibrous root; flexible, cylindrical stalks filled with white marrow, similar to those of the fig tree, four fingers long and of the thickness of the little finger; leaves like those of the grape vine in the length of the coarse, thin stem; an oblong, red flower from which the fruit emerges, formed of three coral-red triangular buds; edible and filled with black seeds. It is by nature very cold, humid, and salivurus; such that drinking the water in which its powdered root or stalk has been soaked for some time rapidly cures those suffering from diarrhea or any other disease which comes from a hot source, and also relieves painful urination and inflammation of the eyes. It is native to cool or slightly warm climates, as the mexican and the texcocan, and of rural humid lands. It flowers in August, and with these, together with its fruits and fallen leaves, are stored the roots to be used during the rest of the year.

The editors of the 1942 edition of Hernández's botanical work (Hernández 1942:1:127-28) identify this as *Malvaviscus drummondii*, and characterize it as a

[English translation] bush 1.5 to 3 meters high, with rounded, stringy, obtuse or sharp crenu-lated leaves 4-9 cm long, commonly angular or slightly lobulate; liner-spatulate bractlets; red corrola from 2-3.5 cm long.

The fruit is edible either raw or cooked.

We believe that the other variety of this plant, which Hernández indicates might be called white, may correspond to *Malvaviscus candidus* DC, because this species has white petals. . . . According to Stanley, Palmer indicates that the boiled flowers of this plant are used locally as a remedy for deafness, and that the flowers in an infusion of alcohol serve as a drink to prevent coughs and colds.

Del Atatapálcatl, o tiesto puesto en las aguas (Hernández 1959a:48)

Llaman los mexicanos a esta hierba *Atatapálcatl*, porque es parecida a tiestos o tepalcates puestos sobre las aguas de los lagos. Es propia de las lagunas, corrientes lentas y aguas estancadas, lo mismo que las demás especies de ninfea, a cuyas variedades también parece pertenecer, aunque las hojas son mucho más pequeñas y carece de tallo y de flor. Tienen las hojas pedúnculos semejantes a los de ombligo de Venus, gruesos, redondos, lisos, rojizos, enroscados cerca del nacimiento, y de cuya parte inferior salen raíces semejantes a cabel-los que se afianzan en el limo y casi en el agua misma; las hojas son gruesas, redondeadas, medianas, de un verde oscuro por encima y más pálido por debajo, y flotan sobre las aguas a la manera de las de potamogeton o de ninfea. Carece de sabor y olor y es de temperamento húmedo y refrescante, debido a lo cual podría usarse sin inconveniente en substitución de la ninfea común. Quita, aplicado, las inflamaciones y erisipelas; tomado en dosis de una dracma mitiga las fiebres de los niños, y dicen que arroja así la enfermedad a la cabeza provocando erupciones; ayuda a guardar la castidad, y se opone, en fin, a todos los vicios que provienen de calor y sequedad. Subsiste todo el año y durante todo el año se arranca y se utiliza. Es propio de clima templado o un poco frío, como el mexicano, y nace . . . en las lagunas.

[English translation] The mexicans call this plant *Atatapálcatl* because it has the appearance of potsherds placed on the lake surface. It is native to the lakes, and to places of slow current or ponded waters, like the other species of water-lily, to whose varieties it also seems to belong, although its leaves are much smaller and it lacks both a stem and a flower. The peduncular leaves are similar to those of the Venus naval wort, thick, rounded, smooth, reddish, twisted near the base, and from whose lower part extend hair-like roots that attach to the mud and seemingly to the water itself; the leaves are thick, rounded, medium-sized, dark green above and paler below, and float on the water surface like those of the *potamogeton* or the water-lily. It lacks taste and odor and is of a damp and refreshing nature, such that it can be readily used as a substitute for the common water-lily. When applied to the skin, it cures inflamations and erysipelas; when drunk in a drachm [1/8 ounce] dose it reduces fevers in children, and they say that it casts out head sickness causing eruptions; it helps maintain chastity, and thus opposes all those vices that derive from heat and dryness. It grows year-round and is pulled up and used throughout the year. It is native to a cool or slightly cold climate, like the mexican, and it grows . . . in the lakes.

The editors of the 1942 edition of Hernández's botanical work (Hernández 1942:1:152) identify the plant as *Pistia stratiotes* Linn., and characterize it as a

[English translation] floating aquatic plant; leaves in the form of a wedge or oval-wedge rosette, from 8-23.5 cm long, or less; flowers displayed in short spadixes; the masculine, in the upper part, have only two united stamens; the feminine with one ovary or several; it flowers rarely. According to Dragendorff, the plant is useful for treating dysentery, diabetes, hemorrhoids, and abscesses.

Del segundo Atatapálcatl (Hernández 1959a:48)

También nace en los lagos el *segundo Atatapálcatl*, y flota y nada en las mismas aguas; es algo parecido a la lechuga que llaman rizada, y tiene raíces rojizas parecidas a cabellos; las hojas son pequeñas, surcadas de nervaduras rectas, carnosas y no muy diferentes de las de llantén. Es de naturaleza fría y húmeda, y quizás es el *stratiotes* que describe Dioscórides o congénero suyo. Nace en los lagos y aguas estancadas de todas las regiones, calientes, templadas o frías.

[English translation] The *segundo Atatapálcatl* also grows in the lakes, and floats and moves about in the same waters; it is somewhat similar to curled lettuce, and it has reddish, hair-like roots; the small, fleshy leaves are creased with straight nervatures, not very different from those of the plantain. It is by nature cold and damp, and it may be the *stratiotes* described by Dioscórides, or a related species. It grows in the lakes and ponded waters in all warm, cool, or cold regions.

The editors of the 1942 edition of Hernández's botanical work (Hernández 1942:1:153) consider this plant to be the same as the previous (*atatapálcatl*).

Memoriales de Fray Toribio de Motolinia (**Motolinia 1967, 1971**)

This mid-sixteenth-century writer describes the harvesting and processing of lacustrine algae in western Lake Texcoco (Laguna de México):

Críanse sobre el agua de la laguna de México unos como limos muy molidos, y a cierto tiempo del año que están más cuajados, cójenlos los indios con unos redejoncillos de malla muy menuda, hasta que hinchen los *acales* o barcas dellos, y a la ribera hacen sobre la tierra o sobre arena unas eras muy llanas con su borde de dos o tres brazas en largo y poco menos de ancho, y échanlos ahí a secar: echan hasta que se hace una torta de gordor de dos dedos y en pocos días se seca hasta quedar en gordor de un ducado escaso; y cortada aquella torta como ladrillos anchos, cómenlo mucho los indios . . . anda esta mercaduría por todos los merdcaderes de la tierra, como entre nosotros el queso . . . es bien sabroso, tiene un saborcillo de sal, y creo especialmente que a este cebo vienen a esta laguna de México grandísima multitud de aves de agua, y son tantas, que por muchas partes parecen cuajar el agua: esto es en el invierno, en el cual tiempo los indios toman muchas aves destas. . . . [Motolinia 1967:327-28]

[Cited and translated to English by Ortiz de Montellano 1990:104] There breeds upon the water of the Lake of Mexico [western Lake Texcoco] a sort of very fine slime [algae], and at a certain time of the year when it is the thickest, the Indians gather it with very fine nets until their *acales*, or boats, are full. On shore they make a very smooth plot 2 or 3 brazas [3.4-5.1 m] long and a little less wide on the earth or on very fine sand. They throw it [the tecuitatl, algae] down to dry until it makes a loaf 2 *dedos* [3.6 cm] thick. A few days later it dries to the thickness of a used ducat [coin]. The Indians cut this loaf into wide bricks and eat a lot of it and think it good. This merchandise is carried by all the merchants of the land as cheese is among us. Those of us, who share the tastes of the Indians, find it very tasty. It has a salty flavor. I think particularly that this substance is the bait which brings great multitudes of birds to the Mexican lagoon. There are so many, that in many parts it looked like a solid lake made up of birds. This happens in winter and the Indians harvest many of the birds.

La Conquista de México (Gómara 1987:186)

Most of the following quote refers to the harvesting and use of algae:

Pocas cosas vivas dejan de comer . . . lombrices, piojas, y hasta tierra, porque con redes de malla muy menuda barren, en cierto tiempo del año, una cosa molida que se cría sobre el agua de las lagunas de México, y se cuaja, que ni es hierba, ni tierra, sino una especie de cieno. Hay mucho de ello y cogen mucho, y en eras, como quien hace sal, los vacían, y allí se cuaja y seca. Lo hacen tortas como ladrillos, y no solo las venden en el mercado, sino que las llevan también a otros fuera de la ciudad y lejos. Y dicen que a este cebo vienen tantas aves a la laguna, que muchas veces en el invierno la cubren por algunos sitios.

[English translation by Farrar 1966:341] There are few things they do not eat . . . worms, lice, even a sort of earth, for with nets of very fine mesh they collect, at a certain time of year, a soft substance which breeds on the water of the lakes of Mexico, and they thicken it, though it is neither plant nor earth, but a sort of mud. It is plentiful and they collect a lot of it; they empty it out on floors, as if they were making salt, and there it thickens and dries. They make it into cakes like bricks, which they sell, not only in the market . . . but carry it to others outside the city [of Mexico], and far off. They eat this as we eat cheese. . . . They say that so many birds come to the lake for this food, that often in winter some parts are covered with them.

Tratado Curioso y Docto de las Grandezas de la Nueva España (Ciudad Real 1976:111)

This late sixteenth-century writer describes the aquatic resources of western Lake Texcoco (Laguna de México) in the following terms:

La Laguna de Mexico . . . es de mala agua . . . no cría pescado ninguno que valga nada, pero cría mucho caza de patos y otras aves, y cázan las los indios . . . que cercan gran parte de la laguna donde ellas, especial los patos, van a dormir en los henares y zacatales, con redes puestas en unos palas hincados algo altas, y . . . espantan los patos que duermen por allí, y . . . quedan presas de los pies en las redes. Sácase desta laguna zacate para los caballos . . . deste hay todo el año . . . también se saca gran suma de moscas a manera de hormigas o gusanillas, las cuales venden las indias en los mercados para el sustento de los pájaros que en México tienen enjauladas . . . y cogen estas moscas los indios y las indias con unas redecillas en las partes que no está honda la laguna, de la cual también sacan muchos huevecillos de moscas de que . . . hacen algunos guisados que comen y tienen por muy gustosos.

[English translation] Lake Mexico has bad water . . . and there are no good fish there, but there is much hunting of ducks and other birds by the indians . . . around much of the lake where these birds, especially the ducks, come to sleep in the reed beds, with nets placed on high poles thrust into the lake bottom, and . . . they frighten the ducks that sleep there, and . . . the birds are captured by their feet in the nets. They harvest grass and reeds from the lake for their horses . . . the year round . . . also they collect great quantities of flies, like ants or worms, which the indians sell in the markets as food for the caged birds in Mexico City . . . and these flies are netted by the indian men and women in the shallow parts of the lake, from whence they also collect many fly eggs from which . . . they make certain dishes that they eat and consider very good.

Crónica Mexicana (Tezozómoc 1944:425)

In the following passage, Tezozómoc describes Moctezuma's (the Aztec ruler at the time of initial Spanish contact in 1519) triumphal procession back to Tenochtitlán following a military victory in late prehispanic times:

y llegados a la orilla de la gran laguna [Texcoco] le estaban esperando muchos lugares y partes de pescadores, que parecía no haber laguna, de tantas canoas que venían de gentes al recibimiento del rey y venían con infinito pescado blanco los de Mixquic, Cuitlahuac, Culhuacán, Iztapalapán, Mexicatzingo y lagunas dentro Aztahuacán, Acaquilpán, Chimalhuacán, y otros pueblos que están a las orillas de la laguna con todo género de patos, ranas, pescado, *xohuilli, yzcahuitle, tehuitlatl, axayaca, michpilli, michpeltetein, cocolin, ajolotes, anenez, acocozillin,* y la diversidad y género de aves de volatería. . . .

[English translation] and [Moctezuma and his entourage] having arrived at the shore of Lake Texcoco, there were awaiting him so many fishermen from different places that the lake was scarcely visible because of the great numbers of canoes filled with people who had come to receive the king, and they came with great quantities of white fish those from Mixquic, Cuitlahuac, Culhuacán, Iztapalapán, Mexicatzingo and from Aztahuacán, Acaquilpán, Chimalhuacán and other lakeshore villages bringing all kinds of ducks, frogs, fish, *xohuilli, yzcahuitle, tehuitlatl, axayaca, michpilli, michpeltetein, cocolin, ajoles, anenez, acocozillin,* and a great diversity of flying birds. . . .

Relaciones Geográficas (Acuña 1985, 1986a, 1986b)

These are compilations of a royal questionnaire distributed to local administrators throughout New Spain in 1579-1582, seeking information about individual indigenous communities. The most recent publication of these questionnaires is that edited by Acuña (1985, 1986a, 1986b); there is an earlier edition edited by Paso y Troncoso (1905). Below

I list the lakeshore (or near lakeshore) communities (see Fig. 2.2 for locations) for which some mention is made of harvesting or using aquatic plants or animals.

Chimalhuacán (southeastern shore of Lake Texcoco)
   Las mantenimientos que usaban eran maíz, ají, frijol y otras legumbres de la tierra, y los mismos usan ahora; y [usaban] de pescado, poco mayores q[ue] los albures de Castilla, y pescadillo menudo, y otras chucherías q[ue] se crían en esta laguna, de diferentes maneras. [Acuña 1985:165]

   [English translation] Their foods were maize, ají, beans, and other cultivated vegetables, and they use the same nowadays; and [they ate] fish, somewhat larger than the Castillian dace, and small fish, and other local lake tidbits that they prepare in different ways.

   [Lake Texcoco] en partes es hondable y, en otras no, y ser el agua della salobre. Los naturales deste pueblo tienen sus canoas de madera para pasar a la d[icha] ciudad [de México], y a otras partes, para sus contrataciones. En algunas tiempos del año es mala de navegar, por las grandes olas q[ue] en ella se llevantan cuando corren los vientos del norte y sur, y sudeste y el noroeste. . . . en ella se crían pescados de dos géneros, el q[ue] llaman blanco y el otro, q[ue] son como albures, y pescadillo menudo, ranas y camaroncillos, y otro género de marisco q[ue] pescan los indios para su sustento y granjerías. [Acuña 1985:166-67]

   [English translation] [Lake Texcoco] is deep in some parts and shallow in others, and its water is salty. The natives of this village travel in their wooden canoes to Mexico City, and to other places where they have business. At some times of the year it is difficult to navigate in the lake because of the big waves which come up when the winds blow from the north and south, and from the southwest and northeast. . . . two kinds of fish live in the lake, one which they call white, and the other that is like the dace, and there are also small fish, frogs, and small shrimps, and other kinds of lake creatures that the indians fish for their sustenance and to trade.

   En este pueblo y sus sujetos, los naturales del viven de labradores y pescadores, [y] no tienen otros tratos ni granjerías. . . . [Acuña 1985:168]

   [English translation] In this town and its subject communities, the natives live from their fields and from fishing, [and] they have no other sources of income. . . .

Chiconautla (northeastern shore of Lake Texcoco)
   los indios siembran y cogen maíz y frijoles y chile, y otras legumbres, y pescan y cazan, y desto sustentan. . . . [Acuña 1985:238]

   [English translation] the Indians cultivate maize, beans, chile, and other plants, and they fish and hunt, and from this they sustain themselves.

Culhuacán (southwestern shore of Lake Texcoco)
   Críanse en él arboledas de saces y cañaverales, [y] carrizos que dan en la laguna. [Acuña 1986a:32-33]

   [English translation] They raise groves of willow trees and beds of canes and reeds in the lake.

Su comida ordinaria es maíz y yerbas q[ue] llaman *quilites*, y pescadillas de la Laguna. . . . [Acuña 1986a:34]

[English translation] Their ordinary food is maize and greens, which they call quilites,[2] and fish from the lake. . . .

en la d[icha] Laguna y acequía del d[ic]ho pu[ebl]o, se cría mucha caza de patos, ansares y grullas. . . . las casas del d[ic]ho pu[ebl]o son todas bajas, hechas de piedra y adobes, y que se edifican con barro de la Laguna, que llaman Tlaltzacutle, que quiere decir "engrudo de barro," y las cubren de azotea, con su enmaderami[ent]o, y de Xacales de paja; y no usan cal, por no tenerla. Cercan sus casas con setos de cañas. [Acuña 1986a:35]

[English translation] on the lake and lakeshore there is much hunting of ducks, geese, and cranes. . . . the houses of the town are all low, built of stone and adobes cemented with clay from the lake, which they call Tlalzacutle, which means "clay cement," and they cover them with flat roofs made of wood and straw, using no lime because they do not have any. They surround their houses with cane fences.

Ixtapalapa (south shore of Lake Texcoco)

La granjería de los dichos naturales . . . es llevar a la . . . ciudad de México yerbas, que ellos llaman zacate y tule, para vender, en unas canoas largas a manera de barquillos. Crían aves y gallinas y, de la dicha Laguna, tienen caza de ansares y patos, y otros géneros de avecillas. [Acuña 1986a:38]

[English translation] The natives make their living by carrying large boat-loads of reeds and canes for sale in Mexico City. They raise fowl and hunt geese, ducks, and other kinds of small birds.

en algunos lugares cerca de la Laguna, hay temporadas, que es desde fín de septiembre hasta marzo, grullas, ansares, patos, zarapitos, garzas [y] carvejones. [Acuña 1986a:41]

[English translation] in certain places near the lake, from the end of September until March, there are cranes, geese, ducks, whimbrels, herons, and birds of prey.

Mexicalzingo (southwest shore of Lake Texcoco)

en la laguna cercana . . . hay a temporadas, que es desde octubre hasta marzo, ánsares, patos, zarapitos, garzas, corvejones y algunos aves de rapiña, sin las que hay todo el año. [Acuña 1986a:46]

[English translation] in the nearby lake . . . seasonally, from October until March, there are geese, ducks, whimbrels, herons, corvejones and several types of birds of prey, not including those that are present throughout the year.

las cercas y atajos son de cañas y carrizos, ... Sírvase este pueblo, en su contratación del zacate, con canoas a manera de chalupillas. [Acuña 1986a:46]

[English translation] the fences and alley borders are of canes and reeds, ... The people acquire grassy forage with small boats or canoes.

---

[2]Garcia Sanchez (1998:54) distinguishes six different categories of "aquatic quelites" used in indigenous cooking.

Citlaltepec (or Zitlaltepec, northern shore of Lake Zumpango)

los dichos naturals no tiene género de animal doméstico, si no es perrillos pequeños. Aves tienen gallinas, patos, y ánsares, ... Suelen venir por Navidad grúas, ánsares, y otros géneros de aves, y en este pueblo hay de ordinario, patos reales bravos, corvejones, cuervos, buharros, gavilanes, halcones, mochuelos, gaviotas, garzas y codornices y otros muchos génereos de aves campesinas. . . .

Tienen los deste pueblo grandisimos aprovechamientos desta dicha laguna, y los demás que en contorno della y de las demás estan, porque toman grandísima suma de pescado blanco . . . Y, asimismo, toman otras generas de pescados . . . y muchas ranas, y grandísima suma de patos, ánsares, grullas, garzas y otros géneros de aves, que toman con redes y lazos de que son muy aprovechados y sacan mucha suma de dinero. Y no lo son menos, de las esteras que hacen de tulle o "juncos" que por la vera de las dichas lagunas hay, de las cuales de ordinario traen estos indios mucha cantidad en canoas. . . . Usan anzuelos para pescar, y redes. Tienen, en las . . . lagunas, muchos y diversos géneros de yerbas y raíces, con que se sustentan. . . . [Acuña 1986a:201-2]

[English translation] these natives lack any kind of domestic animals, except small dogs. Of birds they have fowl [probably chickens and turkeys], ducks, and geese. . . . At Christmas time come cranes, geese, and other kinds of birds, and here there are usually ducks, cocks, crows, owls, hawks, falcons, red owls, gulls, herons, and quail and many other kinds of native birds.

The inhabitants of this village, and others around the lakeshore, derive great benefit from the lake because they catch great quantities of white fish . . . and other types of fish . . . and many frogs, and great numbers of ducks, geese, cranes, herons, and other kinds of birds, which they skillfully capture with nets and snares and from which they earn much money. And, not the least, are the mats that they make from reeds or rushes that grow along the lakeshore, and which the indians usually carry about in great quantities in canoes. . . . They use hooks and nets for fishing. There are in the . . . lakes great quantities of many different kinds of plants and roots, from which they subsist. . . .

Las naturales de este pueblo y sus sujetos tienen, por principal trato y granjería, vender pescado y esteras y otras cosas que de la dicha laguna sacan de cosas de caza, lo cual se venden unos a otros, y a españoles que entre ellos siempre andan tratando y contratando. . . . [Acuña 1986a:204]

[English translation] The natives of this town and its subject communities have, as their main business and source of income, the selling of fish and reed mats and other things that they acquire from hunting in the lake, which they sell to one another, and to the spaniards who are always going around buying and selling. . . .

Tequizistlán (northeastern shore of Lake Texcoco)

Los naturales de Acaltecoya, sujeto de Tequizistlán, tratan en pesquería y aves de caza, de que se pagan su tributo. [Acuña 1986a:244]

[English translation] The natives of Acaltecoya, a dependent community of Tequizistlán, exploit fish and waterfowl, which they use to pay their tribute.

Texcoco (ca. 2.5 km east of the eastern shore of Lake Texcoco)

sacan della [from Lake Texcoco] los indios, sus vecinos, muchas y muy ordinarios provechos. Lo primero es mucha caza de aves, que toman con redes, y el pescadillo que cogen, de que se mantienen casi todo el año, y un género de comida que llaman *tecuitlatl*, que hacen de unas lamas verdes que cría, lo cual, hecho tortas y cocido, queda con un color verde oscuro, que llaman los españoles "queso de la tierra." Cría otro género de comida que se llama *ezcahuitli*,[3] que hacen de unos gusanillos como lombrices, tan delgados y tan cuajados por su multitud y espesura, que apenas se puede juzgar si es cosa viva o no; y otra que llaman *ahuauhtli*, que también comen ya los españoles los viernes, y que son unos huevecillos de unas mosquillas que se crían en ella; y otra que se llaman *michpillin* y, otra, *cocolin*. Aunque las más destas comidas no comían, ni al presente comen, personas principales, sino pobres y gente miserable. [Acuña 1986b:104]

[English translation] the nearby indians take from the lake great quantities of foodstuffs. Most important is the hunting of birds and little fish, which they catch with nets, and from which they maintain themselves the year round, and a type of food that they call *tecuitlatl* that they make from certain types of green slime, and which, made into cakes and cooked, takes on a dark green color, and which the spaniards call native cheese. There is another type of food called *ezcahuitl*, which they make from tiny worms, so compacted that it is difficult to tell whether or not the mass is a living thing; and another food which they call *ahuauhtli*, which the spaniards also eat on Fridays, and which are eggs of certain lake flies; and another which they call *michpillin*, and another, *cocolin*. Although most of these latter foods nowadays are only eaten by poor, miserable people.

The Uppsala (Santa Cruz) Mid-Sixteenth-Century Map (Figs. 3.16 and 3.17)

This important document has been published and discussed at some length by Apenes (1947) and Linne (1948). My figures 3.16 and 3.17 are adapted from Apenes' rendition (1947: Lamina 2). This map graphically depicts many of the hunting, fishing, and netting activities described in the other sixteenth-century texts. Clearly visible (Fig. 3.17) are (1) hunters in canoes using pronged spears; (2) fishers in canoes using hooked lines; (3) hunters catching ducks in large nets strung above the water surface; (4) men walking [in shallow water?] and carrying long-handled nets; (5) men scooping the water surface with long-handled nets; and (6) men walking along the sides of what appears to be a long, low, partly submerged barrier made of interwoven reeds. Berres (2000:33) cautions that these depictions of hooking fish may not be valid for precolumbian times: on this point he cites zoologist Meek's (1904: liii) assertion that most indigenous fish in the Valley of Mexico will not "take the hook." On the other hand, Ciudad Real (1976:2:77) observed in 1586 that on Lake Pátzcuaro (a large lake in western highland Mexico) the Indians "pescan con cañas y anzuelos y con redes" [fish with poles and hooks and with nets].

Figure 3.17 clearly shows two distinct sections of the lakebed separated by the reed(?) wall/barrier noted above: (1) an outer section (apparently shallower water), in which clusters of reeds or rushes occur, and within which waterfowl are being netted, along with some other activities being carried out by men in boats; and (2) an inner section (presumably deeper water), in which aquatic plants are absent, and where activities other than waterfowl netting are being carried out. This reed "wall" apparently functioned as a kind of artificial barrier to deliberately separate deeper and shallower bodies of lake water, each of which may have been most appropriate for different types of procurement activities. John Staller (pers. comm. 2004) suggested that such a barrier might have

---

[3]This substance was also fed to dogs whose meat was intended for human consumption (Acuña 1986b:111).

Figure 3.16. Uppsala (Santa Cruz) map of the Valley of Mexico in the mid-sixteenth century (adapted from Apenes 1947: Lamina 2). North is to the right.

Figure 3.17. Enlarged section of the map shown in Figure 3.16, showing the eastern half of Lake Texcoco and adjacent piedmont, extending from Chimalhuacán in the south (left) to Chiconautla on the north (right) (adapted from Apenes 1947). *1*, men spearing (fish? salamanders?) from a canoe; *2*, man fishing(?) with a pole and line; *3*, man capturing waterfowl in large, upright nets suspended from poles; *4*, man with a push-net over his shoulder; *5*, man pushing a net through the water (to capture insects?); *6*, two men engaged in uncertain activity (building or repairing the reed barrier?).

functioned to enhance the effectiveness of fish poison within a ponded area, as is often done in northwestern South America (Heizer 1949). Figures 3.10 and 3.11 also illustrate techniques of netting waterfowl and fish in Lake Texcoco during the sixteenth century.

Linne (1948:127-28) offered an interpretation of the map's several depictions of duck hunting in boats (in the passage below he refers to an area of the drawing that does not appear in the section of the map that I have selected as Fig. 3.17). Linne was convinced that the men depicted throwing spears at swimming waterfowl were using *atlatls* to propel the pronged spears.

> *[English translation]* In the canoe we are looking at, one of the men manages the oar while the other is recovering the bird pierced by the lance. On board the following canoe another hunter prepares to throw his spear, while his companion is directing the course of the boat, which is necessary because the intended prey, three ducks, is almost invisible. . . . The spear has three points, which is the most common type. Without any doubt an *atlatl* was used to propel the spear, in spite of the fact that it can't be distinguished in the drawing. Nevertheless, the hunter always propels the spear from its rear end, which excludes the possibility that he is throwing it directly by hand. Furthermore, the distance between the hand and the end of the shaft corresponds to the length of an *atlatl*. [Linne 1948:127-28]

Book of the Gods and Rites and The Ancient Calendar (Duran 1971 [ca. 1581])

Fray Diego Duran describes the ritual that accompanied annual festivities honoring Tlaloc, the god of water, during late precolumbian times. His account supplements that of Sahagun (1970, 1981) (see above) by noting the importance of the associated ritual at the Tlaloc shrine atop Mount Tlaloc, some 30 km to the east of Tenochtitlan. The cosmological significance of Lake Texcoco clearly stands out in Duran's account, just as it does in Sahagun's.

> At dawn the lords celebrated the Feast of Tlaloc on the mountain (this mountain of Tlalocan) [a prominent hill, ca. 30 km east of Tenochtitlán] with . . . solemnity and lavishness . . . , in great haste since they wished to be present at the sacrifice of the waters. [While these rites were being performed at the top of Cerro Tlalocan], those who had remained in the city [of Mexico], where the image of the god . . . was kept in the temple of Huitzilopochtli, prepared for the same feast of the waters. This was especially true of the priests and dignitaries of the temples and of all the youths and boys who lived in seclusion and in the schools. . . . All these games and festivities were carried out in an [artificial] forest set up in the courtyard of the temple in front of the image of the god Tlaloc. In the middle of this forest was placed a very large tree . . . called Tota. . . . This indicated that the idol was the god of the woods, forests, and waters. When the news arrived [that the lords who had been on Mount Tlaloc] were descending from the mountains and drawing close to the waters to embark in the canoes which awaited them, this solemnity and feast ended in the lagoon. These [canoes] were as numerous as the lords, chieftains, and men who had made the journey, and they covered the shores of the lake. . . .
>
> . . . before the actual day of the feast of this god a small forest was set up in the courtyard of the temple in front of the shrine of the idol Tlaloc [in Tenochtitlán]. There were placed many bushes, little hills, branches, and rocks, all of which seemed the works of nature, yet were not arranged in imitation of nature. In the midst of this forest was set a tall tree of luxuriant foliage [Tota], and around it were four smaller ones. . . . Once the great tree and the four small ones had been set up in the form of a square with Tota in the center, from each of the small trees emerged a twisted straw rope, attached to the large one in the center. . . .

When the great pole or tree had been set in place, together with the smaller ones and the penitential ropes, the high priests and dignitaries, dressed up in their pontifical robes . . . carried forth a little girl seven or eight years old in a covered litter, . . . the priests carried this girl on their shoulders, enclosed within the covered litter. She was dressed in blue, representing the great lake and other springs and creeks. On her head she wore a garland of red leather, and on top was a bow-knot with a blue tuft of feathers. The little girl was carried within the covered litter into the [artificial] forest and was set down. Then a drum was brought forth, and everyone was seated, without dancing; then they sang various chants before the girl. This chanting lasted until news arrived that the lords had completed their offerings and sacrifices on the mountain [Mount Tlaloc], and were now ready to board their canoes. Having received this news, [the people] took the child in her litter and sent her off in a canoe. At the same time the great tree was removed, its branches were bound again, [and] it was placed on a raft in the water. The music and singing did not cease, and innumerable canoes [filled with] women, men, and children [who desired to] see the feast went along with her to the middle of the lake swiftly. Then they arrived at the place called Pantitlán, where the lake had its drain. Occasionally a tremendous whirlpool appears when the water is sucked down. . . .

When the great lords on the one hand and those of the city on the other had arrived at that place, the great tree called Tota was taken and was thrust into the mud next to the spring or drain. Its branches were untied, and it filled out again. Then [the people] took the child within the litter and slit her throat with a small spear (used for killing ducks), and her blood was allowed to flow into the water. Once [the blood] had flowed, she was cast into the waters, right into the whirlpool. It is said that the latter swallowed her so that she was never seen again. After the little girl had been cast in, the sovereigns came to make offerings, one after the other, and so did the lords. They offered as many rich things (such as jewels, stones, necklaces, and bracelets) as had been given on the mountain. These were thrown into the lake in the same place where the girl had been cast. Here each year such quantities of gold, stones, and jewels were cast that it was a marvelous thing to see.

. . . [The sacrifice] and offerings terminated, together with the other ceremonies. . . . In grave silence all returned to the city. In this way the feast ended. But the ceremonies did not, since *the peasants and the common men continued them in their tilling and sowing in the fields, in the rivers, springs, and streams* [emphasis added]. . . .

The tree of which I spoke was left fixed there until it rotted and fell. And since each year they set up a new tree, it is said that there were so many dried ones next to the spring [at Pantitlán] that finally they had to place them farther away owing to lack of space. This is true because I remember that, on crossing the lake by canoe many times, I saw the great hoary tree trunks rising out of the water. . . . [Duran 1971:160-65]

Relación de Texcoco (Pomar 1891 [1582])

Juan Pomar described the expanse of Lake Texcoco that lay between Texcoco and Mexico City in the late sixteenth century. He observed that the lake

es muy amarga, y muy peor sin comparación que la de la mar; y con no ser grande su hondo á respecto de los grandes y muchos ríos de agua dulce que en ella entran, no se mejora ni convierte de la dulzura de ella, antes de está y permanence siempre su amargura natural; y lo otro que aunque entran en ella otros ríos, y que alguna vez crece por muchas agues, no sobrepuja de su ser ordinario arriba de una vara de medir, de donde se presume que tiene algunas vías y aberturas por donde se vacía y desagua, porque si algún año es algo falto de lluvias, mengua tanto que yo me acuerdo que por la sequedad del año apenas se podia navegar por ella; porque yendo por ella en una canoa á la ciudad de México ví una abertura de peña tosca que corría casi por medio de ella de Norte á Sur, y ancha de una braza y en partes más y menos, llena de cieno, por donde debe sumirse el agua de ella, . . . No cría ningún género de pesdcado, si no es á las bocas de los ríos, del agua de los que en ella entran, . . . los géneros de patos y ánsares y otras aves de agua que en ella hay, vienen, según dicen, de la Florida, y no duran más de cuanto dura el invierno; pero con todo su maldad todavía sacan de ella los indios sus vecinos muchos y muy ordinaries provechos. Lo primero es la mucha caza de aves que toman con redes, y el pescadillo que cogen, de que se mantienen casi todo el año, y un género de comida que llaman *tecuitatl*, que hacen de unas lamas verdes que cría, lo cual hecho tortas y cocido, queda con un color verde oscuro, que llaman los españoles queso de la tierra. Cría otro género de comida que se llama *ezcauhtili*, que hacen de unos gusanillos como lombríces, tan delgados y tan cuajados por su multitude y espesura, que apenas se puede juzgar si es cosa viva ó no. Y otra que llaman *ahuauhtli*, que también comen ya los españoles los viernes, y que son unos huevecillos de unas mosquillas que se crían en ella; y otra, que se llama *michpitlin* y *cocolin*; aunque las más de éstas no comían ni al presente comen personas principales, sino pobres y gente miserable. No se cría sal del agua de ella, ni aun salitre bueno, porque el que se da en sus riberas no sirve de más de para hacer jabón. [Pomar 1891:54-55]

[English translation] it is very salty, although less so than the sea; and its depth is not great and its waters remain saline in spite of the numerous freshwater rivers that flow into it, and despite the abundant inflow of water, the depth of its water usually does not exceed a yard, which must mean that there are openings through which the water flows out, because I remember that in some dry years it was scarcely possible to navigate by canoe; once, when traveling by canoe to Mexico City, at about the center of the lake I saw an opening formed by rough rocks and filled with mud, through which the water must drain away underground. . . . The only fish are found at the mouths of the rivers where they enter into the lake. . . . all the ducks and geese and other waterfowl in the lake apparently come from the north, and only remain during the winter months; but in spite of this, the Indians who live around the lake take from it many kinds of useful products. First are the many waterfowl that are netted and the fish that are caught, with which they sustain themselves for almost the entire year, and a type of food called *tecuitatl*, which they prepare from some green ooze that they harvest, from which they make cakes that, when cooked, are dark green in color, and which the Spaniards call native cheese. Another type of food is called *ezcauhitli*, made of little worm-like grubs, so tiny and so densely and thickly packed together that it is scarcely possible to tell whether they are alive or not. And there is another food which the Indians eat, called *ahuauhtli*, which the Spaniards also now eat on Fridays, and which consist of the eggs of small lacustrine insects; and other foods called *michpitlin* and *cocolin*; although these are only consumed by poor people.

Tratado Curioso y Docto de las Grandezas de la Nueva España (Ciudad Real 1976 [1580s])

Antonio de Ciudad Real, a young Spanish friar, observed Lake Texcoco in November 1585, about two months after the end of the rainy season.

La laguna de México en que entran estas acequias es de mala agua y de malo y pestilencial olor, que no hace poco daño a la cibdad, especialmente cuando en verano se seca algo della; por partes tiene siete leguas y más [ca. 30 km] de traviesa, y muchas más de largo; no cría pescado ninguno que valga nada, pero cría mucho caza de patos y otras aves, y cázanlas los indios con una curiosidad extraña, y es que cercan gran parte de la laguna donde ellas, especial los patos van a dormir en los henares y zacatales, con redes puestas en unos palos hincados algo altas, y a la mañana antes que sea de día espantan los patos que duermen por allí, y como van a volar quedan asidos y presos de los pies en las redes. Sácase desta laguna zacate para los caballos, que es la yerba que comen, y desta hay todo el año, llávanla en canoas por aquellas acequias arriba a las plazas y allí la venden; también se saca gran suma de moscas a manera de hormigas o gusanillos, las cuales venden las indias en los mercados para el sustento de los pájaros que en México tienen enjaulados los españoles y aun los indios, y cogen estas moscas los indios y las indias con unas redecillas en las partes que no está honda la laguna, de la cual tembién sacan muchos huevecillos de moscas de que las criollas, que son las nacidas en esta tierra, hacen algunos guisados que comen y tienen por muy gustosos. También con el agua desta laguna y otros materials que (según dicen) no son para gente asquerosa, hacen sal los indios de aquella comarca, y la venden por toda la tierra; aunque es morena y se hace como dicho es. . . . Hay en aquella laguna entre otras, una isla que llaman el Peñol, y en ella unos baños de agua caliente que aprovechan para muchas enfermedades . . . cuando hay mucha seca se puede pasar a pie junto a este Peñol e isla. [Ciudad Real 1976:1:111]

[English translation] The Lake of Mexico [Lake Texcoco], into which these canals [mentioned earlier] lead, has bad water and a bad and pestilential odor that is harmful to the city, especially in the summer when it dries up somewhat. In places it is seven leagues or more [ca. 30 km] wide, and much longer; there are no fish worth anything in the lake, but there is much hunting of ducks and other birds, and the Indians hunt them in a very curious way by surrounding a great part of the lake where the birds, especially the ducks, go to sleep in the marshes, with nets placed high on poles, and in the early morning of the next day, before daylight, they frighten the sleeping ducks which then attempt to fly away and are trapped by their feet in the nets. They take plants from this lake for the horses, which is what they usually eat, and this is available all year, and they take it in canoes to the town plazas and sell it there; they also collect large quantities of insects, like ants or little worms, which the Indian women sell in the markets for use as feed for the caged birds kept by the Spaniards, and even by the Indians. The Indian men and women collect these insects with nets in those parts of the lake that are not too deep, and they also collect large quantities of insect eggs which the creole people, those born in this country, eat in several dishes which they consider very tasty. Also, with the water of this lake, and with other materials as well . . . the Indians of the area make salt and sell it throughout the region. . . . There is an island in the lake, one of several, called the Peñol, where there are hot baths to which many sick people go . . . [and] when it is very dry you can walk on foot to this island.

Summary and Conclusions

The sixteenth-century sources offer considerable information on the economic importance of aquatic products in the Valley of Mexico. Most of the resources mentioned are animals, including very large quantities and varieties of waterfowl, mainly seasonal migratory species but also some year-round residents. Several kinds of fish and fish eggs, several kinds of edible aquatic insects and insect eggs, and a range of amphibians, reptiles, and crustaceans are also mentioned. Except for migratory ducks, which were available in prodigious numbers only during the winter months, the other fauna appear to have been more readily available year-round, although this is not wholly clear. Both Cortés (1963:73) and Sahagun (1969:3:147) note the availability of waterfowl eggs in urban marketplaces, and Sahagun observed that they were consumed in omelettes and stews.

Waterfowl were hunted and trapped in various ways, especially with nets, snares, and well-designed approach-and-follow tactics that tired the birds so that they were unable to fly away from the approaching hunters, who then simply seized, speared, clubbed, or netted them. Fish were speared, hooked, or netted. Insects were collected with a variety of nets. The production of insect eggs was facilitated through the construction of nurseries in shallow waters where the eggs were deposited on conveniently placed reed bundles inserted into the lake bottom, or on thick submerged "ropes." It is difficult to quantify the annual harvests of lake fauna on the basis of the sixteenth-century documents. However, more detailed information from the nineteenth century indicates that sixteenth-century harvests were very substantial (see below).

Only one lake plant, algae, is frequently mentioned as a food source, although the seeds, stalks, and roots of three or four other types of aquatic plants are described as edible (e.g., Fig. 3.13). There are also references to the use of reeds, rushes, and cane as important raw materials for floor and wall mats and houselot fences. Several lakeshore towns specialized in making reed mats (Gibson 1964:336). There is even a hint that lake brine was used for cooking, without being transformed into crystalline salt (e.g., Hernández's reference to "agua nitrada" in the preparation of edible insect paste [1959b:390]).

Wooden canoes are often mentioned as essential for many kinds of hunting and collecting on and around the lakes. Netting and spearing of fish and waterfowl were commonly carried out in canoes, for example. These boats were also commonly used for transporting lakeshore residents, together with their harvested ducks, fish, reeds and reed mats, and aquatic insect products, to places where they paid their tribute/taxes in the form of these materials, or to urban marketplaces where they exchanged aquatic products for complementary agricultural and craft goods. Canoes also were used to transport heavy construction materials (e.g., rock, adobes, sod blocks) from place to place around the lakeshore. Reed boats are not mentioned.

The sixteenth-century sources do not provide many details about the specific spaces and facilities where aquatic resources were prepared and processed. Nevertheless, there are some general hints about such activities as storing, drying, thickening, grinding, cooking, and mixing. Masses of algae, for example, were sun-dried on flat lakeshore surfaces approximately 3-5 m on a side.

The occasional mention of "water folk" (e.g., Sahagun 1963:31, 33, 36, 65; 1970:37) suggests specialization in the exploitation of aquatic resources by lakeshore communities. Although some sixteenth-century lakeshore dwellers were described as combining farming and fishing, the products of aquatic specialists would have nicely complemented those of full-time agriculturalists living farther inland—as references to market exchange of aquatic and agricultural products indicate. The occasional mention of the individual ownership of fishing and algae-collection plots (e.g., Gibson 1964:339-40; Hernández 1959b:408-9) further testifies to the economic importance of aquatic resources and lacustrine specialists in the post-hispanic sixteenth-century economy. The implications of such early-Colonial lacustrine territoriality for prehispanic economy and polity remain uncertain, but there is good reason to suspect that controlled access to specific lake and marsh locales existed prior to European contact.

Barlow's (1949) study of the *Códice Mendocino* reveals little mention of aquatic products in the tribute levied by the Aztec Triple Alliance on the eve of European contact. Only one tributary province contributed a significant quantity of such materials, and these were exclusively in the form of reed mats and seats. This contrasts strongly with the large quantities of agricultural products from many localities within the Valley of Mexico and around its peripheries that were provided as tribute to the Triple Alliance. If aquatic products were so important in the prehispanic economy of the Valley of Mexico, why did they not find a more significant place in the tribute lists, comparable to that of cultivated crops (foodstuffs, cotton, agave fiber, etc.)? Does this reflect a Spanish prejudice against foods that, in European minds, were regarded as fit only for impoverished, low-status Indians? In this regard, it is important to remember that although the *Códice Mendocino* was drawn and formatted in indigenous, prehispanic style, it was prepared during the early post-conquest years under Spanish administration (Barlow 1949).

Sixteenth-century sources also reveal the cosmological significance of Lake Texcoco, especially its importance in water symbolism connected with rituals and ceremonies associated with Tlaloc and other water-related deities to ensure adequate water supplies. The most important of these rituals were carried out at the beginning of the rainy season—obviously a critical juncture in the annual hydrological cycle. These sixteenth-century documents have inspired a series of important ethnohistorical and archaeo-astronomical studies by modern scholars (e.g., Arnold 1999; Aveni 1991; Broda 1971, 1991; Carrasco 1991; Tichy 1983).

In addition to hilltop shrines around the lakeshore margins (Tichy 1983), human sacrifices and other offerings were made at three primary shrines in southwestern Lake Texcoco, at and around the island hill now called Peñon Viejo or Peñon de los Baños, formerly called Tepetzinco (Fig. 2.2): Tepetzintli, Poyauhtlán, and Pantitlán. The latter locale, purported to be a great whirlpool on the lakebed, and possibly the source of a major spring, was particularly important in this regard. Broda (1991:85) suggests that this triply sacred locale may have "delimited an eastern demarcation separating, maybe, the domains of Tenochtitlán from those of Tetzcoco."

Broda (1991:97-98) also calls attention to the distinction in Aztec cosmology between saline Lake Texcoco and the remaining freshwater lakes in the Valley of Mexico. She suggests that Huixtocihuatl, the goddess of salt, was also the patroness of salty water and of saltmakers, and that this goddess "seems to have been the personification of the salty waters of Lake Texcoco [and, by extention, of the sea], in contrast to the sweet waters of the other parts of the lake that were personified by Chalchiuhtlicue [the 'wife' of Tlaloc]."

The activities at these three major lakebed shrines were performed at the highest levels in the sociopolitical hierarchy, but the sixteenth-century sources also mention the active participation of commoners, and they hint that related rituals were performed by commoners at their own (much less well described) festivities honoring water deities, presumably at other localities in and around the lake. If Broda's insightful suggestion about the role of lakebed shrines in formally demarcating the border between the sociopolitical domains of Tenochtitlan and Texcoco is correct, might not smaller lakebed shrines, associated with communities at lower levels of the overall hierarchy, demarcate local community territories in a similar fashion? The frequent mention of burning incense and offerings of "green stones" and human sacrifices hints at some potential archaeological manifestations of these rituals. These manifestations should include, especially, objects of greenstone, incense-burning ceramic vessels, and human bone.

Another, highly original, perspective on the early sixteenth-century cosmological role of Lake Texcoco comes from Jill Furst (1995), who speculates that

The *ihiyotl*—the spirit that was wind, light, and odor—is probably the Central Mexican version of the will-o'-the-wisp. Certainly the Mexica were living in the right environment to see this phenomenon: a shallow, boggy lake was the perfect environment for marsh gas. . . .

If the *ihiyotl* was indeed a methane fire and the *ignis fatuus* [a European term denoting supernatural spirits associated with mysterious nocturnal lights], the Mexica probably saw it as a glowing, elusive entity drifting over the lake surrounding Tenochtitlan. The environment favored the formation of the methane necessary for the *ignis fatuus*, and during the rainy season, the gas could have easily ignited because of residual static electricity. The flames burned cold, unlike the warm and protective hearth fire known to the Mexica or the internal heat of the *tonalli*. Mesoamericans probably associated cold fires with the underworld and the dead. . . . [Furst 1995:162-64]

The Seventeenth-, Eighteenth-, Nineteenth-, and Twentieth-Century Sources

The most useful primary works I have consulted are (in order of original publication date) those of Vetancurt (1971 [1698]), Ajofrín (1986 [1760s]), Clavijero (1964 [1780]), Alzate (1831 [1780s]), Mayer (1844), Poumaréde (1859), Tylor (1861), Orozco y Berra (1864), Cowan (1865), Bishop (1883), Peñafiel (1884), Ober (1884), Duges (1888), Herrera (1895), Beyer (1969 [ca. 1920]), Ancona (1933), Apenes (1943), Smith and Smith (1971), Ortega (1972), Saenz and Posadas del Río (1978), Pérez (1985), Tortolero (1993), Roush (2005), and Aguilera (2001).

In his comprehensive archival studies, Gibson (1964:336) found that throughout the Colonial period the weaving of reed mats was an important activity in Xaltocán, Zumpango, Citlaltepec, "and many other lakeshore towns where the reeds (*tule*) were found." Gibson (1964:339-40) also determined that during the seventeenth and eighteenth centuries

[t]he freshwater lakes contained the fish called *xohuilin* (*juile*), and several species under the general description *iztacmichin*, or *pescado blanco*. None was of large size, the *pescado blanco* being 8 or 9 inches [ca. 18 cm] in length, with the preferred *amilotl* being slightly larger. The salt-water fish, notably white or yellow *charales*, were smaller. The most successful fishing of the salt-water lakes was to be found where springs or the mouths of fresh-water streams reduced the salinity, as near Zumpango and Ecatepec, or in parts of Lake Citlaltepec [northwestern Lake Zumpango]. *Pescado blanco* were caught in the waters of Xaltocán, at Coyotepec on the shores of Lake Zumpango, and even in the artificially dammed laguna de Ozumbilla [eastern Lake Zumpango] in the seventeenth century. . . .

. . . Salt fish were not unknown in native markets, but it is likely that the difficulties of preservation restricted the area of trade. The known notices refer only to the sale of fish in Mexico City and neighboring towns. . . . an estimate of the early seventeenth century [relates] that over a million fish were being taken annually from Lake Chalco and Lake Xochimilco [freshwater lakes in the southern Valley of Mexico].

Professional Indian fishermen are reported from Cuitlahuac, Huitzilopochco, Mixquic, Chalco, Mexicalzingo, Mexico City, and many other communities near the fresh-water lakes. A number of them are associated also with the salt-water communities, including Texcoco, Chimalhuacán, Tequisistlán, Chiconauhtla, Zumpango, Citlaltepec, and Xaltocán. . . . *fishing jurisdictions were as carefully demarcated and as jealously guarded as land jurisdictions in native society* [emphasis added].

Increasing conflict between Spanish and Indian fishermen gave rise to many disputes that were ultimately settled in Colonial courts during the sixteenth and seventeenth centuries (Gibson 1964:340).

Gibson (1964:341-42) also found that *"[w]aters for duck hunting, as for fishing, were included in the jurisdictions of individual towns"* [emphasis added]. Some lakeshore towns rented out their marshlands to duck hunters, and the annual duck consumption in Mexico City during the eighteenth century was estimated at between 900,000 and 1,000,000 birds (Gibson 1964:343).

Teatro Mexicano (Vetancurt 1971)

Writing in the late seventeenth century, Vetancurt describes six different varieties of aquatic reeds (tule) that served many different functions in and around Lake Texcoco:

> sobre aquellos cespedes se cria cantidad de enea, que llaman tule, que es de muchas maneras: ay tule que sirve par alas bestias de yerba, ay tule para hacer esteras, otro que sirve de colgar las puertas de los Templos, y se forman arcos para las fiestas, otro por ser mas denso sirve para hacer toldos para los que andan en canoas, ay cañizales, o carrizales, de donde se saca cantidades de cañas, que sirve a los Indios para hacer los paredes de sus chosas, y las cercas de sus corrales, y ay otro genero de tule mas grueso, y alto que el que dan a las bestias, que sirve de techos para sus casas, que ellos llaman sácales. . . . [Vetancurt 1971:33]

> [English translation] many different kinds of reeds, which they call tule, grow in abundance in the marshes: one type of tule serves as food for animals, another to make mats, another to hang up on the Temple doors and to form arches for fiestas; another, which is more dense, serves to make shelters for use while traveling in canoes; there are places where they harvest quantities of other reeds with which the Indians make the walls of their huts and the walls of their corrals; and another type of reed, thicker and taller than those which they feed to their animals, serves to make the roofs of their houses, which they call *xacales*. . . .

Diario del Viaje a la Nueva España (Ajofrín 1986)

Francisco de Ajofrín, a young Spanish friar, describes his trip by boat from Lake Xochimilco into Mexico City in the mid-1760s:

> Este mismo día, por la tarde, me embarqué en la canoa. . . . Nos amaneció en la laguna, y la serenidad de la mañana con su natural frescura, me ofreció la gran diversion de ir viendo tantos pueblitos y haciendas como hay en la laguna y sus inmediaciones, y la hermosa variedad de aves, patos, gansos, ánades, etc. que trafican por sus aguas y junto con las frescas arboledas que hay en las inmediaciones, forman un objeto deliciosísimo a la vista. . . . Llegase a esto la multitud de canoas y piraguas que se Cruzan por todas partes. Ya estaba compuesta la compuerta de Mexicalzingo y pasamos sín trabajo, como también otra compuerta que hay antes, cerca del pueblo de Qalhuacán [Culhuacán]. . . .

> Las lagunas de México dan más carne que pescado, porque crían patos con grandísima abundancia y de mucho regalo, gansos, ánades, y otras mil avecillas grandes, medianas y pequeñas, todas delicadas al gusto, pero el pescado, poco y malo.

> El modo de coger los patos es singular, se meten los indios todo el cuerpo, excepto la cabeza, en el agua, se ponen una gran calabaza en la cabeza que queda fuera, y luego acuden a ella los patos, pensando que es alguna peña, y sacando un brazo, los van cogiendo con este engaño. También los matan con escopeta. . . . .

En Mêxico se van los mosquitos al agua como en España al vino. En las lagunas se crían a nublados, aunque no son dañosos ni mordaces, los cogen para los canaries y otros pájaros, y los venden a costales en Mèxico. Cerca de los baños del Peñon . . . se crían tantos mosquitos que impeden andar, y se cogen a puñados con que no es de admirar se venden a costales y a celemínes. [Ajofrín 1986:160-61]

[English translation] That same day, in the afternoon, I embarked by canoe. . . . We woke up in the lake, and in the morning freshness I was diverted in seeing so many little settlements and farms in and around the lake, and the great variety of birds, ducks, geese, etc. which move about on the waters, and the groves of trees on the lakeshore, all of which forms a beautiful sight. . . . Added to this the multitude of canoes and pirogues that pass by everywhere. The flood-gate at Mexicalzingo had been repaired and so we passed it without difficulty, likewise the other flood-gate that comes before, near the village of Qalhuacán [Culhuacán]. . . .

The lakes of Mexico provide more meat than fish, because ducks are so abundant and productive—geese, ducks, and many other kinds of birds, large, medium-sized, and small-sized, and all delicious to the taste—but fish are few and of poor quality.

They capture ducks in a very singular fashion: the Indians submerge themselves, all except their heads, in the water and place a large gourd on their heads that stays above water, and then the ducks approach them, thinking that the gourd is some kind of rock, and the man then seizes a leg of the duck and captures it by this deception. They also kill ducks with shotguns. . . .

In Mexico the water flies come to the water as they do to wine in Spain. In the lakes there are huge masses of them, although they are not dangerous and do not bite. They capture them for pet birds, and sell them in sacks in Mexico City. Near the Peñon de los Baños there are so many water flies that one can hardly walk there, and they simply collect them by handfuls and sell them in sacks and measures.

História Antigua de México (Clavijero 1964)

Clavijero (1964:28, 38, 43) noted the abundance of aquatic birds and lake fish in the Valley of Mexico in the late eighteenth century, and mentioned five types of edible lacustrine insects. His most detailed information concerns the *axaxayácatl,*

una especie de mosca palustre del lago de México [western Lake Texcoco]. De los innume- rables huevecillos que ponen estas moscas en la enea y espadaña del lago, se forman unos grandes costras que traen en cierto tiempo los pescadores para venderlas en el mercado. Este huevo que llaman *ahuauhtli,* comían comunamente los mexicanos y al presente es plato común en las mesas de los españoles. Tiene casi el mismo sabor que el huevo de pescado. [Clavijero 1964:43]

[English translation] a type of marsh fly in Lake Texcoco. From the innumerable eggs that these flies deposit in the reed and rush beds around the lake, there form large layers which the fishermen bring at certain times of the year to sell in the marketplace. These egg deposits, which are called *ahuauhtli,* are commonly eaten by both the mexicans and the spaniards. It has the same flavor as fish eggs.

Regarding fish, Clavijero (1964:81) noted that in the Valley of Mexico,

[l]os ríos y lagos tienen los pescados blancos de 3 o 4 especies; las carpas, las lizas, las truchas, las trillas, los surieles, los bobos, los robalos, los barbo o bagres, los dorado, las jaibas, las corvinas, los langostinos, los cabezudos, las mojarras, las anguilas, lox *axolotes,* y otros.

[English translation] the rivers and lakes have 3 or 4 species of white fish; carp, skates, trout, mullet, surieles, bobos, robalos, bagres, dorados, jaibes, bass, shrimps, chubs, mojarras, anguilas, *axolotes*, and others.

Lake fishers employed a variety of tools (Clavijero 1964:235):

Los instrumentos más comunes de que se servían los mexicanos para la pesca, eran las redes; pero usaban también de anzuelos, arpones, y mazas. . . .

[English translation] The most common implements which the mexicans used for fishing were nets; but they also used hooks, harpoons, and clubs. . . .

Clavijero (1964:234) also took note of the numerous aquatic waterfowl in the Valley of Mexico, and of the techniques used to hunt them:

hay en las lagunas de México . . . una increible multitud de patos, gallaretas y otras aves acuátiles. . . . mantenían nadantes sobre las aguas a donde acudían estas aves algunas calabazas huecas para que, familiarizándose con ellas, no se ahuyentas en al tiempo de la caza. Entraba el cazador en el agua y ocultando bajo de ellas todo el cuerpo no llevaba fuera más de la cabeza enmascarada en una de esas calabazas; los patos llegaban a picarla y el cazador los cogía por los pies y las zambullía, y de esta suerte apresaba con suma facilidad cuántos quería.

[English translation] in the lakes around Mexico City there are an incredible number of ducks, widgeons, and other aquatic birds. . . . [the hunters] leave floating on the lake surface, in spots where the birds congregate, hollow gourds that are left in place during the hunting season so that the birds become accustomed to them. The hunter enters the water and hides beneath the hollow gourds, with only his head above water, where it is hidden by the gourds; the ducks come to pick at the gourds, and the hunter seizes them by the feet and pulls them under water, and in this fashion he easily seizes as many as he wishes.

Clavijero (1964:86) emphasized the importance of exchange of complementary products between lakeshore fishers and others who lived farther from the lake:

El pescado que cogían y las esteras que tejían de la enea que lleva el mismo lago, permutaban por maíz para su sustento, por algodon para su vestido, y por piedras, cal, y madera para sus edificios. . . .

[English translation] The fish that they caught and the mats that they wove from the rushes that grow on the same lake, they exchanged for maize to eat, for cotton to make their clothing, and for rocks, lime, and wood to build their houses. . . .

Gacetas de Literatura de México (Alzate 1831)

Alzate (1831:3:246) noted that aquatic insects and their eggs were being collected on the lakes near Mexico City during the 1780s. One variety was particularly abundant,

[English translation] an aquatic fly . . . whose eggs serve here as food, and which is called *aguautle* . . . the indians are accustomed to collecting these eggs. . . . This fly (which only serves as food for caged birds, for which purpose it is collected) never leaves the water, only coming to the surface from the bottom. . . .

Mexico As It Was and As It Is (**Mayer 1844**)

On the morning of October 7, 1841 (at the end of the rainy season), Brantz Mayer and several companions embarked from the eastern edge of Mexico City on a boat journey to Texcoco across the width of Lake Texcoco. He described this trip as follows:

We . . . rendezvoused at the gate of San Lazaro, where the canal enters the city. . . . In half an hour we found ourselves on board a flat-bottomed scow, under an awning of mats stretched over saplings. . . .

For nearly a mile from the city gates the canal leads through a tangled marsh, tenanted exclusively by mosquitos. . . . I scarcely ever suffered so much as in reaching the waters of the lake through these foul and desolate fens. We, however, soon found our way out of them, stopping for a moment at the Peñon Viejo [originally Tepetzinco, now Peñon de los Baños], a small volcanic hill . . . rising from the plain, where there are warm baths. . . .

On attaining the lake itself, the view was exceedingly beautiful. The expanse is a clear and noble sheet, reflecting on its calm bosom every hill and mountain of the valley. . . . Yet it is singular, that, sounding in the deepest central part of the lake, we obtained *but two feet and a half of water!* [0.76 m] [emphasis in original]. The boatmen poled the entire distance of twelve miles [19.2 km], and on every side we saw fishermen wading along in the lake, pushing their boats as they loaded them with fish, or gathered the "flies' eggs" from the tall weeds and flags, that are planted in long rows as nests for the insects. These eggs (called *agayacatl*) were a favorite food of the Indians long before the conquest, and, when baked in *patés*, are not unlike the roe of fishes, both in flavor and appearance. . . . they are not despised even at fashionable tables in the Capital.

Father Gage [Thomas Gage, a seventeenth-century cleric] at page 111 of his Travels, says that "at one season of the year, the Indians had nets of mail with which they raked off a certain *dust* that is bred on the water of the lake of Mexico, and is kneaded together like unto oats of the sea. They gathered much of this and kept it in heaps, and made thereof cakes like unto brick-bats. And they did not only sell this ware in the market, but also sent it abroad to other fairs and markets afar off; and they did eat this meal, with as good a stomach as we eat cheese; . . . and they did hold the opinion that this scum of fatness of the water is the cause that such great numbers of fowl cometh to the lake, which in the winter season is infinite."

This was written in the seventeenth century, and "*infinite*" still continues to be the number of wild fowl with which these lakes and the neighboring marshes are covered during the winter. . . . the plains and the waters seem actually peppered with them.

There can of course be but little skill in sporting among such clouds of birds, and the consequence is that they are slain for the market, by persons who rent the best situated shooting-grounds from the proprietors of the lake margins. The gunners erect a sort of infernal machine, with three tiers of barrels—one, level with the marsh or water, another slightly elevated, and the third at a still greater angle. The lower tier is discharged at the birds while they are setting, and this of course destroys a multitude; but as some must necessarily escape the first discharge, the second and third tiers are fired in quick succession, and it is rare indeed that a duck avoids the wholesale slaughter. From 125,000 to 200,000 annually load the market of Mexico, and form the cheapest food of the multitude. . . .

It was near four o'clock when, under the slow impulse of our polers, we approached the eastern borders of the lake. . . . we disembarked on the waste-like quay, among the sands and marshes. . . . [Being unable to procure transport from the quay into Texcoco, Mayer and his companions were obliged to walk a considerable distance over difficult marshy terrain into town.] [In the course of this walk] [o]ur anxiety was greatly increased by the loss of one of our party in the darkness among some morasses, and by the rise of a considerable stream that crossed the road near the town. We however waded the brook, and, [reached their destination at] about eight o'clock. . . . [Mayer 1844:217-19]

Desagüe del Valle de México (**Poumaréde 1859**)

This mid-nineteenth-century writer (1859:471-72) noted the huge quantity of organic material that accumulated in Lake Texcoco, the product of human, animal, and plant wastes. This organic mass often built up on the lake surface in the form of a

> [English translation] thick foam that the winds bring together and move towards the shores, where it continues rotting, giving off the most offensive stench that could affect the olfactory sense.
>
> These circumstances . . . result in the transformation of the waters of Lake Texcoco and Lake San Cristobal into a type of broth . . . [which] has attracted millions of flies that come to these lakes . . . in search of food, and these insects deposit their eggs on the beds of lake plants that cover parts of the lake surface, . . . generally these eggs germinate easily in the lake waters, producing larvae which form, together with the aid of the materials they expel, a common organic mass somewhat similar to the sponges obtained on the sea coasts. . . .
>
> . . . the eggs, the larvae and the organic mass are eagerly sought after as food by certain indigenous inhabitants of the valley [of Mexico]. The eggs are sold in the Mexico City market with the name of *ahuautle*, which are generally eaten as cakes flavored with spicy chile. The larvae, with the special name of *puchi*, . . . are mixed with maize dough . . . [in the form of] tamales . . . [and] are consumed in these places by the inhabitants of certain lakeshore communities. When cooked, it appears as a gelatinous material which must be highly nutritious.

Anahuac: or, Mexico and the Mexicans, Ancient and Modern (**Tylor 1861**)

On a visit to the town and environs of Texcoco, on the eastern side of Lake Texcoco, during the spring (late dry season) of 1856, Tylor (1861:156) noted that

> a favorite dish here consists of flies' eggs fried. These eggs are deposited at the edge of the lake, and the Indians fish them out and sell them in the market place. . . .
>
> The flies (*Corixa femorata* and *Notonecta unifasciata*) which produce these eggs are called by the Mexicans *axayacatl* or "water face." . . . The eggs themselves are sold in cakes in the market, pounded and cooked, and also in lumps *au naturel*, forming a substance like the roe of a fish. This is known as . . . *ahuauhtli* . . . "water wheat."

Memoria para la Cartografía Hidrográfica del Valle de México (**Orozco y Berra 1864**)

This writer describes the vast numbers of waterfowl that inhabited the lakebed zones in the Valley of Mexico during the mid-nineteenth century (Table 3.4).

> [English translation] The ducks are found in all the lakes, and even in places in the Valley [of Mexico] where water has been ponded. Migratory birds come in considerable numbers in the winter, and at least some species disappear for the entire summer. Of these there are at least 20 kinds. [Orozco y Berra 1864:147]

During the winter season, when the migratory waterfowl were most abundant on the lakebed, professional hunters rigged outward-facing circles of dozens of crude shotguns (*armadas*) in places where ducks were accustomed to feed—similar devices had been described by Brantz Mayer (1844) two decades earlier (see above). These devices, triggered all together by a man hidden some distance away at the end of a long string, were

Table 3.4. Orozco y Berra's (1864:148-49) categories of waterfowl in the Valley of Mexico.*

Category	Orozco y Berra's Comments
canauhtli	generic term for all waterfowl
concanauhtli	largest of the waterfowl
xomotl	
huexocanauhtli	
quetzaltecololton	
metzcanauhtli	
atapalcatl, or iacatextli	
tzitzicoa	
xalcuani	
colcanauhtli	
chilcanauhtli	
yacapatlaoac	
oactli	
nepapantototl	
tzinitzcan, or teutzinitzcan	
tlauhquechol, or	
teuhquechol	
tlalacatl	goose
atotoli	gallina de agua (water hen)
cuachilton	
xacozintle	
colin, or coquiacolin	
atzitzicuilotl	chichicuilote
aztatl	heron
axoquen	
acoiotl	
acitli	liebre de agua (water hare)
tenitzli	
cuapetlaoac, or	
quepetlanqui	
tolcomoctli, or ateponaztli	
cohuixin	
yoxixoxouhqui	
acachichictli	

*Most of these were denoted by identical or similar terms in the sixteenth century (Hernández 1959b; Sahagun 1963).

apparently capable of killing up to 2400 birds in a single massive firing. It was through such practices that over a million ducks entered the Mexico City marketplace each year (Orozco y Berra 1864:150).

Orozco y Berra (1864:150) asserts that the only fish in saline Lake Texcoco at the time of his observations were found in places where freshwater streams entered the lake. In such places

> *[English translation]* are found *juiles*, and small fish, white or yellowish, that they call *charales*.

Orozco y Berra also provided a detailed description of the preparation, in the shallow waters of Lake Texcoco, of nurseries where the eggs of the aquatic insect *axayácatl* were deposited and subsequently harvested.

[English translation] The indians form small bundles of reeds, which they place in shallow parts of the lake at intervals of about one meter, in such a way that one end of the reed bundle rests on the lake bottom, while the other end projects above the surface. The female *axayacatl* comes there to deposit its eggs, and soon not only do the eggs cover the entire reed bundle, but they also form bunches of eggs lying one atop the other. Once the egg-covered reed bundles are pulled out of the water and dried, they are shaken over a cloth; the eggs fall off with this action, it being sufficient to brush the reeds with the hand in order to loosen those eggs that may have remained attached. The product thus prepared is known as *ahuautle*. . . . *Ahuautle* is considered an appropriate food for those days in which religious rules prohibit the use of meat; it is prepared and eaten in several ways, ground up and mixed with chicken eggs, as cakes fried in grease, that are either eaten alone or in particular dishes, such as *revoltillo*, a favored and obligatory dish on festive occasions, such as Christmas and Easter. *Ahuautle* has a taste similar to that of fish caviar. . . .

The larva that forms from the egg is a small white or yellowish worm; it is collected in great quantities, and is prepared by cooking the entire insect in maize husks, or grinding them into a paste, and thus taken to market wrapped in husks. This product is called by the mexican name of *puxi*, and is reputed to be a very good food. [Orozco y Berra 1864:152-53]

In another passage, Orozco y Berra referred to masses of insect matter, which he believed to be larval forms of the *axayacatl* (*axaxayacatl*) that became concentrated in large masses that floated in the shallow lake water in the form of

[English translation] a nest composed of innumerable little cellular units, that is similar in form, although not in consistency, to certain sponges. By means of circumstances unknown to us, these nests rise to the surface of the water where the indians collect them and cook them in maize husks, in which form they have the appearance of a gelatinous material, which should be very nutritious. This culinary product is not eaten by city people, but by the indigenous inhabitants around the lakeshore. . . . [Orozco y Berra 1864:153-54]

According to Orozco y Berra, some species of lacustrine insects were so abundant in the mid-nineteenth century that they were used as agricultural fertilizer:

[English translation] There is in this lake a small black fly, known by the indians with the name of *requesón*, and which appears to be the *chiltón* of the [ancient] mexicans: it is so abundant that in flight the insects form veritable clouds. When they die the insects remain scattered on the water's surface, and the wind pushes them to the shore where they are collected, and from where the natives take them to use as fertilizer in their fields. . . . [Orozco y Berra 1864:154]

Orozco y Berra (1864:153) also noted that lake algae (locally called *espuma del agua* or *cuculito del agua*) were then still being collected and consumed by Indians. Deevey (1957:227) suggested that Orozco y Berra may have confused some types of insect larvae with algae.

Curious Facts in the History of Insects (Cowan 1865)

Citing several now-obscure zoological studies, Cowan recounted a number of mid-nineteenth-century observations of aquatic insect egg use in the Valley of Mexico.[4]

---

[4]These same sources are also cited at some length by P. Simmonds (2001[1859]:308-11).

In the *Bulletin de la Société Impériale Zoologique d'Acclimation*, M. Guérin Méneveille has published a paper on a sort of bread which the Mexicans make of the eggs of three species of heteropterous insects.

According to M. Graveri, by whom some of the Mexican bread, and some of the insects yielding it, were brought to Europe, these insects and their eggs are very common in the fresh waters of the lagunes of Mexico. The natives cultivate, in the lagune of Chalco, a sort of carex called *touté*, on which the insects readily deposit their eggs. Numerous bundles of these plants are made, which are taken to a lagune, the Texcuco, where they float in great numbers in the water. The insects soon come and deposit their eggs on the plants, and in about a month the bundles are removed from the water, dried, and then beaten over a large cloth to separate the myriad of eggs with which the insects have covered them. These eggs are then cleaned and sifted, put into sacks like flour, and sold to the people for making a sort of cake or biscuit called *"huautle,"* which forms a tolerably good food, but has a fishy taste, and is slightly acid. The bundles of carex are replaced in the lake, and afford a fresh supply of eggs, which process may be repeated for an indefinite number of times. . . .

"The insects which principally produce this animal farinha of Mexico," says a writer in the *Journal de Pharmacie*, "are two species of the genus *Corixa* of Geoffrey, hemipterous (heteropterous) insects of the family of water-bugs" . . . (*Corixa femorata* and *C. mercenaria*). . . . The eggs of the two species are attached in innumerable quantities to the triangular leaves of the carex forming the bundles which are deposited in the waters. They are of an oval form with a protuberance at one end and a pedicle at the other extremity, by means of which they are fixed to a small round disk, which the mother cements to the leaf. Among these eggs which are grouped closely together, there are found others, which are larger, of a long and cylindrical form, and which are fixed to the same leaves. These belong to another larger insect . . . (*Notonecta unifasciata*).

It appears from M. Virlet d'Aoust, that in October the lakes of Chalco and Texcuco, which borders on the City of Mexico, are haunted by millions of "small flies," which, after dancing in the air, plunge down into the water, to the depth of several feet, and deposit their eggs at the bottom.

"The eggs of these insects are called *hautle* (*haoutle*) by the Mexican Indians, who collect them in great numbers, and with whom they appear to be a favorite article of food. They are prepared in various ways, but usually made into cakes, which are eaten with a sauce flavored with chillies." [Cowan 1865:275]

Old Mexico and Her Lost Provinces (Bishop 1883)

William Bishop journeyed from Mexico City across Lake Texcoco to the city of Texcoco in about 1880. His chatty account of this trip, comparable to the same voyage undertaken by Brantz Mayer some four decades earlier (see above), provides a good feel for the nature of this body of water and of the transport across it of people and goods in the late nineteenth century.

My next journey was by lake across Texcoco to the old capital of that name. I had hoped to take [the passenger boat] *El Nezhualcoyotl*, which lay in the mud by the Garita of San Lazaro. . . . The *Nezahualcoyotl* was . . . a long, rusty, gondola-like scow, devoted exclusively to passenger traffic. We took instead a freight-boat of much larger and heavier build, *La Ninfa Encantadora*, ...

A cabin sheltered the passengers and some budgets of goods. . . . The canal of San Lazaro on this side extends about a league to the lake. It is very much less attractive than that of Chalco. Its terminus in the city is the point of a most animated and Venetian-like market scene, but one earns his pleasure in dealing with this canal at the expense of a bad odor. Six men put a sort of harness on themselves and dragged us along, plodding on the tow-path,

Figure 3.18. Poling a freight-passenger boat across Lake Texcoco, ca. 1880 (Bishop 1883:165).

as Russian peasants drag their boats in some of their rivers. A man on horseback with a tow-rope also assisted on the other side.

The water, shoal in the beginning, shoaled more as we went on, till we were aground on flats in the edge of the lake. The city sewage was aground with us. . . . The teocalli-like [i.e., pyramid-like] Peñol [Peñon de los Baños], where there had been warm baths, was close at hand. Sky and water were of an identical blue; the shallow expanse reflected the circuit of dark and purplish foot-hills and great snow-peaks beyond as perfectly as if it had been as deep as they were high.

Our crew walked for an hour in the mud, pushing against long poles projected from the sides, before we could be said to be fairly afloat. Then they came on board and poled the rest of the way. They walked up an inclined plane, carrying the poles over their heads, and came down, pushing, with them supported against their shoulders, in a bold and striking motion [Fig. 3.18]. It was eight o'clock [AM] when we set out, four [PM] when we reached the mouth of the short branch canal which makes up to Texcoco. . . .

. . . We met other packets like our own, loaded with people [one appears on the left side of Fig. 3.18]. A considerable part of the cargoes was the fine large red earthen jars and dishes we saw at Mexico, which are made at Texcoco. . . .

Then we fell in with one of the curiosities of the lake . . . swarms of the *mosca*, a little water-fly, so thickly settled on the water that we took them for flats and reefs. They resemble mosquitoes, but neither sting nor even alight on the boat. They are taken in fine nets and carried to Mexico, as food for the birds; and they have eggs, which are sold in the market and made into tortillas, which are said to be very palatable.

The shores are encrusted with a native alkali, which has its share in the production of the disagreeable odors. Peasants gather the crude product and load it upon donkeys, to carry to a salt and soda works, and a manufactory of glass, situated at Texcoco. [Bishop 1883:163-64]

Memoria sobre las Aguas Potables de la Capital de México (Peñafiel 1884)

Peñafiel reported the results of his detailed examination of a sample of water in Lake Texcoco taken

[English translation] at a point intermediate between Chimalhuacán and the Peñon los Baños [Fig. 2.2] . . . . on its surface we observed an infinite number of the larvae, that produce *ahuautle*, measuring between 1.5 and 2 centimeters in length. . . .

. . . According to what we saw, we calculate that there are 200 larvae in each square decimeter of lake water; consequently, 20,000 larvae per square meter, and 3,650,000,000,000 larvae in the whole of Lake Texcoco. The weight of each larva, dried at 108°F, is about 5 milligrams, which gives us a total weight [in the whole of Lake Texcoco] of 18,250,000 kilos; the weight of 100 *ahuautle* eggs, dried at the same temperature, is 6 milligrams; calculating at 100 eggs per square decimeter, would give a total of 109,500 kilos for the entire lake, which added to the weight of the larvae, would give us 18,359,500 kilos of material in this immense deposit; and we are confident that our calculations, rather than being exaggerated, actually are less than the true figures. [Peñafiel 1884:129-30]

Travels in Mexico and Life Among the Mexicans (Ober 1884)

Frederick Ober traveled extensively in the environs of Mexico City during the late nineteenth century. He reported that

[t]he best fishing on the lakes is near the town of Ayotla [near Tlapacoya in northeastern Lake Chalco, Fig. 2.2] . . . where the poor people subsist almost entirely upon the products of the water and marshes . . . [the] marsh fly called *axayacatl* (*Ahuatlea mexicana*), which deposits its eggs in incredible quantities upon flags and rushes, and which are eagerly sought out and made into cakes which are sold in the markets. . . .

These cakes . . . are sold in the markets to this day, and the black heaps of the *ahuauhtli*, or "water wheat," may be frequently seen dotting the mud flats about the lakes, Tezcoco especially. The insects themselves (which are about the size of a house-fly) are pounded into a paste—as they are collected in myriads—, boiled in corn husks, and thus sold. The eggs, resembling fine fish roe, are compressed into a paste, mixed with eggs of fowls, and form a staple article of food. . . .

The Indians of the Mexican lakes have a systematic method, by which they plant bundles of reeds a few feet apart, with their tops sticking out of the water. The insects deposit their eggs upon these reeds in such quantities that they not only cover them, but depend in clusters. When completely covered, these bundles are removed from the water, shaken over a sheet, and replaced for a fresh deposit. *Paxi* are the larvae of the *axayacatl*, yellowish-white worms, which are also eaten, being prepared for the table in various ways. [Ober 1884:339]

Batracios del Valle de México (Duges 1888)

Duges identified two frog species that were still commonly eaten in the Valley of Mexico during the late nineteenth century: *Rana montezumae* and *Rana halecina* Kalm.

[English translation] Rana montezumae . . . It lives mainly in ponded waters. Its flesh is excellent, and the Indians who sell it in the markets of Mexico City break its leg bones so that it can be kept alive without being able to escape.

Rana halecina Kalm. Its flesh is delicious. These frogs deposit their eggs in June and July, and sometimes earlier. . . . [Duges 1888:138-39]

Fauna del Lago de Texcoco (Herrera 1895)

Herrera was interested in the potential for commercial development of the aquatic resources in the Valley of Mexico. He made several detailed observations in the urban marketplaces and in the surrounding lake zones.

> *[English translation]* I have counted 300-400 insects in each gram of the "mosco" [dried insect product] that the indians sell in Mexico City. . . . it is common that each of these ambulatory merchants [in the Mexico City marketplace] carries 12-24 kilos of this material [dried "mosco"], that is to say 4,800,000-9,600,000 bodies of *Coryza* [*Ephydra hians*]. . . .
> . . . some years ago this product was exported to France for the purpose of feeding pheasants and other birds. [Herrera 1895:44]

Herrera also observed that *Ephydra hians* was so abundant in and around Lake Texcoco that

> *[English translation]* sometimes the crushed bodies of these insects lubricate the wheels of the locomotives so that these machines slip in place and are unable to advance. [Herrera 1895:45]

The prodigious quantities of these insects also made possible their use as agricultural fertilizer (as Orozco y Berra, 1864, had also noted some thirty years earlier), and Herrera reported an experiment aimed at evaluating this potential.

> *[English translation]* Sr. Segura planted maize seeds, some in land fertilized with requezón [bodies of *Ephydra hians*], others in unfertilized land. The result was very conclusive; all the fertilized plants developed with unusual vigor. The plants in unfertilized land were rickety and weak.
> Sr. Segura determined that requezón contains 29% organic matter and 61% mineral material. [Herrera 1895:46]

Herrera listed fourteen species of waterfowl (ducks) that had been reported from Lake Texcoco a few years previously by Villada (Table 3.5). Villada had also noted two species of herons and one species of goose.

Herrera attributed the great abundance of waterfowl on Lake Texcoco to the high natural fertility of these birds. According to his studies (1895:60-61), each mature female duck was capable of laying up to 180 eggs per season, from which several batches of young might be hatched in a single breeding season. Herrera estimated that the million birds slaughtered annually for the Mexico City market could easily have been supplied by only 50,000 breeding pairs, without any long-term diminution of the overall duck population on Lake Texcoco.

Herrera provided additional details on the same *armada* duck-hunting technique mentioned decades earlier by Mayer (1844) and Orozco y Berra (1864) (see above). In the 1890s the annual duck-hunting season began in November.

> *[English translation]* the first [armadas] are prepared at the Peñon Viejo [Peñon de los Baños], about 8 kilometers to the east of Mexico City [Fig. 2.2], and from there they are extended into distinct shooting spots. . . . by the middle of the same month [November] new ones are established in ponds of water that have formed fortuitously between the Villa de Guadalupe

Table 3.5. Villada's identification of duck species on
Lake Texcoco, as listed by Herrera (1895:51).

Scientific Name	Common Local Name
Anas boschas	concanauhtli
A. strepera	colcanauhtli
A. americana	xalcanauhtli
A. carolinensis	cuicuitzcatl
A. discors	metzcanauhtli
A. cyanoptera	chilcanauhtli
Dafila acuta	tzitzihoa
Spatula clypeata	tempatlahoac
Aythya vallisneria	coacoxtli
A. americana	
A. collaris	talalactli, tezoloctli
Erismatura rubida	atepalcatl
Anser albifrons	tlalalacatl
Dendrocyana fulva	tziquiotl

and Tlalnepantla [north-northwest of Mexico City]. . . . [at each armada] it is possible to fire
the guns up to 3 times per week, and at least once a week. . . . [Herrera 1895:55]

Recognizing that by the 1890s ducks were no longer being hunted in the traditional
manner in the Valley of Mexico, Herrera noted contemporary hunting practices then still
employed on Lake Pátzcuaro in west-central Mexico. He suggested that these techniques
might have been used around Lake Texcoco in earlier centuries:

[English translation] a large number of indians in small boats cooperate in this task, and they
proceed immediately to the place where a large group of ducks is clustered: they begin by
surrounding the ducks and then they follow them very carefully for a very long time, obliging
them to swim away continuously without rising into flight; the birds finally begin to tire and the
indians then capture them with harpoons, or sometimes simply seize them with their hands.

[Another traditional duck-hunting technique] . . . consists of [subtly] moving a group of
ducks to a canal or narrow waterway enclosed by a giant net, which is arranged in such a
way that, at the opportune moment, the mouth of the net can be quickly closed to entrap the
birds. . . . [Herrera 1895:55-56]

Notes upon the Ethnography of Southern Mexico, Part 1 (Starr 1900)

During an 1898 fieldtrip to Lake Pátzcuaro in western Mexico, Frederick Starr observed
the dugout canoes then in common use for hunting ducks and for transporting people.
This is the most complete description known to me of dugout canoes used on the highland
lakes in Mexico during the nineteenth century. Starr also briefly described the *atlatls* and
spears used for duck hunting, and the nets used for fishing in Lake Pátzcuaro.

The canoes used on the lakes are dugouts; they range from hunting canoes for one man to
travel canoes that will carry eight or more persons. At the stern they are cut almost square;
at the bow trimmed to slope from the water upward; they are wide and flat-bottomed below;
the walls are rather thin, thicker below than above, and almost vertical inside; there are
buttressing pieces left at two or three places on the bottom which serve as strengthers and
for seats; the bow not only rises, but also narrows, and a buttress block left in it serves as
a foot-rest for the steersman. Paddles, cut from a single piece of wood, with a beautifully
rounded blade some eight inches in diameter, and a handle three feet [91 cm] or so long,

serves for propulsion; . . . women paddle as well as men. . . . The steersman, sitting high perched in the bow, uses a paddle similar to the others, but with a lengthened handle, which passes through a rest or loop made by lashing a crooked stick to the upper edge of the canoe on one side. Gum from pine trees is used for caulking cracks or splits in the canoes. . . .

In hunting ducks a spear-throwing stick [*atlatl*] is used. . . . This is simple, about two feet [61 cm] long, with two holes for the fingers, a groove in which the spear shaft lies and a peg against which the butt rests; there is also a hook below the end for dragging floating spears to the canoe. The spears are made of long canes with two or three divergent iron points firmly bound in. . . . The nets used for fishing are long seines and great dip nets. It is said that the fish of the lake will not take bait. In making nets a special wooden handle is used. [Starr 1900:11]

Through Southern Mexico (Gadow 1908)

In the course of two summer trips during 1902 and 1904, Hans Gadow encountered substantial numbers of larval salamanders (*axolotl*) for sale in the Mexico City market-place. He also learned about their habits in freshwater Lake Xochimilco:

The fishermen who punted us about in dug-outs knew all about the *axolotl*: how they bred early in the spring, about February; how their eggs were fastened singly to the water-plants; how soon afterwards the little larvae swarmed about in thousands like other tadpoles; how they grew at a great rate, always remaining dark and never becoming piebald or marbled over with yellow, until by the month of June they were all grown-up, ready for market. . . . Later in the summer they take to the rushes, and in the autumn they seem to become scarcer. . . . Sometimes they are caught in nets, more frequently they are speared with a pronged fork. [Gadow 1908:11]

La tiradera (atlatl), todavia en uso en el Valle de México (Beyer 1969)

During his visit to Atenco on the northeastern shore of Lake Texcoco in about 1920, Hermann Beyer found that the *atlatl* was still used by duck hunters in the nearby lake. This implement was used to hurl cane spears tipped with iron nails at the birds, usually from boats. The *atlatl* was well known in precolumbian Mesoamerica in the early sixteenth century (Nuttall 1891), and had probably been commonly used for millennia prior to that time as a weapon and a hunting implement. Beyer's inquiries revealed that duck hunters in other lakeshore villages near Atenco also used the *atlatl*, although mainly for dispatch-ing birds already wounded by the discharge of multiple shotguns in rigs similar to those described in the nineteenth century. Beyer learned that such duck-killing devices were often used in lakeshore settings purposively flooded by the villagers to attract waterfowl. Visiting Atenco some fifteen years later, in 1934, Sigvald Linne (1937; 1948:127, 130) found several *atlatls* in the possession of men who knew how to use them, but at that time these implements were no longer employed for duck hunting because the water level in the lake had dropped to a point where it was no longer feasible to use boats. One of these men demonstrated for photographer Bodil Christensen how the *atlatl* had formerly been used with a pronged spear for duck hunting (Plate 3.1).

Beyer (1969:424) described the Atenco *atlatl* and its use:

[English translation] The Atenco *atlatl* is the the simplest of this kind of implement, made of a wooden pole hollowed out longitudinally. The hollowed-out portion terminates at the

Plate 3.1. Demonstration of how the *atlatl* was formerly used for duck hunting with a pronged spear, near Atenco on the eastern shore of Lake Texcoco, late 1930s. Photo by Bodil Christensen, courtesy of Irmgard Johnson 1994.

top of the instrument, before the tip, leaving a small conical piece of wood that supports the base of the cane dart which is placed on the implement. The middle and index fingers hold the dart in place, while the other fingers steady the lower, or anterior, section of the dart.

Another variant, somewhat more comfortable, is also used in this region. This has a finger hold, formed of two loops of wire, gripped by the index and third fingers.

El Ahuautle de Texcoco (Ancona 1933)

L. Ancona (1933) provided details on the traditional processing, sale, and use of edible aquatic insects during the early decades of the twentieth century.

[English translation] The insects are placed in baskets, where they are dried in the sun. Prepared in this way, they are commonly sold in the streets and marketplaces of the city, as "insects for birds." Well pounded and ground up, they are sold in small cakes . . . not only in the markets of Texcoco, Chimalhuacán, Xochitenco, Sochiaca and Los Reyes, but even in Mexico City itself. . . . The *ahuautle* eggs . . . are also commonly consumed by local people: they are sold during the months of May, June, and July, and when fried they provide a delicious food with a taste like shrimp. In their dried state they are stored in homes for months until they are used for the preparation of a delicious Christmas Eve dish, *revoltijo.* . . . In the communities bordering Lake Texcoco the people help support themselves by collecting and exporting the *ahuautle* eggs and insects, which are sent to several places in England and Germany to supply feed for fish hatcheries. [Ancona 1933:63]

The Pond in Our Backyard (Apenes 1943)

Ola Apenes (1943:18) described and photographed several techniques for the collection and processing of aquatic insects on Lake Texcoco in about 1940.

> After being caught, the insects are emptied out on the ground in large squares formed by rows of dried grass, and left to die [Plate 3.2]. Although the insects are able to fly, they lose their strength from the dryness and heat, and are unable to escape. . . .
>   Other men are drying out a black mass which they pour from *ayate* bags [made from maguey fiber: *ixtle*] [Plate 3.3]. . . . it is a larva called *requezón* (*pochi*). . . . It is found in great quantities near the edge of the water and used as fertilizer.
>   [In order to facilitate the deposition of insect eggs, the fisherman] . . . binds bundles of rush and sets them in the shallow water at regular intervals [Plates 3.4 and 3.5]. There is one long straw tied around the bundle with a knot in the free end of it. This end is pressed with a stick into the sandy lake bottom so the catch will not drift away. . . . The bundles are left in the water for about two weeks. . . . At that time the bundles are taken up, dried, and the eggs shaken off.

Apenes (1943:18) also described the "desaguadero" fishing technique:

> A man standing in the mud with rolled up trousers is scooping water with a bucket, and when you get nearer you see that he is emptying a little pond which he has formed by building up a low wall of mud. . . . the fish which happen to be in the pool will soon find themselves on dry land.

Synopsis of the Herpetofauna of Mexico. Vol. 1: Analysis of the Literature on the Mexican Axolotl [larval form of salamander] (Smith and Smith 1971)

Smith and Smith (1971: x) note that

> [o]nly in Mexico has the *axolotl* or any of its confamilials been used notably for food. . . . In the markets of Xochimilco, Zumpango, Toluca, Pátzcuaro and many other cities and villages . . . they are sold both roasted (ready to eat) and alive. At times in the past they were a staple in the local diet; now they are often an occasional delicacy. Home (1824:420) notes that in June [of that year in the early nineteenth century] his friend "Mr. Bullock saw them in the [Mexico City] market in thousands for sale," taken from Lake Texcoco. They are now [ca. 1970] found in the markets in much smaller numbers.

Smith and Smith (1971: xx) noted a Colonial-period reference to the preparation of salamanders for food:

> Customarily it gives wholesome and pleasing sustenance, similar to the meat of eels, prepared in several ways, fried, roasted, and boiled, but the Spanish . . . usually eat it boiled, with much pepper and cloves, and with some chile; the Mexicans prefer them with chile alone, ground or whole. . . .

Smith and Smith (1971: xx) indicate that today, salamanders

> are prepared with tomato sauce, in sweet sauce, with chile, as tamales, with squash flowers, and as stuffed tortillas. The recipies call for them to be boiled, fried, steamed and shredded, and for heavy seasoning with onion, garlic, and chile. The animals are prepared for cooking

Plate 3.2. Drying insects near Chimalhuacán in the late 1930s. © Museum of Ethnography, Stockholm, Sweden. Photo: Ola Apenes.

Plate 3.3. Drying *requezón* near Chimalhuacán in the late 1930s. © Museum of Ethnography, Stockholm, Sweden. Photo: Ola Apenes.

Plate 3.4. Demonstrating the use of a *polote* near Chimalhuacán in the late 1930s. © Museum of Ethnography, Stockholm, Sweden. Photo: Ola Apenes.

by evisceration, decapitation, skinning, and mashing. In some recipes they are cooked until the bones can be removed before completion of the dish.

La Pesca en el Medio Lacustre y Chinampero de San Luis Tlaxialtemalco (Pérez 1985)

Pérez made his primary field observations in 1984, and his account is supplemented with memories from his own childhood at this same locality on the south shore of Lake Xochimilco during the early 1960s, and by the memories of older residents of the community. Although he focuses on the freshwater chinampa district in Lake Xochimilco, his observations should have relevance to traditional life on and around Lake Texcoco. Pérez provides the only ethnographic description known to me of how turtles and molluscs were harvested.

Plate 3.5. Inserting *polotes* near Chimalhuacán in the late 1930s. © Museum of Ethnography, Stockholm, Sweden. Photo: Ola Apenes.

As recently as the early 1960s, fish and other aquatic fauna flourished in the canals between the chinampa fields, and comprised an important component of the domestic economies of *chinampero* families who resided there. Pérez reports (1985:113) that older residents recalled that during the violent years of the revolutionary period (1911-1918), when agricultural production was severely reduced, many people subsisted largely from aquatic products harvested from the canals. Although fishing was always secondary to chinampa agriculture, even as late as the mid-twentieth century there were several different kinds of fish readily available, along with a variety of other aquatic fauna (*acocil* [a small crustacean], salamanders, frogs, tadpoles, molluscs, turtles, and several kinds of aquatic insects [known locally as *padre, cucaracha, mecapal, and ahuauhtli*]). At least nine varieties of waterfowl were also hunted and locally consumed.

Figure 3.19. Capturing and cooking turtles in the sixteenth century (Sahagun 1963: Fig. 198).

For fishing, the following implements were employed: (1) a small circular or ellipitical net with a wooden handle, mounted on a wooden frame, operated by a single fisher; (2) a large rectangular net (*chinchorro*), measuring some 3-4 m long, usually fastened on wooden poles, operated by two or more men; (3) a harpoon (*fisga*) with a wood or cane handle measuring 3.5-4 m long, with 8-13 iron prongs mounted in a circular configuration at one end, used by a single individual, usually for larger fish, frogs, and salamanders; (4) an iron hook (*anzuelo*) at the end of a cord tied to the end of a cane handle; and (5) a large circular net (*tarraya*), 8-10 m in diameter, with sinkers tied around the circumference. The chinchorro and tarraya nets were used only in the major canals with their larger expanses of water. Fishing was done either afoot in shallow water, in canoes in deeper water, or afoot from dry land at the edges of chinampa fields.

Pérez (1985:118) describes another fishing technique (the *encierro*, or enclosure) that Apenes (1943:18) had earlier noted at Chimalhuacán (as mentioned above):

[English translation] within a ditched area a type of dam formed of tightly joined aquatic plants is made so as to form an encircling barrier extending from the bottom of the ditch up to the water surface. Once the fish inside the barrier sense that they are trapped, they jump about very notably. The fishermen then thrash the enclosed water with their feet so that the fish grow faint from lack of oxygen. Using their hands or a small net, the fishermen then extract the fish from the enclosure and place them in a container with a little water.

Similar enclosures were made in ponded areas in swampy terrain when fish were seen there. The fishermen moved into the center of the enclosure with their nets, if the water was deep, or simply seized the entrapped fish by hand.

Pérez (1985:124) describes harvesting lacustrine molluscs (*almeja*). These bivalved species measured about 5 cm long and were black or brown in color, similar to oysters in general appearance. These bottom-dwelling molluscs were collected from canoes in shallow water,

Table 3.6. Number of fishermen in the Valley of
Mexico, 1895-1910.

Lake	1895	1900	1910
Chalco	41	0	5
Zumpango	390	17	67
Texcoco	—	4	118

(Adapted from García Sanchez 1998:95)

with the fisher looking carefully into the water to distinguish them in the mud at the bottom of the canals. When seen in this fashion, they were simply seized with the bare hand. Net fishing was not practicable because the molluscs lived in the mud on canal bottoms.

Turtles were common in the chinampa canals well into the 1960s, and, while they tended to be small, as recently as 1982 one measuring 30 cm long was captured near San Luis Tlaxialtemalco (Pérez 1985:125). Turtles lived in thickly vegetated areas along the canal banks, and they were usually captured by hand when the animals came out to sun themselves. The animal was killed by decapitation, and then placed bottom-up atop a cooking fire, or boiled in a pot, until the meat was cooked (see Fig. 3.19 for Sahagun's sixteenth-century illustration of the same processes).

Haciendas, pueblos y gobierno porfirista: los conflictos por el agua en la región de Chalco (Tortolero 1993)

García Sanchez (1998:95) cites an early twentieth-century census of fishermen in the Valley of Mexico that was included in a study by A. Tortolero (1993) (Table 3.6). It is not clear what these "fishermen" were actually fishing for, but I assume, as does García Sanchez, that most of them were interested in commercially saleable species of fish. However, some of them may well have been involved in collecting aquatic insects and/or insect eggs. The number of fishermen working in Lake Texcoco as late as 1910 is surprisingly high, but I am puzzled about why there was apparently no fishing reported there only fifteen years earlier, in 1895. In any event, these figures indicate that the aquatic economy was still viable in the Valley of Mexico during the early twentieth century. These census data correspond well with Meek's (1904: liii [cited in Berres 2000]) report of "commercial fisheries" in the Valley of Mexico during the early twentieth century, "with white fish dried in large quantities" (Berres 2000:32).

Study of the Edible Algae of the Valley of Mexico (Ortega 1972); *The Xaltocán Fish in the Twentieth Century: An Ethnoarchaeological Study* (Roush 2005); *Algunos Aspectos de la Cultura del Lago de Zumpango* (Aguilera 2001)

These three studies describe some aspects of the procurement and processing of aquatic resources during the 1940s through the mid-1970s at Xaltocán, a community in central Lake Zumpango-Xaltocán in the northern Valley of Mexico. At that time, a remnant, diked lake of some 850 hectares, and up to 4.5 m deep in some places, still existed. After 1980 this was completely drained, although some areas were subsequently reflooded with treated sewage water (*agua negra*) (Aguilera 2001:74).

Traditional harvesting of algae in the Valley of Mexico has virtually vanished. However, a generation ago, Ortega (1972) described what must have been one of the very last occurrences of this activity at Xaltocán. The algae, locally referred to as *cocol*, were collected and prepared in the following manner:

> The Xaltocano fishermen gather *cocol* from puddles and canals when it is mature . . . when the layer of algae is rather thick. They collect it by hand, using fine-mesh nets. . . . They wash the algae to get rid of the mud, then grind it up in . . . *molcajetes* [ceramic or stone mortars, used with a pestle], and supplement it with parsley, epazote . . . , chile, and lard. Finally, they steam it in cornhusks. The finished product, cooked, has a red-brown color, a strong aroma, and a moist flavor. [Ortega 1972:164]

Based on her own observations in the early 1990s and interviews with older people about their memories of earlier times, Roush (2005) provides additional information about the preparation of aquatic products at Xaltocán. In addition to the *cocol* discussed by Ortega, Roush notes that lake fish, salamanders, frogs, tadpoles, freshwater shrimps, and aquatic insects and insect eggs were harvested around Xaltocán prior to the final drainage of the surrounding remnant lake in the mid-1970s. Once netted or speared, these foods were typically mixed with seasonings (salt, cilantro, chile) and cooked in *tamal* form in corn husks, or wrapped in maguey tissue as *mixiotes*, and baked in large batches on a ceramic or metal *comal* placed atop a stone, brick, or oil-drum oven. The inhabitants of Xaltocán sold many of these prepared aquatic products in local and regional markets, where their offerings were well known. A modified form of this activity, using imported fish, persists through the present day at Xaltocán.

Roush also describes a technique (one that I have not found in any other source) formerly used by Xaltocán fishermen for harvesting aquatic insect eggs (*ahuauhtle*). Small floating "rafts" made of buoyant grass or reeds were placed in appropriate spots for a period of time during which the insects deposited their eggs on the plant surfaces. These rafts were periodically dragged from the water onto the shore to dry out, after which the accumulated eggs were shaken off onto cloths.

Aguilera provides a good description of traditional fishing techniques employed by Xaltocán fishermen during the 1940s through the mid-1970s. Some of the fish sought at that time were large, recently introduced species (e.g., carp). Most of the fishing was done with a large net managed by a small group of men working in groups of three boats:

> *[English translation]* The fishermen used . . . a net—of Spanish origin—for their activity. . . . The common net measured about 50 meters long by 1.6 m wide. At intervals along the upper side of the net they fixed a line of wooden floats in the form of bars, triangles, circles, or butterflies. The lower part of the net is the "drag." Here they hung lead weights from a line, at intervals of 15-40 cm according to the depth of water and the current, in order that the net would rest on the bottom of the lake and the fish could not escape. In the center of the net was the "naval" made of the finest mesh that served to capture the fish and smallest animals. Ball-like floats made of wooden poles with attached lead weights at the upper and lower ends were placed on either side of the net. The "fasteners," lines attached to the tops and bottoms of the floats, were pulled in order to close up the net.
>
> Above the net's "naval" there was an "ear," a handle with which the fishereman could hold up the fish-filled net, or drag it along through the water. In the 1970s it was possible to

obtain ready-made nets, although these did not last long because of the poor quality of the string. Don Pedro Vicenteño [the author's informant] and his father wove their own nets with special needles that they made themselves, preparing the lead weights, the floats, . . . everything. With a bundle of string weighing 50 kilograms, which cost 60 pesos, Don Pedro wove a net that lasted a month in daily use.

At the time when fishing was at its peak, the Vicenteños had two nets, one of coarse mesh for large fish manipulated by father and son together, and the other of finer mesh for small fish that was handled by hired men. . . .

Each casting of the net was done with three canoes, two to carry the net and the third to carry the fish. First the net was stretched out in a straight line, each end tied to a ring at the tips of the canoes. Then two men placed themselves on either side of the net, while another three men spaced themselves equidistantly along the length of the net, one of them at the "naval." This is a tedious task that took an hour or more to perform since great care was necessary not to break the long net. As soon as the net was extended, it began to fill with fish. The men in the canoes began to gradually close up the net. When the net was felt to be sufficiently heavy, they closed it up entirely; this operation also required more than an hour.

The fishermen then gathered up the net into the canoes alongside and at the same time seized the fish by hand. After closing up the net, they placed the fish in the third canoe that was divided with branches into compartments for each different kind of fish, or they placed the fish in separate baskets that served the same purpose. . . .

Fishing began in February and March, although the most productive months were April and May, when the water was clearest. The fishermen left home in the early morning, and even at night if they wanted to make money. During the rainy season, from June to September, the water was turbid, and for that reason there were fewer fish that could be caught at night. In the winter fishing began about mid-morning when the water was lukewarm. There was little fishing activity in December and January, when the water level was at its lowest. Fishing generally took place when the moon was waxing, since the fish were attracted into the open water by the effect of the moon; but if the fish would not come out, the fishermen repeatedly struck the surface of the water near the marshes in order to force to fish to come out and move towards their nets. . . .

A net cost about 150 pesos, which was a large sum of money for the time and considering the economic capacity of most fishermen. This meant that the possession of a net and the other necessary equipment—burros to carry the fish on land, canoes and baskets—was a communal enterprise. Since the work itself was communal, the various household heads themselves were also the fishermen. [Aguilera 2001:76-82]

Aguilera also describes a variety of traditional smaller nets formerly used by Xaltocán fisherman. These included nets placed across the width of irrigation canals to trap fish that swam into these waterways from nearby lake or streams. Some fishing was also done with small drag nets, up to 2 m in diameter, that were pulled along the lake bottom by individual men wading in shallow water. Another common technique was a small, lightweight net, typically measuring 70 m in diameter and 1.2 m long, that was manipulated, usually from a canoe, so that it floated just below the water surface in order to capture fish swimming at that shallow depth. Some fishermen continued to use iron-pointed barbed harpoons for spearing larger fish from canoes. Such harpoons were constructed in the following manner:

[English translation] The harpoon consisted of an "oar" or rod made of cane or wood, to which was affixed by a hoop of wire or string, three or four hooked points made of iron spikes about 30 cm long that served to capture the fish. The wooden or cane harpoons measured

from 1-1.5 meters in length and were used to capture the bearded carp that could weigh up to eight kilos. . . . [Aguilera 2001:80]

Extracción y aprovechimiento del ahuauhtle (Hemiptera: Corixidae) del Lago de Texcoco (Saenz and Posadas del Río 1978)

During the 1970s a part of the huge solar evaporator, "El Caracol" (at the Sosa de Texcoco commercial soda-producing plant at the northern edge of Lake Texcoco) (see Plate 4.2), was adapted for the large-scale production of *ahuauhtle* (insect eggs) for and by the inhabitants of several adjacent lakeshore villages. This enterprise was abandoned about 1990.

> *[English translation]* the *ahuauhtle* collectors prepare bundles of grass and reeds to form an "anchor" that serves to fasten the grass to the muddy soil using an iron rod.
>
> Using wooden canoes, the grass bundles are distributed in lines that literally surround a great part of Section A of "El Caracol." These bundles remain submerged for approximately two weeks, being removed after that period in order to expose them to the sun's rays and dry out the *ahuauhtle* to facilitate its separation from the grass by manual shaking.
>
> . . . the *ahuauhtle* generally is ground on a metate in order to convert it to a powder similar to flour. In its simplest form, this "flour" is then mixed with water and salt, forming a dark dough that is then cooked in oil or lard.
>
> The resulting "cake" acquires a consistency like that of fried beef steak. Its fine and delicate flavor is similar to that of dried shrimp. [Saenz and Posadas del Río 1978:129-30]

Summary and Conclusions

Throughout the historic period the open waters and marshlands of Lake Texcoco continued to provide very substantial quantities of the same foods and raw materials that had been significant in the sixteenth century. Furthermore, these resources continued to be collected, hunted, or harvested with much the same techniques and organizational infrastructure as those described in the sixteenth-century sources (e.g., netting, spearing with *atlatls*, snaring, following and trapping, insect-egg nurseries, individual or community ownership of fishing and collecting territories, and market exchange between lake fishers and inland agriculturalists). Water-borne transport of people and goods across Lake Texcoco continued until about 1900.

Throughout the historic period many hundreds of thousands of waterfowl, perhaps substantially more than one million, annually made their way into the urban marketplaces. Even if the average edible meat per bird amounted to only 0.25 kilo (Tables 4.8 and 4.9), this would have meant an annual consumption of perhaps 250 metric tons of high quality animal protein. Although there is little mention of their use in post-sixteenth-century sources, waterfowl eggs probably continued to provide an additional significant source of protein, nutrients, and calories, just as they had in the sixteenth century.

Other estimates hint that annual harvests of edible insect products might have amounted to many hundreds, or even thousands, of metric tons. The documented use for agricultural fertilizer of masses of lacustrine insects periodically washed up along the shorelines indicates the prodigious quantities of this aquatic resource that were available as recently as the 1930s. The potential annual harvests of fish, larval salamanders, frogs, turtles, crus-

Plate 3.6. Harvesting and drying reeds (*tules*) for making mats, near Chimalhuacán in the late 1930s. © Museum of Ethnography, Stockholm, Sweden. Photo: Ola Apenes.

taceans, molluscs, algae and other aquatic plants are more difficult to quantify, but these also would have been very considerable, probably amounting to at least many hundreds of metric tons annually.

The nineteenth- and early twentieth-century sources reveal that most of the lake resources exploited in the sixteenth century continued to be used widely and intensively in the Valley of Mexico in subsequent centuries. Similar products, similar uses, similar extractive and processing technology, and similar importance of market exchange between aquatic, agricultural, and craft producers characterized the regional economy over these four centuries. As in the sixteenth-century sources, marsh reeds and rushes are often noted as raw material for mats (Plate 3.6) and housing (Plates 3.7 and 3.8), and there are also some suggestions that these same plants were used for food. Many aquatic food products were effectively dried for long-term storage, greatly facilitating the accumulation and exchange of surpluses from one year to the next.

Albores' (1995) and Sugiura's (1998) recent ethnographic studies of the surviving modern use of aquatic plants for food in the nearby Toluca basin (see Chap. 6) suggest clearly that such plants were also formerly important sources of food in the Valley of Mexico, just as Sahagun (1963) and Hernández (1959a) indicated for the sixteenth century. There are numerous historic references to the use of lacustrine algae from Lake Texcoco for food.

Plate 3.7. Shelters made of reed mats, Lake Xochimilco chinampa district, ca. 1900. Arrows point to reed-mat shelters. © Museum of Ethnography, Stockholm, Sweden. Photo: Gustat Cedergren Collection.

Plate 3.8. Houses made of reed mats, Lake Xochimilco chinampa district, ca. 1900. © Museum of Ethnography, Stockholm, Sweden. Photo: Gustat Cedergren Collection.

Table 3.7. Summary of the documented techniques for the procurement and processing of aquatic resources in the Valley of Mexico, 1500-1970.

Resources	Availability and Procurement Techniques	Processing Techniques
waterfowl	Netting, noose-trapping, spearing (with atlatl), and pursuing until the birds tire and can be seized or clubbed. Canoes were in common use. Stationary nets on high poles were also employed. Both individual and cooperative techniques were used. Primarily a winter activity.	No information.
waterfowl eggs	No information. Some eggs available year-round, although the greatest abundance would have been in the winter months when migratory species were most abundant.	Cooked in omelettes and stews.
fish	Netting, spearing, and hooking from canoes or afoot; also in artificial pools that are emptied of water by hand. Apparently a year-round activity. Seemingly a significant, but secondary, lacustrine resource.	Wrapped in maize husks and cooked on a griddle (comal). Small fish cooked in an olla.
fish eggs	Netting in shallow water, either afoot or in canoes. Apparently a year-round activity(?).	Cooked in metal or clay vessels.
aquatic insects, both larval and adult forms	Netting in shallow waters, either afoot or in canoes. Primarily during the summer months, but apparently there was some exploitation year-round.	May be stored in large vessels preparatory to drying. First sun-dried on prepared lakeshore surfaces, then ground into paste, before cooking with other foods or alone in the form of tamales wrapped in maize husks. Some stored in "large vessels" prior to usage. Some varieties were wrapped in maize husks and cooked in salty water. Others were salted and toasted on plates or comales.
insect eggs (ahuauhtle)	Eggs were deposited in prepared "nurseries" consisting either of reed bundles inserted into shallow water, or of thick "ropes" placed in the water, or of large submerged cloths. The ropes or bundles or cloths were removed, dried, and the attached eggs shaken off onto cloths and stored in large vessels (probably ceramic). Mainly a summer, rainy-season activity, but some were probably available year-round.	Stored in "large vessels" preparatory to drying. The dried eggs were ground into paste, preparatory to cooking with other foods or for the preparation of tamales wrapped in maize husks. The dried eggs could be transported in large sacks. The product could be stored for at least several months.
salamander larvae	Netted or speared.	Fried, roasted, or boiled, usually with seasonings.
turtles	Captured by hand along thickly vegetated canal banks and in marshlands.	Decapitated and then roasted in their shell on a fire, or boiled in a pot.
algae	Netted on water surface, or removed from there with scoops, both afoot and from canoes. Apparently a year-round activity(?).	Sun-dried on prepared surfaces on the lakeshore, then formed into thin "loaves" or cakes. Wrapped in leaves it could be stored for up to a year.
reeds (for mats)	No information, but presumably individually cut with knives or sickles.	Probably dried on the lakeshore (Pl. 3.6). Used for mats and houselot fences, and parts of some species were probably eaten.

Table 3.7 cont.

other aquatic plants	Little information. One species was "grubbed up in the mud." Some species were seasonal, while others were available year-round.	Limited information. Some mention of cooking seeds, stalks, and roots in ollas (Fig. 3.13), and of leaching roots in wood ashes, and making "tortillas" cooked on griddles. Some plants were eaten raw.
ceremonies associated with water deities	Ritual performances and offerings at several places on and around the lakeshore, and in mid-lake in southern Lake Texcoco (especially at Pantitlán).	Cutting reeds, dancing and chants, and other ritual performances. Deposition of offerings, including sacrificed humans, greenstones, and burned incense.

Overall Summary and Conclusions

Most lakeshore communities were involved in the exploitation of lacustrine resources throughout the historic period. In most cases, the inhabitants of these communities were dependent on the nearby lakes, ponds, and marshes for much of their subsistence and income; they typically exchanged their surplus production of aquatic products for complementary agricultural and craft goods in nearby urban marketplaces. Harvesting territories—especially for waterfowl, fish, reeds, and algae—were carefully defined and controlled by individuals and local communities. The notable importance of Lake Texcoco in indigenous cosmology at the time of Spanish contact must also be considered when attempting to interpret the archaeological record: the common practice of depositing offerings, at lakebed shrines dedicated to water deities, of greenstone objects and sacrificed humans, with accompanying incense burning, for example, would have produced such material remains as jadeite beads, jadeite or serpentine figurines or celts, incense-burning ceramic vessels, and human bone. The great cosmological significance of Lake Texcoco in prehispanic times appears to have been lost during the subsequent Colonial period as an imported Christian cosmology was firmly imposed by the Spanish administration.

The highlights of the historic-period information on the procurement and processing of the most important aquatic resources in the Valley of Mexico are summarized in Table 3.7.

The use of wooden boats for many kinds of activities is well documented in the Valley of Mexico. However, I have found no historical references to the use of reed boats in this region. Apparently, all boats described historically have either been dugouts (seemingly illustrated in several sixteenth-century sources [e.g., Figs. 3.5, 3.6, 3.9, 3.11, 3.14-3.17] and described in use during the later nineteenth century on Lake Pátzcuaro) or vessels made from wooden planks. This corresponds to a similar lack of ethnographic references to reed boats for the nearby Toluca region and for the Marsh Arabs in the Tigris-Euphrates delta, but differs markedly from descriptions of reed boats in common use in the U.S. Great Basin, the Titicaca Basin (see Chap. 6), and on several African lakes (see Chap. 2). I continue to wonder why reed boats are apparently used in some of the world's marshlands but not in others. I also wonder if such negative evidence really means that reed boats were not used in the Valley of Mexico, or in the Tigris-Euphrates delta, during earlier, prehistoric periods. I do not believe that we should assume that this was necessarily the case. However, if reed boats were not used in the Valley of Mexico in historic or in prehispanic times, then one potentially important use of marsh reeds would have been absent, and we might expect a correspondingly lower concern with communal or individual control over reed beds.

Also interesting is the apparent absence in the Valley of Mexico of historically documented marshland camp sites—temporary residences for activities that require stays ranging from overnight to several weeks, or even longer. Even so, as we will see in Chapter 5, dozens of such camps were used by insect collectors at Chimalhuacán during the 1930s—primarily for drying the harvested insects on patches of dry ground around the edges of the lakeshore. I wonder if the lack of reference to camps in the historic documents necessarily means that they did not exist in those earlier times. Such ephemeral features may simply have failed to attract the notice of earlier writers, most of whom were city people and/or foreigners who lacked an intimate knowledge of many indigenous practices. In Chapter 2 we saw that such temporary encampments are well known for Lake Chad in north-central Africa (Plate 2.1), and in Chapter 6 we will find that they are described for the U.S. Great Basin, the Titicaca Basin, and the Tigris-Euphrates delta, but not for the nearby Toluca region just west of the Valley of Mexico. In the Toluca region, forays into the marshlands were usually launched at daybreak from permanent shoreline settlements, with a return to the home base before nightfall; occasional night-time hunting and fishing expeditions were similarly arranged so as to avoid any encampments away from the main shoreline settlement.

The apparent dearth of historically documented temporary marshland camps in the Valley of Mexico and the Toluca region might signify that local communities had access only to aquatic resources relatively close to their settlements in areas where aquatic territories were formally delineated at the local and regional levels. If such an occupational pattern can be projected back into prehispanic time, then archaeological traces on the lakebed surface itself would be subtle.

– 4 –

Species Identification

It is still difficult to precisely identify the aquatic fauna and flora described in the sixteenth-century sources. As noted in Chapter 3, several nineteenth- and early twentieth-century scholars have made significant progress in linking the surviving modern aquatic plants and animals with those described in the historical documents. However, greater precision is needed to better explicate the relationships between the behavior, productivity, and nutritional importance of specific plants and animals on the one hand, and their procurement and use by humans on the other. To this end I now consider the main contributions of biological science since the 1930s.

Aquatic Insects

L. Ancona appears to have been the first professional biologist to observe the ecology and utilization of aquatic fauna in Lake Texcoco. He identified the insect species that were being collected by local fishermen during the early 1930s, noting that the Hemípteros were especially abundant (Table 4.1). Ancona observed that, for the aquatic insects of this zone,

> *[English translation]* [t]he permanent pools, ponds, canals, and springs which are found in the vicinity of Sochiaca, Chimalhuacán, Xochitenco, Texcoco and the Chapingo hacienda [a few km south of the town of Texcoco] . . . offer good refuge during the dry season, and from those places these insects later extend over the entire lake surface. [Ancona 1933:53]

Ancona noted that the insects are most abundant in waters 30-50 cm deep with abundant aquatic vegetation. Under natural conditions, several different insect species deposit their eggs on the submerged portions of the aquatic plants. In such a rich and ecologically complex environment, the developing larvae of various insect species feed upon each other's eggs, including those of species not consumed by humans.

> *[English translation]* The most nutritious places for the corixids are the submerged parts of the reeds . . . that border the hatching places and the lake margins. Here they [the corixids]

Table 4.1. Aquatic insects collected for food by fishermen in Lake Texcoco, identified by Ancona (1933:53).

Family Category	Genus and Species	Comments
Coleópteros	*Rhantus mexicana* Dug. *Megadytes fallax* Aubé *Hydrophillus insularis* Cast. *Tropisternus oculatus* N. *Tropisternus tinctus* N. *Thermonectes basilaris* Harr. *Gyrinus parcus* Say.	
Hemípteros	*Ranatra americana* Mondt. *Hydrometra martini* Kirk. *Gerris marginatus* Say. *Trichoxorixa parvula* Champ. *Graptocorixa abdominalis* Say. *Krizousacorixa azteca* Jaex. *Krizousacorixa femorata* Guér. *Notonecta unifasciata* Guér. *Corisella mercenaría* Say. *Corisella texcocana* Jaez.	 produces ahuauhtle produces ahuauhtle produces ahuauhtle produces ahuauhtle produces ahuauhtle

are mixed together with the eggs of *Gyrinus*, *Tropisternus*, and . . . *Hidrófilos*. Several species of *Spirogyra* . . . are enmeshed in the tiny intervening spaces that provide a magnificent refuge for the larvae and aquatic insects belonging to the genus *Ephydra*, which in their turn provide a rich source of food for the insects that produce *ahuautle*. Floating on the surfaces of the lake and, especially, in the standing pools and canals that persist during the dry season, are found gelatinaceous masses of clear green and dark green color comprised of *Vaucherias* and *Ciaoficcas* belonging to the genuses *Oscillaríz* and *Nostoc*: the gelatinaceous secretions of the latter provide a good food for *Gyrinus* and even for the corixids. [Ancona 1933:54-56]

Ancona detected significant seasonal variability in the proportions of different edible aquatic insects in Lake Texcoco (Table 4.2). Some eggs are apparently available year-round, although they become more abundant at the onset of the rainy season (May). At that time, fishermen began to insert the reed bundles, upon which the eggs are deposited in abundance, in the most favorable breeding grounds. The fishermen also submerged coarse cloths, measuring about 100×60 cm, upon which eggs were deposited during the rainy season (Ancona 1933:62). The average egg density was 66 per cm^2 of water surface (Ancona 1933:59).

Ramos-Elorduy and Pino (1989:6-7) provide a comprehensive list of insect species consumed in ancient and modern Mexico. The lacustrine insects on this listing include members of three orders, five families, six genera, and nine species (Table 4.3). In the last column of Table 4.3, these authors attempt to link the modern insects with those named and described in the major sixteenth-century sources; this is often a complicated and uncertain task. The same authors (1989:49-55) also provide some useful nutritional information (Tables 4.4 and 4.5). These nutritional data indicate that edible aquatic insects from Lake Texcoco have been a significant source of proteins and essential amino acids for both modern and prehispanic populations. The protein content is among the very highest of several dozen categories of Mexican foods (including several kinds of meat) listed by

Table 4.2. Seasonal variability in proportions of edible aquatic
insects in Lake Texcoco.

Dry Season (Oct.-May)	
Species	%
Krizousacorixta azteca Jaez.	72
Notonecta unifasciata Guér.	18
Krizousacorixta femorata Guér.	7
Corisella texcocana Jaez.	2
Corisella mercenaria Say.	1
Wet Season (June-Sept.)	
Species	%
Krizousacorixta azteca Jaez.	31
Notonecta unifasciata Guér.	33
Krizousacorixta femorata Guér.	12
Corisella texcocana Jaez.	7
Corisella mercenaria Say.	17

(Ancona 1933:57-58, 61-62)

Ramos-Elorduy (1987:115). These edible lacustrine insects are also rated relatively high in calcium, phosphorous, riboflavin, and niacin (Ramos-Elorduy 1987:117-19). In their studies of the caloric content of some edible Mexican insects, Ramos-Elorduy and Pino (1990:68) find that *Ephydra hians* contains 3348.70 kilocalories per 1000 grams, while the eggs of this same species contain 3182 kilocalories per 1000 grams—both values on par with that of wheat, and exceeding that of chicken.

Ramos-Elorduy and Pino (1989:58-59) also provide some suggestive data on aquatic insect seasonality and relative abundance (Fig. 4.1). These data indicate that although the number and availability of these insects peak during the spring and summer months (especially March through July), there is a measure of year-round availability, and even some minor fall and winter peaks.

Although I know of no comparable studies in Mexico, there is some indication that the periodicity of the abundance of some aquatic insect species in Lake Victoria (highland eastern Africa) is related to lunar cycles. Corbet noted that

[d]espite the constancy of their environment, certain aquatic insects in Lake Victoria exhibit periodic emergence. In the mayfly, *Povilla adusta*, emergence is closely synchronized and occurs shortly after full moon. On the other hand, most swarms of "lake flies" (unidentified Chironomidae and Chaoborus) have been reported to occur shortly after the new moon. [Corbet 1958:330]

Corbet studied the behavior of thirty-seven species of aquatic insects in Lake Victoria to test whether their abundance might be linked to lunar cycles. He found that only four species, in addition to the mayfly, "showed a periodic fluctuation in numbers correlated closely with the age of the moon." His observations led him to conclude that the "emergence and reproduction of many aquatic insects in equatorial lakes need not be cyclical . . ." (Corbet 1958:330). The extent to which periodic abundance of some aquatic insects in Lake Texcoco may be linked to lunar cycles remains an open question.

Table 4.3. Edible aquatic insects exploited in ancient and modern Mexico.

Order	Family	Genus	Species	Sixteenth-Century Name
Hemiptera	Corixidae	*Krizousacorixa*	*azteca* J.	axayacatl, or mosco
Hemiptera	Corixidae	*Krizousacorixa*	*femorata*	axayacatl, or mosco
Hemiptera	Corixidae	*Corisella*	*mercenaria* S.	axayacatl, or mosco
Hemiptera	Corixidae	*Corisella*	*edulis* J.	axayacatl, or mosco
Hemiptera	Corixidae	*Corisella*	*texcocana* J.	axayacatl, or mosco
Hemiptera	Notonectidae	*Notonecta*	*unifasciata* G.	axayacatl, or mosco
Hemiptera	Belostomatidae	*Abedus*	*ovatus* S.	ahuihuilla, or ahuihuitla
Coleoptera	Dytiscidae	*Cybister*	*explanatus* L.	atopinan, or atopina
Diptera	Ephydridae	*Ephydra*	*hians* S.	izcahuitl, escahuitli, ocuiliztac, poxi, amoyot, or michpilli

(Adapted from Ramos-Elorduy and Pino 1989:6-7, 15-17, 9-20, 29-31; Ramos-Elorduy and Pino 1996)

Table 4.4. Protein content of some edible aquatic insects.

Insect	% Protein	% Protein Digestible	% Total Digestible
Corixidae: ahuauhtle (eggs)	56.55	89.34	61.56
Corixidae: axayacatl (adult)	62.80	98.02	86.95
Abedus ovatus S. (adult)	67.69	no data	no data
Ephydra hians S. (larvae)	35.81	no data	no data

(Adapted from Ramos-Elorduy and Pino 1989:49, 54, 55; slightly different figures are given in Ramos-Elorduy 1987:90, 106, and Ramos-Elorduy et al. 1984:71-72)

Table 4.5. Essential amino acid content of some edible aquatic insects.

Insect	Essential Amino Acid* Content (mg/16 g)	FAO Daily Requirement (mg)
Krizousacorixa spp. and *Notonecta* spp.	43.6	—
Corisella spp.	38.9	—
Ephydra hians	50.62	—
—	—	36.0

(Adapted from Ramos-Elorduy and Pino 1989:51-52; Ramos-Elorduy et al. 1984)
*These amino acids include isoleucine, leucine, lycine, metionine + cisteine, phenylalanine + tironsine, threonine, triptophane, and valine.

Salamanders

Sahagun (1963:62) and other sixteenth-century writers referred to the amphibious creature, the salamander, as the *axolotl*. It is the larval form that is sought after as human food. According to Smith and Smith (1971: x), three variants of this animal have survived in freshwater Lake Xochimilco (*Ambystoma mexicanum*), in the shallow, saline remnants of Lake Texcoco (*A. tigrinum*), and in the brackish remnants of Lake Zumpango (*A. lacustris*). Closely related variants continue to be abundant farther west in highland Mexico, in the Upper Lerma drainage and in Lake Pátzcuaro. Furthermore,

[i]t is clear that the larvae of the ambystomatid salamanders, particularly those related to *Ambystoma tigrinum* . . . are a highly propitious source of food . . . , since they can develop in enormous numbers in stagnant waters that would not support fish. [Smith and Smith 1971: x]

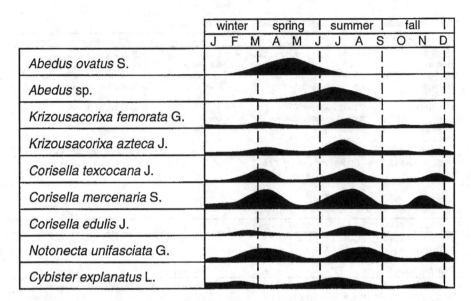

Figure 4.1. Seasonality and relative abundance of some edible lacustrine insects (adapted from Ramos-Elorduy and Pino 1989:58, Cuadro 7).

Waterfowl

By the mid-twentieth century, following many decades of severe decline produced by habitat destruction, waterfowl in the Valley of Mexico had been reduced to only eight common types (Table 4.6), although smaller numbers of other species continued to be present (Table 4.6A). A 1952 census provides some sense of their relative quantity (Table 4.7). The weights of these and other native waterfowl are compiled in Tables 4.8 and 4.9. Species identifications are not always consistent in the different listings, but I take this to reflect relatively minor quibbles between specialists. These waterfowl occupied the full range of ecological niches potentially available to them in the Valley of Mexico—for example, some are "dabbling or surface feeding ducks," while others are "diving ducks" (Berres 2000:35).

Chichicuilotes (not listed in Tables 4.6, 4.6A, or 4.7) are still fairly abundant on and around the remnants of Lake Texcoco. These birds are members of the Charadriidae family (plovers), and are commonly known in English as "killdeer"; they probably are *Charadrius vociferous* (Kent V. Flannery, pers. comm. 2001).

Sahagun (1963) and Hernández (1959b) both identified waterfowl species that reared their young within the Valley of Mexico in the sixteenth century (Table 4.10). As far as I can determine, three of those mentioned by Hernández remain unidentified in the modern literature and cannot be cross-listed with Sahagun's compilation; consequently, they may be duplicated in Table 4.8. In addition, *Charadrius vociferous* (killdeer) is a

Table 4.6. Common waterfowl in the Valley of Mexico in the mid-twentieth century.

Nahuatl name	Common Name (Spanish)	Scientific Name	Comment
tlalalácatl	ganso gris	*Anser albifrons*	present in winter
cuacoztli	pato coacostle	*Aythya valisineria*	present in winter
tzitziua	pato golondrino	*Anas acuta tzuitihoa*	present in winter
metzcanauhtli	cerceta de alas azules	*Anas discors*	resident year-round, but most abundant in winter
iztactzonyayauhqui	pato de carreteras	*Aix sponsa*	present in winter
zolcanauhtlih	pato de collar	*Anas platyrhynchos*	present in winter
chilcanauhtli	cerceta canela	*Anas cyanoptera*	
amanacochi	pato chillón jorobado	*Bucephala albeola*	present in winter

(Adapted from Martin del Campo 1955:68)

Table 4.6A. Comprehensive list of waterfowl species present in the Valley of Mexico during the twentieth century.

Family	Common Name	Genus and Species
Dendrocygnidae (whistling ducks)	fulvous whistling duck	*Dendrocygna bicolor*
	black-bellied whistling duck	*Dendrocygna autumnalis*
	white-fronted goose	*Anser albifrons*
	Canada goose	*Branta canadensis*
	green-winged teal	*Anas crecca carolinensis, Anas cerceta aliverde*
	Mexican mallard (pato mexicano)	*Anas diazi*
	northern pintail (pato golodrino norteño)	*Anas acuta*
	blue-winged teal	*Anas discors*
	cinnamon teal (pato castona)	*Anas cyanoptera septentrionalium*
	northern shoveler (pato cucharon norteño)	*Anas clypeata*
Anatidae (swans, geese, ducks)	gadwell (pato pinto)	*Anas strepera*
	American wigeon (pato chalcuam)	*Anas americana*
	canvasback (pato coacoxtle)	*Aythya valisineria*
	redhead (pato cabecirrojo)	*Aythya Americana*
	ring-necked duck (pato piquianillado)	*Aythya collaris*
	lesser scaup (pato boludo menor)	*Aythya affinis*
	bufflehead (pato monja)	*Bucephala albeola*
	ruddy duck (pato tepalcate)	*Oxyura jamaicensis*

(Adapted from Berres 2000:35)

Table 4.7. Counts of migratory and year-round waterfowl on Lake Texcoco in January 1952.

Common English Name	Scientific Name	Number	Comment
blue-winged teal	Anas cyanoptera & A. discors	2550	migratory, winter residence only
green-winged teal	Anas carolinensis	4580	migratory, winter residence only
pintail	Anas acuta	15,900	migratory, winter residence only
baldpate	Mareca americana	910	migratory, winter residence only
gadwall	Anas strepera	460	migratory, winter residence only
shoveler	Spatula clypeata	8100	migratory, winter residence only
canvasback	Aythya valisineria	580	migratory, winter residence only
redhead	Aythya americana	460	migratory, winter residence only
white-fronted goose	Anser albifrons	5	year-round resident
coot	Fulica americana	2100	year-round resident

(Adapted from Leopold 1959:139, 142)

Table 4.8. Mean adult live weights of Lake Texcoco waterfowl species identified by Martin del Campo (1955) and Leopold (1959).

Species Common English Name[a]	Mean Adult Weight (grams) (from Dunning 1984)	Weight Range (grams) (from Dunning 1984)
Anas cyanoptera or Anas discors cinamon teal or blue-winged teal	female: 363 male: 409	female: up to 499 male: up to 549
Anas acuta northern pintail	female: 986 male: 1035	n.d.
Anas strepera gadwell	female: 849 male: 990	n.d.
Anas platyrhynchos mallard	overall: 1082 ± 129	overall: 720-1580
Anas clypeata/Spatula clypeata[b] northern shoveler	female: 590 male: 636	female: up to 726 male: up to 908
Aythya valisineria canvasback	female: 1190 male: 1249	n.d.
Aythya americana redhead	female: 990 male: 1100	n.d.
Anser albifrons greater white-fronted goose	overall: 2587	overall: 1920-3220
Fulica americana American coot	female: 560 male: 724	female: 427-628 male: 576-848
Aix sponsa wood duck	female: 635 male: 681	female: up to 908 male: up to 907
Bucephala albeola bufflehead	female: 334 ± 23.2 male: 473 ± 32.8	female: 297-374 male: 424-551
Charadrius vociferous[c] killdeer (chichicuilote)	female: 101 male: 92.1 ± 10.4	n.d.

[a]English common names from Dunning (1984) and the National Geographic Society (1999).
[b]Identified as *Anas* by Dunning (1984).
[c]Identified by K.V. Flannery, from photographs.

year-round resident of the Valley of Mexico, producing eggs locally. Although neither Sahagun, Hernández, nor any other writers known to me specifically mentions the collection of waterfowl eggs, as noted in Chapter 2, Cortés (1963:73) and Sahagun (1969:147) mentioned the availability of waterfowl eggs in the Tenochtitlán marketplace in the sixteenth century. Waterfowl eggs were obviously a significant food source during their breeding season. During our archaeological surveys in July 2003 in central Lake Texcoco, we saw numerous nests with eggs of aquatic waterfowl in a federally protected wildlife reserve (Plate 4.1).

I have not found much detailed information about the number of eggs that waterfowl typically produce during a single breeding season. As noted in Chapter 3, Herrera (1895:60-61) asserted that one female duck of the type resident in Lake Texcoco during the late nineteenth century was capable of producing up to 180 eggs in a season. However, I take this as a potential maximum figure, seldom realized in practice. In their discussion of waterfowl in the U.S. Great Basin, Raven and Elston (1988:342) indicate that "[e]ggs are produced until a successful hatch occurs." This generalization conforms to descriptions of waterfowl breeding behavior in *The Birds of North America Online* (Cornell Lab of Ornithology 2005), which indicate that most species produce more than one hatch per season, and most will produce new clutches of eggs if the contents of an existing nest are robbed or destroyed. Table 4.10 provides some idea of the quantity of food available from waterfowl eggs.

Plate 4.1. Clutch of 10 duck eggs (species uncertain) in central Lake Texcoco, July 2003. Scale = 25 cm.

Table 4.9. Mean adult live weights of Lake Texcoco waterfowl species identified by Dibble and Anderson from Sahagun (1963), and not noted by Leopold (1959) or Martin del Campo (1955).

Species Common English Name	Mean Adult Weight (grams) (from Dunning 1984)	Weight Range (grams) (from Dunning 1984)
Anhinga anhinga anhinga, or water turkey	overall: 1235 ± 54.8	n.d.
Aechmophorus occidentalis western grebe	overall: 1477	overall: 795-1818
Rynchops niger[a] black skimmer	female: 255 male: 344 ± 38.7	n.d.
Mycteria americana wood stork, or wood ibis	female: 2050 male: 2702	n.d.
Porphyrula martinica purple gallinule	female: 215 male: 257 ± 27.1	n.d.
Pluvialis squatarola[b] black-bellied plover	overall: 220 ± 24.4	n.d.
Recurvirostra americana American avocet	overall: 316	n.d.
Grus canadensis brown crane, or sandhill crane	female: 2982 ± 19.0 male: 3350 ± 22.3	female: 2450-3300 male: 2700-3700
Nycticoras nycticorax black-crowned night heron	overall: 883	overall: 727-1014
Gallinago gallinago[c] Wilson snipe, or common snipe	female: 116 male: 128	female: up to 156 male: up to 156
Phalaropus lobatus[d] red-necked phalarope, or northern phalarope	female: 35.0 male: 32.0	female: 29-35 male: 29-33
Egretta thula[e] snowy egret	overall: 371 ± 25.0	n.d.
Egretta caerulea[f] little blue heron	female: 315 male: 364 ± 47.1	n.d.
Probably *Pelecanus erythrorhynchos*[g] American white pelican	overall: 7500	n.d.
Anas crecca common teal, or green-winged teal	female: 318 male: 364	female: up to 409 male: up to 454
Lophodytes cucullatus hooded merganser	female: 540 male: 680	female: up to 680 male: up to 910
Oxyura jamaicensis ruddy duck	female: 499 male: 590	female: up to 635 male: up to 816
Podiceps nigricollis[h] eared grebe	overall: 297	overall: 218-375
Larus pipixcan[i] Franklin's gull	overall: 280 ± 9.69	overall: 220-335

[a]Dibble and Anderson identify this as *A. negra*.
[b]Dibble and Anderson identify this as *Squatarola squatarola*.
[c]Dibble and Anderson identify this as *Capella gallinago*.
[d]Dibble and Anderson identify this as *Lobipes lobatus*.
[e]Dibble and Anderson identify this as *Leucophoyx thula*.
[f]Dibble and Anderson identify this as *Florida caerulea*.
[g]Dibble and Anderson identify this as *Atotolin*.
[h]Dibble and Anderson identify this as *Colymbus nigricollis*.
[i]Dibble and Anderson identify this as *Larus franklini*.

Table 4.10. Types of waterfowl that reared their young within the Valley of Mexico, according to Sahagun (1963) and/or Hernández (1959b).[a]

Species	Average Number of Eggs per Nest	Average Weight of Individual Fresh Eggs (including shell)[b]
concanauhtli, goose, *Anser albifons*	3-5 (Baicich and Harrison 1997:73)	128 grams
quachilton, American coot, *Fulica americana*	6-9 (Baicich and Harrison 1997:120)	29.2 grams
tolcomoctli, American bittern, *Botaurus lentiginosus*	4-5 (Baicich and Harrison 1997:60)	?
icxixoxouhqui, American avocet, *Recurvirostra americana*	4 (Baicich and Harrison 1997:129)	32 grams
atapalcatl, ruddy duck, *Oxyura jamaicensis*	6-10 (Baicich and Harrison 1997:88)	74 grams
pipitztli, probably Franklin's gull, probably *Larus pipixcan*	3 (Baicich and Harrison 1997:152)	36 grams
acachichictli, western grebe, *Aechomophorus occidentalis*	3-4 (Baicich and Harrison 1997:52)	?
acacálotl, cormorant, species uncertain	?	51 grams
azazahoactli [unidentified in modern literature]	?	?
amacozque [unidentified in modern literature]	?	?
atotolquíchil [unidentified in modern literature]	?	?
killdeer, *Charadrius vociferous*	4 (Baicich and Harrison 1997:126)	?

[a]The killdeer (chichicuilote, *Charadrius vociferous*) has been added to this list.
[b]From Cornell Lab of Ornithology (2005).

Fish

Modern investigators have identified up to fourteen indigenous species of lake fish in the Valley of Mexico; members of the Cyprinidae family are the most numerous in recent times (Table 4.11).

Citing Aguirre (1955:56-58), Ortiz de Montellano (1978:617) noted that dried *charales* (*Chirostoma* spp.) from Lake Texcoco are 61.8% protein by weight, and that 100 g of their flesh contain 60 mg of niacin (some three times the daily minimal adult requirement) and 3200 IU of vitamin A. C. Phillips (2002, citing Ensminger et al. [1995], Pennington [1998], and Ronzio [1997]) provides additional information on the nutritional value of fish:

Fish provide vitamins A, D, B1 . . . , B2 . . . , a 100-gm portion of fish . . . would have provided 67 usable calories and a range of important nutrients such as niacin, iron, calcium, and zinc. . . . most fish contain 18-20% protein, of which 85-95% is digestible (Ensminger et al. 1995). . . . Fish comprises a high quality, "complete" protein, meaning that it contains all the amino acids humans need for proper nutrition (Ronzio 1997:369). Fish meets or exceeds the recommended daily intake of five of these amino acids. . . . with a 3-ounce (85 gm) portion of lean white fish providing over 20 gm of protein (Pennington 1998:332-37), a modest portion of fish could make a substantial contribution to daily protein needs (63 gm for adult males, and 50 gm for adult females [Ronzio 1997]). [Phillips 2002:49-50]

Table 4.11. Indigenous lake fish in the Valley of Mexico.

Family	Genus	Species
Cyprinidae	*Algansea*	*tincella*
Cyprinidae	*Aztecula*	*vittata*
Cyprinidae	*Evarra*	*eigenmanni*
Cyprinidae	*Evarra*	*bustamantei*
Cyprinidae	*Evarra*	*tlahuacensis*
Goodeidae	*Girardinichthys*	*innominatus*
Goodeidae	*Girardinichthys*	*viviparus*
Goodeidae	*Neoophorus*	*diazi*
Goodeidae	*Skiffia*	*variegata*
Goodeidae	*Skiffia*	*lermae*
Atherinidae	*Chirostoma*	*regani*
Atherinidae	*Chirostoma*	*jordani* ["charal"]
Atherinidae	*Chirostoma*	*estor estor*
Atherinidae	*Chirostoma*	*humboldtianum* ["charal"]
?	*Zoogeneticus*	*minatus*

(Adapted from Alcocer-Durand and Escobar-Briones 1992:176; Alvarez and Navarro 1957:57; Berres 2000:29; García Sanchez 1998:50; Martin del Campo 1955:60-61; Meek 1904:778; Seurat 1900:406)

Table 4.12. Clams, aquatic snails, frogs, and small crustaceans in the Valley of Mexico.

Clams	Snails	Frogs	Acocil (a crustacean)
Anodonta impura	*Physa osculans*	*Hyla exima*	*Cambarus mexicanus*
Sphaerium subtransverum	*Planorbis tenuis*	*Rana montezuma*	*Cambarellus montezumae*
Valvata humeralis	*Limaea attenueta*	*Rana pipens*	
	Succinea campestris	*Rana halecina*	

(Adapted from Alcocer-Durand and Escobar-Briones 1992:178)

Miscellaneous Lacustrine Fauna (Molluscs, Crustaceans, Snails, Frogs)

Substantial quantities of a small bivalve mollusc (for which we were unable to secure species identification) are netted in Chimalhuacán today (see Chap. 5). Alcocer-Durand and Escobar-Briones (1992:178) indicate that three species of freshwater clams and four species of lacustrine snails were once common in the Valley of Mexico (Table 4.12).

Algae (*Spirulina geitleri*)

This multicelled alga was usually referred to as *tecuítlatl* by sixteenth-century writers (e.g., Sahagun 1963:65; Hernández 1959b:408-9). Santley and Rose (1979) considered its implications for prehispanic demography in the Valley of Mexico. The nutritional value of this food is outstanding. According to Furst (1978:60), for example, it is 65-70% protein by weight, "a higher percentage than any other natural food . . . ," and it contains all eight essential amino acids. Dillon and Phan (1993:103) report that "the essential amino

Plate 4.2. Northern Lake Texcoco in 1954, showing the commercial evaporation facility at Sosa de Texcoco, S.A. (El Caracol). Courtesy Cia. Mexicana de Aerofoto, S.A.

acids comprise 47% of the protein." Gallegos (1993:135-37) also notes the high vitamin and mineral content of *Spirulina*. Furthermore, because of its cellular structure, algae is highly digestible without chemical or physical processing (Dillon and Phan 1993:105). Notably, the area of a

> pond devoted to the cultivation of *Spirulina* can produce 125 times as much protein as the same amount of area devoted to corn, 70 times as much as to farmed fish, and 600 times as much as to cattle. [Furst 1978:62]

Since the 1960s *Spirulina* has been commercially produced at the La Sosa de Texcoco,[1] a large evaporation plant on the north side of Lake Texcoco that was also used for soda production (Plate 4.2). By the 1970s, the pilot program had succeeded in producing about one metric ton per day of dry *Spirulina* (Furst 1978). By the early 1990s, annual production had expanded to 600 metric tons (amounting to 14 tons of protein per year per hectare) from this evaporation facility of some 800 hectares (Gallejos 1993:135). The overall potential production is far higher because *Spirulina*

> multiplies rapidly, dividing three times daily, and flourishes in waters that are too salty for irrigation or human consumption. All that is needed is the right amount of solar radiation[2]

---

[1]All production at this plant was abandoned after the mid-1990s.
[2]Durand-Chastel (1980:54) notes that Lake Texcoco receives an average of 140 kilocalories/cm/year of solar irradiation.

Plate 4.3. Remnant of marsh environment in southeastern Lake Texcoco, near Chimalhuacán, Sept. 1967. Arrow points to man hunting ducks. This area is now completely urbanized.

and a high level of salinity. The Valley of Mexico . . . has about 240 days of sunshine per year and the water of Lake Texcoco has a pH factor between 9 and 10, which indicates a high salt content. Under these conditions, a single hectare can produce from 12,000 to 20,000 kilograms of dried protein [12-20 metric tons] per year from *Spirulina*. [Furst 1978:63]

Under ideal conditions, the potential daily output of protein from *Spirulina* on 500 hectares of Lake Texcoco would amount to 48.8 metric tons (48,835 kg) (Furst 1978:64).

Durand-Chastel (1980:57) and Gallegos (1993:137) observe that the *Spirulina* produced by La Sosa de Texcoco also contains substantial quantities of several essential minerals, many of them in significantly higher proportions than in other common plant foods: calcium, phosphorous, iron, sodium, chloride, magnesium, manganese, zinc, potassium, copper, and chromium.

Other Aquatic Plants

Long-term drainage has increased the levels of salinity and alkalinity in the lakebed and lakeshore zones of Lake Texcoco relative to precolumbian times. These changes in salinity, alkalinity, and humidity, together with gradual conversion to agriculture of large sections of the lakeshore zone since 1911, have produced substantial changes in the types of wild vegetation that have characterized the region over the past 150 years

Table 4.13. Characteristic aquatic facies plants of Lake Texcoco.

Genus and Species	Common Spanish Name and Reference	Common English Name and Reference
Aganippea bellidiflora	estrella de agua (Sanchez 1968:435)	
Cyperus Bourgaei	tule grande (Sanchez 1968:67)	tule (Orme 1990:77)
Eleocharis Dombeyana		spikerush (Orme 1990:77)
Hydrocotyle verticillata	ombligo de Venus (Sanchez 1968:286)	whorled marsh pennywort (USDA*)
Juncus balticus	tulillo (Sanchez 1968:91)	baltic rush (Orme 1990:77)
Jussiaea repens	verdolaga de agua (Sanchez 1968:277)	floating primrose (USDA)
Leersia hexandra	(Sanchez 1968:44)	southern cutgrass (USDA)
Polygonum hydropiperoides	chilillo (Sanchez 1968:145)	swamp smartweed (USDA)
Polygonum punctatum	venenillo, chilillo (Sanchez 1968:146)	dotted smartweed (USDA)
Sagittaria macrophylla	hoja flecha (Sanchez 1968:30)	arrowhead (USDA)
Scirpus lacustris	tule (Sanchez 1968:70-71)	tule bulrush (Orme 1990:77)
Scirpus pungens		tule bulrush (Orme 1990:77)
Scirpus californicus	tule redondo (García Sanchez 1998:52)	California bulrush (USDA)
Typha latifolia	espadaña, tule (Sanchez 1968:26)	cattail (Orme 1990:77)
Typha angustifolia	tule ancho (García Sanchez 1998:52)	narrowleaf cattail (USDA)
Nymphaea sp.	cabeza de negro, nenúfar, ninfa (Sanchez 1968:167-68)	water lily (Orme 1990:77)
Potamogeton pectinatus	(Sanchez 1968:27)	pond weed (Orme 1990:77)
Myriophyllum hippuroides	(Sanchez 1968:280)	western watermilfoil (USDA)
Azolla caroliniana		Carolina mosquitofern (USDA)
Eichhornia crassipes	lirio de agua, jacinto, cucharilla, huauchinango (Sanchez 1968:90)	common water hyacinth (USDA)
Lemma minor	(Sanchez 1968:75)	duckweed (Orme 1990:77)
Lemma gibba	(Sanchez 1968:75)	duckweed (Orme 1990:77)
Lemma valdiviana	(Sanchez 1968:76)	
Wolffia columbiana	(Sanchez 1968:77)	Columbian watermeal (USDA)
Ceratophyllum demersum	(Sanchez 1968:168)	coon's tail (USDA)

(After Rzedowski 1957:26-27)
*United States Department of Agriculture

(Rzedowski 1957:23-24). Although it is difficult to quantify these changes, Rzedowski (1957:25) estimated that there are now many fewer water-loving plants in the lakebed-lakeshore zone than there were prior to the mid-nineteenth century.

Rzedowski divided the mid-twentieth-century lakebed-lakeshore vegetation into two main groups (facies): Aquatic and Terrestrial. His aquatic plants (Table 4.13) are found primarily along canals and ditches, at the mouths of streams that empty into the lake, and in small areas of permanent water around springs and remnant lakebed ponds (Plate 4.3)—all very restricted habitats today, but obviously much more common in precolumbian times before external drainage began. Rzedowski's principal aquatic plants include *Typha* spp. (cattail), *Juncus* spp. (rush), *Scirpus* spp. (tule, or bulrush), *Nymphaea* spp. (water lily), and *Lemma* spp. (duckweed) (Rzedowski 1957:26-27; also, Sanchez 1968).

Rzedowski's terrestrial lakebed-lakeshore plant facies is strongly dominated by a single species: *Distichlis spicata* (*zacahuistle*, a sharp-edged grass). Over the past century this aggressive species has advanced steadily across the increasingly dessicated lakebed, limited only by the high alkaline content of the innermost lakebed zones. These latter zones characteristically lack vegetation entirely (Plate 4.4). Minor components of Rzedowski's terrestrial facies include *Suaeda nigra* (*romerillo*), *Atriplex linifolia* (ink-

Plate 4.4. Saline lakeshore plain on the eastern side of Lake Texcoco, showing expansion of *Distichlis spicata* vegetation and bare ground, July 1988.

weed, or *quelite de puerco*), and up to eight other species (primarily chenopodium and portulaca) (Rzedowski 1988:361).

Conclusions

The modern biological data on aquatic resources in the Valley of Mexico clearly indicate that:

(1) These animal and plant resources were varied, abundant, and intensively exploited.

(2) Aquatic fauna were a significant component of the diet, in terms of both energy and nutrition. The high quality and quantity of proteins available from these aquatic sources is especially impressive, perhaps particularly in the case of edible aquatic insects.

(3) Except for algae—an extraordinarily important source of calories, protein, and minerals—there is less information about the dietary significance of aquatic plants. Nevertheless, there is some indication that the starchy stalks and roots of several aquatic plant species have been important as food; these same plants have been important since the mid-sixteenth century as fodder for domestic animals. The economic importance of reeds and rushes as sources of raw materials for mats, baskets, and house construction is quite clear.

(4) Although there appears to be some seasonal variation in the availability of aquatic resources (most particularly in the case of migratory waterfowl), it is equally clear that many were available year-round.

– 5 –

Collecting and Processing Aquatic Fauna at Chimalhuacán in 1992

Although this chapter focuses on aquatic insects, the *pescadores* (fishermen) at Chimalhuacán also harvest small fish and molluscs that live in the shallow lake remnants. Sometimes these animals are netted together, sometimes separately. Because of their close association, I include them all in my discussion. In this chapter I first present the local folk taxonomy used by my informants, and link this taxonomy to that of professional zoologists discussed in Chapter 4. I then describe in detail the activities I observed at Chimalhuacán in 1992. Unless otherwise noted, all references to present and past time are relative to August 1992.

Folk Taxonomy of Collected Aquatic Fauna

Five categories of aquatic insects are presently collected (Table 5.1): (1) *Mosco* (Plate 5.1); (2) *Palomero* (Plate 5.2); (3) *Cuatecón* (Plate 5.3); (4) *Tejoncito* (Plate 5.4); and (5) *Chipirín* (Plate 5.5). Most of these are said to be available year-round, although their distribution is more restricted during the dry season when many lakebed ponds dry up. Sometimes "mosco" is used as a generic term to refer to all collected aquatic insects. One type of mollusc, a tiny bivalve locally called *Arneja* (Plate 5.6), is also still deliberately netted during the rainy season (I never learned its species identification or its use). This mollusc is sometimes netted separately, but more commonly together with insects and/or fish in locations where they co-occur. *Mosco* and *cuatecón* are considered acceptable for human consumption, as was formerly another type, *requezón* (see below). However, only a small proportion of these potentially edible insects is consumed by people today. Most of the catch is sold to market wholesalers in Mexico City who, in turn, resell the product to urban pet stores as food for caged birds. *Mosco* eggs (*ahuauhtle* or *ahuauhtli*) (Plate 5.7) are also collected and sold as a high-priced delicacy food for human consumption.

One type of small fish, *charalito* (*Chirostoma* spp.), is still commonly netted, mostly in the deepest remaining waters in the central part of the old lakebed. These are seldom more than 3 cm long (Plate 5.8). Occasionally these fish are netted together with insects.

Four large samples of these local insect categories, sorted by my informants, were identified by Richard C. Froeschner[1] (Table 5.2). Froeschner's identifications indicate that although there has been some admixture of different species in the samples I provided, "mosco" is the adult stage of *Corisella edulis*, "cuatecón" is the adult stage of *Notonecta unifasiata*, "tejoncito" is probably the nymph stage of *Notonecta unifasiata*, and "palomero" is probably the adult stage of *Buenoa uhleri*.

Two of the most common species collected today at Chimalhuacán are known popularly in English as the "waterboatman" and "whirligig beetle" (Kent V. Flannery, pers. comm. 1992).

According to my informants, until the 1970s and before the lakebed ponds dried up as much as they have in recent years, three other categories of insects were also collected: *maranito*, *pulga* (*michipitl*), and *requezón* (*poche*) (Table 5.3).

Requezón were once so abundant that they were used as agricultural fertilizer as late as about 1940 (Apenes 1943:18), just as they had been in the nineteenth century (see Chap. 3). My informant, Sr. Peralta, collected large quantities of *requezón* until about 1980, but he reports they have become quite scarce since then. Quite by chance, while passing through the area in September, 1967 (near the end of the rainy season), I observed a man collecting, drying, and bagging these insects along the lakeshore a few km west of Chimalhuacán (in an area that has subsequently become part of Ciudad Netzahualcoyotl, a vast urban sprawl that is now the third largest city in Mexico). My 1967 photographs (Plates 5.9 and 5.10) indicate that the insects were netted (probably much as described below), drowned in small rectangular ponds (ca. 2 × 4 m in area) at the water's edge, spread out on adjacent ground surfaces to dry for a few hours, and then scooped into large bags for transport to market in Mexico City. Apparently, much commercial *requezón* was formerly collected by specialists referred to as "chales." When he saw my 1967 photographs, Sr. Peralta thought that the individual looked like one of the *chales* he remembered.

Today the collection of lacustrine insects peaks during the rainy season months. However, prior to the 1970s, when lakebed ponds were larger and more enduring, there was apparently less seasonality in collecting them.

The Collecting Nets

The Two Types of Net: Common and Special

Most netting is done with the "common" net (Plate 5.11). A "special" net is used for catching *charalitos* (small fish) in the deepest waters of central Lake Texcoco (Plate 5.12). The special net is adapted for use in Lago Nabor Carillo, a large artificial lake of recent origin in central Lake Texcoco from which water is periodically discharged through large tubes to maintain uniform lake size and depth. The special nets are placed across the mouths of these underwater discharge tubes, where they capture the numerous small

---

[1]Richard C. Froeschner, Dept. of Entomology, National Museum of Natural History, Smithsonian Institution, Washington, D.C.

Table 5.1. Categories of presently collected aquatic fauna.

Category	Characteristics	Use
mosco	insect; available year-round in shallow ponds	dried for birdfeed, ground fresh for human food
palomero	insect; available year-round in shallow ponds	dried for birdfeed
cuatecón	insect; available year-round in shallow ponds	dried for birdfeed, ground fresh for human food
tejoncito	insect; available year-round in shallow ponds	dried for birdfeed
chiripín	insect larvae; available June-Sept. and Dec.-Feb., mainly in deeper waters	dried for birdfeed
ahuauhtle	mosco eggs; available year-round in shallow ponds, most abundant in rainy season	dried or fresh for human food
arneja	bivalve mollusc; mainly available June-Nov. in shallow ponds	dried for birdfeed(?)
charalito	small fish; available year-round in ponds	dried or fresh for human food

Table 5.2. Identifications by Richard C. Froeschner of four vials of informant-sorted insect specimens collected near Chimalhuacán.

Category	Identification
vial 1: "mosco"	Corixidae: *Corisella edulis* (Champion) 300-plus adults and nymphs Notonectidae: *Buenoa uhleri* (Truxal) 4 adults and 2 nymphs Notonectidae: *Notonecta* 2 unidentifiable nymphs, probably *N. unifasciata* (Guérin-Méneville)
vial 2: "cuatecón"	Notonectidae: *Notonecta unifasciata* (Guérin-Méneville) 76 adults Corixidae: 1 very young nymph, unidentifiable
vial 3: "tejoncito"	Notonectidae: *Notonecta* 235 unidentifiable nymphs, probably *N. unifasciata* (Guérin-Méneville) Notonectidae: *Buenoa uhleri* (Truxal) 38 adults, 2 nymphs Corixidae: *Corisella edulis* (Champion) 21 adults, 51 nymphs
vial 4: "palomero"	Notonectidae: *Buenoa uhleri* (Truxal) ca. 230 adults Notonectidae: *Notonecta* 1 unidentifiable nymph, probably *N. unifasciata* (Guérin-Méneville) Corixidae: *Corisella edulis* (Champion) 7 adults, 22 nymphs

Table 5.3. Categories of formerly collected lacustrine insects.

Category	Characteristics	Use
maranito	small, "shrimp-like" creature, mainly available June-Nov. at edges of lakebed ponds	dried for birdfeed
pulga (michipitl)	small, wingless insect, found year-round at edges of lakebed ponds; sold live	live food for pet turtles and fish
requezón (poche)	worm-like larvae; mainly available June-Nov. in shallow water at edges of lakebed ponds	dried for birdfeed, fresh for human food

Plate 5.1. *Mosco* insect type. Scale in mm.

Plate 5.2. *Palomero* insect type. Scale in mm.

Plate 5.3. *Cuatecón* insect type. Scale in mm.

Plate 5.4. *Tejoncito* insect type. Scale in mm.

Plate 5.5. *Chipirín* insect type. Scale in mm.

Plate 5.6. *Arneja* mollusc type. Scale in mm.

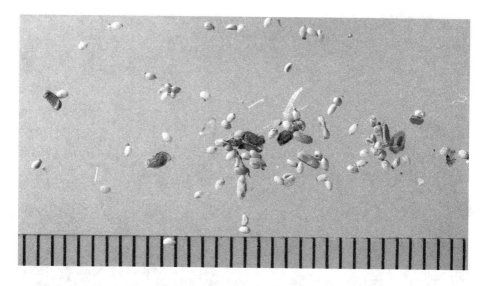

Plate 5.7. *Ahuauhtle* (*mosco* eggs). Scale in mm.

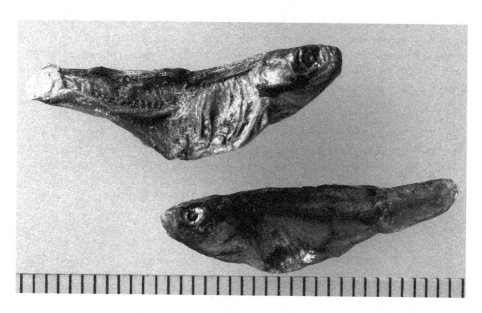

Plate 5.8. *Charalito* fish. Scale in mm.

Plate 5.9. Collecting and drying *requezón*. Sept. 1967.

fish that flow out with the water. Because they must withstand the substantial force of the rushing water, the special nets are made of unusually strong material, a sort of thick twinelike netting (Plate 5.13) securely fastened to an oval-shaped metal rim measuring about 50 × 60 cm. When in use, the net's metal rim is securely tied around the discharge tube's mouth. The special net is obviously adapted to uniquely modern circumstances.

The common net, which is pushed through still water by the walking *pescador*, is made of finer fabric, and has a rigid rectangular opening defined by a framework of wooden sticks. Both the common and special nets are funnel shaped, with a wide opening and a long, tapering tail tied at the small end; the total length commonly ranges from 2.5 to 3 m. This elongated funnel shape functions to securely trap the captured insects and fish inside the net. Very similar nets were in use at Chimalhuacán and nearby lakeshore villages in the 1930s (Ancona 1933:62-63; Apenes 1943; Linne 1948:134).

Making the Common Net

Figure 5.1 shows the different component parts of the common net (Table 5.4). Today all netting is made from two grades of commercial nylon fabric purchased in Mexico City: a common grade for the bulk of the net, and a stronger grade for the *cuchillas grandes* and *cuchillas chicas* pieces. Until the 1960s, all the netting was made from maguey-fiber (*ixtle*) cloths (*ayates*), purchased in Mexico City markets in individual pieces measuring about 1 × 1 m (Apenes 1943:18). The individual *ayates* were sewn together with large needles

Plate 5.10. Bagging dried
requezón. Sept. 1967.

and heavy cotton thread. My informants told me that a typical maguey-fiber net required
seven 1 × 1 m *ayates*, including one constructed of extra heavy thread for making the
cuchillas pieces. Today the component pieces of nylon cloth are cut into triangular form
and sewn together with strong thread. My description is based on a net made for me by
Sr. and Sra. Peralta (Plates 5.14-5.19). The overall length of the finished net is 2.6 m.

Prior to about thirty years ago, when the lakebed pools were deeper, larger, and longer
lasting, the long tails of the nets were usually made of a lighter cotton cloth (called *manta
de cielo*). This gave the net added buoyancy and ensured that its full length would float
near the water surface, where most of the insects lived, rather than dragging along near
the bottom in contexts where the *pescadores* waded through water that was commonly
waist to chest deep.

Plate 5.11. Common net.

Plate 5.12. Special net.

Plate 5.13. Detail of special net fabric.

The net is made in two separate parts: (1) the *redina*, and (2) the rest of the net. The *redina*, which needs to be especially strong, continues to be separately handmade with thick cotton thread and a special wooden hooking tool (*aguja de tejer redina*) (Plate 5.20) in combination with a simple wooden stick (*cucharita*, ca. 25 cm long, about the size and form of a common wooden pencil). Formerly the Peraltas made their own *redinas*, and sometimes even supplied them to other *pescadores*. The usual procedure was to obtain raw cotton in the market, spin it into thread, and then use the hooked tool and stick to form a coarse-mesh piece of netting; the complete process took several days. Now, however, the Peralta family has lost its *redina*-making skill and must purchase what it needs. Good *redinas* are becoming increasingly difficult to find, and used ones are often repaired for as long as possible.

The main raw material for the net is a single piece of cloth measuring 6 × 3 m (a *pieza completa*).[2] As noted above, a much smaller piece of stronger cloth (whose dimensions I did not record) is also needed for making the *cuchillas grandes* and *cuchillas chicas* components—these are placed at points of special stress, and so must be stronger than the rest of the net. The only tools needed for making the body of the net are a measuring device, a pair of scissors, a large steel needle (for sewing the tough *cuchilla* pieces), a smaller steel needle (for sewing the rest of the pieces), and some strong thread. Two people usually work together, one to hold the pieces while the other sews them together. A third person may sometimes assist in the cutting, sewing, or measuring operations.

[2]Cost: 80,000 pesos (ca. U.S. $26) in the Mexico City market.

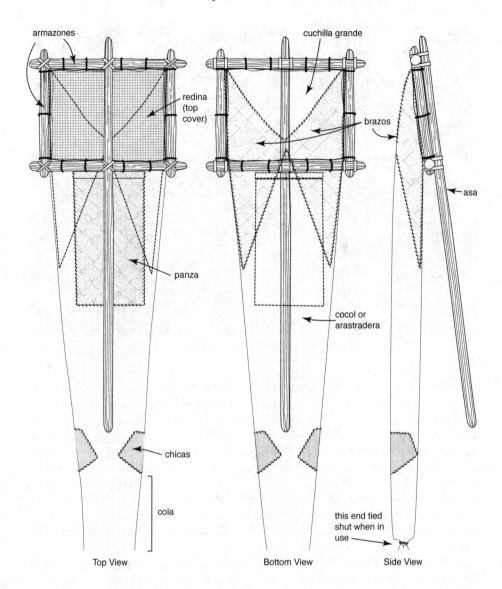

Figure 5.1. Components of common net: top, bottom, and side views.

Table 5.4. Components of the common net (see Fig. 5.1).

Component	Description and Function
asa	wooden handle, 209 cm long, 3 × 5 cm in cross-section
armazón	the wooden frame that forms a rigid net opening measuring 40 × 105 cm; the net is tied to the frame with several pieces of strong string
redina	strong, coarse netting covering the net opening; functions to keep out floating debris
cuchilla grande	strong cloth that absorbs much of the force of the water passing through the net
brazos	long pieces of ordinary cloth
panza	rectangular piece of cloth, to help maintain net form
cocol (atrastradera)	long triangular piece of ordinary cloth forming the bulk of the net
cuchillas chicas	small pieces of strong nylon cloth to slightly widen and strengthen the net funnel, and to keep it from bunching up at points of particular stress
cola	the long end piece, of ordinary cloth

The component pieces are cut from the main cloth bolt, using the scissors and the measuring device. As the work progresses, the partly finished sections are laid out on the floor to check their fit and make necessary adjustments. The opening of the completed net is hemmed with thread and a narrow strip of cloth. This strengthens the net opening and facilitates its attachment to the wooden frame. The net can usually be completed in 4 to 5 hours (using a purchased *redina*), although the netmaking is sometimes spread out over a longer period as other household tasks compete for attention.

Using the Common Net

The *pescador* pushes the net through the water by its long handle, so that it moves parallel to the pond surface with the long tail trailing along behind (Plates 5.21 and 5.22). The net skims the uppermost few centimeters of the water, capturing the insects and small fish that inhabit the surface and near-surface zone. When moving from one "fishing" locality to another, the *pescador* doubles the net over and secures it inside the wooden frame so that the insects or fish trapped inside will not escape (Plate 5.23). If the harvest is large, the contents of the net are poured into a large bag (Plate 5.24). The net is usually deployed in water less than 50 cm deep, but it can be used at depths up to about 120 cm (chest high). The net will normally last only about one month before it needs to be replaced. The stronger maguey-fiber nets apparently lasted for up to a year with frequent patching.

The quantity of insects netted on any given day is quite variable. However, with reasonable luck, Sr. Peralta can usually fill a large bag (Plate 5.24) in a day's work. The length of a work "day" also varies, but it typically involves 5-6 hours of netting in the lake, and another hour or two drying the insects at home. Sr. Peralta estimated that the contents of the large bag shown in Plate 5.24 weigh about 30-40 kilos wet, and approximately 15-16 kilos when dried.

Photographs taken in the late 1930s show that some insect-collecting practices were similar to those of today, while others were quite different. At that time, as today, some men worked alone, pushing their nets through the shallow water (Plate 5.25). Others,

Plate 5.14. Making new common net: beginning of process.

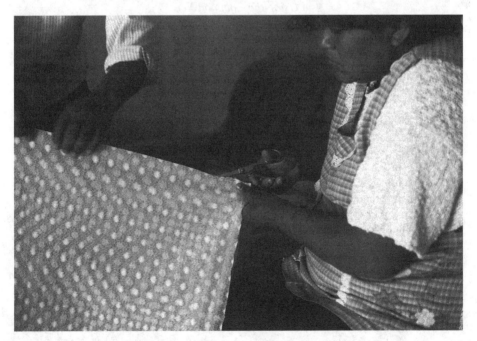

Plate 5.15. Making new common net: measuring and cutting fabric.

Plate 5.16. Making new common net: pieces in process of being sewn together.

Plate 5.17. Common net, showing *cuchilla grande* component.

(*Above*) Plate 5.18. Common net, showing *cuchilla chica* component.

(*Facing page*) Plate 5.19. Making new net: completed project.

(*Below*) Plate 5.20. Hooking tool, formerly used to made the *redina*.

however, worked in groups of 6-10 men (*en cuadrilla*) (Plate 5.26). I do not know under what circumstances group-netting versus individual-netting may have been preferred. The 1930s photographs also indicate that some nets were much larger than those of today, and some were double-tailed (Plate 5.27). These photographs also show that the *pescadores* carried their harvests in baskets or bags slung across their shoulders (Plates 5.25 and 5.26). Canoes were formerly the usual mode of movement of fishermen and their gear (Plate 5.28 and cover photograph); today these boats have been replaced by bicycles (Plate 5.29). The working boats were of two types: (1) larger vessels, *chalupones* (an example appears in the background of Plate 5.25), used for a wide variety of lakebed/lakeshore work, including insect collection; and (2) smaller vessels, *chalupas* (Plate 5.28), used only in netting and hunting birds. Both types were made of wooden planks carefully fitted and nailed together by specialist local carpenters.

Drying the Netted Insects

The netted insects are brought back to the *pescador*'s home in large bags or folded-over nets, alive and dripping wet. The insects to be consumed at home, or locally within the community, are always prepared in their fresh, living state, so a small number may be set aside in a small bag for this purpose. The rest are dried for sale as birdfeed. Because the netted insects would simply fly or crawl away if spread out to dry while still alive, they must first be drowned by immersing an insect-filled bag in a plastic bucket filled with water. This bucket, measuring about 25 cm in diameter and 40 cm high, is adequate for most drowning operations. For unusually large batches, Sr. Peralta uses the cement tub in which his wife washes clothes and dishes. The insects are poured into a plastic-mesh bag and placed under water for 10 to 30 minutes.

The dead insects are then spread out in a thin, even layer atop the flat roof of the family's home (Plate 5.30). Drying can be effective only on dry, sunny days; if clouds and rain do not interfere, two hours are sufficient. Unexpected rain can cause serious problems so every effort is made to dry the insects on rainless days. Because different insect types command different prices (Table 5.5), a dried batch containing more than one type is usually sorted before being offered for sale (Plate 5.31). The dried insects are scooped by hand into strong bags to be carried on the public bus into Mexico City.

Drying practices have changed a good deal since the early 1970s. Up to that time, when the lake remnants were larger and more enduring, the common practice was to erect small temporary huts, built of perishable materials and used for sleeping and meal preparation and storage, along the edges of the lakebed ponds at some distance from the village. Here the *pescadores* would live for several days at a time while netting and drying the insects in the vicinity. There were formerly dozens of such quarters around the pond perimeters, many of which would be occupied at intervals over the year. As noted in Chapter 3, the insects were simply placed to dry on the bare ground surfaces near these huts (e.g., Plate 5.9). A 1930s photo (Plate 3.2) indicates that some individual drying areas, measuring a few meters on a side, were surrounded with low brush walls that probably prevented the insects from blowing away in the wind (Apenes 1943:18).

(*Above and below*) Plates 5.21 and 5.22. Pushing net through water.

Plate 5.23. Partially filled net, folded in use. Scale = 50 cm.

Plate 5.24. Bagging collected insects.

Plate 5.25. A *pescador* with his insect net near Chimalhuacán in the late 1930s. Note how the individual ma-guey-fiber cloths are sewn together in triangular pieces to form the net. Also note the boat in the background (upper right). © The National Museum of Ethnography, Sweden. Photo: Ola Apenes.

Plate 5.26. Group of men netting insects "en cuadrilla" near Chimalhuacán in the late 1930s. © The National Museum of Ethnography, Sweden. Photo: Ola Apenes.

Plate 5.27. Example of double-tailed net used for netting insects near Chimalhuacán in the late 1930s. Note how the individual maguey-fiber cloths are sewn together in triangular pieces to form the net. © The National Museum of Ethnography, Sweden. Photo: Ola Apenes. (Originally published in Apenes 1943:16.)

Plate 5.28. Canoe transportation near Chimalhuacán in the late 1930s. Photographed by Bodil Christensen. Courtesy of Irmgard W. Johnson 1994.

Plate 5.29. Bicycle transport for a modern fisherman.

Plate 5.30. Drying insects on flat house roof.

Plate 5.31. Sorting dried insects into types.

Table 5.5. Prices paid for dried insects.

Category	Approx. Price (pesos/kilo)
cuatecón	30,000
palomero and tejón	40,000
mosco	60,000

(Aug. 1992 exchange rate: ca. 3050 pesos/U.S. $1)

The *Ahuauhtle* Nursery

Most insect eggs are acquired from specially prepared nurseries. Eggs are deposited naturally on whatever solid surfaces are available, including plants and rocks. Formerly there were many lakeshore reeds and masses of other aquatic vegetation that probably served as natural nurseries (see Chap. 3). Today, however, there is very little natural vegetation (and virtually no rocks) in the remnant lakebed ponds, and so the *pescador* must provide suitable surfaces for egg deposition if he hopes to harvest large quantities of them. Such practices may well have been followed in earlier times simply to provide better and more predictable egg-nursery locations. As noted in Chapter 3, virtually identical nurseries were described in and around Lake Texcoco during the mid-nineteenth century (Mayer 1844:218; Orozco y Berra 1864:152-53) and in the 1930s (Ancona 1933:56-57; Apenes 1943:18; Ramos-Elorduy 1987:122-23).

The traditional nursery is formed of rows of U-shaped bundles (*polotes*) of long grass, each bundle with a tail that is rammed into the lake bottom with a strong wooden stick or iron rod. The length of the tail is adjusted so that the U-shaped bundle floats just at the surface of the water. Most nurseries today are in water about 25 cm deep, although it is apparently possible to establish them in water up to 1 m deep. Occasionally pine boughs, brought in from higher ground to the south, are used instead of the grass bundles. Formerly, bundles of reeds were sometimes used. The insects deposit their eggs in these convenient locations, from which the *pescadores* collect them at intervals of 1 to 4 weeks. The *polotes* are replaced after the wear and tear of a few harvests.

In making a new nursery, the first step is to find grass that is sufficiently long and abundant. This grass should be at least 50 cm long, although lengths of 60 to 80 cm are better. Today such high grass occurs only along the edges of large drainage ditches that cut through the lakebed area (Plate 5.32). This material is pulled up by hand, and formed into loose bundles about 6 to 8 cm in diameter. The ends of two bundles are joined together with twine (Plate 5.33) and the elongate bundle bent to form the "U." A third bundle is attached at right angles at the point where the first two bundles are joined together (Plate 5.34). The completed *polotes* (totaling about 70 in the case I observed) are then tied together in a large bundle (Plate 5.35) and backpacked over to the nursery location (Plate 5.36). It took Sr. Peralta about 1.5 hours to collect the grass and make 70 *polotes*, enough for the new nursery he was preparing.

The next step is to insert the *polotes* at the nursery locale. A long wooden stake—about 70 cm long and 3 cm in diameter, with a notch at the lower end—is used to ram each *polote's* tail firmly into the lake bottom (Plates 5.37 and 5.38). Because of its greater weight, an iron stake is better for this task than a wooden one. The wooden (or iron) stake functions only to push the *polote* tail into the lake-bottom mud; the stake is then immediately withdrawn and used to insert the rest of the *polotes*.

Sr. Peralta inserted 66 *polotes*, spaced about 1 m apart, in a single long line (Plate 5.38); the end of the line was "capped" by a short row of four additional *polotes* inserted at right angles to the main line (the capping row measuring 5 *polotes* long). It took him about a half hour to perform this work. After about one week, the *polotes* are periodically inspected (Plate 5.39) until there are sufficient eggs deposited upon them to warrant harvesting and drying (Plate 5.40). It is commonly believed that thunder encourages egg deposition, and this is one local explanation for why eggs are more abundant during the rainy season.

In recent years, some *pescadores* have begun to use plastic-mesh bags, instead of the traditional grass *polotes*, as egg nurseries. Twenty or thirty individual bags are tied together to fashion lines measuring 50-60 cm wide and up to 40 m long (Plates 5.41 and 5.42). This method is somewhat less labor intensive than making and inserting the grass *polotes*, and the plastic mesh will last a long time. Sr. Peralta, however, insisted that the traditional grass *polotes* are far superior in their ability to attract and secure egg deposition, and so he continues to use them. Long strips of coarse cloth were also used as *ahuauhtle* nurseries in Lake Texcoco during the 1840s (Cowan 1865:275), and 1930s (Ancona 1933:62), and so this alternative *polote* technique may also have been common in earlier historic, and perhaps even prehistoric, times.

Harvesting and Drying the *Ahuauhtle* (Insect Eggs)

Eggs from individual *polotes* are harvested and dried at intervals of 1 to 4 weeks. The egg-laden *polotes* are pulled from the water and laid out to dry in the sun for 2 to 3 hours on the nearest dry ground surface (Plate 5.43). The dry eggs are then shaken from the *polote* onto a piece of fine cloth, and carried to the *pescador's* house for storage until sale or use. It is critical that the eggs, once dried, be collected and bagged immediately so that they will not be dislodged by rain or wind from the grass or plastic mesh. In 1992 a *cuartilla* (4 sardine tins) of dried *ahuauhtle* sold for 80,000 pesos (ca. U.S. $26). Sr. Peralta estimates that one harvest of the 70 *polotes* in his new nursery (described above) will yield about 6 *cuartillas* of eggs.

Pescadores who use plastic-mesh nurseries pull the long lengths of plastic bags from the water, and dry them on the nearest dry ground (Plates 5.44 and 5.45). The dried eggs are then shaken onto fine cloths, and carried away to a safe place.

Plate 5.32. Collecting grass for making *polotes*.

Plate 5.33. Tying two grass bundles together to form a *polote*.

Plate 5.34. A completed *polote*. Scale = 50 cm.

Plate 5.35. A bundle of completed *polotes* being tied together for transportation to nursery.

Plate 5.36. Carrying bundles of *polotes* to nursery.

Plate 5.37. Demonstrating how the tail of a *polote* is rammed into the lake bottom.

Plate 5.38. Inserting *polotes* into the nursery.

Plate 5.39. Inspecting *polotes* to check for deposited eggs.

Plate 5.40. Detail of insect eggs deposited on a *polote*.

Plate 5.41. Using plastic-mesh bags as egg nurseries.

Plate 5.42. Plastic-mesh bag with deposited eggs.

Plate 5.43. Drying *polote* fully laden with deposited eggs.

Plate 5.44. Drying egg-laden plastic-mesh bags.

Plate 5.45. Drying egg-laden plastic-mesh bags.

Preparing the Edible Insects and Fish for Human Consumption

Because they are "clean"—that is, hatched from eggs deposited on vegetation near the lake surface—three categories of insects are considered fit for human consumption: *mosco*, *cuatecón*, and *requezón*. Because the other types seem to originate in the muddy lake bottom, they are regarded as "dirty" and thus unfit for human food. The edible insects are prepared for consumption while they are in their fresh, living state. It is believed that dried insects lack food value for humans, and so none are ever eaten. Because they cannot be stored alive for more than a day or two, the insects are eaten only as they become available. Diana Kennedy visited the Peralta family some months after my own study. She recorded several of their insect recipes, in more detail than I present here, in the most recent edition of her well-known Mexican cookbook (Kennedy 1998:459-61). Very similar preparation techniques are described for the mid-nineteenth century (Orozco y Berra 1864:153)

All three insect types are prepared for consumption in the same basic manner. The first step is to grind them into a paste by taking a few handfuls of the living creatures from the storage bag, washing them quickly in a small pot filled with clean water, tossing them onto the stone *metate* (a massive stone grinding platform), and quickly reducing them to a paste with a few rapid passes of the *mano* (a cylindrical grinding stone). This washing and grinding process is a very rapid one, accomplished in less than half a minute, and there is apparently never a significant problem with insects escaping their fate by crawling or flying away. In preparing *requezón*, it is necessary to separate the hard and soft components of the paste on the *metate* after the grinding operation: the hard component consists of the indigestible insect shells.

The insect paste is then combined with a variety of chopped seasonings (most commonly cilantro, onion, garlic, epazote, chile, or salt); other vegetables, chicken eggs, or pieces of meat can be added if they are available. The mixture is placed in a moistened maize husk and cooked for about a half hour on a *comal* (a thin ceramic or metal griddle) over a low fire. The mixture can also be placed inside *tortillas* and cooked on a *comal* as *tacos*. The *tamal de mosco* is still a common food in *pescador* households.

The small netted fish (*charalitos*) can be prepared in the same way: reducing handfuls of fresh, living fish (bones and all) to paste on the *metate*, and preparing the paste in *tamal* or *taco* form. *Charalito* is also sun dried, and in that state can be stored for months. *Charalito*, either in fresh or in dried form, can also be prepared as a sort of stew (*mixmole de charal*), which involves slow-cooking for about an hour in a pot mixed with potatoes, nopal leaves, and a variety of seasonings (chile, onions, cilantro, and salt).

Insect eggs (*ahuauhtle*) are prepared in much the same way. Most commonly, a sardine-tin filled with dried *ahuauhtle* is sifted through a coarse cloth to remove impurities. The clean *ahuauhtle* is then quickly reduced to a paste on the *metate* (four expert swipes with the *mano* are sufficient). The paste is mixed with chicken eggs and seasonings (onion, chile, cilantro, and salt), and the mixture fried in a pan to produce an omelet-like dish. The seasoned *ahuauhtle* paste can also be prepared as *tacos* or spread atop *gorditas* (fried maize dough). Because it fetches such a high price in the market, very little *ahuauhtle* is consumed at the *pescador*'s home.

Sra. Peralta informed me of an interesting belief associated with preparing the insect paste: it should not be done in the presence of a crying child or other loud noises, and the grinder herself should be in a good frame of mind—otherwise, the paste will turn to water.

Netting Waterfowl

Until about fifty years ago, waterfowl were abundant on and around Lake Texcoco, and depictions of them even entered into popular mural imagery during the 1930s (Plate 5.46). Linne (1937, 1948:126-38), Rojas (1985:43-80), and García Sanchez (1998:97-104) provide comprehensive ethnographic and historic perspectives on this formerly important resource. Today few waterfowl remain, although small flocks of *chichicuilotes* (members of the Charadriidae family [plovers], probably *Charadrius vociferous*, known in English as "killdeer"[3]) are sometimes seen (Plate 5.47), and a few migratory ducks still appear (Plate 5.48). Nevertheless, Sr. Peralta was able to provide the names of nine types of ducks and four types of *chichicuilotes* that were fairly common up until the 1950s (Table 5.6). Ducks were apparently most abundant between September and April, while *chichicuilotes* were especially numerous from August through October. Some types of both categories were also available at other times of the year. As noted in Chapter 4, during our archaeological surveys in central Lake Texcoco in May-August 2003, we found that waterfowl eggs were abundant in nests throughout this federally protected ecological reserve (Plate 4.1).

Photographs from the 1930s indicate that many waterfowl were still being harvested from Lake Texcoco two or three generations ago. The *chichicuilotes* were usually trapped in long nets made of maguey-fiber twine (*ixtle*) stretched between high poles in nesting and feeding areas (Plates 5.49 and 5.50). Some of the much larger ducks were also netted in this fashion (Plate 5.51). The bird-netters moved about the lake in small boats that they poled through the shallow waters during the early morning hours (cover photograph).

Through the 1930s professional duck-hunters rigged circular frameworks of crude shotguns in favorite nesting or feeding areas in and around Lake Texcoco (Plate 5.52). Once the ducks had settled onto the lake surface around these mechanisms, the guns would be fired in unison with a long string pulled by a trigger-man hidden in the reeds nearby, and scores of birds could be slaughtered at one time. Such a mechanism appears on the lower left-hand side of the 1930s drawing shown in Plate 5.46. As described in Chapter 3, similar devices were in use during the nineteenth century (Herrera 1895:55; Mayer 1844:219; Orozco y Berra 1864:149; Ward 1981 [1828]:163). Decoys, formed of football-sized rocks seated atop tripod supports of reed stakes pushed vertically into the lake bottom, were sometimes used to lure ducks to such hunting grounds in the 1930s (Plate 5.53).

---

[3]Kent V. Flannery (pers. comm. 2001) informs me that these birds are "resident in Baja California south to Guerrero and Guanajuato, occurring extensively elsewhere in winter. The problem is that sometimes common names like 'chichicuilote' may be applied to more than one species, depending on region."

Plate 5.46. A 1930s photo of a painted window mural showing waterfowl in Lake Texcoco. Photographed by Bodil Christensen. Courtesy of Irmgard W. Johnson 1994.

Plate 5.47. Small flock of *chichicuilotes*.

Plate 5.48. Captive duckling.

Plate 5.49. Netting *chichicuilotes* near Chimalhuacán in the late 1930s. © The National Museum of Ethnography, Sweden. Photo: Ola Apenes. (Previously published as Fig. 4 in Linne 1940:127, and as Fig. 35 in Linne 1948:132.)

Plate 5.50. Boys with netted *chichicuilotes*, near Chimalhuacán in the late 1930s. © The National Museum of Ethnography, Sweden. Photo: Ola Apenes.

Plate 5.51. Duck caught in a net near Chimalhuacán in the late 1930s. Photographed by Bodil Christensen. Courtesy of Irmgard W. Johnson 1994.

Plate 5.52. Duck hunters rigging a duck-killing mechanism (*armada*) on Lake Texcoco in the late 1930s. Photographed by Bodil Christensen. Courtesy of Irmgard W. Johnson 1994. (Originally published in Apenes 1943:16.)

Plate 5.53. Decoys (rocks on reed stakes) used to lure ducks on Lake Texcoco near Chimalhuacán in the late 1930s. © The National Museum of Ethnography, Sweden. Photo: Ola Apenes.

Table 5.6. Local names for types of waterfowl formerly abundant on Lake Texcoco.

Ducks	Chichicuilotes
garabito	blanco
golondrino	chate
bocón	monjita
sarceta	cuatecón
gallinita	
chantito	
chaparra grande	
chaparra chico	
perro de agua	

Summary and Conclusions

A few *pescadores* continue to collect five types of aquatic insects, one species of mollusc, and one species of fish from shallow remnants of Lake Texcoco near Chimalhuacán. The eggs of one or more of these insect species are also collected. Until recently, three additional types of aquatic insects were also harvested. These lacustrine creatures are caught in large, handled nets fastened on wooden frames that are pushed by a man walking through the shallow water. Three of the insect types are still eaten by local people, although most of the harvest is now sold as birdfeed in Mexico City; the insect eggs are considered a delicacy food for humans. Although insect collecting peaks during the rainy season months (June-September), some continues year-round in the few ponds that survive the dry season. The once-abundant waterfowl have largely vanished and are no longer a significant resource.

In addition to netting insects and fish, the infrastructure of the lacustrine *pescadores* includes egg nurseries and lakeshore (or roof-top) drying surfaces. Formerly there were dozens of small lakeshore huts that served as temporary living quarters for *pescadores* while they collected and dried their harvests at some distance from their permanent village homes. *Pescadores* formerly used wood-plank boats to move around the lake during the course of their work. The *pescadores* consume a large quantity of cloth for making their nets. Today the netting is commercial nylon fabric; formerly nets and carrying bags were made from maguey fiber (*ixtle*). Large quantities of *ixtle* were also formerly consumed to make the long nets stretched between poles to capture waterfowl. I have no information regarding the former significance of cotton fiber in aquatic resource exploitation at Chimalhuacán. However, the need for lighter nets that would float near the water surface may have required significant use of cotton-fiber netting for some types of insect harvesting.

Prior to about fifty years ago, the lacustrine insect, fish, and waterfowl resources of Lake Texcoco were a much more significant economic resource than they are at present. In Chapter 6, I will expand the scope and comparative perspective of my inquiry by considering the traditional exploitation of aquatic resources in several other parts of the world.

$-6-$

Comparative Perspectives
The Documented Use of Aquatic Resources in Other Regions

In this chapter I discuss traditional procurement, processing, and use of aquatic resources in several areas of the world (Fig. 6.1) for which useful information is available, and where commercial or industrial exploitation had not yet significantly encroached. My objective is to develop better analogies for the use of aquatic resources, and for the archaeological implications of that use, in the precolumbian economy of the Valley of Mexico. I begin with the Upper Lerma drainage (the Toluca region) just west of the Valley of Mexico, with brief references to Lake Pátzcuaro and Lake Cuitzeo farther to the west, and to the Tlaxcalan marshes to the east. I then examine three more distant areas whose traditional marsh-lake adaptations have been relatively well described: the Great Basin in the western U.S., the Titicaca Basin in southern Peru and adjacent western Bolivia, and the Tigris-Euphrates delta in southern Iraq and adjacent Iran. I conclude with a description of traditional fishing along the shoreline of Lake Chad, in western Chad.

The Upper Lerma Drainage (Toluca Region), Mexico

Before they began to be extensively drained in the 1940s and 1950s, the vast marshes south and east of Toluca provided rich harvests of aquatic plants and animals, including most of the same species present in the nearby Valley of Mexico (Albores 1995; García Sanchez 1998; Sugiura 1998, 2000; Sugiura and Serra 1983) (Fig. 6.2). The close proximity of these two regions (which have similar geology, geomorphology, soils, altitude, climate, aquatic vegetation and wildlife) means that the unusually rich twentieth-century ethnographic data from the Toluca region should have direct applicability to the Valley of Mexico, where ethnographic descriptions of the exploitation of aquatic resources are generally less comprehensive. The principal environmental difference between the Valley of Mexico and the Upper Lerma drainage is that the latter region lacks the saline lake-marsh environment of Lake Texcoco. In addition, the Toluca region, with its floor at about 2550 m asl, is about 300 m more elevated than the Valley of Mexico.

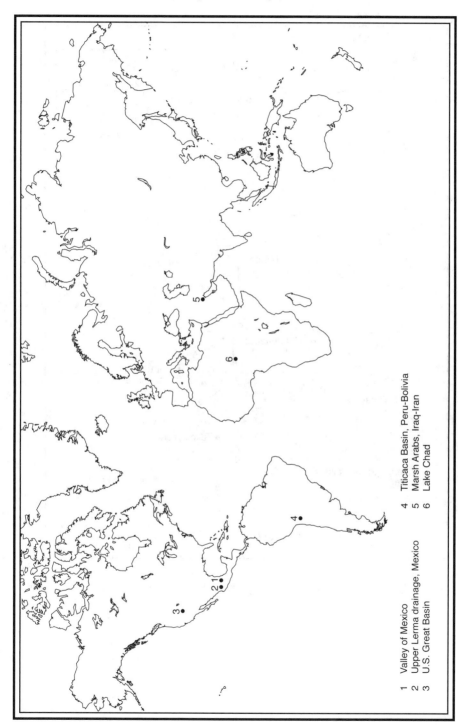

1 Valley of Mexico
2 Upper Lerma drainage, Mexico
3 U.S. Great Basin

4 Titicaca Basin, Peru-Bolivia
5 Marsh Arabs, Iraq-Iran
6 Lake Chad

Figure 6.1. World map showing locations discussed in text.

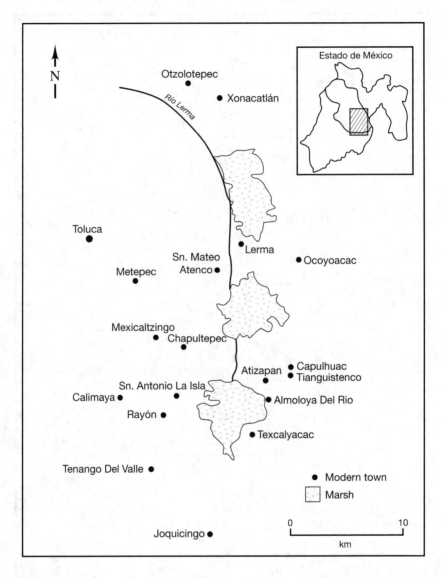

Figure 6.2. The Upper Lerma drainage (adapted from Albores 1995:63). The shaded areas are marshlands.

Table 6.1. Categories of useful aquatic plants in the Upper Lerma drainage.

	Scientific Names of Common Species
Type I: plants that grow in standing water	
reeds, rushes, canes	Scirpus sp., Typha sp., Juncus sp.
submerged plants	Potamogetonáceas sp., Microphyllus sp., Utricularia vulgaris, Ceratophyllum demersum
microscopic plants, usually found submerged in canals	Spirogira sp., Oedogonium sp., Lemma sp., Wolffia sp., Azolla Carolina, Spirodela polyrhiza
floating plants	Limanthemum humboldtianum, Nymphae flavor-virens, Eichornia crassipes, Spiranthes sp., Limnobium stoloniferum
Type II: plants that live in shallower standing water in marshes and canals	
	Eleocharis palustris, Leersia hexandra, Typha latifolia, Sagittaria macrophylla, Echinochloa holciformis, Scirpus lacustris, Hydrocotyle vulgaris
Type III: plants that live along the edges of canals and standing water	
	Amaranthus hybridus, Taraxacum officinale, Datura stramonium, Solanum rostratum

(Adapted from Albores 1995:75-76)

Aquatic Foods and Their Preparation

In Tables 6.1-6.4, I have compiled ethnographic information about the useful aquatic plants and animals in the Upper Lerma drainage. Traces of several of these resources have been found in archaeological deposits in different parts of the area, dating from Formative through Epiclassic times (ca. 600 B.C.-900 A.D.) (Sugiura and McClung de Tapia 1988:122-23).

The diets of modern people who continue to harvest the remaining marshlands illustrate the traditional importance of aquatic resources in this region. Sugiura and Serra (1983) observe that typically two meals are eaten each day, a morning *almuerzo*, and an early evening *comida*. For the morning meal,

[English translation] [i]n the comal, besides tortillas, they are accustomed to cook eggs in different ways, as well as tamales of fish, frogs, tadpoles, or carp . . . [and also] . . . a pot with different stews containing beans, fava beans, meat, *quelites*, etc.

And for a typical evening meal,

a spicy soupy stew comprised of different kinds of fish or frogs was eaten. . . . Sometimes *ahuauhtli* [insect eggs] in meatball form were eaten with large quantities of tortillas and plenty of salt and chili. . . .
. . . *papa de agua* and *cabeza de negro* were boiled or roasted. Salads were made with *berro*, tender *tule* roots, *paletaria*, *carretilla*, *cresón* or *atalquelite*, *jarra* and *amamalocote*. Different kinds of aquatic birds, such as ducks that were abundant in winter, were cooked. [Sugiura and Serra 1983:19-21]

Sugiura (1998) observes that fish, tadpoles, and frogs are commonly prepared for consumption in the form of tamales:

[English translation] These *tamales* lacked maize dough, but simply involved wrapping pieces of fish, a scoop of minnows, a scoop of tadpoles or frog pieces in dry maize husks . . . , flavored with salt, garlic, slices of onion, sprigs of *epazote* and spicy chili, and baked on a comal. [Sugiura 1998:191]

Most marsh plants are prepared for consumption with little processing. *Jara, berro de palma*, and *atlaquelite* are simply enfolded raw into tacos (rolled-up tortillas). Similarly, the tender roots and stems of reeds (tule) "are eaten raw by pulling off the plant's root or tender stalk and chewing it to extract the juice, afterwards tossing aside the fibrous quid." Other edible plants, and duck eggs, require only simple boiling in water or heating on a comal:

[English translation] one or two kilos, or more, of *papa de agua* and *cabeza de negro*, were cleaned and cooked in salted water before being eaten. Sometimes *cabeza de negro* was baked and eaten in the fields while cutting animal fodder . . . , duck eggs were eaten boiled and *zacamichis* were toasted on the comal and eaten with salt. [Sugiura 1998:196]

Albores (1995) emphasizes the traditional *primary, year-round* importance of aquatic plant and animal foods in the diets of indigenous communities in the Upper Lerma marshlands:

[English translation] With the exception of *zacamiche* and *alacrancito*—which were the only seasonal species in the marsh—carp, *ajalote, juil*, frogs, white fish, *acocil, salmiche*, "*támbula*," *atepocate, mojarra, criolla, espejil, charal*, salmon, "*cucaracha*," "*padrecito*," "*habita*" and *almeja* were eaten year round. Carp, *juil*, and white and black fish were eaten in tamales, fried or cooked with *chilacas*, onion and field or marsh herbs; *acocil* was boiled, as was *salmiche*—which could also be toasted—for the preparation of salads; frogs, tadpoles, and *ajolote* were cooked—in pie form—with eggs, tomatoes and chili. Aquatic birds were cooked year-round, although their consumption increased between August and March, especially after October, when the migratory species appeared. They were prepared as a *mole* or in a sauce of squash seeds, and as tamales. Similarly, there came to the table numerous aquatic plants, among which stood out *papa del agua*, several types of *berro, jara, chichamol*, *apaclolillo, cebolla morada, rezones, chivitos* and *mamalacote*. [Albores 1995:301]

Tools and Implements for Hunting and Collecting Aquatic Resources

The traditional aquatic tool kit is relatively simple (Table 6.5). The most costly items are boats (*chalupa/chalupita*) and the large rectangular nets (*chinchorro*). In addition to their relatively high initial costs, boats and nets both require considerable maintenance and have a relatively short use-life. The importance of nets is particularly notable, and a considerable quantity of maguey fiber (*ixtle*) was formerly used to make these nets. In contrast, bows and arrows and blow-guns appear to have been virtually absent.

General Modes of Hunting and Collecting

There are two basic modes of harvesting aquatic resources: (1) afoot in shallower water (up to about 1.2 m deep), on solid ground along the edge of standing water, or

Table 6.2. The seasonal availability of useful aquatic plants in the Upper Lerma drainage.

Availability (+ = available) by Month (beginning with January)

Plant (Common local names)	Species	J	F	M	A	M	J	J	A	S	O	N	D
atlaquelite	*Hydrocotyle ranunculoides*	+	+	+	+	+	+	+	+	+	+	+	+
berro de palmita	*Nasturtium officinales*	+	+	+	+	+	+	+	+	+	+	+	+
berro macho	*Beruha erecta*					no data							
berro redondo	*Hydrocotyle sp.*					no data							
cabeza de negro ♣	*Nymphae flevo-virens, or Nymphae mexicana*		+	+	+								
jaltomate	*Saracha jaltomate*								+	+	+	+	+
jara	*Bidens bigelovii*	+	+						+	+	+	+	+
lengua de vaca	*Rumex crispus*			+					+	+	+	+	+
paletaria											+	+	+
papa de agua ♣	*Sagitaria mexicana*	+	+	+	+	+	+	+	+	+			
quelite	*Amaranthus hybridus*				+	+	+	+	+				
quintonil					+	+	+	+					
tule redondo	*Schoenoplectus californicus*	no data, but most available during rainy season (June-Sept.)											
tule ancho	*Typha latifolia*	+	+	+	+	+	+	+	+	+	+	+	+
xocoyol, agritos	*Oxalis corniculata* L.		+	+	+	+	+	+	+	+			

(Adapted from Sugiura and Serra 1983:18, Tabla 1; Sugiura 1998:139-41)
♣ indicates items most important as food.

Table 6.3. Availability of aquatic fauna (apart from waterfowl) harvested in the Upper Lerma.

Months Collected (+ indicates primary availability)

Item	J	F	M	A	M	J	J	A	S	O	N	D
ahuauhtli (insect eggs)									+			+
acociles (small crustacean) (*Cambarellus moctezumae*)	+	+	+	+	+	+	+	+	+	+	+	
ajolotes (salamanders)	+	+	+	+	+	+	+	+	+	+	+	+
atepocates (tadpoles)			+	+	+	+	+	+				
juiles (fish)				+	+	+	+	+				
pescado blanco (fish)		+	+	+		+	+	+	+	+		
xalimichis (fish)		+	+	+	+	+	+	+	+	+		

(Adapted from Sugiura and Serra 1983:20, Tabla 3)

Table 6.4. Species of waterfowl hunted in the Upper Lerma drainage.

Local Names	Species Name
golondrino, rocio macho	*Aythya affinis*
xalcuani, rocio hembra	*Aythya marila*
cuaco macho	*Aythya americana*
sarceta pinta	*Anas crecca*
hembra de golondrino	*Anas acuta*
cuchara macho, cuchara grande	*Anas clypeata*
xalcuani hembra	*Anas penelope*
sarceta pardo	*Anas discors*
golondrino macho, chiflador	*Anas platyrhynchos*
xalcuani macho, xalcuani chico	*Anas americana*
chaparro	*Bucephala albeola*
sarceta colorado	*Anas cyomoptera*
pato real	*Anas diazi*
ansar macho	*Chen caerulescens*
ansar, anser	*Branta canadensis*
ansar macho	*Anser albifrons*
tildillo	*Charadrius vociferus*
ronco	*Calidris alba*
aparradores, chichicuilote	*Charadrius canatus*
pata larga, chichicuilote	*Tringa flaripes*
gallareta americana	*Recurvirostra americana*

(Adapted from Sugiura and Serra 1983:19, Tabla 2)

from artificial platforms built of earth and aquatic vegetation in especially favorable places in deeper water; and (2) from canoes in deeper water. Some procedures combined canoe-based and pedestrian activities. For example, hunters or collectors might travel in canoes from their home base to good harvesting locales, where they would then carry out their work afoot, returning home in canoes at the end of the day. These activities may be carried out by individuals working alone, or by groups working in cooperative operations. Techniques appropriate for specific types of aquatic plants and animals will be briefly described below.

Aquatic Plants—Availability, Procurement, and Processing

Food plants include surface (e.g., tules), deeply rooted (e.g., *tule, jara, papa de agua, cabeza de negro*), and freely floating species (e.g., *berro de palmita, berro macho, berro redondo*). The different characteristics of these plants require different kinds of harvesting and collecting techniques.

Collecting the papa del agua and cabeza de negro

The rhizomes of these rooted marsh plants have been particularly important as food. They are most abundant during the winter and early spring months, thus nicely complementing the agricultural cycle. The plants usually occur in clusters, measuring 5-100 m in diameter, with the plants' leaves floating visibly upon the water's surface. According to Sugiura (1998),

[English translation] the collection of *papa del agua* was restricted to the period when the plant's rhizomes matured, principally in the months from October to January. . . . the collectors went out into the marshes specifically to harvest *papa del agua*. To secure the *papa*, the collectors immersed their arms below the water's surface, following the plant's stem

Table 6.5. Tools and their functions in the exploitation of aquatic resources in the Upper Lerma drainage.

Tool	Use
chalupa	Larger wooden-plank canoe, accommodating 2 persons, used mainly by full-time specialists. Widely used for a variety of hunting, collecting, and transport tasks.
chalupita	Smaller wooden-plank canoe, accommodating 1 person, used mainly by non-specialists. Widely used for a variety of hunting, collecting, and transport tasks.
remo	Wooden paddle, 1.1-2 m long, for propelling canoe in deeper water.
garrocha	Wooden pole, 2.5-4 m long, used for poling canoe in shallower water, and for mounting large rectangular nets in standing water.
fisga	Spear or harpoon, with 1-6 metal prongs up to 30 cm long, and a wooden handle 3-4 m long. Used for spearing frogs, salamanders, some waterfowl, and larger fish. Shorter spears may be used with an atlatl.
macla	Elliptical dip net measuring 1.2-1.5 m long with wooden handle ca. 1.5-2 m long, with a variable diameter depending on the species being netted. Typically net mesh opening is 1-1.5 cm. Operated by a single person for netting smaller fish, frogs, tadpoles, insects, etc.
chinchorro	Large rectangular net, generally 3-4 m long and 1.5-2 m wide, set on standing wooden poles above water level to capture waterfowl, or submerged for netting fish.
cajete	Small ceramic bowl or jar, containing burning wood as a flare for attracting frogs at night. Usually placed in front of the canoe atop several rocks.
hachón	Another type of flare used in night-time frog hunting. A ceramic vessel filled with burning wood and suspended by a wire from an iron bar in front of the canoe.
hoz	Iron sickle with wooden handle, used for cutting reeds.
anzuelo	Metal hooks used in fishing.
sling	Used to hurl small stones for killing some species of waterfowl. Typically made of twisted sheep's wool or of ixtle fiber.
wooden club	About one meter long, used for killing waterfowl by powerful blows to the head.
bag, basket, bucket, or pot	For holding and transporting fish and waterfowl, either carried while afoot or placed in a canoe.

(Adapted from Albores 1995:207-21)

down to the root buried in the muddy sediment at the bottom; then they pulled the *papas* to the surface and, once out of the water, they pulled out the entire root of the plant; the harvested *papas* were then placed in bags or tossed into containers. The roots of the plant were then discarded into the marsh, and in this fashion the area of their production expanded over time. [Sugiura 1998:184]

In somewhat deeper water,

[English translation] the collector walked around in the water, moving his feet so as to separate the *papas* from the root and speed up the extraction. The collector sensed with his feet where he should move in order to secure more *papas*, because the muddy water prevented him from seeing what he was doing. [Sugiura 1998:186]

In water too deep for wading, collectors in boats worked the plants free from the bottom with long poles and gathered them as they floated to the surface (Sugiura 1998:187).

The harvesting, processing, and uses of reeds and rushes (tule)

Tules are important for making mats for house floors, sleeping surfaces, roofs and walls, and for wrapping dead bodies for burial; they are also used to make a variety of baskets, rain capes, decorative items, fans, houselot fencing, and buoyant rafts (Albores 1995:245-64; García Sanchez 1998:107-15; Sugiura 1998:204-5), or for tempering in pottery (Sugiura 1998:142) and adobe bricks (Albores 1995:252). In addition, significant quantities of the tender roots and stems of tules were often eaten.

García Sanchez (1998:115) emphasizes the importance of the different characteristics (size, color, suppleness, texture, buoyancy, strength, durability) of various types of reeds used for making sundry products. At least four types of reeds were commonly used for different types of implements: *tule redondo, tule ancho, tule bofo, and tule triangular.* People who harvested reeds had to know which varieties of tule were best suited for specific purposes, where these reeds grew, and how to recognize and harvest them properly. As noted in Chapter 3, this highly specialized knowledge about reeds had been observed by at least one seventeenth-century writer in the Valley of Mexico (Ventancurt 1971:33).

Large quantities of tule reeds for mat-making were generally cut with iron sickles, primarily during the rainy season months (mainly June-September, although into October for some variants) when the plants tended to be green and supple. After October, most reeds were too hard, dry and brittle, and tended to have an undesirable yellowish color. Both large and small reeds were harvested; only the dark colored plants were not utilized. Mature tules up to two meters long were harvested either by individuals, wading afoot or operating in small canoes, or by cooperative groups of 5-6 men using a single large boat operated by one man (in which the harvested reeds were piled and hauled away), with each other member of the harvesting team using his own small canoe for maneuvering through the reed stands and cutting the plants.

García Sanchez (1998) reports that during the winter dry season months, the reed beds were commonly burned over, with four major objectives:

[English translation]
(1) to exterminate the insects that inhabited the reed beds. . . .
(2) to enable the ashes . . . to serve as fertilizer for the new reeds, so that they would develop more strongly.
(3) taking advantage of the hunting season, to frighten and seize the ducks that nested amongst the reeds.
(4) to keep the canals, ditches and waterways through which canoes moved free of vegetation. . . . If these routes were not cleaned at least once a year, a major problem arose because of the great difficulty in managing the boats. [García Sanchez 1998:119-20]

I have no detailed information about how tule stands were apportioned to individuals or reserved to specific communities, or about how such arrangements may have been formally administered. Nevertheless, Albores (1995:254) implies that members of individual villages held some type of communal right to harvest reeds in particular places. Dense stands of tules controlled by a single community typically measured two kilometers long. García Sanchez (1998:121) reports that during the early and mid-twentieth century, good duck-hunting spots were rented to outsiders by individual and community owners in the fall and winter months. Similarly, during the summer, desirable marsh areas were rented for reed harvesting by specialists who made mats, baskets, fans, and so on.

Tule harvesting tended to be undertaken in day-long shifts from the harvesters' home villages, with departure at first morning light and return at dusk. According to Albores (1995:256), tule harvesters carried with them only a few tortillas to eat during their day's work, securing most of their food by opportunistic snacking on the edible marsh plants they encountered.

Sugiura and Serra (1983) outline nine consecutive steps in tule harvesting and processing preparatory to making mats:

[English translation] (1) Choosing and cutting the tall reeds; (2) tying them up in bundles; (3) forming rafts with the tied-up bundles; (4) transporting them along the Lerma River to the mat-making location; (5) taking the bundles out of the water; (6) leaving them piled up for two weeks until they turn yellow; (7) separating out the yellowed reeds; (8) placing bunches of reeds to dry in the sun for 10 days, gathering them up each night to prevent them being dampened by rain or dew; (9) selecting out the quantity of dried reeds needed to make a particular product. [Sugiura and Serra 1983:22]

Albores (1995) describes the sequence of tule harvesting and processing in detail:

[English translation] Group harvesting of the reeds. [Once the harvesters arrive at their place of work] they separated and each man grasped an arm-load of reeds. The harvester encircled a batch of reeds with one arm and held them against his chest, using his free arm to cut them with a sickle [Fig. 6.3a].

The reeds were cut off at the lower part, and sometimes, right there in the reed bed, the flowering top parts of the reeds might be detached at the most convenient height; some harvesters, on the other hand, preferred to cut off the top part of the reeds after they have returned home with the harvested reeds, or to carry out only a part of this top-cutting operation before transporting the reed bundles.

Bundling and piling the reeds. Each armload bundle of cut reeds was then tied up and placed in the water [Fig. 6.3b, c]. The buoyant, tied-up bundles might be left in place to be collected the following day. However, when only a few reeds were cut, the bundles were prepared for transport right after they were tied up.

Making reed rafts. The reeds were made into rafts by tying the bundles together one by one in a line [Fig. 6.3d, e]. These lines could be very long, comprising up to 20 or 30 bundles.

Transport. The first reed bundle in the line was tied to the end of a canoe operated by one of the reed cutters so that the long raft formed by the line of bundles could be towed [Fig. 6.3e]. The other reed cutters followed along in their canoes and oversaw the safe movement of the reed raft. [In some cases, the reed bundles were piled into large boats for transport (Fig. 6.3f).]

In cutting and transporting the reeds, the groups worked three or four days per week; one day was dedicated to cutting and bundling, and the next day they made the reed raft and towed it to San Mateo [the home village]. These same operations were then repeated throughout the week.

Drying. After cutting, it was necessary to sun-dry the green reeds so that they would turn yellow and be ready for weaving. There were three types of drying in the village.

(1) Directly on the ground surface. The most common drying technique was to place the reeds outside the houses, in the yards and along the streets. The reeds were laid out to form fans or circles, squares, or wheels [Fig. 6.3g, h].

(2) Raised platforms [Fig. 6.3i]. The reeds were placed across wood-pole supports formed into lines up to 40 or 50 meters long.

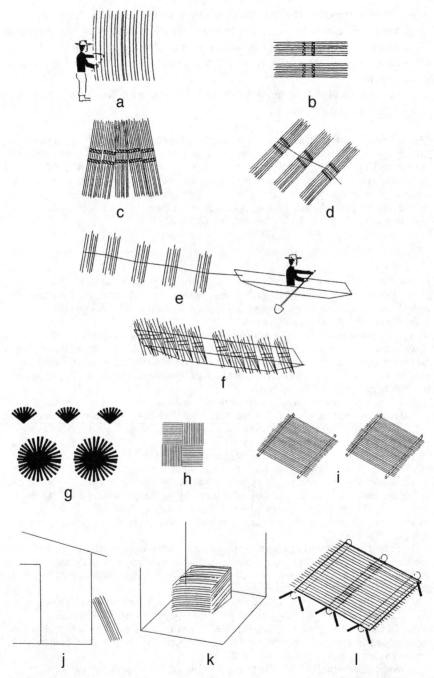

Figure 6.3. Sequence of tule harvesting and processing in the Upper Lerma (adapted from Albores 1995:258, 261).

(3) Against a wall [Fig. 6.3*j*]. In certain parts of the village . . . when there was no more room in the streets for drying, the reeds were leaned up against the house walls.

In the morning the reeds were taken outside the house to be dried in the sun, and they were brought in again at night to a room where they were laid out in large stacks [Fig. 6.3*k*]. During the drying period, great care was taken to prevent the reeds from getting wet, because in this damp state the reeds turned black and were no longer useful for weavings. When rains threatened, the entire household helped to collect the drying reeds and bring them indoors.

Drying lasted from 15 to 20 days, depending on the size of the reeds and the weather. During the time it was necessary to turn the individual drying reeds over in order to ensure a better and more rapid drying process. The reeds that turned yellowish were separated out, leaving only the green reeds to continue drying.

[Mat-]Weaving platform. When they were dried, the reeds were then laid out across a raised platform measuring about four meters long [Fig. 6.3*l*]. These platforms were made of wooden poles arranged transversally upon three wooden supports. The platform could extend up to the roof and was generally installed in the room where the weaving was to take place. [Albores 1995:256-62]

Aquatic Fauna—Availability, Procurement, and Processing

Table 6.6 indicates the aquatic fauna (apart from waterfowl) consumed in the Upper Lerma drainage, and the implements with which different animals were captured.

Fishing

Many fish were consumed fresh, while some were sun-dried and stored for later use (West 1948:55). Traditional fishing included both individual and collective techniques. Although some fishing was carried out year-round, several important species were most abundant during the summer months (Table 6.3).

Sugiura (1998:144-69) and Albores (1995:221-28) describe a variety of individual and collective fishing techniques that were best suited for different species and different types of aquatic environments. I summarize these in Table 6.7 and Figure 6.4. Foster (1948:102) and West (1948:54) note that during the 1940s on Lake Pátzcuaro, collective fishing from boats involved using nets measuring 100-150 m long and 8 m wide, commonly with a 2 cm mesh. Foster also reports the use of gill nets (with mesh size 0.7-2.8 cm) that were sometimes joined in lengths of up to 250 m. These large nets involved wooden floats and unworked-stone sinkers. Fishing on Lake Pátzcuaro was carried out mainly during the dry season, from November through May.

Individual fishing was often done afoot in shallow water and from solid ground or artificial platforms along the edges of standing water:

[English translation] Fishing for *acocil* and *atepocate* generally occurred on foot, outside the canoe, because these species were usually found near the edge of the marsh. Once in the water, the fisherman walked forward, pushing the net ahead of himself while supporting the base of the net handle against his chest [Fig. 6.4*a*]. [Albores 1995:211]

Table 6.6. The technology used in harvesting aquatic fauna (apart from waterfowl) in the Upper Lerma drainage.

Common Spanish or Local Name and English Name	Scientific Name	Capturing Implements*				
		1	2	3	4	5
acocil (a small, shrimp-like crustacean)	*Cambarellus montezumae*	+				
ahuilote (pescado blanco, white fish)	*Chirostoma* sp.	+				
ajolote (larval salamander)	*Ambystoma mexicana*			+		
almeja (mollusc)						+
atepocate (frog tadpole)		+				
carp (introduced fish species)	*Cyprindidae* sp.	+	+	+	+	+
cucaracha (insect)						+
charal (small fish)	*Chirostoma* sp.	+				
espejillo		+				
habita		+				
juil (fish)	*Cyprinidae* sp.	+		+	+	
mojarra		+				
padrecito (insect)						+
picaro (dragon fly larvae)						+
popochas (fish)		+				
rana (frog)				+		+
salmiche (fish)	*Chirostoma* sp.	+				
támbula (fish)	*Godeidae* sp.	+				
zacamiche (insect larvae)						+

(Adapted from Albores 1995:203, Cuadro 3)
*1 = *macla* (handled dip net, used by one person); 2 = *chinchorro* (large rectangular net mounted on upright poles); 3 = *fisga* (spear, or harpoon); 4 = *anzuelo* (hook); 5 = *a mano* (by hand)

Table 6.7. Individual and collective fishing techniques in the Upper Lerma drainage.

Activity and Environmental Context	Technique
Individual Techniques (adapted from Sugiura 1998:144-62)	
Fishing in deep, clear water, from a canoe.	Handled net, using water current to guide fish into the net.
Fishing in open water, deep or shallow, from a canoe.	Harpoons and hooked lines.
Fishing in shallow open water, on foot.	Pushing handled nets; harpoons.
Fishing in canals, shallow water, on foot.	Pronged spears and handled nets.
Catching frogs, and sometimes fish, in shallow water.	Seizing the animals by hand.
Collective Techniques (adapted from Sugiura 1998:162-69)	
Fishing from boats in open water, with large nets.	Multiple boats, with large nets stretched between boats.
Fishing from boats in open water, with small nets.	Multiple boats, with small nets operated from each boat. Person in one boat disturbs the water surface with rocks or sticks to agitate fish so that they move towards the other boats where they are netted.
Fishing on foot from shore, and in shallow water of ponds or canals cut through reeds.	Multiple individual nets, using rocks or sticks to agitate water surface to move fish towards nets manipulated by other fishermen.
Fishing on foot from shore, and in shallow water of ponds or canals cut through reeds.	Erecting small reed or mud dams toward which fish are directed, by men who agitate the water surface with sticks, towards men with small handled nets standing in front of the dam.

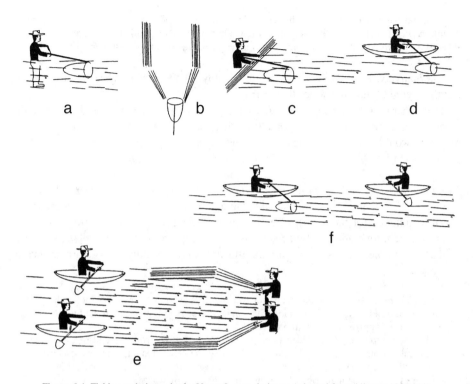

Figure 6.4. Fishing techniques in the Upper Lerma drainage (adapted from Albores 1995:212).

Individuals also fished from the edges of the water, using barriers (*presas*) constructed of reeds and other aquatic vegetation anchored with stakes to the marsh bottom and placed so as to direct fish into a net placed at the terminus of the weir barrier (Fig. 6.4*b*).

> *[English translation]* [These weirs] were set up in ditches that canalized water from higher parts of the zone toward the lake. These dams were generally made by those who could not go out into the lake because they lacked canoes, and [by everybody] on those occasions when fish were especially abundant in the ditches. . . . [Albores 1995:211]

Alternatively, a fisherman working afoot might place himself adjacent to flowing water atop an artificial platform constructed of piled-up mud and aquatic plants. In such a setting, the fisherman simply dipped his net into the water and waited for fish to swim into it (Fig. 6.4*c*).

Fishing in canoes was carried out in a variety of ways. Different techniques were employed depending on whether the fisherman could see the intended prey, or whether the fish remained invisible below the water surface:

> *[English translation]* When the fish was visible . . . the net was dipped into the water with a forward movement, and then pulled out with the fish inside. When the prey could not be seen,

the fisherman stuck the net into the water alongside the canoe and waited until a fish came into it [Fig. 6.4*d*] . . . and its weight was felt. Then, the net was pulled out . . . and the fish tossed out directly into the bottom of the canoe, or into a container. [Albores 1995:211]

Alternatively, a man in a canoe might employ a barbed spear (*fisga*) when fishing during daylight hours for larger fish or frogs.

Two fishermen in their separate canoes might work together. One would approach the other, agitating the water with his paddle so that the fish would move toward the second man who would hold a net alongside his canoe so as to capture the alarmed fish as they passed by (Fig. 6.4*f*).

Example of specialized technique for capturing pescado blanco (white fish)
Due to their distinctive habitats and behaviors, different species of fish required different techniques for their most effective capture. Albores (1995) describes one such ingenious technique adapted by specialists for the capture of "pescado blanco," a particularly desirable species. This example illustrates the diversity of specialized fishing techniques.

[English translation] White fish were netted using a pole some four or five meters long to which reed bundles were affixed along its length. These reed bundles were tied to the pole at intervals of approximately half a meter.

The pole with the affixed reed bundles was secured at the forward end of the canoe, held firmly in place with a flat board placed so that the reeds floated on the water surface. The bundles were made of white-colored reeds, those parts of the plants, measuring about a meter in length that had originally been submerged below water. . . .

The white-colored reeds were used so that the sunlight they reflected during the movement of the approaching canoe would frighten the fish into a carefully placed handled net. This type of fishing could only be carried out on bright, sunny days when the light not only revealed the fish but also enabled the fisherman to see sufficiently well to entrap the fish in his net.

The fisherman worked alone, seated in the middle of his canoe, bearing with him his net and a paddle for propulsion in deep water. Supporting the net in his right hand, the fisherman paddled slowly with his left hand. Sighting a group of fish, he placed his net in the water and awaited the arrival of the fish. The latter, frightened by the sun's reflection, immediately swam toward the net that was properly placed so as to anticipate their movement. [Albores 1995:221-22]

Use of weirs
Canoes were commonly used with weirs (*presas* or *corrales*) in collaborative efforts involving two or more boats and multiple individuals. This technique might be carried out in open water, or in places where drainage canals or ditches emptied into large areas of standing water. The weirs were essentially V-shaped barriers constructed of aquatic vegetation secured to the bottom with wooden stakes or reeds.

[English translation] The *corral* was a trap formed by two arms made of aquatic plants that converged to form an opening where nets were placed. This trap formed a triangular space on the water's surface such that the fish entered from the base of the triangle and moved toward its point, where they were entrapped in the waiting nets [Fig. 6.4*e*].

The fishermen made the *corrales* from marsh plants. . . . The plants were pulled together to form the arms of the *corral* by men standing in water no more than neck deep—since most of the fishermen could not swim, they could not make such *corrales* in deeper water. The *corral* arms measured about 10 cm thick and from 12 to 15 meters in length, depending on the size of the fish school they expected to encounter. The *corral* arms needed to extend from the water surface to the bottom of the lake so that no fish could escape from below.

From one to four nets were placed across the space at the point of the *corrales*, each net supported by stakes driven into the lake bottom with a wooden oar. The nets were linked together at the top and from the sides and interwoven tightly with aquatic vegetation so that no fish would be able to escape. In addition, aquatic vegetation was placed around the nets and their supports in order to camouflage them and thus deceive the fish.

Once the *corrales* were prepared, some fishermen remained afoot beside the nets, while others got into their canoes and caused the fish to move into the trap. To this end they began to whistle, sing, and shout, while rhythmically pounding the bottoms of their canoes with their feet in order to frighten the fish and make them move into the *corral*. . . . Once the fish had reached the nets, two men standing in the water closed up the front of each net in order to entrap the fish within. . . .

The same person who had emplaced the net also emptied it of fish and cleaned away the adhering plants in order to leave the net ready to use in the next *corral*. The captured fish were put into one of the canoes designated for this purpose. Meanwhile, the rest of the fishermen looked for other places to construct a new *corral* and repeated the operation during the course of the day's work.

. . . In shallow water, the fishermen frightened the fish while on foot, instead of from their canoes. . . .

Depending on the size of the *corral* and the number of fishermen, the arms of the *corral* were constructed in greater or lesser time, and correspondingly fewer or more *corrales* were emplaced during a day's work. With eight or 10 fishermen, it took 10-15 minutes to make a *corral* and about 20 minutes to finish the whole procedure. On the other hand, groups of five or six fishermen needed four hours to make six *corrales* with three or four nets per *corral*.

At the end of a day's work, the catch was divided between the participants using plates, jars or wooden trays (about 40 cm wide and 70 or 80 cm long) to measure out the fish. Each fisherman brought with him three or more five-kilo buckets to hold his share of the fish. Each fisherman returned home in his own canoe. [Albores 1995:224-27]

Night-time fishing

According to Albores (1995:227-28), this is always done in canoes in clear water free of aquatic vegetation, using a one-handled dip net (*macla*). This technique is primarily effective for fish that swim near the surface. Fishermen may operate either alone or in pairs. In the latter procedure, one man startles the fish by the noise of his canoe and so directs them toward the net of the second man waiting in the other boat. A single fisherman working alone simply poles or paddles his boat through a likely spot in the water, holding the net over one side to entrap the fish that he hopes to encounter.

Indigenous fish farming on Lake Pátzcuaro

A very important perspective on indigenous fishing in west-central Mexico comes from Arturo Argueta's (2005) recent study of a traditional P'urhépecha (Tarascan) community on the shores of Lake Pátzcuaro. Here, indigenous fisherfolk, concerned with maintaining a long-term fish population, construct "nurseries" of tree trunks and branches in certain protected areas along the lakeshore. These nurseries protect the eggs from disturbance

Table 6.8. Individual and collective waterfowl-hunting techniques in the Upper Lerma drainage.

Context and Activity	Technique
Individual Techniques (adapted from Sugiura 1998:169-75)	
Hunting afoot in shallow water.	Stalking birds and killing them with slings, sticks, clubs, pronged spears, or simply by hand.
Setting pole-noose traps in shallow water.	Large numbers of cord nooses are looped onto wooden poles (80-200 cm long) and set into the lake bottom, at an angle of about 20°-45°, at a suitable depth to ensnare individual swimming birds returning to their nesting grounds in the evening after feeding during the day. Traps are visited in early morning and reset as needed. Typical trap density = 150 per 2500 m².
Hunting birds encountered while fishing from canoes.	Killing birds with sticks, stones, or pronged spears.
Collective Techniques (adapted from Sugiura 1998:180-83)	
Netting waterfowl in shallow waters near where they nest or feed. Both smaller and larger birds may be taken in this way.	Stretching nets, ca. 10 m long and 1.5 m wide, placed at the right height above water between two poles in shallow water where feeding or nesting birds can be frightened by hunters and driven into the nearby entangling nets [Fig. 6.5a].
Trapping small birds with sticky gum smeared on marsh vegetation in shallow, clear waters near birds' feeding grounds. Higher reeds and other vegetation may be cleared from the trap area.	Hunters hide in nearby reeds and attract birds with simulated calls. When approaching birds become entangled in glue, hunters rush out to kill them with sticks and/or bag them alive in net sacks. The vegetation is then cleaned of adhering old glue and feathers, and re-glued. Used mainly during fall and winter months.

by wind and water current that could cause the egg masses to drift onto land, or into unprotected stretches of open water, where they would die. The nurseries are deliberately guarded while the young fish are in their early stages of development to prevent them from being exploited prior to their maturation, and to ensure that sufficient numbers survive for another breeding season. Argueta believes this tradition of fish conservation is rooted in prehispanic practices. As Argueta notes, the parallels with insect-egg nurseries on Lake Texcoco are striking.

Waterfowl—Hunting and Egg Collecting

Although most bird hunting is now done with firearms, Sugiura (1998:169-83) and Albores (1995:234-45) describe many traditional techniques that were commonly practiced in the region until the 1950s. The vestiges of similar techniques have been reported for Lake Pátzcuaro in the 1940s by Foster (1948:106-7) and West (1948:51). These included hunting waterfowl from canoes using *atlatl*-propelled spears. Hunting involved both individual and collective techniques (Table 6.8) in open ponds and lagoons, in reed-filled marshland, and in more enclosed or restricted spaces (e.g., canals). A variety of stalking, driving, spearing, snaring, trapping, and netting practices were employed. These practices might be undertaken while wading in shallow water, while swimming in deeper water, or from boats. Because there were so many different waterfowl species

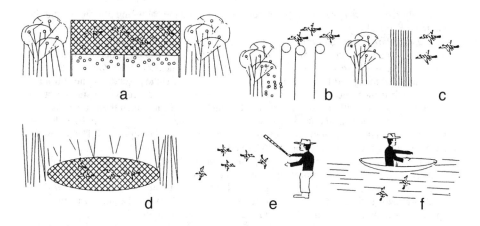

Figure 6.5. Waterfowl-hunting techniques in the Upper Lerma drainage (adapted from Albores 1995:265).

available, with varied feeding and nesting habits, hunting was productive in virtually all types of marshland environments. Although waterfowl hunting was primarily a fall and winter activity, some species were available year-round. Waterfowl eggs were widely collected during the late winter and spring breeding seasons, as they were in the Cuitzeo marshlands farther west (e.g., Williams 2005:12-13).

Collective hunting techniques included netting large and small birds, and trapping smaller birds (especially *chichiquilotes*) with sticky gum (*liga*) thickly smeared on reeds in the nesting grounds. The latter technique was not suitable for large waterfowl with sufficient strength to break free of the glue. The glue was prepared from certain tuberous plants that grow wild on the surrounding hillslopes, and an experienced hunter could ensnare over 400 birds per day in this way (Sugiura 1998:182). Entrapping waterfowl in nets on Lake Texcoco during the late 1930s is illustrated by Linne (1940, 1948:130-33) (Plates 5.49 and 5.51).

Albores (1995) provides additional useful detail on hunting waterfowl:

[English translation]
Waterfowl were hunted by day and night, on land, on the water surface, or under-water. . . . The principal auxiliary implements used were canoes, oars, and harpoons. . . .

Hunting with the harpoon. Waterfowl were hunted with five-pronged harpoons, either in canoes or afoot in shallow water.

Snares [Fig. 6.5*b*]. . . . Hunting ducks with snares was undertaken at night, in shallow water where the seeds of abundant *apipilote* plants provided good feed for the birds. In such places between 100 and 150 wooden stakes were fastened to the bottom surface; a cord made of twisted horse- or ox-hair was fastened to each stake.

The cord was approximately 60 cm long and was fastened to one end of the stake, while a loop, about 15 cm in diameter, was formed at the other end and remained floating on the surface of the water, where the duck became entrapped within it. If the head, wing, foot, or neck of a feeding duck came within the loop the bird was trapped, either strangling itself or simply remaining a prisoner. The snares were checked the following afternoon, and the hunter collected his prey.

Hunting with a rectangular net [Fig. 6.5*a*]. The rectangular net measured between 20 and 50 meters long by about 1.25 meter wide. . . . The net was emplaced in shallow water with abundant plants whose seeds were sought as food by the ducks. The net was supported on oak stakes that measured 1.5 m high, with about 30 cm of the stake pushed into the bottom of the lake, while the three lowermost rows of the net extended below the water surface. A net that measured some 40 meters long required about 20 stakes, to which the net was laced.

The net was put up at about six in the afternoon and remained in place all night so that the birds feeding in the evening might become entrapped within the net openings. The following days the hunters returned, at about 5 AM, to collect their prey from the net. . . .

The circular net [Fig. 6.5*d*]. [The net] was rigged with cords to form a type of collapsible net . . . that closed when pressure was applied. This net measured about 3 or 3.5 m in diameter. It was placed in open water surrounded by marsh plants, and wheat or *apipilote* seeds—a favorite food of the ducks—were tossed out as bait. When the ducks saw the open space in the marsh, they would descend in search of food and then, when coming in contact with the net, they become entangled within it as pressure from the birds' bodies caused it to close up and entrap them.

Bird-lime [Fig. 6.5*c*]. Some birds, such as the *chicuilote*, were hunted with bird-lime [a sticky, glue-like substance]. This technique was practiced in very shallow parts of the marsh . . . with less water than places where nets were used.

. . . the bird-lime was obtained from a type of root that was ground up and boiled in a little water . . . and then 100-200 thin wooden stakes, measuring 20-50 cm long and too thin to be noticed by the birds, were acquired. . . . Before setting out from home, the hunters dipped each stake in the container that held the bird lime, and these stakes were piled together and taken out to the marsh. The stakes were then emplaced about 10-15 cm apart within the same area, each stake individually inserted into the lake bottom.

In order to attract the *chicuilotes*, five or six stuffed birds were set out as decoys on the water, and up to 10 if the hunting area measured more than 3 m in diameter. The stakes and decoys were set out in the morning, and in the afternoon the hunter hid himself behind the bordering plants, and when a flock of birds appeared, which might number 40, 50 or 100 *chicuilotes*, he whistled, imitating the voice of the female birds in order to attract the males. When the *chicuilotes* came into contact with the glued stakes they immediately became entangled as their feathers adhered ever more tightly to the glue as they struggled to free themselves. In this fashion, the birds were captured alive, and immediately the hunters fastened their wings together and strung them on a pole [Plate 5.50]. . . .

Stick [Fig. 6.5*e*]. Waterfowl were also hunted with a wooden stick that measured approximately one meter long, with which up to 20 birds were struck and killed in quick succession while they were on the ground and not in flight.

Sling. Hunting birds with a sling was done on the surface of the marsh. This homemade instrument was made from maguey fiber or with wool threads. . . .

By hand [Fig. 6.5*f*]. . . . this was done at opportune times, such as when a bird came out of the marsh after immersing itself to hide or to feed. . . . [Albores 1995:234-43]

Although the collecting, availability, and use of waterfowl eggs are not described in detail, they were collected in substantial quantities during bird hunting and, more casually, at other times (Sugiura 1998:141-42, 185). García Sanchez (1998) provides a general sense of the importance of waterfowl eggs in the traditional marshland economy:

[English translation] Since winter is the reproductive period of almost all the migratory waterfowl species (and also of the permanent residents), collecting duck eggs is a task . . .

that women and children could perform, and it was an activity that readily complemented fishing and harvesting aquatic vegetation.

Collecting eggs requires knowledge that is not well documented but that is amply manifested in the activity itself, such as knowing which kinds of eggs can be eaten, or not, according to the development of the embryo within. . . . [García Sanchez 1998:104-5]

Other Aquatic Fauna

As noted above, a variety of aquatic insects, crustaceans, and amphibians are collected over the annual cycle (Table 6.3). Many of these are available year-round, but some are most commonly harvested during the summer months.

Acocil (Camberellus montezumae)

According to Albores (1995), this small crustacean, about 6 cm in length, is available year-round along the margins of the marshlands:

[English translation] Fishing for *acocil* was done with a fine-mesh net . . . [with openings that measured] 1.5 cm. . . . One fishing technique consisted of removing the *acocil* from the marsh vegetation by inserting the net into the plants and quickly bringing it out again so as to dislodge the *acocil* into a container. Frequently the *acocil* were found in shallow parts of the marsh, where the fisherman . . . rolled up his pants and got down from the canoe. Once in the water, he placed the net in front of himself, supporting the handle of the net on his chest as he walked forward. [The fisherman commonly carried a basket in which to place his catch.] [Albores 1995:222-23]

Zacamiche (insect larvae)

[English translation] This was obtained during the the rainy season, from June to September, when it was most abundant. . . . The *zacamiche* was found in the marsh grass, especially in . . . a variety of reed that had a sharp, serrated point capable of hurting the fisherman. The *zacamiche* also occurred in another type of marsh grass, called "socanual." After being collected, the living *zacamiches* were placed into large baskets or into large pitchers fitted with tops so that the worms would not escape. [Albores 1995:228]

Picaro or alacrancito (dragonfly larvae)

[English translation] This term denotes . . . an *Odonta* [dragonfly] larvae measuring some six cm long, with a flattened head and small claws, which appeared during the rainy season. . . . It was collected alive by seizing it by the rear part of its body, so that it could not bite, and putting it into a container. [Albores 1995:228-29]

Atepocate (frog tadpole)

[English translation] The *atepocate* is obtained using a fine-mesh net—with openings from 1-1.5 cms—. . . in a manner similar to that of the *acocil*, with the fisherman working afoot, outside the canoe, in shallow parts of the marsh. [Albores 1995:228]

Frog (adults)

[English translation] There were several kinds of edible frogs hunted in the marshes. The diameter of the largest was 15-20 cm, with a weight of up to 1 kilo; the smaller ones measured about 5 cm in diameter. . . .

Frogs were hunted in the middle of the marshes or at their edges, using the small canoe, a wooden pole for propulsion, and two types of pronged harpoons.

Daytime hunting with pronged harpoon. . . . commonly the hunter detected his prey by seeing its eyes projecting above the water surface, the only visible part of the frog's body. At night it was easy to see the frogs because their eyes reflected the brilliant light of the torches that the hunters carried in their canoes. On the other hand, during the day it was difficult to see the frogs' eyes, and so day-time hunting required a high degree of special-ization. In effect, the hunter was obliged to place himself face down in the canoe with his eyes close to the water surface so that he could best see his prey. For greater comfort and to facilitate the hunting operation, the hunter might lie down in the canoe with his harpoon carried in one hand underwater at one side of the canoe, or simply allowed to float on the water's surface.

As he navigated the canoe, the hunter remained alert. Once he sighted a frog, he speared it with the harpoon, and left it floating while he came up in the canoe to seize it. He removed the frog from the harpoon and broke its hind legs so that it could not jump back into the water. . . . The frogs obtained in this manner were placed in a covered, box-like container.

Day-time hunting by observing air bubbles. . . . carried out by individual hunters in canoes within the marshes. This technique consisted of hurling the pronged harpoon at trails of bubbles that appeared on the water surface and that might indicate the presence of a submerged frog.

Day-time hunting by hand. This was carried out during the day in shallow water at the edge of the marsh. . . . The frogs were seized by feeling for them in the mud. Once a frog was grasped in one hand, a second might be held tightly for a moment in the other hand while the hunter pulled the first frog from the water and bit its head and the two hind legs . . . which, although not killing the frog, disabled it and prevented it from moving. If only one frog was caught at a time, the hunter could break its hind legs with his free hand. After thus disabling the frogs, the hunter tossed them onto the bank, where a second person collected them.

Night-time hunting. At night, frogs could be hunted by individuals within the marsh or along its edge. Those who were not specialized frog hunters usually hunted along the edges of the marsh, while the professional hunters worked in both zones. . . . Within the marshes, the night-time frog hunters used a harpoon with five prongs, a small, narrow, one-person canoe with three compartments, and a pine torch. The hunter was seated on a small bench. He carried the harpoon in one hand and poled the canoe with the other. He navigated slowly and silently, since the least noise or disturbance of the water would frighten the frogs away. When he saw his prey, the hunter crouched down and speared the frog with the harpoon. . . .

After the frog was speared, the hunter broke its legs so that it would not jump back into the water, or else he pulled out the spinal cord so that the animal immediately died. The frogs were then placed in buckets or in other containers.

Night-time hunting on solid ground. . . . This collective form of hunting . . . was carried out after a rain, since at that time the frogs were easiest to capture when they came out onto the land next to the shallowest water.

Night-time hunting in shallow water at the edge of the marsh. This was another collective frog-hunting technique. It consisted of following the tracks left by the frogs in the grass to the points where they had entered into the water, from where they could be traced by the trail of bubbles they left on the water surface.

Hunting frogs at the edge of the marsh, on dry land or in the shallow water, was under-taken with the bare hands or with a 5-pronged harpoon. At night a torch was used to provide light. . . . After the frogs were captured, the hunters broke their legs and placed the animals into a basket. [Albores 1995:217-20]

E. Williams (2005:16) indicates that frogs were hunted primarily during the dry-season months in the Lake Cuitzeo marshlands, apparently because they are more difficult to detect during the rainy season when water levels are higher.

Utilization of Aquatic Resources in the Tlaxcalan Marshlands

Much of the marshy floor of the Tlaxcala region east of the Valley of Mexico has been drained for agricultural purposes, and most of the small lakes and marshes that once existed have disappeared. Nevertheless, remnants survive, and the extensive network of drainage and irrigation canals supports aquatic fauna and flora that are still utilized. Today these resources are clearly secondary relative to agricultural products, but they continue to be important in the local economies:

> Of the several types of watercress common in Tlaxcala, *berro chino* (*Nasturtium officinale*) is considered the tastiest and is usually eaten fresh. *Berro palmita* (*Sicon snare*) and *berro redondo* (*Hydrocotyle ranunculoides*), also popular, are eaten raw or cooked. . . . Two water plants produce bulbs (*papas*) which are cooked and eaten: an arrowhead, *acatexcle* (*Sagittaria latifolia*), and a water lily, *tlaquaxona* (*Nymphoea* sp.).
>
> Tlaxcalan farmers shoot scarce waterfowl in all swamps and lake areas. Women and children gather small aquatic animals in *zanjas* [canals] and swamps with nets or porous blankets. Their catch includes *padrecita* (dragonfly nymph), *acocil* (a decapod crustacean), *cucarachita* (nymph of family Belostonitidae), *rana* (*Rana* sp.) [frog], and *carpa* (a small unidentified fish). . . .
>
> Swamp and *zanja* [canal or ditch] plants are used extensively for animal food . . . [and] as green manure when spread on fields. . . . Sleeping mats (*petates*) [are] made from dried *tule* (*Scirpus* sp.) [reeds]. . . . In some instances, *tule* is planted in freshly cleaned *zanjas* to hasten regeneration of the stands. Leaves of *palma* (*Typha* sp.) are woven into chair seats. Bundles of vegetables for market are tied with leaves of *lirio*, a small cattail (family Typhaceae). [Wilken 1970:291-92]

Summary and Conclusions

Ethnographical and historical information provide many details about the technology and sociology of aquatic resource exploitation in the Upper Lerma drainage and neighboring regions in central Mexico. This information from the past century in the Toluca-region marshlands complements the more detailed historical information for the sixteenth through the nineteenth centuries available from the Valley of Mexico. Several generalizations about the procurement and use of aquatic resources in the Upper Lerma drainage stand out as particularly important.

(1) Settlement pattern. There are no reports of temporary camps within the Upper Lerma marshlands from which fishing, hunting, harvesting, collecting, or crafting activities were carried out. All such activities appear to have been undertaken by people who walked or boated from their permanent settlements around the margins of the marshes. Similarly, most activities associated with processing aquatic plants and animals—for example, drying, storing, and weaving reed mats; butchering and preparing waterfowl

and fish—seem to be carried out at the main settlements. Within the marshes, material remains associated with such a settlement pattern are likely to be comparatively few and subtle, although physical traces of permanent settlements on the marsh borders would probably be quite substantial.

Nevertheless, the apparent absence of temporary fishing or hunting camps in the Upper Lerma marshlands cannot necessarily be taken as definitive for either the historic or prehispanic eras. E. Williams (2005:12-13), for example, describes such camps for overnight, or multiday, fishing and hunting expeditions in the Cuitzeo marshes—fishermen either slept in their canoes or in crude huts fashioned from reed bundles.

(2) The dietary importance of aquatic foods for marshland inhabitants. Aquatic plants and animals provide daily food staples throughout the annual cycle for people living in the region. Also impressive is the amount of such foods consumed opportunistically, as snacks, throughout the course of daily hunting, collecting, and harvesting activities in the marshlands. Even in very recent times these foods have provided significant quantities of calories, proteins, and other nutritional elements for thousands of people in the region. At the same time, however, there is little indication that these food products have entered into broader, market-based exchange networks as they once did in the Valley of Mexico. As in the Valley of Mexico, aquatic foods are available throughout the year, but there are definite peaks during certain seasons for different plants and animals (for example, hunting waterfowl in the winter months).

(3) Secondary utilization of aquatic insects or algae. In contrast to the Valley of Mexico, the collection, processing, or consumption of aquatic insects or algae appears to be of no more than secondary importance. I am presently unable to account for this, except to speculate that the water salinity in the Upper Lerma drainage is simply too low to provide a suitable habitat for great numbers of the species that are so abundant in the more saline environment of the central Valley of Mexico. Alternatively, or additionally, since, unlike Lake Texcoco, the Toluca marshes do have an external outlet, the water current, however slight, associated with this external drainage might inhibit some stage of the life cycle of aquatic insects.

(4) The great importance of netting in hunting and harvesting aquatic fauna. A variety of netting techniques are predominant for hunting waterfowl and fish. Spears are predominant only for hunting frogs and salamanders. Spears, snares, and clubs are also employed for hunting waterfowl, and spears are used for some kinds of fish. However, until the recent advent of firearms, netting techniques have clearly been primary. Traditionally such netting, together with a variety of cords for snares and bow strings, have been made of maguey fiber (*ixtle*). This latter material would have been required in very large quantity, especially given the relatively short use-life of netting, being alternatively wetted and dried out through daily use. If the netting was made by the marshland inhabitants themselves, their settlements should have large numbers of spindle whorls, especially the larger sizes suitable for making thick thread and cord (Parsons and Parsons 1990). On the other hand, since maguey (*Agave* sp., the source of *ixtle* fiber) does not flourish in marsh environments, marshland populations may have needed to acquire such material in either raw or processed form through some form of exchange with maguey cultivators and fiber processors living at somewhat higher elevations in the Toluca region.

(5) The great importance of boats in facilitating movement of people throughout the marshlands. Although many kinds of aquatic resources can be exploited on foot in the shallow waters and solid ground of the marshland margins, boats are essential for moving over deeper waters and for hunting, fishing and collecting activities in locales that are often separated by stretches of open water. Interestingly, as in the Valley of Mexico, all boats in use during historic times have been made of wooden planks; there is no mention of reed boats of the type so commonly reported ethnographically in the U.S. Great Basin, the Titicaca Basin in Peru/Bolivia, and the Chad Basin in north-central Africa. The buoyant properties of reeds are well understood, however, as large bundles of harvested reeds are commonly floated from the reed beds to the settlements, towed by men in boats.

(6) The importance of group activities. Although individual hunting, fishing, and collecting are common, it appears that the major harvests of aquatic resources are products of cooperative group activities. These sometimes involve only a pair of people working together, but more commonly, groups of up to a dozen or more cooperate, especially in netting fish and waterfowl, activities that require some people to drive the animals toward the place of entrapment.

(7) Territoriality. Only a few historical details from the Valley of Mexico inform on this important area of inquiry. Similarly, there are a few tantalizing hints, but little detailed information, about the control of access to different kinds of aquatic resources in the Upper Lerma drainage. A few brief statements about local community, or even individual, control of particularly desirable reed beds and duck-hunting locales, and the renting of such places to outsiders, imply some degree of community-level administration of these aquatic resources—*although this control may be mainly a product of the comparatively recent commercialization of reed mats and waterfowl hunting.* Other hints of long-term "ownership" interest in specific marshland locales include the deliberate transplanting of young reed plants into harvested reed beds, and the burning of stands of old reeds so that their ashes might fertilize young plants.

(8) Degree of specialization. Aquatic resources in this region may be acquired either by generalists, who are mainly interested in household subsistence or in minor cash sales, or by specialists, who are more involved in cash sales of reed mats, fish, waterfowl, or frogs, usually through centralized marketplaces. Large work groups, large boats, and large nets are commonly used by specialists, while smaller boats, individual or single-pair cooperation, and small nets or spears tend to be used by nonspecialists. The degree to which certain highly specialized hunting and fishing techniques (for example, the use of "bird lime" glue to capture small waterfowl) may be more characteristic of specialists as opposed to generalists remains uncertain.

The Great Basin, Western U.S.

This vast, arid region contains numerous lakes and marshes of varying size and degree of salinity or alkalinity. Most of these lakes are bordered by marshes, the largest being the vast Stillwater Marsh in western Nevada (Fig. 6.6). The multiple rivers and streams emptying into these lakes contained many plants and animals that were utilized by indigenous people. These aquatic environments support a great variety and abundance of plants and animals that have supplied humans with food and raw materials for millennia (Heizer and Napton 1970; Janetski and Madsen 1990; Kelly 2001; Raven and Elston 1988; Sutton 1995). Many of these same aquatic resources are found in the Valley of Mexico.

However, because the Great Basin is an arid, temperate region, relative to the Valley of Mexico there are more extreme seasonal differences and greater overall aridity. Furthermore, it must be remembered that indigenous people in the Great Basin during the nineteenth and early twentieth centuries were hunter-gatherers who used no pottery and who lived in noncentralized societies at the margins of an expanding Euro-American state, rather than being intensive pottery-using agriculturalists and aquatic specialists at the core of major precolumbian and Hispanic-American states, as in central Mexico. Except in times of unusual scarcity or famine, for example, after pre-Formative times in the Valley of Mexico, domesticated plants would probably have supplied most of the calories and nutrients that were traditionally acquired from wild plants in the U.S. Great Basin. Despite these differences, the Great Basin provides much information about the traditional use of aquatic resources that is potentially relevant to the prehispanic Valley of Mexico.

Aquatic Plants and Animals

The most important aquatic fauna consisted of many species of waterfowl (Tables 6.9 and 6.10), at least four species of fish (Table 6.11), and three species of insects (Table 6.12). A variety of reeds and rushes comprised the most important aquatic flora, although many other plant species were also used as food (Tables 6.13 and 6.14).

Waterfowl-Hunting Techniques

Waterfowl were present in prodigious numbers, especially during the peak seasons (September-November and February-March); some important species were available year-round (e.g., the mud hen, or American coot [*Fulica Americana*]). Up to 100,000 birds have been counted in annual censuses taken in recent years in Stillwater Marsh (Fowler 1992:46). Waterfowl were hunted both individually and in groups, on foot and in boats, during the day or at night, and with a variety of implements, including bows and arrows, spears, and nets (Tables 6.15-6.17). Waterfowl eggs were also commonly collected, especially during the height of the breeding season during the spring and early summer months (March-June) (Loud and Harrington 1929:156).

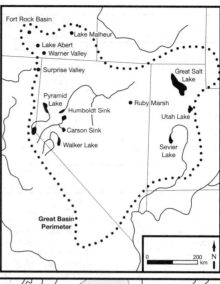

Figure 6.6. The Great Basin, western U.S., showing principal places mentioned in text (adapted from Kelly 2001:3, 101, Figs. 1-1, 5-1).

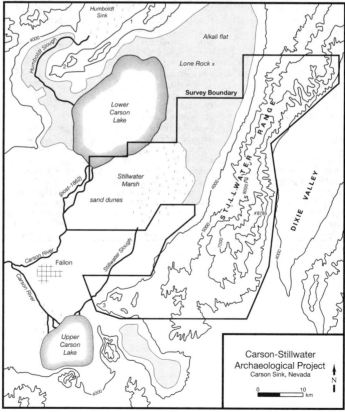

Table 6.9. Great Basin waterfowl.

Of Primary Importance		
Common Name	*Species Identification*	*Comment*
♦mallard	*Anas platrhynchos*	eggs and hatchlings also used
♦northern pintail	*Anas acuta*	eggs and hatchlings also used
♦northern shoveler	*Anas clypeata*	eggs and hatchlings also used
♦cinnamon teal	*Anas cyanoptera*	eggs and hatchlings also used
♦green-winged teal	*Anas crecca*	eggs and hatchlings also used
♦American wigeon	*Anas americana*	eggs and hatchlings also used
♦gadwell	*Anas strepera*	eggs also used
♦redhead	*Aytha americana*	eggs and hatchlings also used
♦ruddy duck	*Oxyura jamaicensis*	eggs also used
♦American coot (mud hen)	*Fulica americana*	eggs and hatchlings also used; up to 20 eggs per nest

Of Secondary Importance		
Common Name	*Species Identification*	*Comment*
common loon	*Gavia immer*	eggs also used
pied-billed grebe	*Podilymkbus podiceps*	eggs also used
♦eared grebe	*Podiceps nigricollis*	eggs also used
♦western grebe	*Aechmorphorus occidentalis*	eggs also used
♦American white pelican	*Pelecanus erythcorhunchos*	eggs and hatchlings also used
great blue heron	*Ardea herodias*	eggs and hatchlings also used
great egret	*Casmerodius albus*	eggs and hatchlings also used
♦snowy egret	*Egretta thula*	eggs also used
♦black-crowned night heron	*Nycticorax nycticorax*	eggs and hatchlings also used
white-faced ibis	*Plegadis chihi*	eggs and hatchlings also used
tundra swan	*Cygnus columbianus*	
Canada goose	*Banta canadensis*	eggs and hatchlings also used
♦white-fronted goose	*Ansere albifrons*	
snow goose	*Chen caerulescens*	
Ross goose	*Chen rossi*	
♦canvasback	*Aythya valisineria*	
common merganser	*Mergus merganser*	
double-crested cormorant	*Phalacrocorax auritus*	
common goldeneye	*Bucephala clangula*	
♦bufflehead	*Bucephala albeola*	eggs also used
♦killdeer	*Charadrius vociferus*	eggs also used
black-necked stilt	*Himantopus mexicanus*	eggs also used
♦American avocet	*Recurvirostra americana*	eggs also used
long-billed curlew	*Numenisu americanus*	eggs also used
semi-palmated plover	*Charadrius semipalmatus*	
♦common snipe	*Gallinago gallinago*	eggs also used
Wilson's phalarope	*Phalaropus tricolor*	eggs also used
California gull	*Larus californicus*	eggs and hatchlings also used
Caspian tern	*Sterna caspia*	eggs also used
black tern	*Chlidonias niger*	eggs also used

(Adapted from Fowler 1992:51, Table 6)
♦ = Also occurs in the Valley of Mexico.

Table 6.10. Average weights of adult waterfowl in the Great Basin (including bone and feathers).

Species	Male Wt. (kilos)	Female Wt. (kilos)
American coot	0.8	0.7
tundra swan	7.3	6.3
Canada goose	4.5	3.7
white-fronted goose	2.9	2.5
snow goose	3.4	2.8
Ross goose	1.8	1.6
green-winged teal	0.3	0.3
mallard	1.3	1.1
northern pintail	1.0	0.9
cinnamon teal	0.4	0.4
northern shoveller	0.7	0.6
gadwell	1.0	0.8
American wigeon	0.8	0.8
canvasback	1.3	1.2
redhead	1.1	1.0
common goldeneye	1.1	0.8
bufflehead	0.5	0.4
ruddy duck	0.5	0.5
surf scooter	1.1	1.0

(Adapted from Fowler 1992:52, Table 7)

Table 6.11. Some indigenous Great Basin fish (none of these occur in the Valley of Mexico).

Common Name	Species Identification	Average Adult Length (cm)	Average Adult Weight (kilos)	Calories/kg
tui chub	*Gila bicolor*	19.8-24.2	0.23	1250
Tahoe sucker	*Catostomus tahoensis*	13.2-22.0	0.34-0.91	956
redside shiner	*Richardsonius egregious*	2.2-8.8	0.006	915
speckled dace	*Rhinichthys oscylus*	4.4-5.5	0.002	814

(Adapted from Fowler 1992:61, Table 9)

Table 6.12. Great Basin aquatic insects used for food.

Common Term	Species Identification	Occurrence
shore fly	*Ephydra gracilis*	found primarily in saline water
✦shore fly	*Ephydra hians* (in 1934 renamed *Hydropyrus hians*)	thrives in both saline and alkaline water
salmon fly	*Pteronarcys californica*	a riverine insect, lives in moving water

(Adapted from Aldrich 1912; Fowler 1990a, b; Sutton 1985)
✦ = Also occurs in the Valley of Mexico.

Table 6.13. Useful Great Basin aquatic plants.

Common Term	Species Identification	Uses
♦common cattail	*Typha latifolia* and *Typha domingensis*	food: edible seeds, pollen, stalks construction: mats, basketry, bags, huts, duck decoys, boats clothing: stalks woven into shirts, caps, leggings, capes
♦hardstem bulrush or tule bulrush	*Scirpus acutus*	food: seeds, pollen, roots and stalks construction: mats, basketry, boats clothing: stalks woven into capes
♦tule bulrush	*Scirpus americanus*	food: edible young stalks, seeds
alkali bulrush	*Scirpus maritimus*	food: edible seeds
triangular-stemmed tule	*Scirpus robustus*	construction: mats
♦circular-stemmed tule	*Scirpus lacustris*	construction: mats
♦three-square tule	*Scirpus pungens*	food: edible seeds
♦spike rush	*Eleocharis* sp.	construction: mats, basketry, cord clothing: stalks woven into capes
♦rush	*Juncus* sp.	food: edible seeds and stalks; sap for beverage construction: mats, basketry, cord, boats clothing: stalks woven into capes
♦pondweed	*Potamogeton natans*	food: edible rhizomes
common arrowhead	*Sagittaria latifolia*	food: edible tubers
♦pond lily	*Nymphaea polysepala*	food: edible seeds and roots dye: seed shells used for black dye
common cane	*Phragmites australis*	food: sap for beverage
pickleweed	*Allenrolfea occidentalis*	food: edible seeds

(Adapted from Barrett 1910; Ebeling 1986; Fowler 1990a; Fowler 1992)
♦ = Also occurs in the Valley of Mexico.

Table 6.14. Nutritional composition of some aquatic plants in the Great Basin.

Species	Calories/kg	% Protein	% Carbohydrates	% Fat
sedge seeds (*Carex* sp.)	2590	10.6	54.9	0.3
♦saltgrass seeds (*Distichlis stricta*)	2540	6.2	58.0	0.4
♦bulrush seeds (*Scirpus paludosus*)	3050	6.5	56.9	6.3
♦bulrush root (*Scirpus acutus*)	630	0.2	15.4	0.30
♦cattail pollen (*Typha latifolia*)	1040	4.9	18.2	1.50

(Adapted from Simms 1985:120, Table 2)
♦ = Also occurs in the Valley of Mexico.

Table 6.15. Implements used in hunting waterfowl in the Great Basin.

Implement	Use
bow and arrow	Arrows typically ringed (usually with pitch and sinew) at the point so that they would deflect from the water surface into flock of feeding or swimming birds. Sometimes small obsidian points used. Different kinds of arrows were used for hunting waterfowl, rabbits, deer, and terrestrial birds. Arrow shafts were usually made from cane. Arrows were straightened using grooved or ungrooved stones: typically "a large, smooth rock...somewhat flattened but not purposefully shaped....[These straighteners] were heated in the fire, and the cane shaft was placed over the stone and then bent in the desired direction" (Fowler 1992:104-5). Chipped stone knives and scrapers were used to smooth the arrow shafts.
long, narrow nets	Placed upright on wooden or cane poles near water surface, designed to capture birds in flight (usually either taking off or landing). Nets typically measured 1.2-1.8 m wide and ca. 15 m long. Made of twined "native hemp" (*Apocynum cannabinum*).
bird decoys	Usually made from reeds, placed in groups simulating feeding birds so as to attract over-flying fowl. Birds were then shot or netted by men hidden in nearby reeds. Decoys were either linked together in groups of 10 or more with twine lines that could be manipulated to simulate movement, or were individually anchored to the bottom with a stone weight attached to the decoy by a string tether.
reed boats	One-man prowed rafts made of bundles of cattails and rushes, used for moving about on the water surface. Boats constructed so as to contain space for placing waterfowl, fish, plants, or other harvested materials. Propelled by hand, or with small reed paddles. Also used in fishing and for other tasks, such as egg collecting, setting out bird decoys or fish lines, and for placing nets to capture waterfowl. One-person boats usually measured ca. 3.6 m long, but larger vessels could measure up to 6.1 m long (for carrying 4-5 people) and even up to 15.2 m (for carrying larger groups).
wood dugout canoes	Made from hollowed-out tree trunks, typically 3.6-9 m long and 25-60 cm wide, propelled with paddles in deeper water and with poles in shallower water. Also used in fishing and for other tasks.
flares	Fires kindled atop a rock hearth in boat to attract nesting or feeding waterfowl.
wooden clubs	For killing birds, especially during group hunts of flightless birds when they were driven ashore.
net or reed bags or reed baskets	For carrying captured birds, either afoot or in boats. A small twined-reed bag was used for collecting and transporting up to 4 dozen waterfowl eggs. Larger bags were used for carrying birds, fish, and duck decoys. These same containers were typically hung on house walls as storage vessels for collected waterfowl, eggs, etc.

(Adapted from Barrett 1910; Fowler 1990a, 1992)

Table 6.16. Waterfowl-hunting techniques in the Great Basin.

Waterfowl	Hunting Techniques
hunting molting (flightless) waterfowl in August (especially the American coot, or mudhen) and flightless hatchlings of other species in mid-summer	Groups of men in reed boats herded birds ashore, where they were captured (sometimes with aid of dogs) and killed with sticks or arrows, or immobilized by breaking their legs. They were then collected into piles and placed in baskets for transport to camp. Alternatively, "...men set double nets—one behind the other—...and then with their tule balsa boats drove the flightless birds towards the open nets. As one net became heavy with entangled birds, it was pulled to the shore, and the birds went into the other. Boats formed a half circle as they grew closer to the nets. When the boats touched, the drive was over..." (Fowler 1990a:141).
hunting waterfowl (capable of flight) with decoys and bows and arrows	"...decoys were set out at the edge of open water in marshes by individual hunters who then concealed themselves in blinds of tules and cattails....They set out 5-10 decoys, either linked together by...strings...or individually anchored in place with a small rock attached to each tether string. Hunters sometimes used voice calls...to attract waterfowl....Once a group [of birds] came within range, the hunter shot at them with special arrows...featuring either a bulbous projection an inch below the tip or a small obsidian point. Hunters apparently aimed at the water just in front of the duck, and either type of arrow would glance up and hit the duck. The hunter then had to swim or wade into the water to retrieve his quarry" (Fowler 1990a:110).
hunting waterfowl (capable of flight) with decoys and nets	"The net was stretched [either upright or at an angle of about 45 degrees] between two poles with one end fastened to the top of one of the poles so that the bottom of the net was at water line. The remaining length of cord went to the hunter concealed in the vegetation, who allowed the cord to slacken so that the net was submerged in the water. When the ducks were attracted...by decoys..., they were suddenly flushed [by men emerging from the reeds]. As they rose from the water, the cord was pulled tight and the net came up to the top of the second pole, blocking the flight path. The ducks hit the net and, as the cord was relaxed, became entangled in it. The entire net could be pulled to shore and the ducks removed. "[for night-time hunting the hunters simply]...set the net loosely on the poles...with the decoys tethered near its base. The ducks became entangled during the night, and the hunters retrieved them the next morning. "...[these netting techniques]...would be most effective with ducks that patter or run across the water on takeoff, rather than those that rise abruptly into the air....On the other hand, nets for geese might be more effectively used as these birds land. With large wing spans, they have to glide in slowly, feet forward, to reduce air speed for landing....[As the geese, attracted by decoys, were landing]...a net might then be raised quickly, blocking their landing and entangling them. They would have a great deal of difficulty reversing their path of descent or attempting to become airborne again" (Fowler 1990a:110-11).
hunting feeding waterfowl with submerged-hunter technique	"...a man could hunt effectively by placing a helmet of moss or other vegetation over his head and walking or swimming through the water into a group of waterfowl....Once among them, the hunter pulled one duck at a time under water by its legs, broke them, and crushed its skull with his hands. He then tucked the duck into his belt. When sufficiently weighted down, he came to the shore" (Fowler 1992:59).
collecting waterfowl eggs	Available during breeding season in spring and early summer. Collected on daily trips to shallow-water marshes in special egg bags made of twined rushes or reeds that held 3-4 dozen eggs, usually by women and children, but sometimes opportunistically by men while hunting in deeper water.

(Adapted from Fowler 1990a, 1992)

Table 6.17. Processing and storing waterfowl and their eggs in the Great Basin.

eggs	Boiled in baskets using hot stones, or roasted under a cooking fire. Sometimes buried in cool mud for later use—could be kept for several weeks in this state (Fowler 1992:55).
cooking, drying, and storing bird carcasses after butchering	If large numbers of birds were netted together, butchering and cleaning would take place on the lakeshore, prior to taking the butchered carcasses back to camp. If only a few birds were involved, they would usually be taken back to the camp for butchering. "Small birds or cut-up portions of large birds with or without bones were placed in baskets with water and heated stones added to boil them....Large birds were usually pit roasted. A fire was made and allowed to burn to coals. The coals were removed and the gutted birds...were placed in the ground and the coals and a layer of sand was used to cover them....Birds with feathers removed were placed between layers of cattail leaves or grass to keep them clean....A variant technique for roasting mudhens and ducks was to encase each with feathers remaining in a layer of clay-based mud. When the mud dried it created a hardened shell around the birds. Several could be placed in a roasting pit side by side. The heat of the fire baked bird and clay, sealing in the birds' succulent juices" (Fowler 1992:60). Dried carcasses usually kept well for a few weeks. Surpluses were often split, sun-dried, and stored for up to a few months in covered, grass-lined pits (see below). Sometimes small brush structures were used for sun-drying the birds or for storing the dried carcasses.
storage pits	Used to store parched seeds, pine nuts, dried waterfowl or rabbits, and dried roots. The pits "were dug to a depth of 0.6 m, or more, into dry ground.... [the pits typically measured] 1-1.5 m in diameter...[and were] lined with dry grass or dry cattail leaves....The materials to be stored...were usually in buckskin sacks....The pit was capped with more cattail leaves and willow branches, and then sealed with mud" (Fowler 1992:100).

(Adapted from Fowler 1990a, 1992)

Fishing

Fishing was a year-round activity, either afoot or in boats. However, because some common species frequently congregated in large schools during the spawning season from April into early winter, fishing tended to be most productive during those months. Techniques varied according to whether the water was still (in lakes or ponds) or flowing (in rivers), whether rivers were running high or low, and whether the water was clear or muddy. Reed boats and wooden dugout canoes were commonly employed in fishing and for moving from one fishing locale to another. Different kinds of bags, baskets, and pots were used as containers for holding and transporting fish (Table 6.15). Fish were harvested using a variety of nets, hooks and lines, weirs and platforms, basket traps, and spears; once collected, they were processed with different types of cutting and grinding implements (Tables 6.18-6.20; Figs. 6.7-6.11 [Fig. 6.7*A* nicely illustrates a simple weir used in the Boston Back Bay that probably resembled those used in the Great Basin]; Plates 6.1-6.3). Fish eggs were also collected and eaten. Although Kroeber and Barrett (1960) were mainly concerned with riverine fishing, their descriptions of fishing technology illustrate tools and practices common throughout the Great Basin (Figs. 6.7-6.11; Plates 6.1 and 6.2). Since freshwater streams flow into Lake Texcoco from its entire perimeter, those fishing techniques in northern California that utilize natural water currents to direct fish into nets and traps should also have some potential applicability to lacustrine fishing in the Valley of Mexico.

Kroeber and Barrett (1960:4) indicate that during the early twentieth century, the most productive fishing locales (e.g., at stream eddies or backwaters, or where streams emptied into lakes or lagoons) tended to be privately owned, while less propitious fishing spots (e.g., open lakes) were usually accessible to all members of a given local group who might want to fish there.

Harvesting and Processing Aquatic Insects

J.M. Aldrich (a professional entomologist) vividly described the vast quantities of edible aquatic insects (*Ephydra gracilis* and *Ephydra hians*) that were available along the shorelines of the Great Salt Lake and Mono Lake during his visits in 1908 and 1911:

There is an alga in the lake everywhere common . . . its pulpy masses rolling up and down the beaches with the waves, and often forming rotting deposits of horrible odor along the upper beach as the level of the lake falls in summer. This I take to be the food of *gracilis*. . . .

It is only in the pupal stage that the inconceivable numbers of the flies present in the lake begins to make an impression on the observer. The puparia are buoyant . . . and they become attached to each other by the hardened and somewhat recurved forks of the anal tube, so that vast masses of them float along together. . . .

The shores of the lake everywhere are more or less covered with windrows of puparia, which frequently form dark ridges that can be seen for a long distance. . . . The fly puparia form a mass filling the water close to shore, and a foot or more deep in the water for some distance; all the dark color in the water and along the edge is simply a collection of millions of puparia.

. . . The adults are found on the surface of the water all over the lake, but along the beaches they gather in large numbers, probably because they emerge there from the windrows of the puparia that wash up. . . . [in 1908] the surface of the water from the shore out to a distance of about 18 feet [ca. 5.5 m] was perfectly covered with the adult flies. They made a black belt along the beach that was visible for several miles. . . . They were crowded closely together, and when disturbed by my near approach, they would rise only a few inches and immediately settle again. They extended up the beach a few feet above the water also, so that the average width of the mass was over 20 feet [ca. 6.1 m]. . . . The minimum estimate I would give is about 370,000,000 flies to the mile [2.2 km] of beach [ca. 25 flies per square inch (4.8 cm²)]. [Aldrich 1912:82-83]

Aldrich (1912:88-89) also noted that two different aquatic insect species (*Ephydra gracilis* and *Ephydra hians*) appeared to be differentially distributed in Great Salt Lake:

While *gracilis* occupied all the water's edge and extended out on the surface of the lake for some distance, *hians* occurred in numbers a little farther up the lake beach, where there were windrows of rotting [alga] material that had been washed up at a higher stage of the water not very long before. The two species seemed not to mix much. . . .

Hians appears to thrive well in both salty waters and alkaline, while . . . *gracilis* confines itself to the former only. . . .

Adults of *hians* have the unusual habit of entering the water and walking about on objects below the surface enveloped in a globule of air. They cannot descend unless they can have some solid object to hold to, as they are quite buoyant when below the surface. . . . [in standing water] the eggs are simply dropped in the water while the fly rests on the surface.

The [*hians*] larvae are generally found near the bottom of the water. They wiggle a good deal, but do not come to the surface for air. . . . it is likely that both larvae and adults generally remain rather close to shore.

The technology of the harvesting and initial processing of aquatic insects is simple. Masses of insects, in both adult and pupal stages, were simply scooped up in baskets from naturally occurring windrows along the lakeshore and from the immediately adjacent shallow water. The edible portion of the dried body—the interior core of the insect, about the size of a kernel of wheat—was separated from the rest of the creature (wings, legs, hard outer casing, etc.) by simply rubbing the bodies between the hands and casting aside the unwanted parts. The edible portion of the insect was then placed directly into bags or baskets and carried to the camp site, where it could be stored for up to several months inside houses. This material could be eaten as is, "like raisins or popcorn" (Essig 1934:184), or ground up with acorns, nuts, berries, and other seeds to form a nutritious breadlike food known as "cuchaba" or "kutsavi" (Heizer 1950). The ground-up insect matter might also be mixed with water to make a soup, fried, boiled to make a mush, or mixed with wheat flour to make bread (Sutton 1988:49).

Sutton (1985, citing Aldrich 1912) describes the rather different technique employed for harvesting and processing the salmon fly (*Pteronarcus californica*), a riverine insect. Although this species apparently is not found in central Mexico, the collecting and processing technology may have some applicability for the latter region, especially at points where streams entered the lakes:

The time for gathering the flies was some time in the early summer. The Indians would place logs across the river in about the same manner that a present-day log or lumber boom is constructed. They would then go up-stream and shake the flies off the willow bushes growing along the banks of the river. The flies falling on the water would float down stream and lodge against the logs in great quantities. As many as a hundred bushels could be gathered in this way in a single day. The Indians used a kind of basket to dip the flies from the water and carry them to the place where they were to be prepared for food.

A pit was dug in the ground [near the harvesting locale] about 1.5-2 feet [50-60 cm] and about 2 feet [60 cm] or more square. Then two layers of stones were placed in the bottom of the pit, each layer being about three inches [6.6 cm] thick. A wood fire was built on these stones and more stones were put around and over the fire. When the fire was burnt out and the stones were hot, all the stones were removed except the bottom layer. Then green tules or coarse grass was spread out on the bottom layer of rocks. The walls of the pit were lined with hot rocks also, and this enclosure was then filled with the flies. . . . before the flies were put into the [pit] oven, they were dumped into large baskets and mashed up and kneaded. . . . The mass is made into loaves like bread and placed in the oven side by side. There may be a half dozen or more layers of these loaves in one oven, with the hot stones placed between the layers. . . .

These were covered with green coarse grass and the whole covered with more hot stones. Water was then poured on the hot stones of the walls of the pit, the hot stones converting it to steam. As soon as the water was poured on, dirt was hurriedly thrown over all to a depth of several inches. The flies were allowed to cook in this manner until the heat was pretty much expended. The dirt and grass were then removed from the top and the mass allowed to cool. When sufficiently cooled, the product was taken from the oven and was ready for use. . . . When cold [and dried], [the] *koo-chuh-bie* is about the consistency of hard cheese, . . . and can be cut into slices with a knife. [Sutton 1985:177]

Although, strictly speaking, grasshoppers are not aquatic insects, these nutritious insects were unusually abundant around the Great Salt Lake in the eastern Great Basin. Sutton (1995:279), for example, citing late nineteenth-century sources, notes that during the late fall

[s]warms of grasshoppers commonly fly over the lake, fall in after becoming fatigued, drown, then wash up on the shore of the lake in huge numbers . . . [at which point they are collected] dried, salted, and ready to eat.

Similarly, Madsen and Kirkman (1988:593) note that around the perimeter of the Great Salt Lake,

[d]uring the summer, [naturally] salted and sun-dried hopper are washed up on beaches to form windrows up to 0.2 × 1.5 × 15 km. Hoppers produce over 3,010 kilocalories per kilo. Digestible proportions have not been determined, but even at a return rate well below the experimental value, optimality models suggest hopper collection should be favored over all other collected resources.

Harvesting and Processing Aquatic Food Plants

The importance of aquatic plants over the millennia in the Great Basin can hardly be overstated. These plants supplied an astonishing variety of foods, shelters (domestic residences, outbuildings, windbreaks, and open-sided structures for shade), boats, clothing (skirts, caps, sandals, rain capes, leggings), waterfowl decoys, blankets, pillows, basketry, mats, bags, and cordage. Aquatic plants were harvested for food throughout the year, although there was a definite seasonal rhythm (Table 6.21). They were harvested afoot or in boats, by persons working individually or in groups. Cutting (knives), scooping (baskets), and carrying and storage implements (baskets, sacks) were commonly involved in their harvesting, processing, and use. Seeds were commonly reduced to a powder with ground stone hulling and grinding tools: smaller, *mano*-like tools used for hulling, shelling, and grinding tasks, and larger, *metate* implements used as support surfaces for hulling, shelling, or grinding.

Loud and Harrington (1929) learned a great deal from an elderly native informant about the traditional use of the stone grinding tools from their archaeological excavations in 1912 at Lovelock Cave, near Stillwater Marsh. These ground stone tools—shellers, grinders, metates, mortars, and pestles—were used for grinding seeds from aquatic and terrestrial

Table 6.18. Fishing implements and their use in the Great Basin.

Implement	Characteristics and Use
dip net	Elliptical or triangular in form. Commonly fixed to wooden poles and operated by one man, either afoot or seated at front of a boat with a two-man crew. Netting usually made from twined "native hemp" (*Apocynum cannabinum*).
gill net with stone sinkers	*Net:* long, linear nets with ca. 4 cm mesh. Netting usually made from twined "native hemp" (*Apocynum cannabinum*) (e.g., Fig. 6.8). *Stone sinkers:* grooved, elliptical or triangular in form, worked or unworked (e.g., Plate 6.2).
large net used with weirs	Set upright on poles below water surface.
hooks on cord lines	*Small hook variant:* "...straight piece of bone pointed at both ends and attached to line by means of sinew and pitch" (Barrett 1910:250). *Large hook variant:* "a bone [or wood] shank with two bone points [placed at] angles of 25-30 degrees with the shank. The three pieces of bone are secured one to another by means of sinew and pitch" (Barrett 1910:251). *Set lines:* Usually 3-7 m long, with hooks suspended about every 25 cm. Hooks baited with grubs. "Set lines extended into the lake from a willow stick driven into the shore. Lines ended with a suspended rock sinker....Tule floats [were] attached at each end [of the line] to keep the lines suspended in the water" (Fowler and Bath 1981:183). Fowler and Bath (1981:183) describe a set line used at Pyramid Lake in 1875 that measured 15 m long and had 75 "tiny composite hooks." "The rod is of cane and the rock sinker at the other end is elliptical but not grooved. Line, rock, and hooks are pitch-covered, probably to protect the cordage. The hooks, roughly 1 cm long, are made of a piece of split willow folded in half with a tiny bone pin in the bite. The willow and bone are then wrapped together with cordage and the loose end is affixed to the line." Set lines in use for lake fishing in 1930 had 3-ply cordage 20-30 m long "...with about 30 barbed bone or greasewood hooks suspended by 3-4 m lines from the main line...such large lines were attached to shore and then a swimmer took the end out into the lake to a favored spot. Here he attached a large circular tule float from which he also suspended a rock sinker. The line could be pulled in from shore" (Fowler and Bath 1981:183-84).
stone mortar and pestle	For grinding dried fish into a powder used to thicken soups and stews.
harpoons	Wood shafts with bone points, used to spear larger fish. *Single-pointed harpoon:* "...a socketed bone head [was] fitted to a sharpened greasewood foreshaft that, in turn, was lashed to a 2-3 m [long] willow pole with dogbane cordage. The barb was of hard bone (deer or coyote) and slightly crescent shaped....The bone barb was drilled and a 40-60 cm length of dogbane cordage was added as a toggle." *Double-pointed harpoon:* "...made with two foreshafts "lashed to opposite sides of the pole" (Fowler and Bath 1981:182).
reed baskets	Used as fish traps and to carry or store collected fish.
wood sticks	For beating sides of boats to make noise to frighten fish and cause them to move in the desired direction, away from the noise and toward a net.
fishing platforms	Usually for high-water fish runs in rivers. "Platforms...were constructed by driving two heavy willow or cottonwood poles into the river bottom near the bank. Another pole was lashed across these and others placed at right angles to the last to form the base of the platform and connect it to the bank" (Fowler and Bath 1981:177).
fishing weirs	Barriers made of saplings and brush secured with poles to the bottoms of rivers or lakes to deflect or halt movement of fish and direct them toward a net or basket trap.
obsidian knife	Fowler and Bath (1981:185) report that fish "were filleted with unhafted obsidian knives [ca. 12 cm long] designed to be held sideways between the thumb and first finger."

(Adapted from Barrett 1910; Fowler 1990a, b, 1992; Fowler and Bath 1981; Kroeber and Barrett 1960. Refer to Figs. 6.7-6.11, and Plates 6.1 and 6.2.)

Table 6.19. Fishing techniques in the Great Basin.

Technique	Procedure
dip netting	*Afoot:* "The net was tied on two sides to two poles, the ends of which reached the bottom of the slough with the net about 6 inches [13.2 cm] above. Sometimes the poles were crossed near the fisherman's stomach and tied in this position. The men walked in the water and scooped up fish with this net....When fish were in the net, the two poles were drawn together at the bottom and the entire piece removed to the bank of the river. There the fish were deposited in a spot of clean ground to dry" (Fowler 1992:61). *From a boat:* "...usually two men go out to fish, one sitting in the stern of the canoe and paddling, the other in the prow and manipulating the net. While the net is being dipped, the fisherman in the stern paddles quite rapidly and makes a great noise, swishing the water back and forth in order to scare the fish near the stern towards the prow. He also has a couple of short sticks with which, just before the net is to be raised, he drums upon the sides of the canoe in order to frighten as many as possible of the fish toward the prow. The fisherman in the prow finally raises the poles and brings up the net,....The cross-bar of the net poles is slipped over the top of the prow so as to prevent the points of the poles from falling back into the water...so that the fish are prevented from jumping over the sides of the net..." (Barrett 1910:249-50). The netted fish were placed in a coarse reed basket carried in the boat.
basket scooping	A variant of the dip-net technique, employed to capture small fish at the water's edge. The fisher "...waded into the water and used the basket to scoop up the fish and then deposit them on the shore where they were sun dried" (Fowler 1992:62).
gill netting	The "...large, linear gill net...[was] set up on sticks across the narrow channels in the lake near the base camp....tui chub...were driven into it by people wading into the lake....Gill nets...were made in several different mesh sizes....a chub net collected at Stillwater in 1929...has 4-cm mesh" (Fowler 1992:61).
basket traps in rivers	*Trap used with weir placed across width of river:* "...the weir was tightly woven to obstruct the passage of fish up-stream. Near the center of the weir, on the downstream side, a trough-shaped willow [basket] trap was securely lashed...[the trap measured] 1.5-2 m long, 2/3 m wide, and 2/5 m deep. It was closed at both ends. Trout coming up the river tried to jump the weir and fell back into the basket" (Fowler and Bath 1981:180). *Double-cone trap used with weir at low water:* The trap was "placed in an opening of the weir, facing downstream, and was fastened to the bottom of the river with [wood] stakes. The fish swam into the basket as they followed the current" (Fowler and Bath 1981:180). *Trap used with two converging weirs:* "...two converging woven fence [weir] wings were built extending somewhat downstream and spanning the river to within 1-2 m of its center. Then from each wing, a 1-1.5 m wall of stones extended straight down river. At the ends of the walls a tubular willow basket trap with squared ends and a center opening was placed [so as to catch the fish as they moved downstream]" (Fowler and Bath 1981:180).
spearing fish from platforms or weirs in low water	"Weirs constructed at angles to the river bank directed fish over an area 1-2 m square purposefully paved with white rocks...[thus making the fish easier to see, especially at night] (Fowler and Bath 1981:181).

(Adapted from Barrett 1910; Fowler 1990a, 1992; Fowler and Bath 1981; Kroeber and Barrett 1960)

Table 6.20. Fish processing, preparation, and storage in the Great Basin.

Activity	Procedure
drying and preparing small fish	The collected fish were usually sun dried on cleared ground at the edge of the water where they were caught. "Once dried, the fish were sacked in woven tule bags and either hung in the shade or buried in pits lined with cattail leaves and capped with freshly cut willows and mud....[Dried] small fish were boiled whole in soups....Small fresh fish were baked in the ashes in packets made by placing them between two layers of cattail leaves and tying the ends of the leaves together" (Fowler 1992:63).
drying and preparing large fish	"...often dried on willow racks in the shade. They were...split length-wise...to facilitate the drying process....The drying procedure was followed only during the winter, when it was cold. Otherwise the fish would spoil" (Fowler 1992:63).
grinding dried fish	"Another way of preparing dried fish for soups and stews was to grind them to powder using the mortar and pestle and then add them as a thickening. Soups and stews with a fish powder base might also contain plant foods...or other animal protein" (Fowler 1992:63). This was an especially important food during the winter season.
drying and preparing fish and fish eggs	After filleting, the fish "were dried on pole platforms. After drying they were placed in a sagebrush bark- or grass-lined pit or left on the platforms and covered with layers of leaves and branches. Chubs, redsides, and speckled dace were sun-dried whole and later ground into powder for soups. Fish eggs were treated similarly. Fresh and dried fish were either roasted in hot ashes or steamed and baked in preheated grass-lined pits" (Fowler and Bath 1981:185).

(Adapted from Fowler 1990a, 1992; Fowler and Bath 1981)

Table 6.21. Food uses of aquatic plants in the Great Basin.

Plant	*Food Use: Harvesting and Processing*
common cattail (*Typha latifolia*)	"Early in the spring, Paiute people went to the marshes for some of their best food of the season. There they harvested the newly emerging culms, or stalks, of cattails. A long piece of rhizome was dug from the mud, and the new shoots broken from it. The leaves were peeled back, revealing a crisp, white stalk beneath. This was eaten fresh and tasted much like celery. "In addition to the new shoots, cattail rhizomes…were gathered in the spring and fall, being at their best in the fall. They were peeled and chewed when fresh, or dried for later use. If they were to be dried, the rhizomes were split into strips. The strips were placed in a greasewood fire, and…the roots were occasionally turned. Roasting helped them retain their flavor. Later they were put into baskets to finish the drying process. Dried pieces were ground into flour and made into mush by stone boiling in baskets. The mush was also formed into cakes that could be roasted in the coals. "In late May and June, when the cattails were beginning to send up green spikes that would later form into brown pollen and seed-bearing heads,…people gathered them for additional food types. The green spikes…were broken from the plants and eaten fresh…. "Another use was made of cattail spikes as the pollen-bearing elements began to mature in early July….Considerable quantities of yellow pollen could be obtained in a short time by bending the spikes and shaking or tapping them into a basket. The pollen was then mixed with water, kneaded, formed into cakes, and baked in the coals between layers of cattail leaves or in small leaf pouches. This provided a sweet bread or cake…which could be sacked and stored for later or eaten fresh at the time…. "Yet another use was made of cattails when the brown seed heads…matured. These were cut from the stalks and taken to an area where the earth had been dampened and packed into a hard, crusted surface. After warming the spikes in the sun, the cattail fluff was removed from the spikes and placed on the ground in a layer about two inches deep. This was set on fire and the mixture stirred until all the fluff was burned. Remaining on the hard-packed earth were thousands of tiny…seeds. These were gathered into a finely woven basketry tray, and the seed was winnowed by gently tossing it in the air during a light breeze. The toasted seeds that remained in the basket had a nut-like flavor. The seed could be further processed by grinding it into meal on a flat milling stone and then stone boiling it into mush. The dry meal could also be eaten with a little water without boiling" (Fowler 1990a:69-72).
bulrush (*Scirpus acutus,* *S. americanu, S.* *maritimus,* and *S.* *pungens*)	The Indians "ate the young shoots raw or cooked. When the bulrush was in flower they collected the pollen and mixed it with meal to make bread, mush, or pancakes. Later, the seeds were beaten off into baskets or pails, ground into a meal, and used in the same way as pollen. The scaly rootstocks, available at all seasons, were eaten either raw or cooked. They might also be dried and pounded into a kind of flour. Indians made a sweet syrup by bruising the rootstalks, boiling them for several hours, then pouring off the sweet liquid" (Ebeling 1986:34). The seeds of Scirpus maritimus (alkali bulrush) were "gathered in considerable quantity during the fall and early winter, when the seed dropped from the plant into the water. It accumulated in windrows along the shore and could be scooped up into…baskets and taken to camp. The seeds were put into baskets, parched with coals, and stored for later use in pits dug into the ground. As needed, the seed was ground into flour and made into mush. Another tule seed, that of the common three-square bulrush…, was also processed. But,…the seeds of this plant do not fall free and float on the water. The stalks were cut and returned to camp with seed heads attached. After drying, the tops were placed on a metate and the seeds worked out with a hand stone. The seeds were ground into flour and made into mush…" (Fowler 1990a:74).

Table 6.21 cont.

rushes (*Juncus balticus*, and *Eleocharis palustris*)	Seeds and roots collected and eaten, much as those of cattails. In addition, rush stems "were cut and soaked in water to remove the sweet sap. After several hours of soaking, the liquid was placed in pitch-covered basketry water jars and allowed to stand. It soon fermented and became slightly intoxicating" (Fowler 1990a:74).
common arrowhead (*Saggitaria latifolia*)	Tubers at the ends of rootstalks, about the size of hens' eggs, were cooked in pits.
pondweed or sago pondweed (*Potamogeton natans*)	"A perennial herb growing in fresh water and rising from rhizomes....The rhizomes are edible. Situated at the bottoms of ponds and streams, the rhizomes are somewhat inaccessible, but if the pond or stream dries up in late summer and autumn, they become much easier to harvest" (Ebeling 1986:33-34). "The women waded into the water and scooped them [the stalks] up with open-twined winnowing baskets. They were then returned to camp and boiled, eaten raw, or dried in the sun and sacked and stored for later use" (Fowler 1992:68).
pond lily (*Nymphaea polysepala*)	Seeds and roots were a staple food.
chufa fatsedge (*Cyperus esculentus*)	"It produces small, nut-like tubers attached to root hairs. In addition to digging these plants to obtain the tubers,...women often probed the ground with their digging sticks looking for the caches of these [roots] made by rodents. A small basket could often be filled with the produce from a single cache....the tubers dry well and are easily stored. They were often boiled to reconstitute them, and the milky liquid drunk along with the tubers" (Fowler 1992:69-70).
misc. additional seed-bearing aquatic plants	"Several [other] seed-producing plants grew along the water's edge or in the alkali flats immediately adjacent to Stillwater Marsh. Included were...curly dock (*Rumex maritimus*), pickleweed (*Allenrolfea occidentalis*), salt bush (*Atriplex argentea*), and seepweed (*Suaeda depressa*). Because all these produce a storable product and were quite common in the area, they were heavily collected..." [especially during the late fall months. The seeds were stored in bags or in underground pits, and] "ground into flour and made into small cakes that were baked in the ashes and could be carried on journeys or stored for later. [These were all] important winter foods" (Fowler 1992:69-70).

(Adapted from Barrett 1910; Ebeling 1986; Fowler 1990a, 1990b, 1992)

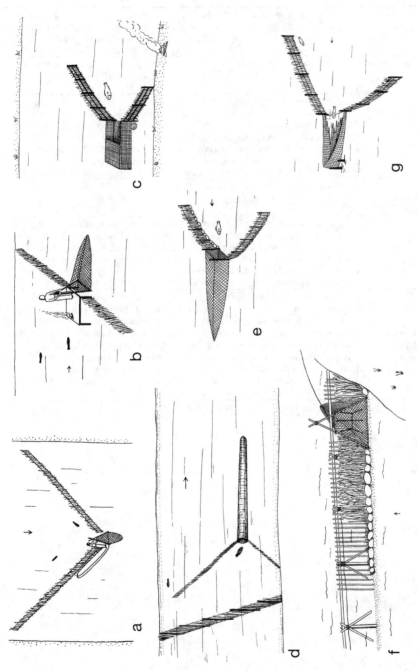

Figure 6.7. Weir fishing in the U.S. Great Basin, adapted from Kroeber and Barrett 1960 (original page and figure numbers as follows): *a*, p. 22, Fig. 4; *b*, p. 21, Fig. 2; *c*, p. 67, Fig. 24; *d*, p. 25, Fig. 10; *e*, p. 24, Fig. 7; *f*, p. 27, Fig. 12; *g*, p. 69, Fig. 27. Note that while most of these weirs are constructed of poles and brush, some have substantial stone weights along the bottom side of the weir.

Figure 6.7A. Reconstruction of a fishing weir in the Boston Back Bay (adapted from Décima and Dincauze 1998:171, Fig. 5).

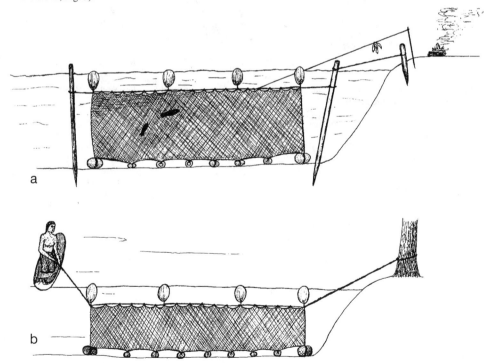

Figure 6.8. Large set nets, U.S. Great Basin, adapted from Kroeber and Barrett 1960 (original page and figure numbers as follows): *a*, p. 50, Fig. 18; *b*, p. 51, Fig. 20. Note stone sinkers along the bottom edges of nets, and wooden floats along the top.

Figure. 6.9. Portable nets used with canoes in the U.S. Great Basin, adapted from Kroeber and Barrett 1960 (original page and figure numbers as follows): *a*, p. 54, Fig. 21; *b*, p. 40, Fig. 15.

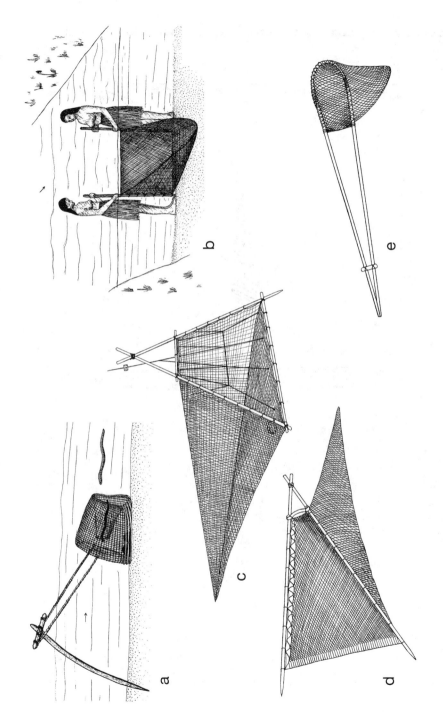

Figure 6.10. Portable nets used while afoot in the U.S. Great Basin, adapted from Kroeber and Barrett 1960 (original page and figure numbers as follows): *a*, p. 70, Fig. 30; *b*, p. 76, Fig. 36; *c*, p. 35, Fig. 13; *d*, p. 45, Fig. 17; *e*, p. 42, Fig. 16.

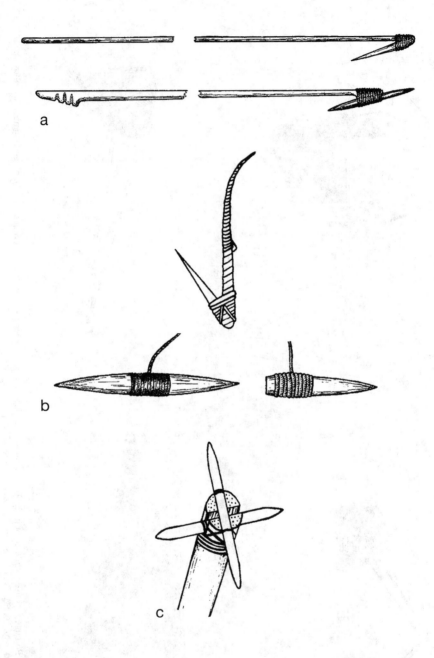

Figure 6.11. Fishing implements used in the U.S. Great Basin, adapted from Kroeber and Barrett 1960 (original page and figure numbers as follows): *a*, gaffs with bone points, p. 71, Fig. 31; *b*, bone fish hooks, p. 83, Figs. 38 (top) and 39 (bottom); *c*, blunt-headed arrow, with bone or wood pieces affixed to prevent piercing, p. 82, Fig. 37.

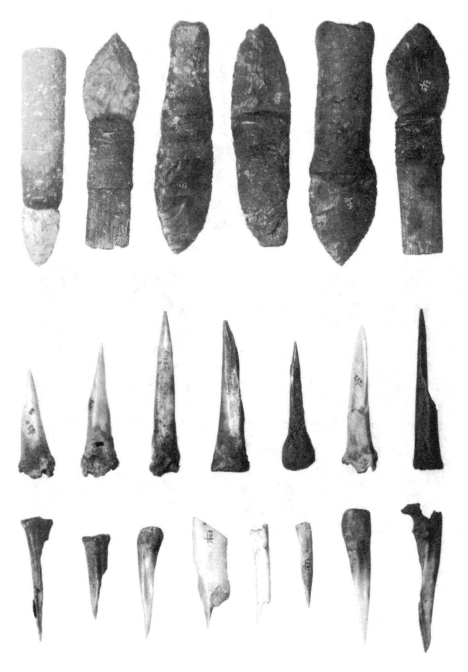

Plate 6.1. Fish butchering tools, U.S. Great Basin. *bottom two rows*, bone awls ("eel slitters"); *top row*, chert "fish knives" with wooden handles (adapted from Kroeber and Barrett 1960:196, Pl. 20).

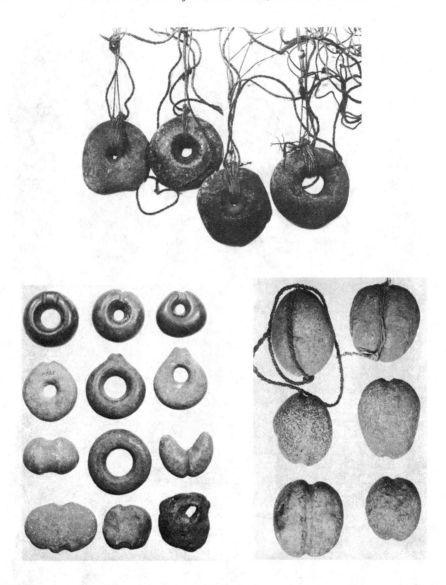

Plate 6.2. Ground stone net sinkers and "anchors," U.S. Great Basin (Kroeber and Barrett 1960:182, Pls. 5*a* and 6). These sinkers weigh 230-671 g apiece, and measure about 9-10 cm in diameter.

Plate 6.3. Reed boat in the Great Basin, 1958 (Fowler 1992:127, Fig. 79).

Plate 6.4. Using reed boat in the Great Basin, 1958 (Fowler 1992:128, Fig. 80).

plants. The seeds were first hulled, using a one-handed "sheller" and metate, and then the kernels were ground to a meal using the two-handed "grinder" (often termed a "mano") and a metate. Other seeds were hulled and ground with pestles in large basalt mortars:

> After the seeds have been hulled and the hulls winnowed out, the kernels are placed on a metate . . . to be ground into meal. The metate is usually oval in shape and was placed on a buckskin or, in more recent times, on a piece of canvas. The seeds were placed on the narrow end of the metate. . . . As the grinding proceeded the meal . . . is gradually driven by the rolling, pushing motion toward the opposite end of the metate . . . , the finished product falling upon the buckskin. [Loud and Harrington 1929:140]

In other cases, the mortar and pestle was used for hulling seeds:

> after the cat-tail seeds had been gathered and the "wool" burnt from them, . . . they were placed in a big mortar "2 feet high" [ca. 60 cm] and the largest sized pestles used in cracking the shells. Then the seeds were again subjected to heat and the shell separated, after which the meal was ground fine on a metate. A band of people, men, women, and children, could produce four or five sacks full of meal by a day's strenuous labor. Often meal from two or three kinds of seeds was mixed with it when it was cooked into porridge. [Loud and Harrington 1929:142]

Some Non-Food Uses of Aquatic Plants

There were two products of particular importance, both made from cattail and rush reeds: boats and houses.

Making and using reed boats (adapted from Barrett 1910; Fowler 1990a; Wheat 1967)

Reed boats were used primarily in two ways: (1) smaller vessels, typically measuring 2.6-3.6 m long, for maneuvering over the water during hunting and collecting activities by one or two persons; and (2) larger vessels, measuring up to 15 m long, for transporting household members and their possessions from one place of long-term residence to another over stretches of open water. During the nineteenth century, such large vessels were also sometimes used to transport war parties (Barrett 1910:256). When in use, reed boats lasted for about a year.

Boats were typically constructed from large bundles of bulrush reeds (usually *Scirpus acutus*) tied together with thick cords made of cattail reeds (*Typha latifolia*); the gunwales were also made of cattails. The rushes provided greater buoyancy, while the cattail ties and gunwales provided greater strength. The boats were usually assembled at the immediate edge of the marsh from which the reeds were cut and dried. Strong, mature reeds, measuring 2.4-3 m in length, were cut during the winter months and piled along the marsh edge, where they were soaked in water for about a half hour to toughen them. Two large bundles of rushes lashed together with cattail cords were used for the smaller boats. Bundles of cattail reeds were then lashed to the back and front of the boat, and additional bunches tied to the sides of the vessel "to keep the harvest of duck eggs, ducks, mudhens, fish, etc. from rolling off the boat . . ." (Wheat 1967:5) (Plates 6.3 and 6.4).

The small vessels were often used to carry gear and the harvested plants and animals during hunting and collecting expeditions in shallow water, while the harvester simply walked, pushing the vessel through the water. Larger boats were usually propelled with poles or paddles, often themselves made of reeds. Fowler (1990a:148) describes the use of a large vessel for both domestic transport and for hunting or fishing:

> This . . . boat, with prow and stern upturned, was used to ferry families across Tulare Lake each spring and fall as they changed campsites. It carried mortars, pestles, bushels of food, skins for bedding, and trade goods, as well as 8-10 persons. . . . Some report that a hole was cut in the middle of Yokuts boats and fishlines suspended through them. A fire for cooking and warming was built on the boat in an earthen hearth a few feet from the hole. Men might stay on such craft for as much as a week, fishing and taking waterfowl.

Making and using reed houses and windbreaks (adapted from Barrett 1910; Fowler 1990a, 1992; Wheat 1967)

Houses functioned for sleeping, storage, and cooking, and as locales for performing several other kinds of domestic activities. The house buildings were typically circular, dome-shaped, and windowless, constructed with a frame of flexible willow poles and a covering of rush and cattail matting. The average building diameter was 3-4.5 m for a structure that could accommodate 5-7 people. Sleeping space was typically in the rear of the house structure, and there was a cooking pit at the center, measuring about 60 cm in diameter and 15 cm deep, which also provided warmth during the cold winter months. The average life of such a house was five years, although that might be extended with adequate repair and maintenance. One of the main factors for abandoning a house locality was access to wood and brush fuel for cooking and heating: long-term occupation would simply exhaust the fuel supplies within reasonable walking or boating distance.

Fowler (1992:94) describes the interior of a typical domestic residence:

> Cooking, such as stone boiling stews and mushes, or roasting small game, might be done on . . . [the central cooking pit] fire, but food might also be prepared outside in a separate fire, perhaps one partly encircled by a brush windbreak. . . . Baskets were hung around the walls . . . from the interior cross members. A man's bow and quiver were stuck in back of a cross member near the door for handy access. A large, bipointed and pinyon-pitch covered basketry water jar was also near the door. . . . A pile of firewood was kept by the entrance as well.

In addition to the main residence,

> [s]emicircular brush windbreaks . . . were used as temporary summer shelters or as kitchens and extra sleeping quarters next to the cattail houses. . . . The brush was piled . . . about waist or shoulder high, and bedding and other camp equipment were placed along the wall on the interior side. Cattail reeds and grass might be scattered to serve as sitting or sleeping mats . . . usually [over an area] 15-25 feet [4.5-7.6 m] across, with a central fire pit. More roasting and cooking could be done here than inside the cattail house because of the size of the structure and its openness. [Fowler 1992:96]

The typical house required 10-15 large willow poles measuring 3-4.5 m long and 0.7-1.4 cm in diameter. Each of these large poles was set upright in a hole dug approximately 20-25 cm into the earth and spaced about 2 m apart around the circumference. A large number of smaller willow sticks would then be tied horizontally in three or four parallel rings at different heights around the circumference of the frame to reinforce it and to support the overlying mat coverings. Adequate spaces were left for a doorway on one side and a smoke-hole in the top. Upright poles were placed at either side of the doorway. The pieces of the frame were tied together with cords made of dried cattails or twisted lengths of sagebark.

Fowler (1990a:115-16) describes how the house frame was covered with cattail matting:

> Once the cattails were cut . . . they were stacked into piles about 3-4 feet [0.9-1.2 m] in diameter. The bundles were then bound with lengths of thick cordage, often made of shredded sagebrush bark. An additional length of thick cordage was tied to each bundle to form a tumpline so that the bundle could be carried on the back. . . .
> Each [cattail] mat required six willow poles about 5-6 feet [1.5-1.8 m] long, and it took 15-20 mats . . . to complete the house. To make each mat . . . , three poles were placed on the ground parallel to each other and roughly one foot [30 cm] apart. Two or more [of the cattail bundles] . . . were then placed across these, butt ends in the same direction, and loosely spread to about a 2-inch [4.4 cm] thickness. The three additional poles were then placed at

the same position as the three underneath, but on top of the cattails. Lengths of dampened and twisted sagebrush bark [or twisted cattail reeds] then joined the sets of poles at four or five intervals along their length so as to secure the cattails between. . . .

Beginning at the bottom of the house next to one of the door posts, cattail mats were secured by their cross members to the framework until an entire row was formed. . . . The mats were allowed to overlap slightly so that rain or melting snow could not leak in. . . . Each mat was tied to each of the house pole uprights and cross-bars wherever the poles and cross pieces intersected. The second tier of mats was added above this row, again slightly overlapping the lower-tier shingle-fashion. . . . In order to further secure the series of mat layers to the house frame, additional lengths of willow [sticks] were joined to one another to create rings that could be placed over the mats at intervals of from 1-2 feet [30-60 cm]. These were then also tied through the mat layers to the house frame underneath.

A separate reed mat was made to cover the door, and another to cover the top smoke-hole during bad weather. Finally, the doorway was topped by "an elongated bundle of cattails, about five feet [1.5 m] long and six inches [15 cm] thick, that was tied horizontally above the door opening. . . . Sometimes two additional bundles [of the same type] were added, one to each side [as additional reinforcements]" (Fowler 1990a:115) (Plates 6.5 and 6.6).

Much less substantial reed-mat and pole structures, either open-side or enclosed, were often constructed near the house to provide additional storage space, shade for outdoor activities (Plate 6.7), or for use as a sweathouse.

Less frequently, houses might be built without mats, by simply tying "small bundles [of reeds or grass] individually to the crossbars of the frame and then holding them in place with encircling bands of willow poles" (Fowler 1990a:123-24) (Plate 6.8).

The Seasonal Round

Aquatic resources were available year-round, although some species of plants and animals were most sought after seasonally. The highlights of seasonal variability are summarized in Table 6.22. Fishing was a year-round activity, as was the collection of many types of plants.

Kelly (2001) compiled a comprehensive list of return rates in kilocalories per hour of time expended in procurement and processing of aquatic and terrestrial food sources in the Great Basin (Table 6.23). These figures indicate that while these rates are generally lower for aquatic than for most terrestrial animal-food sources in this hunter-gatherer economy, aquatic resources had a comparably "efficient" rate of return relative to many terrestrial plant resources. What does not appear in these figures are the comparative dependability, abundance, and accessibility of aquatic plants and animals, and the fact that many of them can be easily and casually accessed close to the home base by women and children.

Plate 6.5. Example of smaller reed-mat hut in the Great Basin, ca. 1890 (Fowler 1992:93, Fig. 40).

Plate 6.6. Example of larger reed-mat hut in the Great Basin, ca. 1890 (Fowler 1992:34, Fig. 21).

Plate 6.7. Example of open-sided shelter for shade in the Great Basin, ca. 1890 (Fowler 1992:98, Fig. 46).

Plate 6.8. Example of small grass-covered hut in the Great Basin, 1958 (Fowler 1992:99, Fig. 47).

Table 6.22. The seasonal round of aquatic resource procurement in the Great Basin.

Month	Activities
January	Hunting waterfowl. Duck decoys set out. Manufacture of reed boats.
February	Hunting waterfowl. Duck decoys set out. Manufacture of reed boats.
March	Hunting waterfowl; collecting waterfowl eggs. Harvest of edible cattail stalks. Manufacture of reed boats.
April	Hunting waterfowl; collecting waterfowl eggs. Harvest of edible cattail stalks.
May	Hunting waterfowl; collecting waterfowl eggs. Collecting cattail seed spikes.
June	Harvest of cattail pollen, stalks, and seed spikes. Collecting waterfowl eggs.
July	Harvest of cattail pollen, stalks, and rhizomes. Collecting waterfowl eggs. Harvesting waterfowl hatchlings.
August	Drives of molting (flightless) waterfowl (esp. American coot). Harvesting waterfowl hatchlings.
September	Collection of insect pupae along lakeshore. Harvest of edible cattail seeds and rhizomes.
October	Collection of insect pupae along lakeshore. Harvest of edible cattail seeds and rhizomes.
November	Harvest of edible cattail seeds. Manufacture of reed boats. Grasshopper harvesting.
December	Harvest of edible cattail seeds. Manufacture of reed boats.

(Adapted from Ebeling 1986; Fowler 1990a, 1992; Heizer 1950; Wheat 1967) Non-seasonal resource procurement (e.g., fishing) is not included here.

Summary and Conclusions

Of the four different marshland groups examined in this chapter, the Great Basin offers the only example of a nonhierarchical, aceramic hunter-gatherer society. The others—in central Mexico, in the central Andes, and in the Near East—have been, for many centuries, economically much more specialized and embedded within larger, more centralized polities, with economies dominated by complementary agricultural or agricultural-pastoral production, and with the common use of pottery vessels for cooking, storage, and other functions. Nevertheless, detailed ethnographic studies of several Great Basin groups indicate many points of technological and organizational comparability with other parts of the world in the traditional procurement and preparation of aquatic resources. Furthermore, archaeological studies of prehistoric aquatic exploitation in the Great Basin are much more extensive than for any other part of the world that we are considering. This combination of detailed ethnography and detailed archaeology offers a unique opportunity to develop expectations about the archaeological manifestations of the ancient aquatic economy in the Valley of Mexico (see Chap. 7).

Table 6.23. Return rates of some Great Basin food resources.

Species	Common Name	Return Rate (kcal/hr)
Anabrus simplex	grasshopper	41,598-714,409
Odocoileus henuibys	deer	17,971-31,450
Ovis canadensis	bighorn sheep	17,971-31,450
Antilocapra americana	antelope	15,725-31,450
Lepus spp.	jackrabbit	13,475-15,400
Thomomys sp.	gopher	8983-10,780
Sylvilagus spp.	rabbit	8983-9800
Typha latifolia	**pollen, cattail**	**2750-9360**
Spermophlus spp.	squirrel	5390-6341
Citellus spp.	squirrel	2837-3593
Anas sp.	**waterfowl, ducks**	**1975-2709**
Quercus gambelli	seeds, gambrel oak	1488
Descurainia pinnata	seeds, tansymustard	1307
Pinus monophylla	seeds, pinon pine	841-1408+
Lewisia rediviva	roots, bitterroot	1237
Elymus salinas	seeds, salina wild rye	921-1238
Atriplex nuttaili	seeds, shadscale	1200
Atriplex confertifolia	seeds, shadscale	1033
Scirpus spp.	**seeds, bulrush**	**302-1699**
Echinocholoa crusgalli	seeds, barnyard grass	702
Lepidium fremontii	seeds, peppergrass	537
Helianthus annus	seeds, sunflower	467-504
Poa spp.	seeds, bluegrass	418-491
Elymus salinas	seeds, wild rye	266-473
Oyzopsis hymenoides	seeds, ricegrass	301-392
Phalaris arundinacea	seeds, reed canary grass	261-321
Muhlenbergia asperifolia	seeds, scratchgrass	162-294
Hordeum jubatum	seeds, foxtail barley	138-273
Carex spp.	**seeds, sedge**	**202**
Typha latifolia	**roots, cattail**	**128-267 ("over 5000 kcal/hr if gathered in winter and processed by boiling")**
Scirpus spp.	**roots, bulrush**	**160-257**
Distichlis stricta	**seeds, saltgrass**	**146-160**
Allenrolfea occidentalis	**seeds, pickleweed**	**90-150**
Sitanion hystrix	seeds, squirreltail grass	91
Gila bicolor	**minnow (with nets)**	**750-7514**

(Source: Kelly 2001:41, Table 3-2)
Aquatic items are in bold face.

The highlights of the ethnographically described aquatic economies of indigenous Great Basin societies can be summarized:

(1) The resources involved. These include a wide variety of aquatic plants and animals utilized both as food and as raw material for making clothing, mats, baskets, houses, and boats. In these nonagricultural societies, many kinds of seeds, roots, rhizomes, and stalks of aquatic plants were intensively collected for food, as were several types of fish, waterfowl, and aquatic insects. Several kinds of reeds were used to build houses; make boats; make mats, baskets, bags, and some articles of clothing; and to construct fish weirs. Although some resources were most available during certain seasons of the year, some aquatic plants and animals were available and used year-round. The diversity and variety of these aquatic resources provided adequate calories and nutrients with

reasonable expenditures of energy for hunting, collecting, and processing. With their abundance of aquatic resources, these marshlands contained the richest source of food and raw materials within this very arid region. Consequently, over the millennia it was to these marshlands that indigenous people tended to concentrate, and with the highest degree of permanence within the Great Basin as a whole.

(2) The technology and organization of aquatic resource procurement. Hunting and collecting activities were both individual and group-based, and were undertaken both afoot, on solid ground along the marsh peripheries or in shallow water, and in reed boats in deeper waters. Relatively large reed boats were also used to move households and their belongings from one place of residence to another (and, in earlier times, to transport raiding parties). Nets (both large, rectangular nets, and small dip nets, usually made of string or twine, but sometimes made of basketry), arrows, spears, clubs, weirs, hooks and lines with their wood or reed flotation devices, and spearing platforms were all employed for hunting waterfowl and fish; masses of aquatic insects were collected in shallow water with basket scoops. Netting often involved the use of stone net-sinkers. Fishhooks were made of one or two sharp pieces of bone affixed to a small piece of wood. Small reed bags were used to gather and transport waterfowl eggs. Bows and arrows with ringed points were used for hunting some types of waterfowl and fish.

Group cooperation was particularly predominant for weir-based fishing, where groups of men in boats would frighten schools of fish along weirs (submerged fences made of reeds and other aquatic vegetation) toward net or basket traps, or where large numbers of flightless waterfowl were driven by groups of men in boats from their feeding or nesting grounds into nets emplaced along the shore where other people secured and killed the birds. Fishing and hunting techniques often required expert knowledge of animal behavior—for example, how and in what direction fish and birds purposively frightened by hunters, or simply moving about on their own, would move, so that traps, snares, and nets could be properly placed. Another particularly ingenious mechanism was the deliberate placement of white stones on the bottom of ponds or rivers to provide backdrops against which swimming fish were particularly visible to fishers armed with spears standing atop adjacent platforms.

Stone and metal (after Euro-American contact) knives were used to cut reeds, usually in areas near the shore where they were dried for making mats, boats, and so on.

(3) The technology and organization of aquatic resource processing. As far as I can determine, once they were acquired, many aquatic plants and animals were brought back to the primary residence for processing. The main exceptions seem to have been the initial butchering of waterfowl and fish, the drying of reeds, and the fabrication of reed boats, all of which usually took place on a piece of solid ground nearest to where the animals and plants were harvested. The final stages of butchering, plus drying, cooking, and storage of fish and waterfowl, were carried out at the places of permanent residence. Butchering of fish and waterfowl was primarily done with stone and metal knives or with sharp bone awls. Insects were simply bagged up along the shore and carried to the permanent camps for drying and storage. Drying was usually on pole frames or on reed mats. Cooking of fish, waterfowl, and some types of insects was carried out in rock-lined

pits. Long-term storage was typically in grass-lined pits, with the foods encased in mud or buckskin bags.

Dried seeds, fish, and insects were usually ground into a flour with ground stone mortars, pestles, manos, and metates. Many foods were eaten in the form of soups, incorporating one or more types of dried food ground into flour, prepared by stone boiling in water-tight baskets.

(4) The settlement pattern. Substantial reed huts dispersed on patches of solid ground throughout the marshlands served as relatively permanent residences. These buildings functioned for sleeping, heating in winter, some cooking, some storage, and some craft activities. Typically, each principal residence would be accompanied by a cluster of subsidiary structures: roofless windbreaks for summertime sleeping and cooking, open-sided sun shades, storage, and sweat-baths. A variety of food processing activities also took place near the main residence. There is little mention of temporary encampments at any considerable distances from the main residence, although large reed boats occasionally served for cooking and sleeping by parties of men engaged in hunting or fishing for several days at a time at some distance from home.

The Titicaca Basin, Southern Peru and Bolivia

Lake Titicaca is a freshwater body, far larger (with a surface area of ca. 8165 km^2) and much deeper (up to 280 m, with an average depth of 109 m [Kolata 1996:26]) than Lake Texcoco, and situated at a much higher elevation above sea level (the water surface is at ca. 3810 m asl). Relative to Lake Texcoco, which has a broad, nearly level lakeshore plain around much of its perimeter, a higher proportion of the Lake Titicaca shoreline rises more quickly to adjacent higher ground, resulting in a generally closer juxtaposition of the lakeshore marshes and large areas of well-drained cultivable land than in the Valley of Mexico. Because it has an external outlet, the water in Lake Titicaca is fresh. Nevertheless, the Titicaca lakeshore zone comprises thousands of hectares of marsh interspersed with shallow open water—an ideal habitat for waterfowl, fish, amphibians, crustaceans, aquatic insects, reptiles, and a variety of aquatic plants, including algae. Levieil (1989:166) estimates that about 13.3% (1086 km^2) of the total surface area of Lake Titicaca comprises marshland with thick stands of macrophyte aquatic vegetation. This aquatic environment closely resembles that of the Valley of Mexico. Interestingly, there is some indication that "the colonization and spread of the most useful and abundant aquatic plant, totora [*Schoenoplectus totora*, or *Scirpus totora*] may have been anthropogenic," caused by the "planting and transplanting by local shore dwelling humans" over the past 3000 years (Kolata 1996:41).

As in the Valley of Mexico, much of the poorly drained land in the Titicaca Basin was converted to agricultural production in prehispanic times by extensive drainage and ridging projects that created thousands of hectares of chinampa-like raised fields (Erickson 1988; Kolata 1996). A highly seasonal average annual rainfall of 687 ± 138 mm (Kolata 1996:26) is quite comparable to that of the Valley of Mexico. A major ecological difference between the two regions in precolumbian times, of course, was the huge potential for camelid pastoralism that existed in the Titicaca Basin—large herds of domestic camelids pastured on the vast grasslands that surrounded the lake (Dedenbach-Salazar 1990; Murra 1965; Webster 1993). Such a major complement to plant cultivation simply did not exist in prehispanic Mesoamerica.

Due to its huge water mass, Lake Titicaca produces a very significant climatic ame-lioration affect around its immediate shoreline. Lakeshore meteorological stations report an average of 320 frost-free days, whereas stations only a few kilometers distant from the lake average only 150 frost-free days (Vacher et al. 1992:511-14). Given the high elevation, this number of frost-free days is remarkable. Vacher et al. (1992:515-16) also note that lakeshore soils offer many advantages for plant growth: relative to nearby inland soils, in lakeshore soils the

> texture is finer, the organic, total nitrogen and potassium contents are twice as high and assimilable phosphorus is five times higher. . . . In the areas closest to the lake shores [un-der the 3860-meter contour], the soil is always wet since the water table lies at a depth of only 30-50 cms. . . . The presence of abundant soil water allows for fast plant growth and germination, even during drought.

These climatic characteristics offer such a unique combination of high agricultural, pastoral, and hunting-collecting productivity that the modern population density in the lakeshore zone is over three times (100 inhabitants/km²) that of nearby areas away from the lakeshore (30/km²) (Vacher et al. 1992:511). Although maize seldom attains high levels of productivity at altitudes above approximately 3000 m asl, ethnographic studies by Sergio Chavez (1999) have revealed that the productivity of modern maize cultivation in the Lake Titicaca lakeshore zone is on par with the highest known levels attained by traditional agricultural practices anywhere in the world.

The marshes and lacustrine zones of Lake Titicaca support a rich assemblage of aquatic flora and fauna that for millennia has been exploited by humans as food and raw materi-als (Browman 1981, 1989). Ethnographers and historians have described the indigenous lakeshore Aymara and Uru-Chipaya communities who focus heavily on marsh and lake resources (e.g., Camacho 1943; Fain 1955; Horn 1984; Ibarra 1962; LaBarre 1941, 1946, 1948, 1951; Levieil and Orlove 1992; Manelis de Klein 1973; Metraux 1935; Ogilvie 1922; Orlove 2002; Palavecino 1949; Posnansky 1932; Tschopik 1946; Vellard 1952, 1992; Wachtel 1986). Most aquatic fauna (including waterfowl eggs) are exploited as food sources by these groups. The indigenous uses of aquatic reeds and rushes are es-pecially varied. The stalks, rhizomes and tuberous roots are used for food as well as for construction (boats, and house walls and roofs), in handicrafts (fans, mats, mattresses, basketry, rope and twine), and as agricultural fertilizer and household fuel.

Some of these same resources continue to be important for modern commercial enterprises, especially fishing (of both native and introduced species) and cattle raising (several types of aquatic plants are harvested in huge quantities for cattle feed) (Leviel et al. 1989; Leviel and Orlove 1990). Vacher et al. (1992:518) estimate that today there is an average annual production of aquatic vegetation for animal fodder of 8 metric tons (dry weight) per hectare of marshland. Using the above-cited figure of 1086 km² (108,600 hectares) as the total marshland zone of Lake Titicaca in which such aquatic plants could potentially be harvested, this might translate to an overall potential productivity of some 869,000 metric tons per year. Such plant material would probably have been suitable for camelid fodder in precolumbian times prior to the introduction of European cattle (Browman 1989:150).

In marked contrast to the Valley of Mexico, I have found few references to the direct human utilization of aquatic insects or other invertebrates from Lake Titicaca, although Park (2001:41, 50) reports modest quantities of aquatic invertebrate remains in archaeological deposits from the lakeshore Formative-period site of Iwawi. The only ethnographic description known to me comes from Posnansky (1932:261):

> *[English translation]* they collect in great quantity . . . tiny transparent shrimp from 2-10 mm in length (*Hidalela palida, robusta*, etc.) that live at the base of the reed roots. They also toast them to make a very nutritious food. . . .

The apparent very secondary significance of aquatic insects and other invertebrates as sources of human food in the Titicaca Basin may relate to the well-developed pastoral economy in that region, in both ancient and modern times. Unlike prehispanic Mesoamerica, domestic camelids (plus cattle and sheep since the mid-sixteenth century) have long supplied much animal protein to inhabitants throughout the region (Orlove 2002; Webster and Janusek 2003). Nevertheless, fish and waterfowl bones have been reported in some abundance from archaeological sites around the shoreline of Lake Titicaca (Capriles 2003; Moore et al. 1999; Park 2001:45-49; Webster 1993:88; Wise 1993). Like the Marsh Arabs (see next section of this chapter), some aquatic resources were thoroughly integrated into the traditional indigenous economy of the Titicaca Basin, despite the importance of well-developed pastoralism.

Traditional Uru Occupation

Sixteenth- and seventeenth-century sources

The numerous historic-period references to the lacustrine-adapted Uru and their ethnic relatives, from the Titicaca Basin southward across the poorly drained highlands of western Bolivia, have been noted by Browman (1981, 1989), Crequi-Montfort and Rivet (1927), Heiser (1978), Palavecino (1949), Posnansky (1932), and Wachtel (1986). These Colonial-period and nineteenth-century documentary sources typically regarded the Uru as both unusual and potentially dangerous—unusual because of their aquatic economy, and potentially dangerous because of the difficulty authorities had in controlling these unruly populations dispersed in trackless swamps.

Writing in 1597, Balthazar Ramírez (cited in Palavecino 1949:70-71) offers a clear picture of Uru settlement some four centuries ago:

> estos hazen sus casas en el agua sobre unas balsas de heno o enea. . . . estas balsas con el tiempo crían por lo bajo sus raíces, y se entrapan y texen de manera que se convierten en

céspedes, y así, echandoles alguna tierra encima, siembran en ellas algunas cosillas que co-men. Mantiénense del pescado de las lagunas ques muncho, aunque no muy bueno; y estas casas son algunas vezes de treinta y quarenta vezinos, más o menos . . . ; llévalas y traelas el viento de un cabo a otro.

[English translation] these people make their homes on the water atop reed rafts. . . . in time these rafts send out roots from their undersides, and these intermingle to create thick mats of vegetation that are converted into agricultural plots by placing a layer of earth on top. They support themselves by catching the lake fish which, although abundant, are not of good quality; and these house lots measure from 30 to 40 meters [long], more or less . . . ; the wind moves them from place to place.

At about that same time, Jorge Acosta (cited in Crequi-Montfort and Rivet 1927:96) noted the importance of aquatic reeds for the Uru people:

Cría . . . gran copia de un género de junco, que llaman los Indios Tótora, de la qual se sirven para mil cosas, porque es comida para puercos, y para caballo, y para los mismos hombres; y de ella hacen casa, y fuego, y barco, y quanto es menester. . . .

[English translation] They raise . . . great quantities of reed, which the Indians call "Tótora," which they use for a thousand things, as food for pigs and horses, and for the people them-selves; and from the reeds they make houses, fire, boats, and whatever else they need. . . .

Another Colonial-period writer, Calancha (cited in Crequi-Montfort and Rivet 1927:97), observed the Uru lacustrine mode of life, their settlement on buoyant platforms made of marsh reeds, and their use of reeds as food:

quando viven en la laguna, son sus casas sobre barbacoas y enea; . . . los Indios Uros nacen, se crían y viven en esta laguna sobre el agua en la enea, que aca llaman totorales, son muy espesos, y deste genero de juncos livianos, aqui abitan sin mas ropa ni cubierta (con ser tierra muy fria) que unas esteras desta enea. . . . comen muchas vezes la carne cruda, y el pescado casi vivo, y las raizes desta totora o enea. No siembran ni tienen labranças, porque la tierra es fria, y por ser tan llano y sin serranias baten los vientos. . . .

[English translation] when they live in the lake their houses are built atop reed platforms; the Uru Indians are born and live in this lake, on floating reed islands that are here called "totorales," and that are very thick and made from living reeds, and here they dwell without any other clothing or covering (in this very cold land) than these reed mats. . . . they often eat raw meat and fish that are half-alive, and the roots of the reeds themselves. Because of the cold, flat, windswept terrain, they do not plant crops and have no agricultural fields. . . .

Writing at the beginning of the seventeenth century, Antonio Herrera (cited in Crequi-Montfort and Rivet 1927:96) observed that

Tiene esta laguna [de Titicaca] de largo treynta y cinco leguas, y quinze de ancho, cria gran copia de vn junco que llaman Totora, que es comida para cauallos [caballos] y puerecos, y les Indios Vros [Urus] hazen dello, casa, comida, y barcos, y quanto han menester. . . . En la laguna se hallaron pueblos enteros destos, que morauan en ella en balsas de Totora atadas a vn peñasco, y quando querian, se mudaua todo el pueblo a otra parte. . . .

[English translation] In this lake [Titicaca] measuring 35 leagues long and 15 wide, there is a great quantity of reeds that they call Totora, which is eaten by horses and pigs, and the Indians make from these reeds houses, food, boats, and whatever else they need. . . . Entire villages of this sort are found on the lake, and here the people live on rafts made of Totora that are tied to rocks, and when they wish they move the entire village to some other place. . . .

Crequi-Montfort and Rivet (1927:100-101) also cite several late sixteenth-century descriptions of the Uru from the *Relaciónes Geográficas*. In one, the Uru were characterized as

gente de poca reputación, á causa de no ser hábiles para el trabajo ni para sembrar, ni tuvieron en su principio pueblos ni concierto en su vivir, ni tenian caciques que les mandasen, sino que cada uno vivia á su voluntad y se sustentaban de lo que pescaban y de las raices de *matara*, ques como junco de España y más grueso; y cuando los ingas vinieron conquistando esta provincia . . . hicieron salir á estos indios Uros de junto al agua y les hicieron vivir con los Aymaraes se les enseñaron á arar y cultivar la tierra, y les mandarin que pagasen de tribute pescado y hiciesen petacas de paja. . . . El modo de pescar destos Uros es una basla de enea, ques el junco, con redes de paja. . . .

[English translation] people of low repute, because they are neither good workers or planters, and even in their principal villages they lack ordered lives, without leaders who command them, and each person does as he pleases and supports himself by fishing and collecting the roots of aquatic plants similar to the reeds of Spain, but thicker, and when the Incas conquered this province . . . they forced the Uru Indians to leave the marshes and live with the Aymaras and learn to plow and cultivate the land, and they commanded them to pay tribute in fish and to make reed containers. . . . For fishing, these Uru use reed rafts with nets made of grass. . . .

Several other observers in the *Relaciones Geográficas* continued in a similar vein (Crequi-Montfort 1927:100-101):

Están en las orillas de esta laguna [de Titicaca] las más poblaciones de indios que hay en el Collao, los cuales llaman indios Uros, gente inútil y ociosa por no querer más que el pescado y aves de la laguna, y la totora que es la raiz de unos juncos que cría la laguna en sus riberas como palmitos, Buenos para comer, . . .
Los indios vros [Urus], son pescadores biven ordinariamente en la gran laguna de Chucuito y en otras, no siembran, ni se mantienen sino de lo que pescan y aves que matan en la laguna, y de totora, que es la rraiz de espadañas que se cría en la laguna. . . .
. . . los vros [Urus] son pescadores que estan poblados al rrededor de la laguna—y estos son maestros de hazer rropa de la tierra y petacas—y esteras y chucos—que son bonetes. . . .
Vros [Urus], la mas bestial gente que el Piru tiene, pues sus casas pegadas à la laguna . . . [de Titicaca], son menos que chozas, ò tugurios, y se sustentan de la rayz de la juncia, que el agua cria como animals inmundos; y algunos viué sobre la misma agua, un vnos como grandes Cespedones, huecos y porosos, que (de la maletía de la laguna y algunoas rayzes que se juntan) se congelan. De manera que el agua facilmente los trae y menea de vna parte a otra. . . .

[English translation] There are on the shores of this lake [Titicaca] the greatest number of Indian communities in Collao, and these are called Urus, useless and lazy people who wish

for nothing other than to fish and hunt lake birds, and to collect totora, the edible roots of reeds that grow like palm trees along the edges of the lake. . . .

The Uru Indians are fishermen who usually live on the big lake at Chucuito and elsewhere, and they do not plant crops but maintain themselves exclusively by fishing and hunting waterfowl, and from the totora, which are the roots of the plants that grow in the lake. . . .

The Urus are fishermen who live around the lake — and they are skilled in making useful clothing and containers from native plants. . . . The Urus are the most bestial people in Peru, living like dirty animals in their houses on the surface of the lake [Titicaca] which are nothing more than huts built atop the roots of aquatic plants; and some live right on the water on great reed rafts, hollow and damp, that have been collected and fixed together. In this manner they easily move around from one place to another on the water. . . .

Nineteenth- and early twentieth-century sources

Travelling through the region in the 1860s, George Squier (1877:309-10) noted that

[a]fter a course of a few miles it (the Rio Desaguadero) [at the southern end of Lake Titicaca] spreads out in a series of shallow lakes or marshes (*totorales*) full of reeds, fish, and waterfowls, in which the remnants of a wild Indian tribe, the Uros, have their abodes. They live on floats or rafts of totora and, it is alleged, subsist on fish and game, cultivating only a few bitter potatoes and ocas in the recesses of the Sierra de Tiahuanaco.

In 1884, Modesto Basadre (cited in Crequi-Montfort and Rivet 1927:102) noted that

[English translation] The Urus have lived, and continue to live, on very large reed rafts, upon which they are sheltered by huts made of *chaclla* reed arches covered with reed matting. The *chaclla* is a thin reed that grows in abundance in sheltered places around the lake, with a yellow flower and seed pods similar to those of the Algarrobo. A primitive oven made of clay serves as a kitchen: the food consists of abundant lake fish, and innumerable waterfowl, and some potatoes and *quinoa* that they obtain in trade from neighboring outsiders. . . .

A decade later, the same author (cited again in Crequi-Montfort and Rivet 1927:103-4) added that

[English translation] The totora reeds, which grow abundantly along these lakes, provide the material necessary for building houses and the rafts upon which they live and to make their boats; and whose roots comprise their food. Usually they go in their boats along the lakeshore; but sometimes, on pleasant days with favorable winds, they sail their boats out to the center of the lake. . . .

The Urus take a great many fish to the market in Puno.

In 1916, Cecil Gosling (cited in Crequi-Montfort and Rivet 1927:105-6) observed that among the Uru

The houses . . . were constructed with a species of "adobe" or sun dried peat and thatched with totora reeds which grow in abundance in the river. These reeds are also used in the construction of the "balsas" or canoes with which they navigate the rivers in their fishing and egg hunting expeditions. These boats are fashioned by binding rolls of the totora together.

Plate 6.9. Uru reed house on Lake Titicaca (© José Miguel Helfer, Quality Postcards, Lima).

. . . Some of them have sails which are also made of the Totora reeds and these frequently travel long distances bartering eggs and fish at the neighboring hamlets. . . .

The poles used for propelling the "balsa" are from 12 to 15 feet [3.6-4.5 m] long. . . . They usually have two prongs at the end, these being spliced on with twine made from some local aquatic plant. . . . these poles are used . . . as a means of propelling the canoes, as a mast when sailing, as a fish spear, and also for the purpose of killing wild fowl when sitting on their nests or within reach. . . .

Their food consists almost entirely of fish and eggs, and they told me that of all waterfowl they preferred the flamingo. . . . This is presumably because of the fat this bird contains.

The Uros consume a considerable amount of coca especially when pushing their canoes through the reeds, which is hard work; they also frequently eat the white shoots of the totora reed growing under water, the taste of which though insipid is not disagreeable. . . .

Their willingness to go into very cold water often up to their waists in search of a wounded bird, and voluntarily to remain in it for some time, without apparent discomfort, attracted my attention as being so opposed to the habits of the [neighboring] Aymara Indians.

The distinctive traditional Uru dwellings, with their walls and roofs formed of bunches of reeds overlain by reed mats (Plates 6.9 and 6.10), are very similar to those described for the indigenous inhabitants of the U.S. Great Basin and the Marsh Arabs of southern Iraq (see other sections of this chapter).

According to Levieil and Orlove (1992), the floating platforms that support Uru settlements are comprised primarily of *kille*, a buoyant substance that forms naturally in

Plate 6.10. Example of an Uru reed house on Lake Titicaca, showing domestic pottery in detached cooking area (©José Miguel Helfer, Quality Postcards, Lima).

the dense lakeshore marshes (this may be the "sun dried peat" referred to by C. Gosling [above] as a component of some Uru houses):

> The mixture of mud, rhizomes and decaying organic matter forms the "kille" or "quilli," with properties similar to that of a sponge. When it is dry it is very light and floats. The floating islands of the Urus are made of great chunks of *kille* which the inhabitants have gathered together and to which they continue to add small pieces. Periodically they throw *totora amarillo* [dried reeds] onto the *kille* so that its surface remains dry. Small *killes* carried away by the wind are hauled by fishermen to their portion of the shoreline, cut into pieces, and used as fertilizer [in agricultural fields]. [Levieil and Orlove 1992:510]

Aquatic Plants—Availability, Procurement, and Use

A wide variety of aquatic plants are used by modern people inhabiting the Lake Titicaca shoreline (Table 6.24). It is not always possible to make precise species identifications of local terms mentioned in historic and ethnographic sources. It appears that the local term *totora* is a generic term for "reed," and includes both *Scirpus* sp. and *Juncus* sp.

Table 6.24. Aquatic plants used in the Titicaca Basin.

Local Terms	Species Identification	Present Uses
llachu, llacho, lakkho, laqo	**Vascular plants:** *Elodea potamogeton, Myriophyllum elatinoides, Potamogeton strictus, Potamogeton pectinatus, Azolla* sp., *Nyriophyllum* sp.	Livestock fodder, handicrafts, cooking fuel. Some parts used as human food.
totora	*Juncus* sp.	Livestock fodder, handicrafts, cooking fuel, construction. Some parts used as human food.
totora verde	*Scirpus* sp. (immature)	The roots and rhizomes (sacca, siphi), and bases of green stalks (chullo) are eaten by humans.
totora amarillo	*Scirpus* sp. (mature)	Construction, handicrafts, fuel.
lima (also chanku, chinka, ch'inqui); lawa (also lank'u or sawsi); cochayuyu (also llalucha, llulluca, chushury, murmunta, urupasha, ururupamacho, upoopoo)	**Algae:** *Chara* spp. (algal stonewort, Charophyceae family); *Cladophora* spp. (green algae, Chlorophyceae family); *Nostoc* spp. (blue-green algae, Cyanophyceae family)	Livestock fodder and human food.

(Adapted from Browman 1981, 1989; Heiser 1978; Horn 1984; Levieil et al. 1989; Levieil and Orlove 1992; Orlove 2002)

Harvesting and transplanting techniques

Truly prodigious quantities of aquatic reeds are harvested today from some sectors of the lakeshore zone, mostly for use as cattle feed and for the manufacture of mats. For example, Levieil et al. (1989:171) note that some 50,000 metric tons were harvested annually from Puno Bay (a relatively small region in the northwestern corner of the lake) in the early 1980s. Indigenous communities accounted for about 2000 metric tons of this quantity (Levieil and Orlove 1992:509).

Harvesting procedures are simple, with different tools and techniques employed for shallow versus deeper water. The peak reed-harvest time is between March and June, during the late rainy season and early part of the dry season. In shallow waters the

[s]horedwellers . . . gather the *llachu* by hand with a sickle or other sharp instrument, wading into the water up to their waists. . . . [Levieil and Orlove 1992:505-6]

In deeper waters,

The main tool for harvesting is a . . . long pole to which a knife has been tied at one end. A villager can use the knifeless end to push a boat or raft through the channels out to a plot of reeds. Standing at one end, with feet firmly planted, he or she . . . inverts the pole, which now serves as a scythe. The villager thrusts it into the water and swings it to slice off several reeds. These actions require some strength, considerable coordination, and a good sense of balance. Moreover, they must be performed rapidly, or else the blade will just push the reeds,

Plate 6.11. Towing bundles of harvested reeds on Lake Titicaca (LaBarre 1946: Pl. 115, bottom).

rather than cut them. For the sweep of the blade to cut a number of reeds, the lower hand on the pole must describe a slightly larger curve than the upper. An experienced cutter also puts some strength of the back and abdominal muscles into the operation by rotating the shoulders and twisting the waist. The lower body plays a part as well: at the same moment that the cutter swings the scythe, he or she must bend the knees . . . in order to compensate for the tendency of the sudden jerk of the heavy tool to make the balsa [reed boat] rock excessively. This work requires not only strength and skill but also patience, since the cutter must repeat the motions again and again, stopping only to retrieve the felled reeds that float on the surface and to propel the balsa through the water to a new spot. [Orlove 2002:179-80]

Totora is harvested much as is *llachu*, taking care never to cut more than 50 cm below the water surface. Cut in this fashion, the stalk will regrow to its former height (averaging 3.8 m) in about a year. Once the reeds are cut,

the totora can be piled up in the harvester's craft or simply on the surface of the water (due to its natural buoyancy) in rafts [formed of the reeds themselves tied together in large masses, or *marayas*] [Plate 6.11]. *Marayas* of 400 *pichus* [individual bundles] (about 5 metric tonnes of totora verde) have been observed sailing over distances of more than 20 kilometers. To transport the totora over greater distances (up to 50 kilometers) . . . [they] use wooden sailing boats about 10 m long, able to carry ca. 150 *pichus*, and which are faster and easier to handle than the *marayas*. . . . [Levieil and Orlove 1992:506]

Totora beds are often replanted after harvest, and natural reseeding is actively encouraged:

> When seeds transported by wind or water reach the shoreline, wave action makes it easier for them to penetrate the earth and mix in with the decaying organic waste. [Levieil and Orlove 1992:507-8]

Orlove (2002:176) describes how reed replanting is done artificially:

> the villagers pole their balsas into areas where the totora is densest. They pull entire plants from the muck at the bottom of the lake, making sure to get a significant mass of roots and rhizomes, and poke around the base of plants that do not come out easily, in order to loosen them. When they have enough plants, the villagers carry them to the planting zones. They wade into the water and use spades to open up spots in which they root the plants. If they wish to plant in water too deep to stand in, they go out in balsas. Once they reach the zone of appropriate depth, they use poles to push the clumps of roots and rhizomes into the lake bottom, or drop into the water clumps that are weighted down with stones.

Food preparation techniques

Parts of many aquatic plants are still consumed, and there are numerous references, extending back to the sixteenth century, to their use as food. Fragmentary archaeological evidence hints at a much longer time depth (Browman 1981:107-8, 1989:150, 157-59; Orlove 2002:132). Heiser (1978:228) observes that one sixteenth-century writer (Cobo 1890)

> informs us that in the area of Lake Titicaca the roots of the totora, which are white and tender, serve as bread for the Indians and are sold in the plazas of their pueblos. Today one may still find the "roots" of the totora sold in . . . Puno . . . [although] it was only the stems that I observed being sold. The culms are pulled from the water and break from the rhizome, and the basal part (20-30 cms long) is eaten raw after the outer layers are peeled away.

Similarly, Browman (1981:107) notes that

> [t]he spongy, white, moist pith of the totora stem is eaten frequently. . . . during low water periods, the rhizomes and tubers of the totora are dug up, and the sweet-tasting starch is highly prized. The *Juncus* spp. plants are similarly utilized.

Some edible aquatic plants were dried so that they could be stored and traded. According to Browman (1981:108-9),

> frequent reference to trade in *cochayuyo* is found in early *visitas* [Colonial documents]. *Cochayuyo* in dried blocks is still traded by remnant llama caravans. Casaverde Rojas (1977:175, 181) identifies *cochayuyo* carried by the Cailloma caravans as being of two varieties of algae and water plants, one collected by the herders from the *bofedales* [marshes] of the punas, and the other coming up from the Pacific coast. . . .

Plate 6.12. Making a reed boat on shore of Lake Titicaca (Tschopik 1946: Pl. 107, bottom).

Nutritional importance

Citing Boyd's (1968) studies of North American specimens of *Scirpus, Juncus, Myrio-phyllum, Potamogeton, Elodea,* and *Chara,* Browman (1981:107-9) finds that

> these aquatic plants are excellent sources of protein, with values ranging from 10-25% [7-8% in the case of *Scirpus* and *Juncus*]. Micronutrients (particularly iron and manganese) in aquatic plants generally exceed levels found in the terrestrial cultigens. *Chara* and *Elodea* are the best protein sources, with 17-21% crude protein and only 0.4-0.8% tannin. *Potamogeton* and *Myriophyllum,* as they mature, have increasing amounts of tannin, up to 7-12%. Tannin interferes with protein digestibility if the concentration surpasses 6-7%. Tannin increases with plant age, while protein content decreases; the amount of available protein is therefore inversely proportional to the age of the aquatic plant.

Construction of reed boats (balsas), mats, and basketry

Orlove (2002:180-81) and Palavecino (1949:77) describe how reed boats (*balsas*) are made. After the totora reeds are cut, they are rafted to a suitable drying place. Here the dried piles are formed into bundles measuring 4-6 m long. Thick wooden hooks and wooden-handled stone hammers are used to compact the reeds and pack them tightly together within their enveloping cords (Metraux 1935: Fig. 24; Orlove 2002:181; Pala-vecino 1949: Lamina XII). The tightly wrapped bundles are fastened together in pairs (Plate 6.12) to make a small craft capable of carrying two people. The wrapping cords are usually made from fibrous grasses (*Stipa ichu*, *Festucha orthophylla*, *Festucha dissiflora*) obtained from nearby hillslopes (LaBarre 1941:514-15). These grasses are spun on spindles, with wooden or ceramic spindle whorls, or rolled into cords on the maker's thigh (Metraux 1935: Fig. 24). Formerly, large balsas, up to 25 feet (7.6 m) long and capable of carrying 8-10 passengers, were also made (Fain 1955:313) (Plate 6.13). Once the reeds are dry, the boat-making process takes 3-4 days. Working balsas have an average use-life of about six months (Fain 1955:313).

Mats and basketry are made by linking individual reeds together with cords looped tightly around each dried reed and drawn closely together (Palavecino 1949:80-81). Orlove (2002:181-82) describes the construction and use of artificial islands composed of matted reeds:

> Some villagers have cut reeds in the large totora beds . . . and made them into enormous mats, hundreds of square meters in area and a meter or so thick [for use as floating islands to support a domestic dwelling]. Once or twice a year, they place freshly cut reeds on the top surface of these islands, to compensate for the gradual rotting of the waterlogged reeds on the bottom. The one-room [rectangular] houses on the floating islands . . . are made from reed mats. Several hundred households live in a dozen or so communities on the floating islands.

Fishing

All indigenous fish in Lake Titicaca belong to two genera: *Orestias* (Family Ciprinodontidae) and *Trichomycterus* (Family Siluridae) (LaBarre 1941:511). These were once very abundant, and the two most sought-after species were "boga" (*Orestias pentlandi*) and "huminto" (*Orestias cuvieri*), both of which lived in the open water. Another indigenous fish ("karache" [*Orestias agassii*, *O. luteus*, and *O. alba*]), that dwelt in the near-shore reed beds, was also intensively exploited (Vellard 1992:495-96). Archaeologically, abundant fish bone has been found in domestic refuse in sites around the lakeshore dating from Formative (ca. 1000 B.C.-A.D. 200) (Capriles 2003:111, 117; Moore et al. 1999) and post-Formative (ca. A.D. 200-1500) times (Park 2001:45-47; Webster 1993:88; Wise 1993).

Trout and *pejerrey* (*Odontesthes regia*) were introduced in 1950 (Vellard 1992:495), and since that time traditional fishing has been radically transformed as indigenous species have declined and commercial enterprises (e.g., as described by Levieil and Orlove 1990:367) have replaced the earlier subsistence-oriented household and local community fishing operations. Nevertheless, a good deal of information is available about traditional fishing. There is a striking general similarity to the fishing techniques described above for the Upper Lerma drainage in Mexico and for the U.S. Great Basin.

Fishing techniques: collective and individual, from boats and afoot, using nets, spears, harpoons, and weirs

The main fishing season was from June until November, although fishing was also done at other times of the year. Much traditional fishing was done collectively, but several individual procedures were also employed, especially for night fishing in boats and for daytime fishing afoot along the shoreline. The techniques varied according to whether

Plate 6.13. Example of a large reed boat on Lake Titicaca (Chavez and Jorgenson 1980: Pl. XVII). Original photo courtesy of Sergio Chavez.

fishing was undertaken during the daytime or at night, in near-shore reed-beds or in deeper, open waters farther from the shore.

There were two types of reed-bed fishing. First, and most common, was day-time fishing in which the fish

> were captured by wading or from small balsas with cotton hand nets . . . or even with the ancient form of hand net made of straw. . . . In shallow water among the submerged macrophytes . . . fish were captured in enclosures . . . made with these aquatic plants. These were made by groups of men who advanced in a circle, piling up a wall of the plants reaching from the bottom to the water's surface. When a circle of 4-5 square meters was thus enclosed, the fish accumulated inside were captured with a landing net. [Vellard 1992:495-96]

In shallow water, sometimes fish were simply seized by hand (Tschopik 1946:522). At night, reed-bed fishing was usually done from a balsa vessel with a lamp fixed to its front. The light attracted the fish close enough to the boat so that they could be speared.

A second type of reed-bed fishing took the form of larger expeditions, during the period of lowest water (August-September), to the large marshes at the mouth of the Desaguadero River (that drained Lake Titicaca to the south). Here, men in groups of balsas, each vessel with two fishermen aboard, speared the larger *Trichomycterus* fish. During such expeditions, "the fishermen's children captured small siluroids [*Trichomycterus*] in the totorales [marshes] . . . with fish traps" (Vellard 1992:499).

When fishing in open waters,

> several boats made of totoras, or balsas, formed a semi-circle and beat the fish towards a central point by striking the water with a stone attached to a rope or with gaffs fitted with a ball of rushes. The fish were driven towards a large pouch-shaped net, the "*kana*" or "*kaana*," held open by stones and totora floats and with a guide wall [a V-shaped weir formed of two walls, some 6-10 m long, of submerged reed bundles tied together and fixed into the lake bottom] that led the fish in. [Vellard 1992:495]

LaBarre (1941:510-11) provides a good description of the type of the two-sided fish weir (or "fish fence") mentioned above:

> Fishing fences . . . of totora bundles stuck in the soft mud of the river bottom were observed several times in the Desaguadero [River, at the southern tip of Lake Titicaca]. They are of the same type that is used in the swampy shallows of southern Lake Titicaca. Palavecino [no reference cited by LaBarre] thus describes their construction:
>   Each of these [reed bundles] is made of 5-6 reeds . . . attached by the upper, thinner part. They carry these bundles in their balsas to the place which appears to them best for fishing, and there build their weir. To drive the bundles of totora into the mud, they use the gaff . . . with which they push their boats. [This is a stout wooden pole with a stubby tripod at the base, so that it will catch on roots and water plants and not sink into the soft mud when the boat is poled along.] . . . The bundle is placed against the gaff, the end of which rests on the ligature of the bundle [i.e., the cord that binds the bundled reeds together]. The whole is thrust vertically into the [lake bottom] earth. The end of the bundle emerges a few centimeters above the surface of the water. They repeat the operation until a sufficiently compact weir is raised to hold the fish. The barrier has the form of an angle which opens in the direction of the current. The two wings are straight or curved slightly inward. They end in an opening

Plate 6.14. Fish weir on Lake Titicaca shoreline (Palavecino 1949: Lamina X*a*).

about a meter wide whose edges, more resistant than the rest of the weir, are made of two [reed] bundles 20 cms in diameter. . . . Facing this passage there is generally an islet of totora which protects the weir from the wind and to which the fisherman can attach his balsa. Here he places the net. He watches the fish that are engaged between the two barriers and thus conducted toward the net which closes the weir. . . . To drive the fish into their weirs, they attach bunches of reeds to a pole and agitate the water up and down.

Tschopik (1946:525) describes another variant of fish weir, with only one wall ("fence"), that was commonly used for night fishing by a single fisherman (Plate 6.14):

The fence, which is one m high, is made of single reeds fastened to a length of grass rope anchored to the bottom so that the reeds float upward. It extends some 20 m perpendicularly from the totora marshes of the lakeshore into open water. The fisherman anchors his balsa at the end of the fence and puts out a conical net 1.75 m in diameter and 1.5 m long, tied into a pole frame. The fences are owned individually and are rebuilt each year.

Fish nets varied greatly in size and form. Both larger drag-nets and smaller scoop nets (dip-nets) were used. The drag-nets were formerly

made of fine, two-ply llama-wood thread. At least one type is of basketry. Nets are fabricated and mended with a small wooden bobbin and a wooden net gauge. Net floats are made of small bundles of totora reeds. Sinkers are either disk-shaped stones grooved around the perimeter or flattish, ovoid stones, perforated from both sides. . . . Fish are usually taken during the day in the "big net," which is some 13 feet [4 m] wide by 26 feet [8 m] deep and is dragged between two one-man balsas. Men in other small balsas paddle around locating schools of fish.

Plate 6.15. Fishing with a small net on Lake Titicaca (LaBarre 1946: Pl. 115, top).

A second [fishing] technique also involves two balsas, which stand parallel with the net between them. The net has the same dimensions mentioned above, with a small opening at the apex for removing the fish. Men in small balsas form a semi-circle and drive the fish by tossing pebbles into the water and lashing it with their balsa poles. . . . [Tschopik 1946:522]

A much smaller drag-net "is towed at night by two one-man balsas. It has a rectangular mouth, some 1.5 m by 1 m, and is 2 m long" (Tschopik 1946:525).

Two types of small drag-nets are also employed by a single fisherman operating from a small balsa. These nets are made of both cord and basketry:

The one-man net has a mouth 1.5 m square and is of equal depth. It is towed by a one-man balsa, and does not require floats because it has a pole attached to the upper edge of its opening.

The basket net is used . . . to take . . . small fish . . . when, from July-December, they lay their eggs in the shallow water of the lake's edge. Each small balsa drags two nets, one on either side. The nets are some 90 cms in diameter and of equal depth. [Tschopik 1946:524]

Several types of scoop (dip) nets have also been reported for traditional fishing in Lake Titicaca. Their use has already been generally noted above, in connection with both reed-bed and open-water fishing. Scoop nets were both circular (conical) and rectangular in form, and were always mounted on a rigid wood-pole frame attached to a wood-pole handle (Plate 6.15). Some were used by fishermen who walked through shallow water in near-shore ponds or along the lake or river shores, either alone or collectively. One type of conical scoop net used in such contexts measured "75 cms in diameter, with a handle 1.5 m long" (Tschopik 1946:525). For night fishing, such nets were used by fishermen carrying lighted flares of dried totora reeds to attract the fish.

Other variants of one-man scoop nets are reported by LaBarre (1941:511, citing Metraux 1935):

> these conical nets are quite large and about all one man can handle. . . . [Metraux also mentions a] smaller rectangular-framed scoop net with a pole handle: "The Indian plunges this rectangular pocket into the water and remains standing or sitting until he sees interesting prey. He begins by lifting his net carefully, then pulls it out of the water with a rapid motion."

Fishing spears and harpoons were used primarily in shallow water, where fish were clearly visible. Tschopik (1946:522) describes a large fish spear with "four unbarbed iron (formerly hardwood) points secured to a 10-foot (3 m) [wooden] shaft with 3-ply cordage of human hair. . . . The fish spear is used only during the day in shallow water along the lake edge." Manelis de Klein (1973:134-35), Palavecino (1949: Lamina XII), and Fain (1955:308, Fig. 6) describe and illustrate different types of harpoons. These implements had either three or eight unbarbed iron or hardwood points tightly bound with twine onto a wooden shaft.

Preparing fish for consumption

According to Vellard (1992:497), "[f]ish . . . were opened and dried in the sun on mats and on the roofs of huts or between layers of hot rocks. . . . " Manelis de Klein (1973:134) notes that "small fish are salted and toasted, and when dried they are carried on long trips. . . . [Larger fish are] salted, cleaned, de-boned and smoked over a fire and stored for times of scarcity" (English translation).

Palavecino (1949:65-66) describes cooking fish in rock-lined pits that measure about 60 cm in diameter and are dug about 60 cm into the ground. The rock lining is heated by building a fire in the pit. Then all the rocks, except the bottom layer, are removed, and alternate layers of fish and hot rocks are placed into the pit. The whole is covered over with a thick layer of earth and reed mats, and allowed to remain until the fish within are well cooked.

Communal fishing and reed-bed territories

Levieil and Orlove (1990) describe communal fishing and reed-harvesting territories along the lake margins. Although much of the fishing associated with these territories is now commercial in nature (that is, undertaken to produce household cash through market sales), these territories are locally defined and administered. The character and administration of these communally managed territories may provide useful analogies for prehispanic contexts, both in the Titicaca basin and in the Valley of Mexico. For this reason, I quote extensively from this account.

> Local communities manage aquatic resources through a system of communal fishing territories. Each communal fishing territory is associated with a specified lakeshore community

and a well defined portion of aquatic space, to which community members have certain exclusive, though informal, rights. Sanctions are brought against outsiders who cross the territory boundaries. . . . These rights focus primarily on two types of resources: (1) the beds of totora reeds, which in most cases consist of plots owned by individuals, and (2) fish . . . [whereby] access to the entire territory is open to all the fishermen in a community. *Such systems of open access within a communal fishing territory, rather than one in which individuals have rights to private fishing spots, are common in settings such as Lake Titicaca, in which fish move from one area to another, and in which the size of fish populations can vary between seasons or years; by contrast, the predictability of totora yields encourages individual ownership of plots* [emphasis added].

The communal fishing territories are approximately rectangular in shape. One edge is made up of the portion of the lakeshore that lies within the community. . . . The width of the territories [extending out into the lake] depends on the width of the totora beds [along the lakeshore]. Where these beds are very narrow or entirely absent, the width [of the fishing territory] is under 5 kms; where the beds are broader [i.e., where they occupy a great distance along the lakeshore], the width [of the fishing territory] extends at most a few hundred meters beyond the outer edge of the [reed] beds. The total area of the communal fishing territories thus tends to be under 30 km^2 . . . the average number of fishermen per community is just under 20. . . .

Most communities restrict totora collection to certain days of the week and months of the year; the responsibility for policing totora beds at other times is assigned to individuals for a year-long term. In this manner, the position of communal fishing territories in which totora grows is either relatively full of community members, who can share the task of watching for outsiders, or quite vacant of community members, so that any distant figure is subject to suspicion. The fishermen can also watch the open-water portions of the territories. Since the average number of trips per fisherman per year is high, over 200, the fishermen have a regular presence in the lake and recognize each other's boats.

. . . the social organization of communities favors the defense of the communal fishing territories. The members of the community know one another well, because of the concentration of the population in the lakeshore zone, with densities exceeding 100 people per square kilometer, and because of the high rate of endogamy [over 50% in-community marriage]. . . . This knowledge of community membership is also increased by the frequent community assemblies and work groups. *Andean communities have defended their collectively held territories for generations; the policing of a perimeter and the expulsion of outsiders are well-developed for fields and grazing lands, and are easily extended to totora beds and fishing grounds* [emphasis added]. [Levieil and Orlove 1990:367-68]

Levieil and Orlove also describe three types of fishing territories (which they refer to as Types 1, 2, and 3) that are based on relative water depth around the lakeshore.

[*Type 1 territories*] . . . are found where the shallow water area extends to a great distance from the shoreline, because of a gentle bottom slope [water depth rarely exceeds 3-5 m]. Present in these areas are aquatic macrophytes, particularly dense beds of totora reeds. Communities with Type 1 [fishing] territories extend their boundaries far into these totora beds and usually . . . claim some open water space, not more than 100-200 meters wide, on their outer edge. . . . The presence of totora reeds in shallow waters greatly simplifies the problem of marking area boundaries within Type 1 territories. The natural channels criss-crossing the totora beds can be used as lateral boundaries and, if necessary, artificially enlarged. In very shallow waters, local people use submerged human-made markers persisting from times in which the lake level was lower, such as paths, ridges, and trenches.

[*In Type 2 territories*] . . . a steeper bottom slope brings the outer edge of the totora reed beds to within a few hundred meters from shore [because reeds do not grow in water deeper than a few meters]. In such cases, local community members claim the totora beds in the shallow waters and an area of open and deeper water a few hundred meters wide, extending out to an area between the 10- and 20-m depth contours. *Natural features such as prominent rocks, hills, or promontories on shore, and small islands offshore, are often used for lateral boundary identification. In a few cases, however, stone constructions on shore also delimit aquatic territories* [emphasis added].

[In *Type 3 territories* a steep bottom slope makes totora beds very narrow, or non-existent]. . . . the 50-meter depth contour provides a good approximation of the outer edge. . . . [in some cases] the communities exclude outsiders from coming within five kms of the shore. Topographic features such as small villages and outstanding rock formations, or human-made markers such as paths, walls, or houses are often used as lateral boundary markers for Type 3 fishing territory areas, since a steep shore elevation makes them visible from a considerable distance. [Levieil and Orlove 1990:372]

The ownership and administration of reed beds vary considerably. According to Orlove,

A few of the [lakeshore] villages . . . have such an abundance of totora, with beds that cover thousands of hectares, that they allow residents to harvest anywhere within the village territory. *In most villages, however, totora plots are much like agricultural fields* [emphasis added]. Rectangular in shape, they can be divided into equal shares at the time of inheritance from parents. They are occasionally sold to relatives or neighbors within the village. It is somewhat more frequent to rent totora beds to people from nearby villages, since the size of the reedbeds varies greatly from one village to the next. . . . There has been a shift in the payment of rent. . . . Through the 1950s and 1960s, renters usually gave potatoes and grain and offered additional gifts of coca leaf and alcohol. In more recent decades, cash payments have become more frequent. . . . [Such personalized rental] ties can last for many years.

Though the increased harvest of green totora [as cattle feed and for mat making] did not change patterns of ownership, it led to increasing disputes over totora theft. Individuals would accuse residents of the same village or of neighboring villages of entering their totora plots and cutting their reeds. The villages held meetings to discuss the problems. . . . A number of villages decided to add a totora guard . . . to the list of community offices. Familiar with the patterns of ownership of plots, these guards would travel through the reedbeds to watch for incursions and theft. Like other such positions, the guard would have a year-long term of office.

To make this work less burdensome and more efficient, the villages established rules for the timing of harvest. They closed the reedbeds to cutting altogether in the middle of the rainy season, since they had learned that totora does not resprout well if it is harvested when the water is most turbid. They also selected certain days for harvest, usually two each week. Each village tried to choose days different from those of its neighbors. . . . This pattern reduced the number of days that the totora guard had to work. It also spread around the effort of defending territory, since all villagers, aware of the days when their neighbors would harvest, would be prepared to look out for trespassers who came across the channels that mark the boundaries between village beds. . . . [Despite the many logistical difficulties involved] the advantages of linking the schedule for totora harvest were evident to all. The dates, since they were established, have rarely changed. [Orlove 2002:188-89]

Table 6.25. Waterfowl recorded around Lake Junín, Peru, in 1967.

Species	Number
Anas versicolor puna	400,000
Gallinula chloropus garmani	316,000
Fulica americana peruviana	45,000
Anas flavirostris oxyptera	33,000
Fulica ordesiaca	22,000
Anas georgica spinicauda	16,000
Plegadis ridgwayi	8000
Oxyura jamaicensis ferruginea	5000
Podiceps chinensis morrisoni	4000

(Adapted from Dourojeanni et al. 1968:3)

Waterfowl—Hunting and Egg Collecting

As in the Valley of Mexico, the majority of waterfowl on Lake Titicaca are migratory birds that spend the winter months nesting and feeding, and then depart. Nevertheless, there are also many year-round residents. Waterfowl hunting is commonly done during the northern hemisphere winter (December-March), although some continues year-round—some of the migratory birds come from the sub-antarctic regions of the far southern hemisphere during the southern hemisphere's winter months (June-August). Hunted birds include "water hens" (American coot), several types of duck, geese, grebes, gulls, loons, herons, and gallinules (LaBarre 1941:512; Tschopik 1946:520), many of the same species that inhabited the Valley of Mexico. Eggs are also collected in some quantity (Fjeldså and Krabbe 1990; Kent et al. 1999; LaBarre 1941:513; Manelis de Klein 1973:134-35; Orlove 2002:199-200), and bird down is spun into thread for making caps and other articles of warm clothing (LaBarre 1941:517). Table 6.25 indicates some of the most common waterfowl species recorded in a 1967 census for Lake Junín, a large lake and surrounding marshland (extending over an area ca. 706 km^2) situated at comparable elevation (ca. 4100 m asl) some 800 km to the northwest in central Peru; these species should be comparable to those found in the Titicaca Basin (for which I have found no precise identifications from modern censuses). Most of these species known for Lake Junín have been identified in archaeological deposits from prehispanic sites around the Lake Titicaca shoreline (Kent et al. 1999:171; Moore et al. 1999).

Hunting techniques

These include both individual and collective practices, afoot or in boats. Birds are trapped, lured into killing places, netted, seized by hand, captured with *bolas* (throwing cords weighted with two wooden balls), or killed with slings or clubs. According to Tschopik (1946:512),

> [d]ucks, grebes, and gallinules are . . . taken with [cord] nooses, a series of which are strung out at an elevation of several inches between two clumps of totora reeds.
> Ducks are lured into the totora marshes by imitating the whistle of the flightless grebe, and by making swishing noises with the hand in the water. Then they are killed with sling-

stones, poles, or bolas. Occasionally they are taken with the big fish net, which is hung over clumps of reeds and pulled down upon the ducks when they swim in.

Further detail is provided by LaBarre (1941:512-13):

men hunting alone in the early morning disguise themselves in bunches of reeds, slowly approach the birds who are still stupefied by the cold of the night, then grab them by the feet, they quickly kill the birds by biting the head or twisting the neck. The Uru are able users of slingshots . . . and they also use bolas made with two large wooden balls and a small, grooved ovoid stone for the handgrip. . . .
   They stretch in selected sites extensive nets, sometimes hundreds of meters long, for birds whose flight is near the surface of the water; the nets are extended below the surface also, to prevent the escape of diving birds. They anchor the nets to . . . clumps of totora set in slightly curved lines. Then hunters in their balsas make much noise and frighten the birds into the almost invisible nets, where they can dispatch them with clubs. . . .

Palavecino (1949:63-64) describes duck hunting with large nets stretched between two upright poles in shallow open water. Such nets are about 30 "brazas" long and 2 "brazas" wide (approximately 30 × 2 m), and are operated by groups of 4-10 men. Palavecino (1949:66) also indicates that waterfowl are cooked, smoked, and dried in much the same manner as fish (see above).

Summary and Conclusions

In the Titicaca Basin—unlike the Valley of Mexico, the Upper Lerma drainage, or the U.S. Great Basin—indigenous people have long had access to domesticated herbivores (llamas and alpacas) as a major subsistence component, along with agriculture and aquatic resources. In this sense, natives of this Andean region are more comparable to the Marsh Arabs (see next section of this chapter). The very secondary importance of aquatic invertebrates in the Titicaca Basin during the historic period is probably related to the readily available sources of animal protein represented by domesticated camelids, and after the mid-sixteenth century, by sheep and cattle. Archaeologically, remains of aquatic reptiles and amphibians are scarce (Moore et al. 1999; Park 2001:41, 50). Nevertheless, the archaeological and historic sources clearly indicate that many kinds of aquatic resources—particularly waterfowl, fish, and reeds—have long played key roles in the economy of the Titicaca Basin.

(1) Complementary economies. Although Lake Titicaca is a far larger and deeper body of open water relative to those found in central Mexico and most of western North America, its lake basin contains huge expanses of marshland that support a rich aquatic fauna and flora around the perimeter of the lake surface, while the open waters of the lake itself support a rich piscine fauna. For centuries, probably millennia, these vast marshlands have been home to the Uru, who reside along the shorelines and atop floating islands comprised of buoyant aquatic vegetation, and whose dwellings and boats are made almost entirely of reed mats and bundles. The historic Uru have had little

direct involvement with agriculture and herding, both of which are carried out by other specialized groups within the basin, who themselves are little involved directly with the exploitation of aquatic resources.

Throughout the historic period, and probably deep into prehistory as well, there have been three complementary, specialized economies in the Titicaca Basin: the aquatic, the agricultural, and the pastoral. This contrasts with the Valley of Mexico, where one of these economies—the pastoral—was entirely lacking until after the 1520s. As in Mexico and North America, the aquatic economy in the Titicaca Basin, while subject to some seasonal variation in resource availability, was essentially a year-round operation. The products of the complementary economies were exchanged and redistributed through markets and a wide variety of interpersonal, interhousehold, and intercommunity exchange networks, many of them noncommercial and deeply embedded in traditional kinship or ritualized systems.

(2) Procurement technology. The traditional technology of aquatic resource procurement in the Titicaca Basin emphasized the netting of waterfowl and fish, with secondary use of pronged spears, cord snares, cord slings, and cord bolas with wooden weights (the latter two are not documented for either central Mexico or the U.S. Great Basin). As in Mexico and North America, some waterfowl are simply seized by hand through stealthy approaches by hunters into nesting and feeding grounds. Interestingly, as in central Mexico but unlike the U.S. Great Basin, the use of bows and arrows for hunting waterfowl or fish is not historically documented in the Titicaca Basin. Nets—both large rectangular devices manipulated by groups of men from boats and held in place by wooden poles, and small dip nets managed by individuals from boats or from the shore—are commonly used with weirs, submerged "fences" made of aquatic vegetation fastened to the bottom surface, that direct the fish into places of entrapment. Reeds are harvested either with sickles in shallow water or with long poles, tipped with sharp knives, in deeper water. Boats, traditionally made from buoyant reeds, are an integral part of aquatic procurement technology—many (probably most) hunting, fishing, and harvesting activities use these vessels to get from place to place, to manipulate nets and weirs, and to transport people and materials throughout the marshes and open water zones.

(3) Preparation and storage technology. Open areas around permanent domiciles seem to be where aquatic resources, once harvested, are prepared for use and stored. Documented activities include drying reeds and making boats in open spaces; drying and salting fish and waterfowl atop poles or rocks; cooking fish and waterfowl in rock-lined pits; and storing dried, salted fish and fowl in rock- or grass-lined pits.

(4) Temporary encampments. I have found no historic period references to temporary encampments within the Titicaca marshlands. Apparently, the exploitation of aquatic resources in this region has typically been conducted from relatively permanent places of residence around the shoreline or on the floating islands within the marshlands. Perhaps the comparative ease with which permanent residences can be maintained on mobile living surfaces accounts for this pattern—that is, when required, permanent residences can be moved close enough to where the hunting, fishing, or reed harvesting activities take place so that people do not have to be away from their homes for more than a few hours at a time.

(5) Territoriality. There is great concern for securing and maintaining access to community fishing grounds and reed beds, and preventing outsiders from accessing these essential resources. Communities expend a great deal of energy in administering and controlling aquatic territories. A high degree of community endogamy facilitates control. Because fish typically move from place to place, fishing locales are not specifically defined or individually "owned." This contrasts with reed beds, which are much more stationary and enduring, and so tend to be "owned" by individuals and inherited much as are agricultural fields on higher ground. In the case of reed beds, community members cooperate in replanting harvested areas to encourage rapid regrowth. Various arrangements safeguard community access (e.g., the deployment of guards who patrol the waters and marshes, and the arrangement of staggered days when fishing, hunting, and harvesting are permitted in different community territories). Also, different kinds of physical demarcations identify the limits of these territories (e.g., prominent landmarks on the shore, including natural topographic formations and artificial [masonry?] constructions, or prominent channels cut through reed beds).

The Tigris-Euphrates Delta, Iraq and Iran

Prior to the politically inspired devastation of this region during the past two decades, the vast marshes at the mouth of the Tigris-Euphrates River covered an area of some 52,000 km². Although the marshes themselves were predominantly fresh water, the soils of the immediately surrounding arid landscape were often characterized by high degrees of salinity or alkalinity. For millennia this watery expanse had been home to a distinctive way of life that combined agriculture around the edges of the marshes with the exploitation of aquatic resources (especially reeds, fish, and waterfowl) and the raising of water buffalo (that fed exclusively on aquatic vegetation) within the marshes. Several descriptions of the Marsh Arabs during the 1950s provide glimpses of their traditional lifeways (Maxwell 1957; Salim 1962; Thesiger 1964, 1979).

Life in the marshes was conditioned by the seasonal rise and fall of water. Each year between April and early July, large areas flooded as the river levels rose with the influx of water from melting snows in the Zagros highlands far upstream. As the floodwaters subsided, areas of open water became marshlands interspersed with ponds and lakes that could only be navigated in boats (Plate 6.16). The water level remained at its lowest ebb between September and mid-October; after October the upland rains began and water levels began to rise once more, culminating in the spring and early summer floods. Salim (1962:6) characterized the marshlands in the following terms:

> Except in the deep water, the marshes are thickly covered with reeds, bulrushes, and floating water plants. Fish and waterfowl abound. The depth of water over most of the marshes is between 4-5 feet [1.2-1.5 m]; in places it is much deeper . . . [up to ca. 6 m]. . . . The area of permanent marsh is probably not more than ¾ of the flood-time marsh [i.e., about 39,000 km²].

Plate 6.16. Navigating the marshlands of the Tigris-Euphrates delta (Maxwell 1957:84-85).

The marshlands contained thousands of "islands." Thesiger (1964:28) characterized these apparently natural features as

[m]any small islands, some only a few yards across, covering an acre [0.4 ha] or more. . . . Some were anchored, others were loose and drifted about. All were smothered under a mass of *qasab* [reeds], here only 8-10 feet [2.4-3 m] high, tall clumps of sedge, . . . brambles, a few small willow bushes, and several different kinds of creeper. Underneath all this was a carpet of mint, sow thistle, willow herb, pondweed, and other plants.

The ground looked solid, but felt rather soggy. Actually it consisted of a layer of roots and decomposed vegetation floating on the surface.

It is unclear whether these "islands" are composed of naturally occurring masses of buoyant vegetation, or whether there may be some artificial component involved, as among the Uru of the Titicaca Basin.

Complementary Marshland Economies

Salim (1962:9) estimated that during the 1950s the Marsh Arab population was approximately 400,000 people. These were subdivided into three semi-specialized and economically complementary groups: about 350,000 "cultivators," about 25,000 "reed gatherers," and about 25,000 "buffalo breeders." The latter two groups resided permanently within the marshlands, well away from solid land. Cultivators, who lived on the edges of the marshes, produced rice, millet, wheat, barley, and a variety of vegetables. The reed gatherers produced reed mats for sale, plus captured fish and waterfowl for their own consumption (Plate 6.17). Waterfowl, although abundant, were apparently not much exploited. The buffalo breeders produced butter, milk, cheese, and dried cattle dung (used mainly for fuel). These groups exchanged their complementary products through markets in the larger settlements and even by means of "mobile canoe shops" that traversed the waterways between scattered marsh dwellers. Social and economic interaction with populations outside the marsh zone were more limited, although through the marketplaces, outsiders provided many essentials such as tobacco, sugar, tea, cloth, and sundry metal implements.

Settlements

Salim (1962:11-14) distinguished four types of marshland settlements:

> *The village* . . . is usually found in the densely populated area, and comprises 100-300 huts . . . scattered [on solid ground] along the edges of the main waterways and over cultivated lands [Plate 6.18]. . . .
> *A mound* . . . an island in the permanent marshes usually taken as a residence either by the reed-gatherers or the buffalo-breeders . . . usually composed of [several] . . . huts lightly constructed of reeds or bulrushes [Plate 6.19]. . . .
> *Floating platforms* . . . [usually made by the buffalo-breeders] in the flood season . . . [constructed of] reeds, bulrushes, and earth. It is large enough to hold a hut, or a few buffaloes, and can be poled from place to place and used as a temporary residence. A group of such rafts may form a settlement [Plate 6.20]. . . .
> *Reed islands* . . . are raised during the high-flood season by layers of bulrushes, reeds, and earth, and are used as residences.

Salim (1962:22) describes one typical large village as consisting "of about 1600 little islands [upon which individual houses were built] stretching in a long narrow belt more than three miles [7.8 kms] in length but only 50-150 yards [15.2-45.5 m] wide."

Of these four settlement types, the "village" and "mound" appear to have been relatively permanent places of residence, while the "floating platforms" and "reed islands" were often occupied primarily during the months of high flood water, or temporarily at other times of the year. Although it is not entirely clear from Salim's description, my impression is that some individual buffalo-breeder and reed-gatherer households may have moved from their homes in a larger, permanent village on the edges of permanent marshlands to more temporary quarters (that is, the floating platforms and reed islands) during the flood season. Presumably, some of these latter types of residential quarters would have been occupied on a more enduring basis in areas that remained as marshland and open water over the entire annual cycle.

Much more temporary encampments are used for fishing expeditions when groups of up to 150 men (more typically 10-18) from a single community may be away from home for several days or a few weeks while netting or spearing fish in bodies of water at some distance from their permanent villages. Such encampments comprise a number of hastily erected reed huts built on natural or artificial islands, quite similar to those on Lake Chad in north-central Africa (see Chap. 2, Plate 2.1).

House Construction

Thesiger (1964:67-68) describes the construction of an artificial house platform in an area of standing water:

> The method of construction was first to enclose an area of water, large enough for the house and yard, with a fence of reeds, perhaps 20 feet [6.1 m] high; next to pack reeds and rushes within this fence; and when the stack rose above the water, to fracture the reeds of the containing fence and lay them across it. . . . [Then they] piled more rushes on top and trampled them down as tightly as possible. When satisfied with this foundation, they built the house, driving the reeds to form the arches individually into the ground, before tying them together in a bundle [see below]. If the floor flooded, because it had sunk or because the water level had risen, the owner had only to lay down several armfuls of newly cut reeds. . . .
>
> For a more permanent site, . . . [they] covered the foundations with mud scooped up from under the water. This they did when the water was at its lowest level, in the autumn, and then only when it was not too deep. They covered the mud with further layers of rushes. . . . Over the years the alternate layers of mud and reeds formed an island. . . .

Salim (1962:72) describes the construction of a reed house. The structure

> is built of bundles of stout reeds and reed mats. The bundles, made of reeds tied with ropes of plaited and twisted reeds, are set at regular intervals in two rows [Plate 6.21], and the heads of each facing pair are bent over and interwoven carefully to form a perfect arch [Plate 6.22]. Thin traverse bundles are bound to the arches, covering the whole structure and ending at a height of about 3 feet [0.9 m] from the ground on each side [Plate 6.23]. A latticework of reeds is then inserted and tied to cover the opening between the lowest transverse bundle and the ground, and to admit air and keep the building cool in summer. Finally the whole framework is covered by large overlapping reed mats [Plate 6.24]. The two end walls are constructed of strong palm trunks covered with reeds and strengthened by vertical bundles with matting and latticework.

Similar techniques are used to construct much larger structures used as community guest houses and other public buildings up to 4.5 m wide and 30 m long (Plate 6.25).

Harvesting Reeds (Principally Phragmites karka)

Mature reeds, standing up to 6 m high above water level, are used for constructing houses and making mats; immature reeds serve as fodder for water buffalos. Most reeds are harvested during short day trips from the main settlement. Occasionally, overnight trips are made to more distant reed beds—these involve temporary camps, much like those used for fishing expeditions. The reeds are usually harvested by a pair of men (or a man and a boy) working together: one to cut the reeds, using a wooden-handled iron sickle with serrated edges (Plate 6.26), and the second to tie the cut reeds into bundles and stack them into a floating platform that is then poled back to the settlement (Plate 6.27). Once back at the settlement, the reeds are split and their outer skins removed (Plate 6.28), and then they are dried preparatory to weaving into mats (Plate 6.29).

Summary and Conclusions

As in the Titicaca Basin, the vast marshes of the Tigris-Euphrates delta have long been home to three complementary economies: the agricultural, the pastoral, and the aquatic. This tripartite, internally specialized economy appears to have great time depth in this region. The agriculturalists occupy substantial permanent settlements on somewhat higher land interspersed between marshes and ponds; most of the pastoralists, with their aquatic buffalo, occupy settlements of variable size and permanence within the marshlands; and the aquatic specialists, focused on fishing and reed harvesting, occupy small settlements, some of which are seasonal, atop floating islands that rise and fall with the annual riverine flood cycle. It is the ebb and flow of the annual flood cycle that determines, in large measure, the occupational pattern of pastoralists and reed-harvesters.

Whatever their economic focus, the distinctive domestic and public architecture of the Marsh Arabs is almost exclusively constructed of reeds. Less enduring residences are built in temporary encampments at fishing and reed-cutting locales too distant from permanent habitations for daily commuting. All movement through the marshes is by wooden-plank boats—even shops move from place to place in such vessels, and the boats themselves sometimes provide living space for several days or longer when groups of men engage in fishing or reed harvesting away from their homes. I have found no record of any use of reed boats in this region. Although they have apparently not been much hunted in recent years, there is a great abundance of potentially available waterfowl in this region.

Plate 6.17. Spearing fish from boats in the Tigris-Euphrates delta (Thesiger 1979:193). The fishermen are awaiting the fish as they move back under the line of approaching boats when they have been driven to a point where dense reeds prevent them from swimming away.

Plate 6.18. Example of a Marsh Arab village in 1974 (Burns 2003).

Plate 6.19. Example of a 1950s Marsh Arab "mound" settlement (Salim 1962: Pl. 8-*A*).

Plate 6.20. Example of a 1950s Marsh Arab "floating platform" settlement (Thesiger 1964:83, Fig. 14).

Plate 6.21. Construction of a 1950s Marsh Arab reed house: early stage, with vertical reed bundles in place (Maxwell 1957:84-85).

Plate 6.22. Construction of a 1950s Marsh Arab reed house: tying the vertical reed bundles together to form arches (Maxwell 1957:84-85).

Plate 6.23. Construction of a 1950s Marsh Arab reed house: tying on the horizontal cross bundles (Maxwell 1957:84-85).

Plate 6.24. A typical 1950s Marsh Arab reed house, with pile of harvested grain covered with pats of buffalo dung in foreground (Maxwell 1957:84-85).

Plate 6.25. A typical 1950s Marsh Arab reed guest house (Salim 1962: Pl. 5-*A*).

Plate 6.26. Marsh Arabs cutting reeds in the 1950s (Salim 1962: Pl. 7-*A*).

Plate 6.27. Marsh Arabs poling buoyant bundles of cut reeds back to their settlement in the 1950s (Salim 1962: Pl. 3-*B*).

Plate 6.28. Splitting and skinning reeds in a Marsh Arab settlement, 1950s (Salim 1962: Pl. 7-*B*).

Plate 6.29. Weaving split reeds into mats in a Marsh Arab settlement, 1950s (Maxwell 1957:84-85).

The Lake Chad Basin, Western Chad

As noted in Chapter 2, Lake Chad is comparable to Lake Texcoco in terms of its latitude, absence of external drainage, numerous in-flowing streams around its perimeter, variable salinity, generally shallow water with considerable variability in depth over time and space, substantial seasonal and inter-annual rainfall variability, extensive marshlands, diverse and shifting aquatic flora and fauna, and long-term desiccation. Archaeological research indicates that aquatic resources have been economically significant for hunters and gatherers, agriculturalists, and pastoralists in this semi-arid region for several millennia (e.g., Breunig et al. 1996; Gronenborn 1998). Although ethnographic descriptions of traditional hunting and fishing in the Chad Basin are scarce, there is at least one detailed and exceptionally well illustrated account of mid-twentieth-century fishing (Blache and Miton 1963) that may have applications to the prehispanic Valley of Mexico.

String nets are used either afoot in shallow water, working in groups or individually (Fig. 6.12), or from individual or multiple boats in deeper water (Fig. 6.13). Nets may be long and rectangular in form (Fig. 6.12a), or small and supported on wooden frames used for dipping or scooping (Fig. 6.12b-g). When used with boats, the nets are typically mounted on wooden frames, and manipulated from one end of the vessel by a man working in tandem with the paddler (Fig. 6.13b, c), or towed from behind two boats (Fig. 6.13d). In deep water men sometimes dive from boats to capture fish using a pair of small scoop nets (Fig. 6.13a). Basketry traps are usually used while working afoot, in shallow water; some are used for scooping up the fish (Fig. 6.14a, c), while others depend upon the current to move the fish into the closed-ended trap (Fig. 6.14b). In Fig. 6.14a, the fisherman also uses a buoyant wooden or watertight basket as a container for his catch.

Fish weirs are also common. Some direct the fish into basketry traps placed where the weir walls constrict (Fig. 6.15a); others force the fish to attempt to leap over the obstructing wall, which invariably causes them to fall into basketry traps placed along the downstream side of the weir (Fig. 6.15b, d). Sometimes the fisherman sits atop a platform alongside the weir (Fig. 6.15c). Another weir variant consists of a circular reed-wall enclosure with a movable door that can be closed by a man pulling a long string from some distance away when he sees that fish have entered the enclosure (Fig. 6.16a). Floating set lines with iron hooks (Fig. 6.16b) as well as diverse iron-pointed harpoons (Fig. 6.17) are used, either afoot or from boats. Many fish are smoked for long-term preservation and exchange: in large ceramic vessels (Fig. 6.18a), in above-ground masonry structures (Fig. 6.18b, d), or in pits dug into the ground (Fig. 6.18c, d). Once smoked, the fish are further dried on wooden poles (Fig. 6.19).

Particularly notable is the striking similarity between the collection and processing of aquatic algae described in the sixteenth-century sources for the Valley of Mexico and comparable activities observed during the 1960s in the Chad Basin. Furst (1978) cites the observations of a 1964-1965 Belgian trans-Saharan expedition (Leonard 1966) that passed through the region around Lake Chad. Here, a variant of algae, *Spirlina platen-*

sis, "morphologically and nutritionally very similar to the Mexican species," was being collected and prepared by the local population (referred to as the Kanembu) (see also Durand-Chastel 1980:53):

> The Kanembu, who get most of their protein from *Spirulina*, wait for winds to push this alga toward the shore, where it collects and becomes concentrated into a thick mash. Women with calabashes ladle the algal mass into circular depressions in the sand where it is dried by the hot sun. As the blue-green sheet gels, the glossy surface is smoothed by hand and marked off into squares. When most of the water has evaporated or seeped into the sand, the squares are pulled up, dried further on mats, and cut into small, flat, brittle cakes. The Kanembu eat *dihe* [the algae] in a thick, pungent sauce made of tomatoes, chili peppers, and various spices poured over millet, the staple of the region. [Furst 1978:62]

These virtually identical (and historically independent) procedures, so far separated in time and space, testify to the remarkable technological convergence that characterizes so many types of resource exploitation in the pre-industrial world.

Indigenous occupation "on the shores of Lake Tschad" is illustrated in a late nineteenth-century drawing (Buel 1890:72) (Fig. 6.20). While this drawing, taken from a popular book about European and North American explorers in Africa, may not be a completely accurate depiction, it does suggest that people lived in clusters of permanent reed-walled and reed-roofed structures resting atop platforms set on wooden poles in the Lake Chad marshlands.

Figure 6.12. Fish netting techniques on foot in shallow water, Chad Basin, Chad (adapted from Blache and Miton 1963). *a*, Planche 3, p. 71; *b*, Planche 25, p. 92; *c*, Planche 7, p. 75; *d*, Planche 25, p. 92; *e*, Planche 24, p. 91; *f*, Planche 22, p. 89; *g*, Planche 17, p. 85.

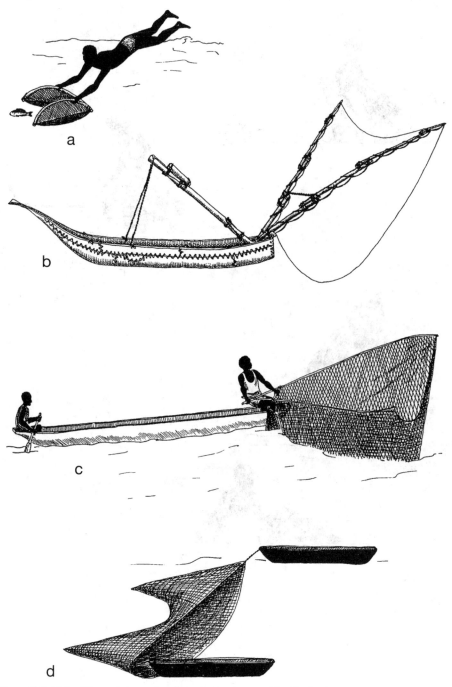

Figure 6.13. Fish netting techniques, from boats in deeper water, Chad Basin, Chad (adapted from Blache and Miton 1963). *a*, Planche 25, p. 92; *b*, Planche 10, p. 78; *c*, Planche 13, p. 81; *d*, Planche 5, p. 73.

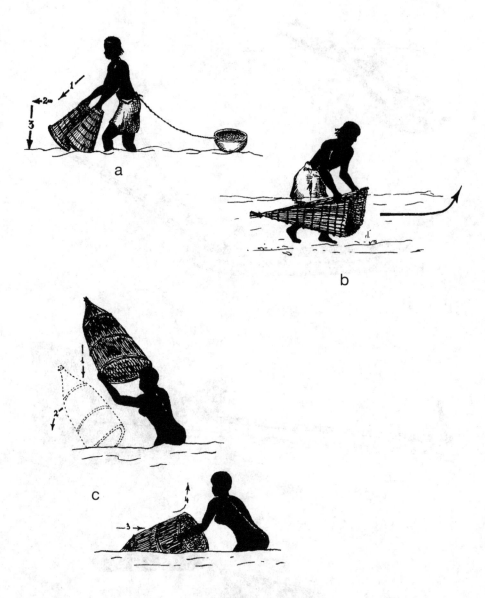

Figure 6.14. Capturing fish with basket traps, Chad Basin, Chad (adapted from Blache and Miton 1963). *a*, Planche 23, p. 90; *b*, Planche 23, p. 90; *c*, Planche 22, p. 89.

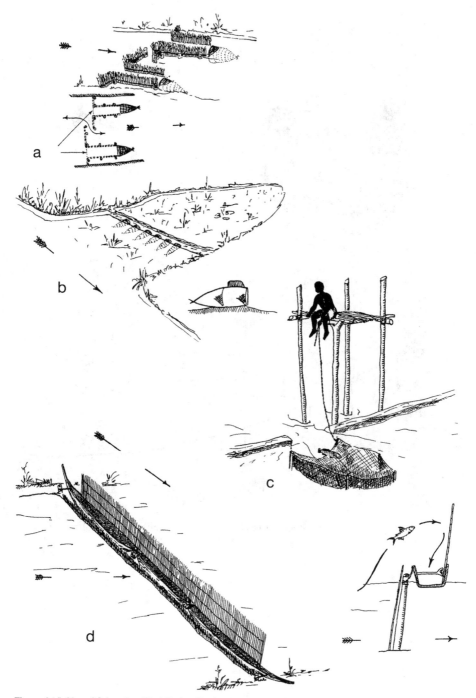

Figure 6.15. Use of fish weirs, Chad Basin, Chad (adapted from Blache and Miton 1963). *a*, Planche 35, p. 101; *b*, Planche 35, p. 101; *c*, Planche 27, p. 93; *d*, Planche 35, p. 101.

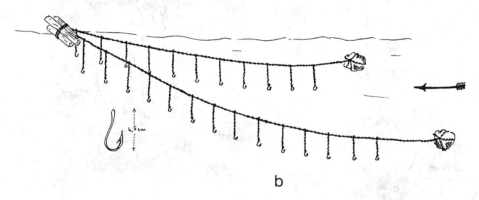

Figure 6.16. Fishing techniques in Chad Basin, Chad (adapted from Blache and Miton 1963). *a*, reed enclosure (Planche 41, p. 107); *b*, floating set lines with hooks (Planche 30, p. 96).

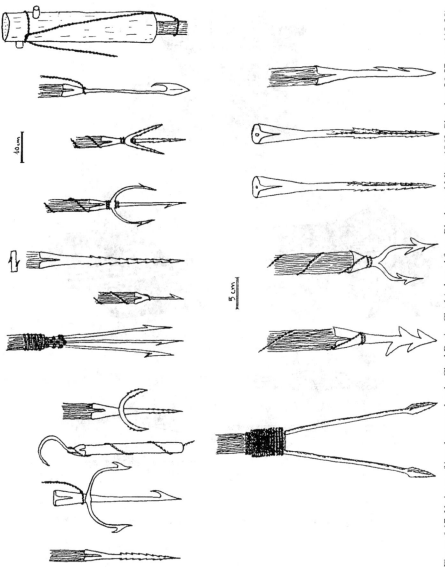

Figure 6.17. Variants of iron harpoon heads, Chad Basin, Chad (adapted from Blache and Miton 1963, Planches 56-57, pp. 119-20).

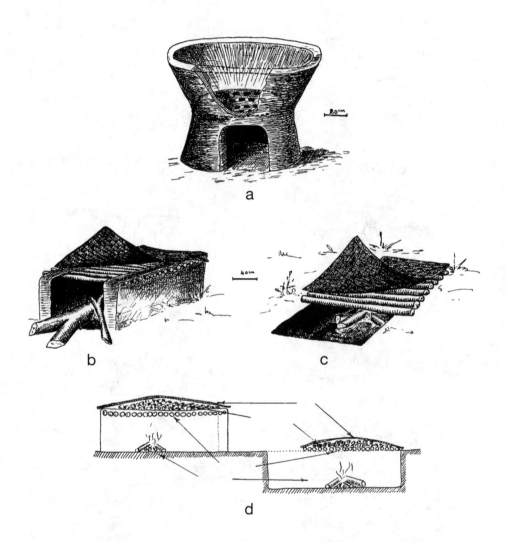

Figure 6.18. Fish smoking techniques, Chad Basin, Chad (adapted from Blache and Miton 1963, Planche 48, p. 113).

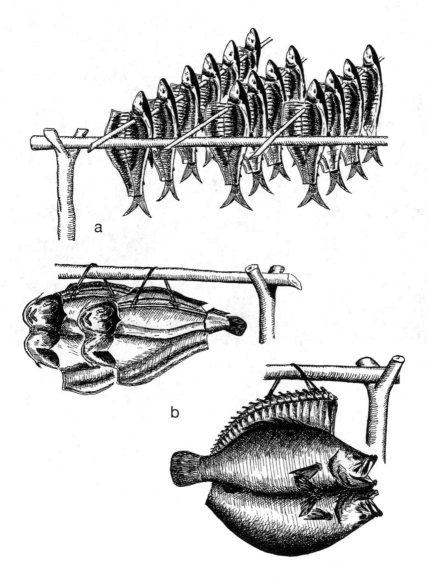

Figure 6.19. Drying smoked fish, Chad Basin, Chad (adapted from Blache and Miton 1963, Planche 49, p. 114).

Figure 6.20. Marsh hamlet "on the shores of Lake Tschad" (Buel 1890:72).

Overall Summary and Conclusions

In this chapter I have discussed aquatic resource exploitation in five different regions outside the Valley of Mexico: the Upper Lerma drainage of the Toluca region in west-central Mexico; the Great Basin of the western U.S.; the Titicaca Basin of southern Peru and western Bolivia; the Tigris-Euphrates Delta of southern Iraq and adjacent Iran; and, more briefly, the Lake Chad region of western Chad. I selected these areas because their traditional aquatic economies had been relatively well described, and because their environmental and ecological characteristics suggested that the details of aquatic resource utilization might, with care, provide useful analogues for the technology and sociology of aquatic resource exploitation in the prehispanic Valley of Mexico, thereby extending those insights more directly based on information from the Valley of Mexico itself (discussed in Chapters 2-5).

Within this large dataset, several general impressions stand out: (1) the diversity of marsh and lacustrine environments over space and time, both within specific regions and between different areas; (2) the striking similarities, both technological and organizational, in procurement and processing of aquatic resources in widely separated regions — similarities that seem to transcend a number of notable differences; and (3) some notable contrasts between aquatic economies that are embedded in larger economies that include a pastoral component (the Titicaca Basin and the Tigris-Euphrates delta) versus those that lack such a component (prehispanic Mesoamerica and the U.S. Great Basin) — apparently, only where pastoralism is absent is there any significant exploitation for food of aquatic insects as a true complement to agricultural production.

The Diversity of Marsh and Lacustrine Environments

Aquatic environments are dynamic, fluctuating, and subject to significant changes over seasonal, inter-annual, and long-term cycles in water level, water flow, water salinity and alkalinity, and fauna and flora. These changes often result in substantial variability in resource availability from place to place, even within relatively small regions and over comparatively short time spans. Specific plants and animals that are abundant in one part of a marsh or lake may not be available in such quantities or proportions a few kilometers distant in the same marsh or lake system at the same point in time. Similarly, a specific lake or marsh locale that has abundant fish, waterfowl, insects, reeds, or algae one year, or during one period, may not necessarily contain such resources in the same quantity or proportion during another year or at another period of time. This expectable resource variability has a number of implications for the archaeological record (see Chap. 7).

On the other hand, whatever the particular disposition and configuration of their resources over space and time, all aquatic environments have essentially the same kinds of plant and animal resources that have, or might have, interested resident human populations in the past: waterfowl, fish, reptiles and amphibians, miscellaneous invertebrates, edible insects, algae, reeds, and a wide variety of plants with edible roots, rhizomes, seeds, stems, or fruits.

Technological and Organizational Similarities and Differences

Although each is unique in some ways, the traditional societies considered in this chapter also reveal a remarkable number of technological and organizational similarities in the exploitation of aquatic resources.

The importance of nets

Most of these societies make ample use of twine/cord/string nets for capturing waterfowl and fish, and often, for harvesting less mobile animal products such as aquatic insects and fish eggs; even some important plant products (primarily algae) are sometimes collected with netting. Although hooks and lines (also made of fiber) are also used for fishing, and harpoons or bows and arrows for hunting birds and fish, these are almost always of secondary importance relative to nets. Nets may be large and rectangular in form, manipulated by groups of men in boats, from the shore, or afoot in shallow water. Nets may also be small, of elliptical, circular, or rectangular form, manipulated by individuals or groups in boats, afoot in shallow water, or from the shore.

Nets, and sometimes baskets, are often employed in conjunction with different kinds of weirs made of wood stakes and reeds or other aquatic brush (occasionally with stone foundations) to entrap fish. Although weirs are most common where water flows in a current, as in a stream or river, lacustrine weirs also occur at points where streams and rivers enter or leave the main body of a lake or marsh. Even where there are no natural water currents, men in boats may move about on the lake surface to agitate and alarm fish or waterfowl and so direct them toward awaiting weirs, nets, and traps. Nets often are held in place with stone sinkers. Because cordage made of natural fibers has a short use-life, due to alternate wetting and drying, very large quantities of string and cord must be constantly acquired to repair and replace worn out nets and lines. We should expect the archaeological record in aquatic environments to reveal a very substantial effort to produce and distribute both twine and netting (see Chap. 7).

The importance of reeds

Apart from their significance as sources of food, these plants are also often used to make a wide variety of essential products: boats, arrow shafts, houses and shelters, mats, bags, baskets, weir walls, and even items of clothing; in societies with a pastoral component, reeds often serve as an important, even major, source of animal fodder. Reed boats, as exemplified in the Titicaca Basin and the Great Basin, can be very large, capable of transporting heavy cargoes of people and their possessions, and even providing facilities for on-board cooking and camping. In some cases, masses of reeds also serve as house foundations, both artificial and natural (where naturally dense concentrations of aquatic plants have compacted to form buoyant platforms that may be extended and deepened by additions of more reeds). Surprisingly, there is no historic record of any use of reed boats in the Valley of Mexico, or in the nearby Upper Lerma drainage. However, the ubiquity of these cheap and convenient vessels in so many other parts of the world makes me doubt that we can assume their absence in central Mexico in prehistoric/prehispanic times. The archaeological record should contain ample evidence for the harvesting and processing of reeds, even where the reeds themselves are rarely preserved (see Chap. 7).

Processing and storing aquatic products
There is less ethnographic information than would be ideal about these essential tasks. The stalks, rhizomes, seeds, roots, or fruits of many kinds of aquatic plants were often consumed casually, as snack foods, as they were encountered during the course of other hunting and collecting activities in lakes and marshes. Waterfowl and fish were often dried, smoked, or salted, and sometimes stored for later use in rock- and grass-lined pits or in bags and baskets inside dwellings; large ceramic vessels might also have served such storage functions, although there is less historic documentation about this. Waterfowl eggs were sometimes preserved for many days or several weeks by packing them in mud and placing them in cool places, in either a cooked or raw state. Smoking and drying of fish or fowl flesh was sometimes carried out within above-ground or subterranean masonry structures, or even in more portable large ceramic braziers. The seeds of many kinds of aquatic plants were often ground into powder with stone mortars, pestles, or manos and metates, as were some aquatic insects. The domestic refuse at places where aquatic resources were processed and/or consumed is likely to contain the bones of fish, waterfowl, reptiles, and amphibians, or the shells of molluscs and waterfowl eggs; the remains of insects, most invertebrates, and many plant foods are much less likely to be found in the archaeological record (see Chap. 7).

The sociology of aquatic technology
In all these societies, aquatic resources are obtained through both individual and communal/group activities. Individuals operate afoot or in boats, using nets, lines, spears, or bows and arrows. Groups of up to a few dozen people, using variants of the same technology, may cooperate, especially when dealing with large flocks of waterfowl (especially flightless waterfowl) that must be persuaded to move onto shore or into awaiting nets to be captured. I have found no documented cases of group cooperation involving more than about three dozen people except for references to cooperative fishing groups of up to 150 men in the Tigris-Euphrates delta. In all documented cases, cooperative groups are composed of closely related people, members of the same local community or an extended household group. There are also hints of long-standing group concerns with aquatic resource conservation, exemplified by the "re-seeding" of reed beds around Lake Titicaca, and by the fish "nurseries" on Lake Pátzcuaro.

Settlement pattern and territoriality
In hierarchical societies with a significant agricultural component, people involved in the exploitation of aquatic resources tend to reside permanently in substantial settlements in and around the marshlands, and to go out from these settlements into the surrounding lakes and marshes on a daily basis, returning to their homes before nightfall. Most processing activity occurs at or near these permanent settlements, although areas of dry ground on unoccupied sections of lakeshores may also be used for drying insects, dry-

ing reeds, or butchering waterfowl. A few temporary camps, either in the marshes or on boats, may be established when hunting or fishing at any distance from their homes, but such camps do not seem to have been common in the societies considered here. On the other hand, and not surprisingly, temporary camps and small-scale settlements (usually small household clusters) are typical of nonagricultural, nonhierarchical societies with an aquatic orientation (such as those in the U.S. Great Basin).

Another notable aspect of occupation in aquatic settings is the extent to which permanent residence, seasonal residence, and temporary camps may be situated on natural or artificial "islands," well removed from sizable expanses of dry land. Natural islands are formed in two main ways: (1) of dunes composed of soil particles distributed by wind action, and sometimes further shaped by waves, water currents, or flooding episodes; and (2) of masses of buoyant aquatic vegetation that accumulate densely in shallow water, and that may be either permananently anchored to the ground surface or detached and rendered mobile as they float about, moved by wind and water currents. The Uru of Lake Titicaca and the occupants of Lake Chad are good examples of the second variant, while the indigenous inhabitants of the Great Basin exemplify the first.

Artificial islands are also of two main types: (1) enlargements of pre-existing natural islands, formed by adding masses of lake-bottom soil, aquatic vegetation and reed matting to the tops and sides of the natural dunes or plant masses, as was done in the Valley of Mexico in late prehispanic times; or (2) completely artificial, as in the case of some Marsh Arabs who construct stationary living platforms in open water by piling up masses of reeds within areas defined by reed fencing.

The archaeological remains of such occupied islands, especially of the floating variety, may well occur in areas that were once covered with open water up to several meters deep, with no necessary relationship to episodes of drought or desiccation. When archaeologists find remains of ancient occupation in low-lying areas where standing water must have been present in the past, they should not assume that such occupation was made possible by a lowering of water level so as to produce dry land.

Another important dimension of societies with a significant aquatic economy is the degree to which lake and (especially) marshland becomes formally incorporated into a community territory. This is best described for the Titicaca Basin in the case of reed beds and adjacent lake areas with abundant waterfowl and fish resources. In many cases, these territories are designated by formal, visible borders, and are patrolled by community police who prevent the incursion of individuals who are not part of the community. It is clear that lake and marshland expanses should be considered in much the same way as agricultural and pasture lands when attempting to comprehend local and regional economy and polity.

$-7-$

Archaeological Implications

In this chapter my primary objective is to develop expectations about the archaeological manifestations of the procurement and processing of aquatic resources in the Valley of Mexico. The numerous important questions about the distribution, redistribution, and consumption of these resources are presently of secondary interest. To this end I integrate the historical and ethnographic information presented in previous chapters both with the known archaeological record in the Valley of Mexico itself and with additional archaeological detail from the U.S. Great Basin, an area for which relevant archaeological information is unusually abundant. I begin with a cautionary tale about how post-depositional processes can disturb and confuse the archaeological record in wetland environments.

Issues of Taphonomy

Aquatic landscapes—lakes, lakeshores, and marshlands—in nearly level terrain like the central Valley of Mexico are subject to periodic incursions and recessions of floodwaters as water levels rise and fall with the annual seasons or over longer climatic cycles. Such water movements, especially those episodes of unusually severe flooding that occur at intervals of years, decades, or centuries, can significantly impact the archaeological record. This is exemplified by conditions in the Stillwater Marsh, Nevada (U.S. Great Basin), following unusually severe floods in 1982-1984 and 1986.

> Floodwaters killed the plants. Waves stripped up to 30 cm of topsoil, exposing the entire horizontal extent of many sites to the surface. Dead bulrush and cattail ringed landforms in windrows. Archaeological material became flotsam as the water eroded cultural deposits. Hundreds of human bones lay scattered across the surface. The bones and cultural debris were eroded from black midden deposits and scores of cultural features that dot each site. The sites also exhibit a veneer of redeposited cultural debris and sediments that blankets

the dune slopes leeward to the principal direction of wave action. Apparently, as the debris-laden waves crested the dunes, water slowed enough to drop its load on the lee side of the landforms. As the water receded from the dunes it etched strandlines in the redeposited sediments, while wave fetch formed windrows of archaeological flotsam on the erosional slopes. [Raymond and Parks 1990:39]

Similarly, Wilke (1978) noted the problems created by wind erosion that he encountered while surveying for archaeological sites around Lake Cahuilla, California, farther west in the Great Basin:

Reconnaissance in the dunes revealed an almost continuous belt of archaeological sites, including shallow middens of *Anodonta* [a local freshwater mollusc] shells, vast scatters of ceramic sherds, burned rocks, and other artifacts, and bones of birds, fish, and other animals. These remains are normally buried within the dunes, but where the anchoring mesquite cover has died, or where the wind has cut into the deposits, the materials are exposed on the surface to be sandblasted into fragments with each new storm. . . . Sometimes when the wind blows strongly from another direction, . . . sites which normally are immense scatters of artifacts and food remains are completely covered with sand and the opposite slopes of the dunes show the only evidence of former occupation. Thus, archaeological reconnaissance in this region is to some extent a hit-or-miss venture, depending on which way the winds have recently blown.
   Since all the heavier materials exposed by deflation of the dunes settle to a common level, items of various ages occur together on the same deflated surface. [Wilke 1978:63-64]

Schmidt (1988:366) provides a graphic illustration of how periodic flooding and wind activity may have impacted archaeological remains in Stillwater Marsh (Fig. 7.1).

These observations exemplify the problems that archaeologists working in wetland environments with low vertical relief are likely to confront as they interpret the material remains of past human activities in these landscapes.

The Essential Elements of Traditional Aquatic Economies

In Chapters 3-6, I considered various aspects of the traditional procurement, processing, and storage of aquatic resources in wetland environments in several parts of the world, all characterized by low vertical relief, abundant marshland, and shallow and oscillating water levels with variable levels of salinity. I addressed the consumption of these resources as components of the diet and as they were transformed into tools, utensils, implements, and shelter. For the Valley of Mexico I also noted the prehispanic cosmological significance of lakes and other bodies of water or water sources (streams, springs), with particular emphasis on lakebed, lakeshore, and marshland shrines where rituals were performed and offerings made in ceremonies dedicated to supernatural forces associated with water supply. Although I did not pursue this cosmological line of investigation outside the Valley of Mexico, there are clear indications that water bodies and water sources were also vital components of ancient Andean cosmology (e.g., Bastien 1978; Duviols 1976; Kolata 1993; Rowe 1980; Sherbondy 1982). I believe we

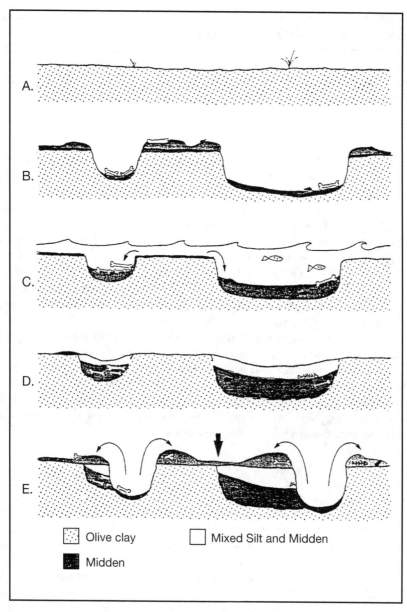

Figure 7.1. The hypothetical impact of periodic flooding and wind activity over time on archaeological materials in the U.S. Great Basin (adapted from Schmidt 1988:366, Fig. 72). *A*, Unmodified surface. *B*, First human occupation. Deposition of bone and stone tools in and around storage pit (left) and house pit (right). *C*, Abandoned occupational surface is inundated by high water. Wave action transports bone and tools. Fish are trapped in house depression. *D*, Wave action and subsequent aeolian processes fill pits with midden and silt. Fish decompose. *E*, Site is reoccupied. Pit excavations truncate earlier occupational features fragmenting and/or redepositing previous cultural and non-cultural accumulations. Note the depression (large arrow) developed between backdirt berms.

can assume that this was the case in virtually all the traditional societies considered in this monograph and throughout the pre-modern world.

My objective in this section is to begin to establish a framework for interpreting the archaeological remains that should permit archaeologists to better understand ancient aquatic economies—particularly in the Valley of Mexico and across highland central Mexico, but perhaps also in other parts of the world.

The Natural Setting

Although each of the regions considered in this study has distinctive physical characteristics, all share some key, interrelated environmental qualities: (1) low vertical relief, shallow water depth, and substantial expanses of marshland; (2) substantial seasonal, inter-annual, and long-term variability in water depth and water-covered area, and in water salinity and alkalinity; (3) substantial variability over time and space in the distribution and configuration of open-water and marshland; and (4) substantial variability over time and space in the distribution and configuration of aquatic flora and fauna. There is also good reason to think that all these environments have been characterized by the existence of "islands" formed of compacted masses of buoyant aquatic plants that have accumulated naturally and that tend to concentrate in localities where the actions of wind, water currents, or human design have driven and emplaced them. Such "islands" may be naturally fixed in place, anchored by roots and branches to other masses of vegetation or to the ground surface, or they may be relatively mobile and capable of being moved about by wind, water, or deliberate human action.

These environmental characteristics have all had a significant impact on how human beings have organized and configured themselves as they sought to exploit aquatic resources and to propitiate the supernatural forces which, they believed, controlled the success or failure of their access to these resources.

The Resources

Although some flora and fauna are unique to particular localities, there is a notable degree of general similarity in the plants and animals that have been exploited by human beings in aquatic environments worldwide (Tables 7.1 and 7.2).

Because many of these plants and animals are dependent on highly specific geophysical and geochemical conditions, their distribution and configuration are in a state of flux over time and space. Any particular locale where specific plants or animals may have been hunted, collected, or harvested at one point in time may, at other points in time, have been a locus for the exploitation of a different set of plants or animals. *Over time this could produce a mixture in the same place of archaeological remains associated with the exploitation of different resources.*

Furthermore, the presence of some of these plants and animals is more stationary and predictable than the presence of others, at least over the short term. For instance, reed beds

Table 7.1. Aquatic fauna and their uses.

Animal	Use
waterfowl and bird eggs	flesh used for food; bone and feathers used for implements and decoration; ritual offerings (?)
fish and fish eggs	food; ritual offerings (e.g., Guzmán et al. 2001)
insects*	food
insect eggs**	food
salamanders***	food
frogs	food
turtles	food; shell used for implements; ritual offerings (?)
misc. molluscs and crustaceans	food; shells used for decoration

*Documented only for the Valley of Mexico, the Upper Lerma, and the U.S. Great Basin.
**Documented only for the Valley of Mexico.
***Documented only for highland Mexico.

Table 7.2. Aquatic flora and their uses.

Plants	Uses
reeds, rushes, canes	stalks, seeds, and roots for food; stalks for mats, houses and other shelters and living surfaces, basketry, clothing, houselot fencing, boats, fans, decorative items, and small spears and arrows
grasses, sedges, water-lilies, and misc. plants	seeds, stalks, roots, and rhizomes for food
algae*	food

*Documented only for the Valley of Mexico and the Chad Basin.

are much more likely to be relatively permanent and enduring in a particular locale than are mobile schools of fish. Because certain animals, such as waterfowl and some insect species, typically live, feed, or breed in close association with specific plant communities (such as reed beds), these animal species are likely to be regularly and predictably found in such places. Similarly, masses of aquatic insects are most likely to wash up year after year on the leeward shores of sizable bodies of open water. These varying degrees of permanence, abundance, predictability, and dependability can have a significant impact on how humans control access to different kinds of aquatic resources. For example, reed beds are more likely to be individually controlled, whereas fishing waters are commonly open to general communal access.

The exploitation of aquatic resources has also involved a series of infrastructural tasks (Table 7.3).

Table 7.3. Infrastructural tasks associated with the exploitation of aquatic resources.

Tasks	Associated Materials	Associated Implements
Building and maintaining permanent shelters	*Dry supporting surfaces*—on shore or on natural or artificial "islands": twine for tying reed bundles and mats to pole framework *Reed structures:* reed bundles, reed mats and brush, with wood-pole framework *Stone and adobe structures:* stone foundations; adobe upper walls; mat roofs; pole roof supports	Hammerstones for pounding poles or canes into surface; knives for trimming reeds and mats, and for cutting twine
Building and maintaining temporary shelters	Brush, or reed mats, with wood poles or canes for support; twine for tying reeds or brush to pole framework	Knives for cutting and trimming canes
Making and repairing boats	*Dugouts:* large logs *Plank boats:* large logs cut or split into planks *Reed boats:* reeds and twine	*Dugouts:* gouging and chipping tools *Plank boats:* cutting and splitting tools *Reed boats:* knives, awls, hammerstones
Making cord or twine	Fiber (ixtle, cotton, etc.)	Scrapers for detaching fiber from encasing plant flesh; spindle whorls
Making and repairing nets	Cord or twine	Awls, large needles
Making and repairing fish-lines and fishhooks	Cord or twine; bone or stone fragments	?
Building and maintaining fish weirs	Poles, brush, twine, netting	Hammerstones for pounding stakes into lake bottom
Making and repairing baskets and bags	Twine, rushes, grasses	Spindle whorls?
Making and repairing spears, arrows, and projectile points	*Spears and arrows:* wood or cane shafts *Projectile points:* chert or obsidian flakes and blades	Knives for cutting and shaping shafts; "spoke shaves" for smoothing shafts; percussion stones and bone punches for repairing stone points
Making and repairing cutting, scraping, puncturing, and grinding tools	Chert and obsidian flakes, and basalt "chunks"	Punching and flaking tools—stone, bone, antler; grinding tools—hammerstones and abrading stones
Making and repairing facilities for drying and smoking fish and waterfowl	*Drying:* dry space on open ground, or wood framework *Smoking:* masonry or ceramic or wood frame over fire	Uncertain
Making and repairing storage facilities	Grass-lined or rock-lined pits; bags or baskets; large ceramic vessels	Uncertain
Replanting reed beds	Placing detached roots into cut-over areas or in shallow stretches of open water	Boats to maneuver; long poles to emplace roots into lake bottom
Territorial definition	Natural or man-made markers, on-shore or in the lake-marsh	Stones, worked or unworked, for building masonry markers; knives for cutting border canals through reed beds

Table 7.4. The technology of procurement, processing, and storage of aquatic fauna.

Animal	Procurement Techniques	Processing Techniques	Storage Techniques
Waterfowl	Netting, noose-trapping, and pursuing until the birds tire and can be seized or clubbed. Decoys and sticky gums sometimes used. Bows and arrows and atlatl spears also used. Large stationary nets set on poles are common. Canoes common but hunting also on foot. Both individual and cooperative techniques. Flightless molting birds may be driven onshore to be clubbed.	Butchering either near place of capture or near residence. Boiled or roasted, sometimes in pits, sometimes encased in mud. Carcasses may be split and sun dried for later use.	When dried, sometimes stored in dry, grass-lined pits, usually in sacks or other containers, for up to a few months.
Waterfowl eggs	Gathering afoot or in canoes working out from home base, or opportunistic appropriation of eggs from nests encountered while hunting or fishing.	Collected eggs brought home in bags, baskets, or other containers. Boiled or roasted.	May be buried in mud for several weeks.
Fish	Netting, spearing, and hooking from canoes or platforms, sometimes on foot, often using pole, brush, or net weirs; hooks on set lines; netting in small artificial pools that are emptied of water by hand. Large rectangular nets and small dip nets both used. Both individual and cooperative techniques employed.	Placement in containers after capture, prior to butchering and filleting. Smoking in masonry or ceramic vessels, or on pole drying frames. Drying on mats, racks, or platforms. Dried fish ground into powder for soups. Roasted, steamed, or baked, sometimes in preheated grass-lined pits.	Dried fish stored in sacks or other containers in houses, or in grass-lined pits near residences.
Fish eggs	Netting in shallow water, either afoot or in canoes.	No good information. Roasted in ashes, or steamed, or baked, sometimes in preheated grass-lined pits. May be cooked in pots.	No information. Probably not stored for any length of time.
Salamanders	Usually speared from canoes.	Brought home in containers. Fried, roasted, or boiled, usually with seasonings.	No information. Probably not stored for any length of time.
Frogs	Speared or seized by hand, either in canoe or afoot.	Hind legs broken after capture to prevent escape. Brought home in containers. Fried, roasted, or boiled, usually with seasonings.	No information. Probably not stored for any length of time.
Turtles	Seized by hand in reed beds, usually while the collector is afoot. Killed by cutting off head.	Baked or boiled in shell.	No information. Probably not stored for any length of time.
Crustaceans and molluscs	Netted, either afoot or in canoes. Some molluscs are collected individually by hand.	No good information.	No information.

Table 7.4 cont.

Insects	Netted, either from canoes or afoot, with dip nets or push nets. Collected in baskets from windrows when washed up on shore.	If living, insects usually first drowned and then dried on flat, dry surfaces (housetops or dry ground on lakeshore). Usually ground to a paste or powder for use as food.	Ground flour may be stored in bags, baskets, or other containers.
Insect eggs	Often collected from artificial "nurseries" prepared from bundles of grass or reeds, either in canoes or afoot.	Shaken from nursery bundles onto dry cloths. Carried home in cloth or container. Dried at home and ground to a paste or powder for use as food.	No information.

Table 7.5. The technology of procurement, processing, and storage of aquatic flora.

Plant	Procurement Techniques	Processing Techniques	Storage Techniques
Algae	Netted on water surface, or removed from there with scoops, both afoot and from canoes. Apparently a year-round activity.	Sun dried on prepared surfaces on the lakeshore, then formed into thin "loaves" or cakes. Sometimes wrapped in leaves.	In bags or ceramic containers.
Reeds* (for non-food uses)	Individually cut with knives or sickles.	Floated from harvesting locale and dried on the lakeshore. Mats and reed boats made on dry ground near residences. Reed housing constructed on dry ground, or on natural or artificial islands.	Piles of dried reeds and mats stored in structures for short periods.
Reeds (for food)	Individually cut with knives or sickles.	Stalks peeled and eaten raw, often as a snack food. Seeds stripped off by hand. Roots and bulbs pulled off by hand, or cut off. Seeds ground up for soups, boiled in ollas or skin bags or impermeable baskets.	Ground-up seeds stored in bags, baskets, or ceramic vessels.
Other plants	Individually cut with knives or sickles. Some detached by hand.	Seeds ground up for soups, boiled in ollas or skin bags or impermeable baskets. Stalks and rhizomes may be simply eaten raw.	Ground-up seeds stored in bags, baskets, or ceramic vessels.

*The term "reed" is here used generically to include reeds, rushes, and canes.

The Technology of Procurement, Processing, and Storage of Aquatic Resources

Despite the obvious differences from place to place in some specific techniques, there is a notable similarity worldwide in the tools, implements, and procedures associated with procuring and processing aquatic resources (Tables 7.4 and 7.5). The procedures imply the need for implements for cutting, scraping, penetrating, grinding, gouging, boiling and storage. These implements would need to be manufactured or acquired, and maintained, repaired, or replaced as they were used. Other implements would be needed to make and repair infrastructural elements (e.g., cord, twine, nets, baskets, bags, boats, shelter, and pottery). In predicting *what* the archaeological manifestations of different activities might be, it is also necessary to consider *where* these material remains might be found in the archaeological record, and *how* they came to be where the archaeologist finds them (e.g., were they lost, broken and repaired in use, broken or used up and discarded, stored for re-use, or moved about by human or natural agencies after they were originally deposited?).

Although organic materials, apart from dense bone and antler, do not generally preserve in the archaeological record outside very arid regions, recent archaeological studies in wetland settings have revealed that a remarkable state of organic preservation can occur in such permanently wet contexts (e.g., Bernick 1998; Parsons et al. 1985; Purdy 2001; Serra 1988).

Settlement Patterns

People who exploit aquatic resources distribute themselves over the wetlands according to the possibilities and constraints of technology, ecology, and sociopolitical considerations (e.g., group territories, access to other resources and services [e.g., marketplaces], security, cosmological associations of particular places, and demands upon the household and community labor forces). The ethnographic and historical sources indicate two main types of wetland occupation:

(1) Residence in relatively permanent settlements, from which people make daily round-trips afoot or in boats into the nearby lakes and marshes. Considerable snacking on aquatic plant foods, as well as some minor meal preparation away from home, may occur on such daily forays. The permanent settlements may be situated along the lakeshore or on natural or artificial islands or platforms within the lakes or marshes. The permanent settlements may be large villages, small hamlets, or diffuse clusters of individual households.

(2) Residence most of the time in relatively permanent settlements, but with the utilization of temporary camps at greater distances from home where a portion of the household or community labor force may spend from a few days to a few weeks at a time in hunting, fishing, collecting, or processing activities. These temporary camps may be occupied regularly or irregularly, and they may be situated on dry ground along the edges of lakes or marshes or on natural or artificial islands or platforms within the lakes and marshes. Temporary encampments may also be on relatively large boats. Some

camps may be used only to prepare food while away from home on day-trips into the lake or marshlands.

The documentary sources from the Valley of Mexico also suggest that sacred places devoted to supernatural forces associated with water may be situated in lakes and marshes. Such places are often marked by shrines where ritual performances take place and where offerings of materials (including human sacrifices) are made. Some shrines are well out in the lakes, in places accessible only by boat, and from whence there is often a full, unencumbered view of the places in the surrounding landscape where other shrines associated with water are situated.

Archaeological Insights from the U.S. Great Basin

The Great Basin is one of the world's archaeologically best-studied wetland regions, with a combination of published archaeological and ethnographic information that may be unequalled. Although, as I stressed in Chapter 6, there are many major natural and cultural differences between the Great Basin and the Valley of Mexico, I am convinced that, used with caution, the rich data from the former region can be relevant to developing expectations about the archaeological manifestations of the utilization of aquatic resources in the latter. In this regard, it is useful to remember that both the central Great Basin and the central Valley of Mexico are large, stoneless areas: whatever stone does occur must necessarily have been brought in and left there by human beings.

In this section I will highlight those archaeological remains from the Great Basin that seem most useful for my purposes. For obvious reasons, I will do no more than skim the surface of the vast literature that exists.

General Character of the Archaeological Record

Excavations and surveys have been undertaken widely throughout the Great Basin since the early twentieth century. Those works that I have consulted include Harrington (1927); Heizer and Napton (1970); Janetski and Madsen (1990); Loud and Harrington (1929); Kelly (2001); Napton (1969); Raymond and Parks (1990); Raven and Elston (1988); and Wilke (1978).

Generally speaking, there are three categories of archaeological "sites" in the Great Basin wetlands (excluding the upland areas, well away from the lakes and marshes): (1) cave and rock shelters in the hills immediately surrounding the main valley floors, which appear to have functioned primarily as places to cache food and equipment, with minimal residence (Hidden, Lovelock, and Humboldt caves are the best known of these); (2) residential sites of varying size and degree of permanence on the valley floors, most of which occur atop slightly elevated dunes, often linear in configuration, some of which appear to be relics of ancient "finger delta" systems at the mouths of in-flowing rivers; and (3) a wide variety of "off-site" remains—lithic and bone artifacts, animal bone, fire-cracked rock, and possible storage pits, mostly situated on low natural elevations, but a few on flat surfaces of old playa lakes—that appear to represent places where many kinds of procurement and processing activities, probably including brief encampments, were undertaken away from permanent residences.

As noted at the beginning of this chapter, the nature and configuration of the archaeological record on the valley floors has been much affected by post-depositional processes. Some regional surveys and excavations in and around Stillwater Marsh, for example, were undertaken after unusually severe flooding episodes in 1982-1984 exposed many archaeological remains that had previously been largely hidden by substantial aeolian deposits. These same floodwaters, of course, substantially disturbed the archaeological materials, truncating some deposits, and eroding and redepositing many others. The 1980s flooding had certainly been preceded by numerous similar events, and so the archaeological record emerges as a palimpsest product of many episodes of past disturbances of erosion and deposition and redeposition, complicated by the activities of many generations of human occupants.

Harrington (1927) provided a good general characterization of the valley-floor sites prior to the 1980s flooding:

> We found the [archaeological] camp-sites scattered over the northern part of the lake-bottom, where the water had been shallowest, and we noticed that the spots selected were usually slight rises in the ground. . . .
>
> One can locate the camp-sites from quite a distance by the stones lying on the surface of the lakebed which is otherwise stoneless; and these on close approach prove to be for the greater part broken mortars, broken or unfinished pestles, metates or grinding slabs, and manos or handstones for grinding the seeds. . . . In addition to these are numerous stones cracked to pieces by fire, countless chips and bits of flint and obsidian; many arrow points, knife blades, and the like . . . ; very rude blades of slate, perhaps for cutting fish; occasional flat disks of stone, perforated in the middle like spindle whorls; a few bowls for straight pipes, made of stone, and some scattered beads made from Pacific Ocean shells. . . . In some places, newly uncovered by the wind, the crumbling bones of rabbits and other food animals may still be seen, and once in a while a human skeleton, originally buried. [Harrington 1927:44-45]

Archaeological Contents of the Cave Caches

These protected deposits, many of them completely dry and little disturbed prior to the early twentieth century, are remarkable for the presence of many kinds of tools and implements, and for the outstanding preservation of organic materials. These include a wide range of stone (ground stone [mostly basalt] and chipped stone [mostly chert and obsidian]) and bone tools (awls, punches, needles), wooden implements (including bows and arrows, harpoons, and digging sticks), basketry, netting, sacking, clothing, twine and cord (including fish lines with attached composite hooks made of small wood and bone pieces lashed together with fine twine), and remarkably realistic duck decoys fashioned of reeds. The ground stone artifacts include net sinkers (both grooved and perforated, some circular and some cylindrical in form), and a great many manos, metates, pestles, and mortars. Chipped stone artifacts include projectile points (larger ones [probably spear points] and smaller ones [probably arrow points]), and a wide variety of bifacial and unifacial flake tools (mostly chert and obsidian) that functioned as knives, scrapers, drills, and gravers.

Loud and Harrington (1929) provide detailed descriptions of two types of ancient fish lines and fishhooks from Lovelock Cave—set-lines with multiple hooks, and individual lines with single hooks. Such descriptions of ancient fishhooks are difficult to come by, and so I quote their description to provide a good sense of the appearance of these implements. It is likely that the true function of such small bone fragments may have gone unrecognized by archaeologists working in central Mexico, even in those few contexts where such fragile artifacts might be preserved:

> The set-line, 22 ft long [6.7 m], . . . is a fine, strong line, apparently of Indian hemp. Strung along its central portion at intervals of about 7½ inches [17 cm] is a series of 5-inch [11 cm] snells [subsidiary cords] made from still finer cord, to which are attached 12 fishhooks. Each [fishhook] consists of a shank of split rush and a barb of bone; the snell being attached at the junction of the shank and barb. . . . To make the hook, the strip of split rush was bent about the bone barb and wrapped tightly with fine cord. The finished shanks are 1 & 1/8 inches long [2.5 cm] on the average. . . .
>
> . . . [Plate 7.1] illustrates another type of fishhook, with a shank of wood to which the bone barb is lashed, the barbs averaging about an inch in height [2.2 cm] and the shanks an inch and a quarter [2.8 cm]. They were not attached to a set-line, but each had a line of its own, a loosely-twisted 2-strand line, apparently of Indian hemp. Barbs [made of small bone pieces] were lashed to the shanks and shanks to the line with fine native cord. [Loud and Harrington 1929:116-17]

An individual fishhook attached to the single line mentioned above is described in further detail (Fig. 7.2):

> [the hook] comprises a section of bone 25 mm long, broken from the side of a pelican ulna or humerus. This bone fragment is acutely sharpened and well polished. A twig of tough wood, 2 mm in diameter, is split in half and folded over the blunt edge of the bone. The extremities of the twig are brought together, pinching between them a cord 0.7 mm in diameter. The cord then spirals about the two halves of the twig, securely binding them to the bone by several half hitches. [Loud and Harrington 1929:41]

Although they are not mentioned or illustrated by Loud and Harrington, other researchers have reported bipolar fishhooks, bone pieces tied to a line in the middle and sharpened on both ends, from other excavated sites in the Great Basin (e.g., Tuohy 1990:148).

The well-preserved cave caches contain virtually complete ancient tool-kit inventories. As will be seen in the next section, a much more restricted subset of this tool kit appears in open sites and off-site occurrences scattered widely over the region.

Valley-Floor Sites

Most of my understanding of open-site archaeology in the Great Basin derives from published reports of surveys and excavations carried out during the 1980s in and around Stillwater Marsh (Janetski and Madsen 1990; Kelly 2001; Raven and Elston 1988; Raymond and Parks 1990). As noted above, most (but not all) of these open sites occur

Plate 7.1. Fishhooks on lines, from Lovelock Cave, U.S. Great Basin (Loud and Harrington 1929: Pl. 51). The bone barbs measure ca. 2.2 cm long.

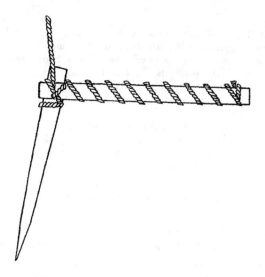

Figure 7.2. Example of a bone fishhook from Lovelock Cave, U.S. Great Basin (from Loud and Harrington 1929:41, Fig. 8). Bone barb measures 2.5 cm long.

atop and alongside slightly elevated natural dunes that rarely rise more than 1 m above the general level of the surrounding terrain. These recent investigations, and many others that I have not cited, have provided a good regional perspective on how the ancient technology cached in places like Lovelock Cave was actually deployed over the wetland landscape.

Raven and Elston (1988:62) describe and assess a fairly typical example of a relatively large site, designated 26Ch1048:

> The surface of the site is marked by the densest concentration of cultural materials encountered during the present testing program. More than 100 circular features [an example from another site is shown in Plate 7.2], many exhibiting slight depressions, are clustered on the central high ground and are scattered on the flats to the west and south; of variable size, a few exceed 3 m in diameter. . . . Both in the immediate vicinity of the features and extending some 100 m to the south occur abundant artifacts of ground stone, fire-cracked rocks [an example of a cluster of fire-cracked rocks from another site is shown in Plate 7.3], and a rich assemblage of bird and mammal bones.
>
> The factors of erosion and redeposition render it difficult to assess the degree to which 26Ch1048 was modified by three years of inundation [early 1980s]. . . . Several of the features . . . appear to have been sheared or planed of their components, while others are probably not true cultural features so much as minor pockets in the gradually undulating terrain that became filled in with redeposited midden. On the other hand, the abundance of cultural debris, including numerous small, light items, and the presence of . . . [a] burned tree stump, the roots of which have not been exposed, argue that volumetric attrition has not been great [some other archaeologists disagree with this view]. [Raven and Elston 1988:62]

Another site, 26Ch1052, is generally similar in appearance, but relative to 26Ch1048, it is smaller and has more dark surface staining and many more shells of a freshwater clam:

> [This site consists of] . . . a discontinuous, darkly stained midden, a field of approximately 50 circular features ranging from 30 cm to 4 m in diameter, and marked by darker staining and occasional depressions, and a scatter of stone artifacts, bones, and shell. Fresh water clam shell (*Anadonta* sp.) constitutes the site's most distinctive attribute, densely scattered over the surface of the ridge and concentrated in windrows along its eastern and western flanks [it remains uncertain whether these shells are natural or cultural in origin, although the authors favor the latter].
>
> The distribution of cultural materials is limited almost exclusively to the elevated surface of the ridge; no features and only isolated fragments of bone and [lithic] debitage occur on the mudflats. It seems likely that most objects on the flats have been redeposited, probably during the [1982-86] flood, from locations higher on the ridge. [Raven and Elston 1988:81]

In their study of 1016 circular features at 51 valley-floor archaeological sites, Raymond and Parks (1990:58) determined that these features ranged from 10 to 580 cm in diameter, with a mean of 142 cm, and with 84% falling into the 51-200 cm range, and a mean of 14 such features per site. Excavations of several of the largest circular features (generally more than 5 m in diameter) at open sites indicate that some apparently represent the remnants of pit houses—several have probable post holes and indications of central hearths (Raven and Elston 1988:147). Most of the excavated smaller circular features seem

Plate 7.2. Examples of typical circular features at an open site near Stillwater Marsh, U.S. Great Basin (photo courtesy of Robert L. Kelly).

Plate 7.3. Example of a typical cluster of fire-cracked rock at an open site near Stillwater Marsh, U.S. Great Basin (photo courtesy of Robert L. Kelly).

to represent storage pits, in different stages of truncation and redeposition by the action of wind deflation and water erosion. Some of these pits appear to have been grass-lined (e.g., Raven and Elston 1988:135), and few are now more than 30 cm deep.

"Off-Site" Archaeological Remains

During his extensive, systematic surface surveys in 1980 and 1981 (before the subsequent floods) of large sections of the valley floors in and around Stillwater Marsh, Robert Kelly and his crew of 10-12 archaeologists, spaced at intervals of 10-15 m, carefully walked over a series of 100 m wide transects that covered about 2% of the total landscape and that aimed to encompass the full range of the region's environmental variability. During fieldseasons in 1985-1987, after the floodwaters had receded, Raymond and Parks (1990) carried out regional surveys in previously flooded areas. Both these surveys recovered the numerous dune-top "sites" briefly considered above, as well as many "off-site" or "non-site" (my terms) localities characterized by diffuse scatters of lithic debitage, lithic artifacts, and fire-cracked rock (Kelly 2001:102-76). These scatters ranged from a few meters in diameter up to much larger areas. Such ephemeral archaeological remains, of course, are subject to the same post-depositional forces that have affected the character of the more concentrated clusters of materials that are more readily characterized as "sites" — indeed, the original locations and configurations of fragile and ephemeral "off-site" remains are likely to be much more altered and confused over time by the forces of wind and water than are those of the more durable "sites."

The interpretation of "off-site" archaeological remains in this region is challenging indeed, and well beyond the scope of this monograph. Suffice it to say that the archaeological record of any wetland area where humans have exploited a variety of aquatic plants and animals is likely to include a very diffuse scatter of the remnants of tools and implements employed in the procurement and processing of these resources. As previously noted, since the central Great Basin, like the central Valley of Mexico, is naturally stone-free, any stone is necessarily the product of cultural activity.

Tables 7.6 and 7.7 list the most common archaeological artifacts from surveys and excavations of open sites in and around Stillwater Marsh and Pyramid Lake in the U.S. Great Basin.

Excavations have revealed abundant remains of aquatic plants and animals (e.g., Kelly 2001:252-80); in addition to abundant bird bone, some egg shells have been recovered (Raven and Elston 1988:15, 95), as well as the remains of molluscs, amphibians, and rodents. Most of the ethnographically utilized species are represented, although many of the archaeological bird bones cannot be identified to the genus and species level. Interestingly, most of the archaeological fish bone comes from very small fish, indicating that most fishing was done with nets and baskets, rather than with hooks and lines (Butler 1996:699; Kelly 2001:280).

Table 7.6. Common stone and bone artifacts from archaeological surveys and excavations in and around Stillwater Marsh.

Chipped Stone (mostly chert, some obsidian)	*Ground Stone* (mostly basalt)	*Bone* (mostly larger bones of birds and mammals)
debitage: flakes and flake fragments	manos	awls
bifacial implements made on flakes, probably mostly	metates	punches
knives and scrapers; a few drills, and gravers	hammerstones	
small projectile points, probably used with bow and arrow	pestles	
large projectile points, probably used with atlatl	mortars	
unifacial implements: utilized flakes of uncertain function	net sinkers	
bipolar cores		

(Adapted from Kelly 2001; Raven and Elston 1988; Raymond and Parks 1990)
Listed in each column in approximate order of numeric abundance. This table does not include fire-cracked rock, which is fairly abundant at some localities.

Table 7.7. Tuohy's* (1990) classification of stone net-sinkers from around Pyramid Lake (Figs. 7.3-7.7).

Net-Sinker Category	*Net-Sinker Variant*
I. Un-modified (Fig. 7.4)	A. Ovate pebble type
II. Perforated (Fig. 7.5)	A. Perforated net-sinker
III. Knobbed (Fig. 7.6)	A. Hook-shaped
	B. Foot-shaped
	C. Ovate
	D. Globular
IV. Grooved (Fig. 7.3)	A. Centrally encircling groove, tapered ends
	B. Centrally encircling groove, rounded ends
	C. Edge grooved, or partially grooved
	D. Single girdled
	E. Double girdled
V. Chipped (few in number, not illustrated)	A. Chipped and battered, roughly rectangular
VI. Notched (Fig. 7.7)	A. Assymetrical with straight sides
	B. Symmetrical, smooth, rectangular
	C. Smooth, ovoid or leaf-shaped
	D. General, irregular shaped
	E. Two-notched
	F. Three-notched
	G. Four-plus notches
VII. Bipointed (not illustrated)	A. Spindle-shaped or bipointed
VIII. Effigy sinkers (few in number, not illustrated)	

*His artifacts classified as canoe anchor-weights, or as large, grooved net-sinkers, are illustrated in Fig. 7.3. No weights given.

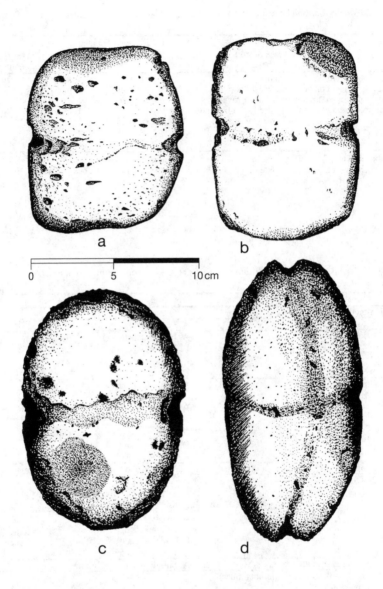

Figure 7.3. Canoe anchor weights, or large, grooved net weights, Pyramid Lake area, U.S. Great Basin (from Tuohy 1990:143, Fig. 16).

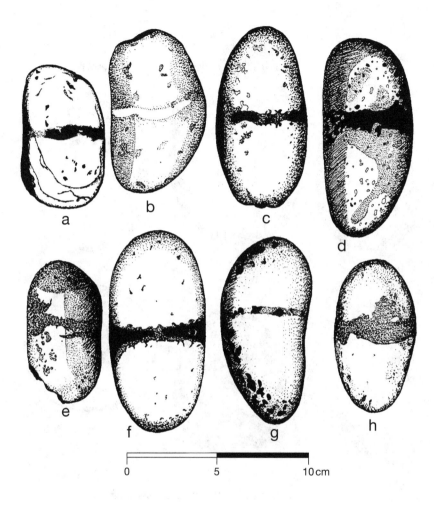

Figure 7.4. Unmodified net-sinkers, ovate pebble type, Pyramid Lake area, U.S. Great Basin (from Tuohy 1990:144, Fig. 17).

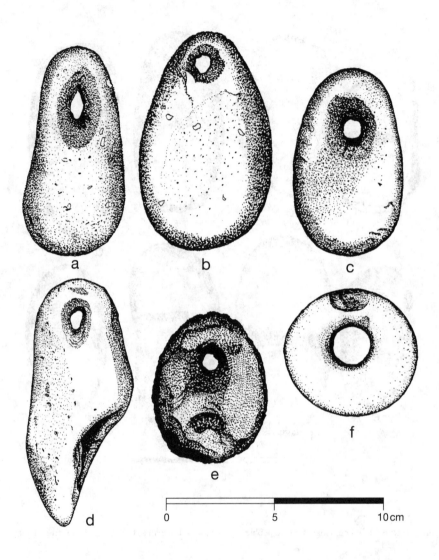

Figure 7.5. Perforated net-sinkers, Pyramid Lake area, U.S. Great Basin (from Tuohy 1990:145, Fig. 18).

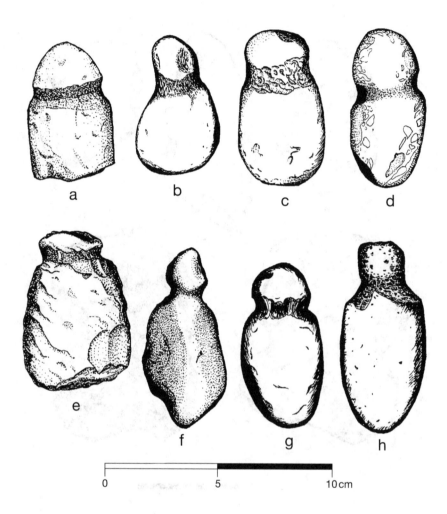

Figure 7.6. Knobbed net-sinkers, Pyramid Lake area, U.S. Great Basin (from Tuohy 1990:146, Fig. 19).

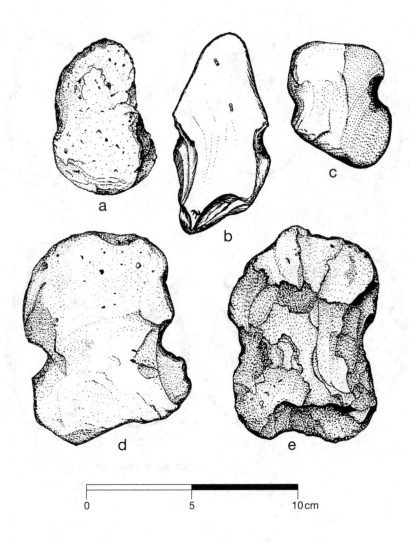

Figure 7.7. Notched net-sinkers, Pyramid Lake area, U.S. Great Basin (from Tuohy 1990:147, Fig. 20).

Potential Archaeological Signatures of Aquatic Resource Use in the Valley of Mexico

Ethnographic and historical information from several parts of the world, and archaeological data from the U.S. Great Basin, suggest a variety of potential archaeological signatures for different aspects of traditional prehispanic aquatic economies in the Valley of Mexico and elsewhere (Tables 7.8-7.16). These expectations are important, not because they are specific and definitive (which they are not), but because they are suggestive of some of the kinds of archaeological evidence archaeologists working in the wetlands of central Mexico should think about and look for as they seek to better understand how these wetlands have been utilized over long periods of time.

Archaeological excavations and surveys in the Great Basin have produced an unparalleled archaeological dataset that bears directly on the past utilization of wetland resources in that region. When these archaeological data are considered with the rich ethnographic and historical information from the same region, it becomes possible to comprehend the long-term utilization of the Great Basin wetlands in a more complete and nuanced way. When these insights are considered together with relevant worldwide ethnographic information and with archaeological remains in the Valley of Mexico, we can make predictions about what different components of the aquatic economy in that region may look like archaeologically. The apparent near-lack of potential archaeological manifestations of aquatic insect use is especially notable. With this in mind, I now turn to the known (that is, published) archaeological record of the Valley of Mexico itself to see how the expectations developed in the first part of this chapter compare with the actual archaeological remains.

Table 7.8. Potential archaeological manifestations of waterfowl use.*

Activity	Probable Implements	Possible Archaeological Manifestations	Predicted Loci
Netting birds in open water, sometimes using decoys. Usually from boats, but occasionally afoot.	Large rectangular nets, held in place by cane stakes or wooden poles, with net-sinkers, and floats, and wooden clubs for killing birds. Decoys made of unworked stone mounted on reed supports, or of stuffed birds, or of reeds formed into bird shape. Hammerstones to drive supporting posts into lake bottom. Sometimes boats and anchoring stones.	Clusters of unworked bird-sized rocks (decoys). Net sinkers of worked or unworked stone, or possibly of ceramic sherds, if lost or discarded in use. Worked or unworked hammerstones, if lost or discarded during use. Boat-anchor stones, if lost or discarded in use.	Areas of open water.
Spearing birds, sometimes using decoys, usually from boats.	Cane or wood spears, tipped with stone, wood, or bone points, used with atlatl. Some decoys made of unworked rocks mounted on reed supports, other decoys made of stuffed birds or reeds.	Stone or bone projectile points, if lost, broken, or discarded in use. Clusters of unworked bird-sized rocks (decoys). Lithic debitage may result from tool repair. Boat-anchor stones, if lost or discarded.	Areas of open water.
Snaring birds with cords or with sticky gum, sometimes using decoys. From boats and afoot.	Cord loops on wood or cane stakes, possibly with flotation devices, sometimes anchored by worked or unworked stones. Wooden clubs for killing birds. Decoys made of unworked rocks mounted on reed supports, or stuffed birds or reeds. Sometimes boats and anchoring stones.	Boat-anchor stones, if lost or discarded in use.	Areas of open water or marshlands where birds typically rest, nest, and feed.

Table 7.8 cont.

Netting birds by driving them onshore, or into enclosed spaces (e.g., canals) and into nets. From boats and afoot.	Unanchored boats. Large nets on wood or cane stakes, wooden clubs for killing birds. Net sinkers may be used. Birds collected in large sacks for transport from killing grounds.	Net-sinkers, either stone or ceramic, if lost or discarded in use.	Lakeshore areas relatively free of marshy vegetation.
Shooting birds with bow & arrow, sometimes using bird decoys. From boats and afoot.	Wooden bow with cord string and cane-shaft arrows tipped with bone or stone points. Decoys made of unworked stone mounted on reed supports, or of stuffed birds or reeds.	Small stone or bone projectile points, if lost, broken, or discarded while in use. Clusters of unworked bird-sized rocks (decoys). Lithic debitage may result from tool repair. Possibly boat-anchor stones, if lost or discarded.	Areas of open water.
Pulling birds underwater while wearing a deceptive disguise, sometimes using bird decoys. Usually afoot.	Decoys made of unworked stone mounted on reed supports, or of stuffed birds or reeds.	Clusters of unworked bird-sized rocks (decoys).	Shallow water, near areas where birds typically rest, nest, and feed.
Butchering captured birds, either near home or in on-shore locales near places of capture.	Chert or obsidian knives and scrapers to gut birds and remove feathers.	Discarded bones, many with cut marks. Large deposits in places of permanent residence; more ephemeral at locales away from residence. Lithic debitage from tool breakage and repair. Some lost or discarded tools.	Lakeshore areas, either in settlements or in isolated places near where birds captured.
Drying and cooking birds. On shore.	Drying on mats in sun; smoking over low fires.	Large hearths—ephemeral outside settlements, or more enduring inside or near settlements.	Lakeshore areas, either in settlements or in isolated places near where birds captured.
Storing birds.	Dried birds placed in lined pits, or inside houses in large sacks or ceramic vessels(?).	Storage pits lined with grass or rock. Large ceramic jars(?).	In or near settlements.
Collecting birds' eggs, either afoot or from boats.	Bags or baskets for carrying eggs back to home base. Boat may be used.	Boat anchor-stones, if lost or discarded while in use(?).	Relatively shallow-water marshlands where birds nest.
Storing birds' eggs.	Buried in mud.	Fragments of broken shell?	In settlements, near residence.
Consumption of birds and eggs.	Ceramic ollas and comales.	Ceramic ollas and comales. Discarded bone and shell fragments.	Domestic middens, in or near residences.

*Here and in Tables 7.9-7.16 I assume the absence of metal and the presence of pottery.

Table 7.9. Potential archaeological manifestations of fish use.

Activity	Probable Implements	Possible Archaeological Manifestations	Predicted Loci
Fishing with weirs, from boats, or from adjoining platform, or afoot.	Wooden stakes and brush, twine, hammerstones to pound stakes into lake bottom. Unworked rocks may be used to reinforce base of weir. Dip nets or baskets to capture trapped fish. Long cords to pull reed barriers in front of circular weirs. Boat-anchoring stones may be used.	Hammerstones if lost or discarded in use. Larger stakes may be preserved in permanently wet settings (e.g., Tveskov and Erlandson 2003). Rock alignments if used to strengthen and stabilize base of weir (e.g., Dortch 1997) or adjoining platform. Boat-anchoring stones, if lost or discarded in use.	Mainly in areas of relatively shallow, open water near lakeshore where inflowing streams produce a water current.
Netting, with large rectangular nets, from boats or afoot.	Nets, multiple boats, containers for captured fish. Net sinkers and floats may be used. Boat-anchoring stones may be used.	Ceramic ollas as containers for fish? Worked or unworked stone net-sinkers or boat-anchoring stones if lost or discarded in use.	Areas of open water.
Netting with dip nets, from boats or afoot.	Nets. Containers for captured fish. Possibly boat-anchoring stones.	Ceramic ollas as containers? Boat-anchoring stones, if lost or discarded in use.	Areas of open water.
Spearing, from boats or afoot.	Atlatl, spear, bag or basket for captured fish. Spears may have wood, cane, or stone points or prongs. Boat-anchoring stones may be used.	Chips from stone points sharpened or damaged in use. Points may occur if used up, broken, or lost in use. Boat-anchoring stones, if lost or discarded in use.	Areas of shallow water in open water or along edges of marsh.
Hooking fish on lines from boats.	Cane rods and lines with composite hooks made of wood, bone, or stone. Boat-anchoring stones may be used.	Bone or stone hook fragments, if lost, broken, or discarded in use. Boat-anchoring stones, if lost or discarded in use.	Areas of deeper, open water.
Hooking fish on set-lines, from shore.	Long line with multiple composite hooks made of wood, bone, or stone. Tied to stake or stone on land and to a stake or anchoring stone in water.	Bone or stone hook fragments, if lost, broken, or discarded in use. Boat-anchoring stones, if lost or discarded in use.	Near-shore areas.
Drying, on shore.	Mats, wood framework.	?	Lakeshore, probably in or near settlements.
Smoking, on shore.	Masonry structures or ceramic vessels for fire.	Stone masonry remnants; large ceramic brazier remnants. Burned earth, ash and charcoal.	Lakeshore, probably in or near settlements.
Preparing dried fish for consumption.	Ground stone or ceramic grinding tools for preparing flour or powder from dried fish.	Ground stone manos, metates, mortars, pestles. Ceramic molcajetes (grinding vessels).	In or near residences.
Storage.	Lined pits, or large ceramic storage vessels.	Rock-lined pits, or large ceramic jars.	Lakeshore, probably in or near settlements.
Collecting fish eggs, afoot or from boats.	Netting or scooping masses of eggs floating at or near surface, using dip nets or baskets. Boat-anchoring stones may be used.	Boat-anchoring stone, if lost or discarded in use.	Areas of open water.
Consumption.	Ceramic olla for cooking.	Ceramic ollas. Discarded fishbone.	Domestic midden, in or near residences.

Table 7.10. Potential archaeological manifestations of aquatic insect use.

Activity	Probable Implements	Possible Archaeological Manifestations	Predicted Loci
Netting insects with push nets, afoot in relatively shallow water.	Handled push net, bag or other container for collected insects.	?	In areas of relatively shallow water, away from settlements
Drowning living collected insects, on shore.	Large basin, enclosed small ponds along lakeshore.	Large ceramic basin.	Lakeshore area, either in settlements or away from them.
Drying collected insects, on shore.	Level, dry surface, probably with small brush "fences" to prevent insects from blowing away.	?	Lakeshore area, either in settlements or away from them.
Preparing insect-egg nurseries, afoot in shallow water.	Twine, bundles of reeds or grass; forked wooden stake to push base of bundle into lake bottom.	?	In areas of shallow, open water.
Collecting eggs from nurseries in shallow water, afoot.	Pulling up reed bundles and shaking sun-dried eggs onto cloth or into bag or ceramic container.	Ceramic jar?	In areas of shallow, open water.
Collecting eggs from submerged "ropes" or reed bundles, from boats in deeper water.	Boat. Pulling up reed bundles or "rope" and shaking eggs onto cloth or into bag or ceramic container. A boat-anchor stone may be used.	Ceramic jar? Boat-anchor stones if lost or discarded in use.	In areas of deep, open water.
Drying eggs.	Dry, level surface, out of wind.	?	Along lakeshore or at or near residences.
Collecting dead insects from windrows deposited along shoreline by wind and wave action.	Basketry scoops, and bags for depositing collected insects.	?	Along lakeshore.
Storing dried insects and insect eggs.	Sacks, baskets, ceramic jars.	Ceramic jars.	In or near residences.
Grinding fresh or dried insects or eggs into paste or powder.	Ground stone manos and metates; or ceramic molcajetes and pestles.	Manos and metates; molcajetes and pestles.	In residences.
Consumption.	Cooking in olla, or on comal.	Ollas and comales.	In residences.

Table 7.11. Potential archaeological manifestations of frog use.

Activity	Probable Implements	Possible Archaeological Manifestations	Predicted Loci
Spearing, afoot or from unanchored boat.	Wood or cane shaft spear, with wood, cane, bone, or stone points.	Small bone or stone chert or obsidian points if lost or discarded in use. Lithic debitage if points repaired or damaged in use.	Lakeshore or marshland.
Catching by hand, afoot.	None.	?	Lakeshore or marshland.
Consumption.	Ceramic olla or comal for cooking.	Ceramic olla or comal. Discarded bone.	Domestic midden, in or near residences.

Table 7.12. Potential archaeological manifestations of salamander use.

Activity	Probable Implements	Possible Archaeological Manifestations	Predicted Loci
Spearing, afoot or from unanchored boat.	Wood or cane shaft spear, with wood, cane, bone, or stone points.	Small bone or stone chert or obsidian points, if lost, broken, or discarded in use. Lithic debitage if points repaired or damaged in use.	Marshland.
Consumption.	Ceramic olla or comal for cooking.	Ceramic olla or comal. Discarded bone.	Domestic midden, in or near residences.

Table 7.13. Potential archaeological manifestations of turtle use.

Activity	Probable Implements	Possible Archaeological Manifestations	Predicted Loci
Seizing by hand.	None.	?	Marshland.
Butchering.	Knife to cut off head.	Chert or obsidian knife or blade, if lost, broken, or discarded in use. Lithic debitage if points repaired or damaged in use.	At place of capture, probably in marshland.
Consumption.	Cooking in shell.	Discarded shell.	Domestic middens, in or near residences.

Table 7.14. Potential archaeological manifestations of mollusc and crustacean use.

Activity	Probable Implements	Possible Archaeological Manifestations	Predicted Loci
Mollusc: seizing by hand from lake bottom, afoot or netting from boats.	Possible use of boat-anchoring stone.	Boat-anchoring stones, if lost or discarded in use.	Marshland or shallow open water.
Crustaceans: netting, afoot or from boats.	Dip nets. Possible use of boat-anchoring stone.	Boat-anchoring stones, if lost or discarded in use.	Open water of varied depth.
Consumption.	Ceramic ollas or comal for cooking.	Ceramic ollas or comales. Discarded shells.	Domestic middens, in or near residences.

Table 7.15. Potential archaeological manifestations of aquatic plant use.

Activity	Probable Implements	Possible Archaeological Manifestations	Predicted Loci
Cutting reeds,* afoot in shallow water.	Knife; twine for tying bundles of collected reeds.	Chert or obsidian flakes or blades (possibly serrated), if lost, broken, or discarded in use. Lithic debitage from tools repaired in use.	Marshlands, areas of shallow water.
Cutting reeds, from boats in deeper water.	Knife mounted at end of wood or cane pole. Twine for tying bundles of collected reeds. Boat and boat-anchoring stone.	Chert or obsidian flakes or blades (possibly serrated), if lost, broken, or discarded in use. Lithic debitage from tools repaired in use. Boat-anchoring stones, if lost or discarded in use.	Marshlands, areas of deeper water.
Transporting reeds by boat from cutting place to places for drying, storing, and mat-making.	Boat and boat-anchoring stone. Twine for tying bundles of reeds.	Boat-anchoring stones, if lost or discarded in use.	Open water.
Drying reeds.	Dry ground on lakeshore; sometimes with wood frames.	?	Lakeshore, probably in or near settlements.
Storing reeds.	Roofed shelter.	Building foundation?, or post-molds of wooden supports?	Lakeshore, in or near settlements.
Making reed mats.	Weaving reeds together, by hand, or using an awl.	Bone awl.	Lakeshore, in or near settlements.
Collecting edible seeds, stalks, roots, rhizomes, afoot or from boats.	Knife for cutting stalks and detaching seeds, roots and rhizomes. Bags or baskets for carrying. Boat-anchoring stone.	Chert or obsidian flakes or blades, if lost, broken, or discarded in use. Lithic debitage from tools repaired in use. Boat-anchoring stones if discarded or lost during use.	Marshlands, variable water depth.
Preparing edible seeds, stalks, roots, or rhizomes for consumption.	Many eaten raw as "snack" foods or in salads. Seeds may be dried and ground to a flour or powder, and cooked with other foods.	Ground stone grinding tools, probably of fine-grained basalt. Ceramic ollas.	Lakeshore, in or near settlements.
Collecting algae, usually afoot.	Dip nets or scoops, made of fine netting or basketry.	?	Open water, of variable depth.
Drying algae.	?	?	Lakeshore, in or near or away from settlements.
Storing dried algae.	Bags or ceramic jars.	Ceramic jars.	In residences.
Consumption.	Ceramic ollas or comales for cooking.	Ceramic ollas or comales.	Domestic midden, in or near residences.

*Used generically to include reeds, rushes, and canes.

Table 7.16. Expectable archaeological manifestations of different types of occupation in wetland environments.

Type of Occupation	Activities and Functions	Expectable Archaeological Manifestations	Loci
Permanent settlements.	Full range of domestic activities, plus some processing and storage of aquatic products.	Possibly slightly elevated settings, but in lower areas if occupation was atop floating islands. Full range of ceramic and lithic implements and debitage. Domestic architecture—stone or adobe house foundations; reed structures; wattle and daub structures. Storage pits.	On lakeshore or on natural or artificial islands in lakes or marshes.
Temporary camps on natural or artificial islands.	Casual shelter. Possible intermittent "re-occupation" of a favorable specific place. Restricted range of domestic activities—e.g., some meal preparation, sleeping accommodations, and some discard of domestic refuse. Specialized activities such as butchering fish or waterfowl; drying insects or algae; drying or smoking fish or waterfowl.	Slightly elevated settings, but in lower areas if occupation was atop floating islands. A few cooking and food processing implements (e.g., ceramic braziers, ollas, and comales for cooking; water jars; ceramic molcajetes or ground stone manos and metates or mortars and pestles for grinding foods. Chert or obsidian flakes and blades for butchering fish or waterfowl, or for cutting reeds and other aquatic vegetation. Lithic debitage if implements repaired or damaged in use. Probably no architectural remains. There may be storage pits on dry ground.	On lakeshore or on natural or artificial islands in lakes or marshes.
Temporary camps, on boats.	Casual shelter. Little or no "re-occupation" of any specific place. Restricted range of domestic activities—e.g., some meal preparation, sleeping accommodations, and some discard of domestic refuse. Some butchering activities.	Diffuse scatter of the artifacts noted immediately above in areas of relatively deep open water where they were discarded, or lost, from boats. Lithic debitage if implements repaired or damaged in use. No elevated setting. No architectural remains. Boat-anchoring stones, if lost or discarded in use.	In open water or in marshlands.
Daily forays from permanent settlements, with return before night-fall.	No domestic activities apart from casual snacking of wild plant foods, and perhaps some minor food preparation—e.g., heating or cooking prepared foods carried from home.	Minimal material remains. Cutting, scraping, puncturing tools for specific procurement tasks—e.g., chert or obsidian flakes, blades, scrapers. Lithic debitage if implements repaired or damaged in use. Comal fragments.	Lakeshore, marshland, or open-water areas.
Shrines associated with supernatural forces, and perhaps with territorial divisions.	Ritual performances and offerings of high-value objects, including human sacrifices. If shrines are in standing water, boats with anchoring stones will probably be used.	Locations may be predictable on the basis of specific natural features (e.g., alignments with prominent hills), or unusual natural phenomena (e.g., whirlpools, springs, rock formations). Potentially marked by presence of offerings of exotica (carved stone, human sacrifices, fine ceramics, incense-burning vessels). There may be stone masonry. Boat-anchoring stones, if lost or discarded in use.	Lakeshore, marshland, or lakebed.

Archaeological Insights into Aquatic Economy and Cosmology in the Valley of Mexico

Published archaeological research from excavated sites in the Valley of Mexico speaks mainly to the consumption of aquatic products; aside from a single study by Serra (1988), there is little information about their procurement and processing. Most available excavated data come from residential sites around the lakeshore, and most of these excavations have been at Middle and Late Formative sites (Table 7.17) (Mc-Clung de Tapia et al. 1986; Niederberger 1976, 1979, 1987; Santley 1977; Serra 1980, 1982, 1988; Serra and Civera 1982; Serra and Valadez 1985; Smith and Tolstoy 1981; Tolstoy 1975; Tolstoy et al. 1977; Tolstoy and Paradis 1970; Vaillant 1930, 1931, 1935), although there is also some information on Middle and Late Postclassic and Colonial-period lakebed and lakeshore sites (Brumfiel 1996, 1997; Brumfiel and Frederick 1992; DeLucia and Brumfiel 2004; Montúfar and Maldonado 1998; O'Neill 1962; Parsons et al. 1985). Regional surveys undertaken in the 1960s and 1970s provide complementary data on settlement patterning for Early Formative through the Late Postclassic periods, primarily in areas outside the former lakebed of Lake Texcoco (Blanton 1972; Parsons 1971, 1974; Parsons et al. 1982; Sanders 1976; Sanders et al. 1979).

As far as I know, the only information from excavated sites on Classic-period consumption of aquatic resources comes from urban Teotihuacan itself, an inland site (Mc-Clung de Tapia 1987; Starbuck 1987). Late Postclassic Otumba, in the far northeastern Valley of Mexico, is the only other inland site for which aquatic plant remains have been reported from excavated contexts (McClung de Tapia and Aguilar 2001). I know of no published archaeological studies of Terminal Formative, Epiclassic, or Early Postclassic occupations with information about the presence or absence of aquatic resources, and, apart from Teotihuacan and Otumba, there is virtually no information about the presence (or absence) of aquatic plant or animal remains at inland sites in the Valley of Mexico. A recent survey in central Lake Texcoco (Parsons and Morett 2004) is virtually the only archaeological study I know of that is oriented explicitly at issues of procurement and processing of aquatic resources in the Valley of Mexico—and the analyses of these materials are still at a very preliminary stage.

Aquatic Fauna and Flora in Excavated Sites

A wide range of aquatic flora and fauna has been identified at many excavated sites (Tables 7.18 and 7.19). Although it is difficult to discern the precise significance of these aquatic resources in quantitative terms relative to other foods and raw materials, it is quite clear from their presence throughout long periods that aquatic resources were economically significant from Archaic through Postclassic times in this region. As far as I know, Santley's (1977:262) identification of abundant carbonized wild rice (*Oryzopsis* spp.) seeds at the Late Formative Loma Torremote site on the shore of Lake Xaltocán-Zumpango in the northern Valley of Mexico is unique in the archaeological record of this region. The presence of this resource at Loma Torremote may be due to this site's location immediately adjacent to the riverine floodplain of the Río Cuauhtitlán, one of

Table 7.17. Valley of Mexico prehispanic chronology.

Date	Period	Phase
1520 A.D.		Aztec III-IV
	Late Postclassic	Aztec III
1350 A.D.		Aztec II-III
	Middle Postclassic	Aztec I-II
1150 A.D.		Aztec I
	Early Postclassic	Mazapan
900 A.D.		
	Epiclassic	Coyotlatelco
650 A.D.		
		Metepec
		Xolalpan
	Classic	Tlamimilolpa
		Miccaotli
150 A.D.		
		Tzacualli
50 B.C.	Terminal Formative	
250 B.C.		Patlachique
	Late Formative	Ticoman
500 B.C.		
	Middle Formative	La Pastora
900 B.C.		El Arbolillo
	Early Formative	Bomba
1200 B.C.		Ixtapaluca
	Preceramic/Archaic	

the largest permanent streams in the region, and one of the largest sources of freshwater flow into the lacustrine system.

Although mats, basketry, and twine made of reeds and rushes have been identified in the waterlogged deposits at the Terremote-Tlaltenco site in northeastern Lake Xochimilco (Serra 1988), in many cases masses of these identified plant materials functioned as artificial platforms of earth and aquatic vegetation upon which living and working surfaces in marshy terrain were constructed. The abundant "vegetal material" in the deeper levels of O'Neill's (1962) excavations at Chalco, and in Brumfiel's excavations at Xaltocán, may have served a similar function as platform fill. Small quantities of aquatic plant remains have been identified at two inland sites: Classic Teotihuacan (McClung de Tapia 1987) and Late Postclassic Otumba (McClung de Tapia and Aguilar 2001). These could have been obtained from local marshy areas, although they might represent exchange or tributary relationships with lakeshore communities.

Tolstoy et al. (1977:100) note that although the American coot (*Fulica americana*) (a year-round resident in the Valley of Mexico) accounts for only about 3% of the total waterfowl residing there during the winter season when so many migratory species are present, this bird represents about 34% of the total waterfowl bone identified in excavated Formative levels at the Zohapilco/Tlapacoya site in northeastern Lake Chalco. This suggests the importance of year-round hunting of waterfowl at this general locality. By extention, this might imply the year-round importance of the exploitation of aquatic resources in general in the Valley of Mexico during Formative times, and probably in later periods as well.

Table 7.18. Aquatic flora identified at archaeological sites in the Valley of Mexico.

Common Name*	Species	Archaeological Site	Period	Environmental Setting	Reference
juncos (sedges, rushes)	Cyperus sp.	Tenochtitlan/ Mexico City	Colonial	western Lake Texcoco, lakebed	Montúfar and Maldonado 1998:99-102, 104-5
tule (reeds)	Scirpus sp.	Tenochtitlan/ Mexico City	Colonial	western Lake Texcoco, lakebed	Montúfar and Maldonado 1998:104-5
juncos (sedges, rushes)	Cyperus sp.	Otumba	Late Postclassic	inland	McClung de Tapia and Aguilar 2001:122-23
tule (reeds)	Scirpus sp.	Ch-Az-195	Middle Postclassic	southeastern Lake Chalco, lakebed	Parsons et al. 1985:65-66
abundant "vegetal material"	n.a.	Chalco	Middle Postclassic	eastern lakeshore of Lake Chalco	O'Neill 1962:40, 44, 259
tule (reeds)	Cyperaceae	Xaltocán	Middle Postclassic	lakebed, northern Lake Xaltocán	Brumfiel 1996:31
tule (reeds)	Scirpus sp.	Teotihuacan	Classic	inland	McClung de Tapia 1987:60
tule (reeds)	Scirpus sp.	Terremote-Tlaltenco	Late Formative	northeastern Lake Xochimilco, lakebed	McClung de Tapia et al. 1986:107; Serra 1988:121-22
tule (reeds or sedge)	Cyperus sp.	Cuanalán	Late Formative	lower piedmont, northeastern shore of Lake Texcoco	Alvarez del Castillo 1982:9
juncos (sedge)	Cyperus sp.	Terremote-Tlaltenco	Late Formative	northeastern Lake Xochimilco, lakebed	McClung de Tapia et al. 1986:107; Serra 1988:121-22
juncos (sedges, rushes)	Cyperus sp.	Zohapilco (Tlapacoya)	Formative	northeastern Lake Chalco, lakebed	Niederberger 1979:133
cattails	Typha sp.	Zohapilco (Tlapacoya)	Formative	northeastern Lake Chalco, lakebed	Niederberger 1979:133
water lentil	Lemma sp.	Zohapilco (Tlapacoya)	Formative	northeastern Lake Chalco, lakebed	Niederberger 1979:133
cattails	Typha sp.	El Terremote (Xo-EF-2)	Early and Middle Formative	northeastern Lake Xochimilco, lakebed	Smith and Tolstoy 1981:426-27
juncos (sedges, rushes)	Cyperus sp.	El Terremote (Xo-EF-2)	Early and Middle Formative	northeastern Lake Xochimilco, lakebed	Smith and Tolstoy 1981:426-27
juncos (sedges, rushes)	Cyperus sp.	El Terremote (Xo-EF-2)	Early and Middle Formative	northeastern Lake Xochimilco, lakebed	Tolstoy et al. 1977:93
water lily bulbs	Liliaceae	Cuanalán	Late Formative	lower piedmont, northeastern shore of Lake Texcoco	Alvarez del Castillo 1982:9
wild rice	Oryziopsis spp.	Loma Torremote	Late Formative	western lakeshore plain of Lake Xaltocán	Santley 1977:262

*The chronologically younger occurrences are listed first within each main plant category.

Table 7.19. Aquatic fauna identified at archaeological sites in the Valley of Mexico.

Common Name*	Species	Archaeological Site	Period	Environmental Setting	Reference
waterfowl	various	Tlatelolco	Late Postclassic	lakebed, northern Lake Texcoco	Martin del Campo 1955
waterfowl	several species	PAX-5/Xo-Az-60	Late Postclassic	northwestern shore of Lake Xochimilco	Castillo 1994:69-73
waterfowl	Family Anatidae	Xaltocán	Middle Postclassic	lakebed, Lake Xaltocán	Brumfiel 1996:29
waterfowl	aquatic birds other than Anatidae	Xaltocán	Middle Postclassic	lakebed, Lake Xaltocán	Brumfiel 1996:29
waterfowl	n.a.	Teotihuacan	Classic	inland	Starbuck 1987:80
waterfowl	n.a.	Loma Torremote	Late Formative	western lakeshore plain of Lake Xaltocán	Santley 1977:254
waterfowl	Aytha Americana, Aythya affinis, Anasplatyrhynchos, Anas spp., Branta canadiensis, Oxyura dominica, Oxyura jamaicensis	Terremote-Tlaltenco	Late Formative	northeastern Lake Xochimilco, lakebed	Serra 1988:243; Serra and Valadez 1985:176
"birds"	n.a.	Zacatenco	Middle Formative	northwestern shore of Lake Texcoco	Vaillant 1930:38
"Mexican duck"	Anas diazi	Zohapilco (Tlapacoya)	Archaic through Late Formative	northeastern Lake Chalco, lakebed	Niederberger 1979:134
redhead	Aythya americana	Zohapilco (Tlapacoya)	Archaic through Late Formative	northeastern Lake Chalco, lakebed	Niederberger 1976:250
shoveler	Spatula clypeata	Zohapilco (Tlapacoya)	Archaic through Late Formative	northeastern Lake Chalco, lakebed	Niederberger 1976:250; Niederberger 1979:134
pintail	Anas americana	Zohapilco (Tlapacoya)	Archaic through Late Formative	northeastern Lake Chalco, lakebed	Niederberger 1979:134
Mexican mallard	Anas platyrhynchos	Zohapilco (Tlapacoya)	Archaic through Late Formative	northeastern Lake Chalco, lakebed	Niederberger 1976:250; Niederberger 1979:134
pied-billed grebe	Podilymkbus podiceps	Zohapilco (Tlapacoya	Archaic through Late Formative	northeastern Lake Chalco, lakebed	Niederberger 1976:250; Niederberger 1979:134
white grebe	Aechmophorus sp.	Zohapilco (Tlapacoya)	Archaic through Late Formative	northeastern Lake Chalco, lakebed	Niederberger 1976:250; Niederberger 1979:134

Table 7.19 cont.

American coot	*Fulica americana*	Zohapilco (Tlapacoya)	Archaic through Late Formative	northeastern Lake Chalco, lakebed	Niederberger 1976:250; Niederberger 1979:134; Tolstoy et al. 1977:100
cinnamon teal	*Querequedula cyanoptera*	Zohapilco (Tlapacoya)	Archaic through Late Formative	northeastern Lake Chalco, lakebed	Niederberger 1979:134
Canada goose	*Branta canadensis*	Zohapilco (Tlapacoya)	Archaic through Late Formative	northeastern Lake Chalco, lakebed	Niederberger 1976:250; Niederberger 1979:134
fish	unidentified	Xo-Az-60/ PAX-5	Late Postclassic	northwestern shore of Lake Xochimilco	Castillo 1994:69-73
fish	n.a.	Chalco	Middle Postclassic	eastern lakeshore of Lake Chalco	O'Neill 1962:45
fish	Class Osteichthyes	Xaltocán	Middle Postclassic	lakebed, Lake Xaltocán	Brumfiel 1996:29
fish Atherinidae family	*Chirostoma humboldtianum, C. jordani, C. regani*	Zohapilco (Tlapacoya)	Archaic through Late Formative	northeastern Lake Chalco, lakebed	Niederberger 1976:250; Niederberger 1979:137
fish Atherinidae family	*Chirostoma* sp.	Terremote-Tlaltenco	Archaic through Late Formative	northeastern Lake Xochimilco, lakebed	Serra 1988:244; Serra and Valadez 1985:182
fish Coodeidae family	*Girardinichthys viviparus*	Zohapilco (Tlapacoya)	Archaic through Late Formative	northeastern Lake Chalco, lakebed	Niederberger 1976:250; Niederberger 1979:137
fish Cyprinidae family	*Algansea tincella, Evarra* sp., *Notropis aztecus*	Zohapilco (Tlapacoya)	Archaic through Late Formative	northeastern Lake Chalco, lakebed	Niederberger 1976:250; Niederberger 1979:137
fish Cyprinidae family	n.a.	Terremote-Tlaltenco	Late Formative	northeastern Lake Xochimilco, lakebed	Serra 1988:244; Serra and Valadez 1985:182
turtle	*Kinosternon* sp.	Xo-Az-60/ PAX5	Late Postclassic	northwestern shore of Lake Xochimilco	Castillo 1994:69-73
turtle	*Kinosternon* sp.	Xaltocán	Middle Postclassic	lakebed, Lake Xaltocán	Brumfiel 1996:29
turtle	*Kinosternon* sp.	Loma Torremote	Late Formative	western lakeshore plain of Lake Xaltocán	Santley 1977:254
turtle	*Kinosternon* sp.	Zohapilco (Tlapacoya)	Archaic through Late Formative	northeastern Lake Chalco, lakebed	Niederberger 1976:250

Table 7.19 cont.

turtle	*Kinosternon* sp.	Terremote-Tlaltenco	Late Formative	northeastern Lake Xochimilco, lakebed	Serra 1988:244; Serra and Valadez 1985:180
salamander	*Ambystoma mexicanum*	Zohapilco (Tlapacoya)	Archaic through Late Formative	northeastern Lake Chalco, lakebed	Niederberger 1976:250
frog	2 species	Xo-Az-60/PAX-5	Late Postclassic	northwestern shore of Lake Xochimilco	Castillo 1994:69-73
frog	Class Amphibia	Xaltocán	Middle Postclassic	lakebed, Lake Xaltocán	Brumfiel 1996:29
mollusc	several species	Xo-Az-60/PAX-5	Late Postclassic	northwestern shore of Lake Xochimilco	Castillo 1994:69-73

*The chronologically younger occurrences are listed first within each animal category.

Ceramic, Lithic and Bone Artifacts in Excavated Archaeological Sites

The same lakebed-lakeshore archaeological sites that contain the aquatic flora and fauna summarized above also contain numerous associated ceramic, lithic, and bone artifacts. However, I am unable to distinguish a definitive "aquatic signature" in these assemblages. The published reports for virtually all these excavated sites indicate the same broad range of lithic and bone artifacts that Tolstoy (1971) and García-Cook (1982) have identified in central Mexico as a whole and ceramic types that have been widely reported in numerous publications from this same region: (1) ground stone assemblages dominated by manos and metates, with a wide variety of secondary categories, including pestles, mortars, polishing stones, stone "balls," and celts, most made of fine-grained basalt; (2) chipped stone assemblages dominated by a variety of obsidian flake and blade tools formed into prismatic cutting blades, a variety of scrapers, knives, and gravers, a variety of projectile points (for which a rough chronological ordering is apparent), and with smaller quantities of similar chert implements; (3) bone-tool assemblages dominated by a variety of awls, punches, and needles made of deer antler, deer bone, and bird bone; and (4) ceramic assemblages dominated by plainwares (ollas, jars, basins, *comales*) and a wide variety of chronologically diagnostic decorated sherds.

Sigvald Linne (1948:135) long ago noted the apparent absence of archaeological fishhooks in the Valley of Mexico. I do not know of any possible fishhooks that have been identified since Linne's time. This is not surprising since, in all likelihood, such implements would have been small bone or wood shafts, sharpened at one end and tied to a small wooden or bone shank. Such tiny, fragile artifacts would simply not preserve, or their actual function would probably remain unrecognized. Even in the U.S. Great

Basin, for example, where fishhooks were common in both historic and prehistoric times, fishhooks are not reported outside caches in protected cave deposits (see above).

The only archaeological study known to me that has successfully identified a distinctive assemblage of artifacts that can reasonably be associated with procuring or processing aquatic resources is that by Serra and her colleagues at the Late Formative lakebed site of Terremote-Tlaltenco in northeastern Lake Xochimilco (McClung et al. 1986; Serra 1980, 1982, 1988; Serra and Civera 1982; Serra and Valadez 1985). These artifacts include (1) bone awls and needles that probably functioned to make mats and baskets (which are abundant in this exceptionally well preserved archaeological deposit), and (2) a variety of stone blades, projectile points, and scrapers, of obsidian and chert, and grinding tools made of basalt, and pottery cooking and storage vessels that presumably performed, at one end of the platform upon which the small Late Formative hamlet was situated, the diverse tasks associated with processing aquatic plant and animal products. The problem is that these same kinds of tools are widely reported in virtually all environmental settings in the Valley of Mexico, where they undoubtedly performed different functions.

The only stone tools that are common at Terremote-Tlaltenco, and not much reported from other localities in the Valley of Mexico, is what Serra (1988:171) refers to as "desfibradores" (fiber scrapers)—trapezoidal ground stone scraping tools that Tolstoy (1971:285) denoted as "square knives," and that Tesch and Abascal (1974) called "azadas" (hoes). These tools are known to be common on the ground surfaces at Late Postclassic sites throughout the northern Valley of Mexico, and almost certainly functioned to scrape maguey fibers (*ixtle*) free of their encasing flesh (Parsons and Parsons 1990:202-3). Nevertheless, aside from Serra's, I know of no other description of these distinctive artifacts from an excavated context in the Valley of Mexico. Their presence at Terremote-Tlaltenco was probably associated with the processing of maguey fiber (*ixtle*) for the manufacture of the nets and cords that fishers, hunters, and collectors of aquatic resources would have needed in abundance, and that would have required frequent repair and replacement over time as the cords rotted through continuous wetting and drying.

Regional Settlement Patterns

Archaeological sites for most prehispanic periods are numerous around the lake margins throughout the Valley of Mexico. This is especially true for localities where well-drained terrain directly borders the lakeshore plain or the lake itself, such as around much of the southern and northwestern perimeter of Lake Texcoco, the southwestern borders of Lake Xaltocán, and the northern, western, and southern borders of Lake Chalco-Xochimilco (Sanders et al. 1979). Such locations are ideally suited for combining direct access to good agricultural land on higher ground with access to aquatic resources in the nearby marshy lakeshore plain and lakebed zones a little lower down. I think it is reasonable to assume that most settlements in such settings maintained this kind of dually focused economic strategy throughout all prehispanic periods. Other parts of the region, however, lack this close juxtaposition of well-drained terrain and marshland: the long eastern and western borders of Lake Texcoco, and the eastern side of Lake Chalco.

The transformation of much of freshwater Lake Chalco-Xochimilco (and smaller areas in Lake Xaltocán-Zumpango) into productive agricultural land (the well-known chinampas) through large-scale drainage projects in Postclassic times (and perhaps, on a smaller scale, as early as the Epiclassic) is relatively well known (Armillas 1971; Coe 1964; Nichols and Frederick 1993; Parsons 1976, 1991; Parsons et al. 1982, 1985; Rojas 1983, 1991; Sanders 1957; Santamaría 1912; Schilling 1983; West and Armillas 1950). More pertinent to my purposes here are those relatively fewer sites situated in the more saline environments of Lakes Texcoco and Xaltocán-Zumpango, well away from any potential agricultural land. The kind of "remote" occupation represented by such sites must represent activities associated with the more specialized exploitation of aquatic resources.

Some of these sites, mostly Late Postclassic in age and with heavy concentrations of Texcoco Fabric Marked pottery, appear to have been primarily associated with saltmaking. These saltmaking sites are especially abundant in the vicinity of Ecatepec, in northwestern Lake Texcoco, and along the eastern and southern margins of Lake Texcoco (Baños and Sanchez 1998; Blanton 1972; Charlton 1969, 1971; Litvak 1962, 1964; Minc 1999; Parsons 1971, 2001; Sanders 1976; Sanders et al. 1979). There are also good indications of several Early Postclassic saltmaking sites around the edges of Cerro Tultepec in Lake Xaltocán (Parsons 1974, 2001:258-59). A much earlier lakebed site, El Tepalcate (Tx-TF-46), a substantial settlement in southeastern Lake Texcoco dating to Terminal Formative times, may also have been a saltmaking locale, although its function remains unclear (Noguera 1943; Parsons 1971:50-51, 2001:261-66). All these presumed saltmaking sites are situated along the lakeshore or at the edges of islands found within the lakes; none are known to exist in those parts of the lakebed far from the shoreline.

There are also many lakebed archaeological sites on Lake Texcoco and Lake Xaltocán-Zumpango that lack any obvious indication of saltmaking. These sites presumably represent places where other aquatic resources were procured or processed. Table 7.20 lists those known lakebed sites that are situated more than one kilometer from well-drained ground and that do not appear to have been associated with either saltmaking or chinampa agriculture—mapped sites on Lake Xaltocán-Zumpango and Cuauhtitlan areas are not included since the final monographs (and thus the final site classifications and numbering sequences) are still in preparation. All the numerous Middle and Late Postclassic sites on Lake Xochimilco and Lake Chalco are presumed to have been directly involved in chinampa agriculture, and so none appear in Tables 7.20-7.23. General maps of prehispanic occupation at "remote" locations in Lakes Xaltocán-Zumpango reveal a pattern of hamlets and small hamlets dating to late Terminal Formative (Tzacualli phase) through Late Postclassic, although with very few Classic-period sites (Parsons 1974; Sanders 1976; Sanders et al. 1979).

Tables 7.21 and 7.22 show how these different lakeshore/lakebed site types are distributed across time. Table 7.21 lists the sites from all three lake systems (Xochimilco, Chalco, and Texcoco), while Table 7.22 shows those for Lake Texcoco only. The relatively high number of "small hamlets" and "hamlets" for the Early Postclassic may be a result of our present inability to distinguish saltmaking sites for this period. The Early

Table 7.20. Surveyed lakebed sites in the Valley of Mexico (excluding Lake Xaltocán-Zumpango) that are more than 1 km from good agricultural land and do not appear to have been associated with either saltmaking or with chinampa agriculture.

Site No.*	Period	Location	Classification
Xochimilco Region			
Xo-EF-1	Early Formative	northeastern Lake Xochimilco	small hamlet
Xo-EF-2	Early Formative	northeastern Lake Xochimilco	hamlet partially excavated by Tolstoy (Tolstoy et al. 1977)
Xo-MF-1	Middle Formative	northeastern Lake Xochimilco	small hamlet
Xo-LF-2	primarily Late Formative	northeastern Lake Xochimilco	Small nucleated village. Excavated by Serra (1988), as the Terremote-Tlaltenco site. A clear focus on aquatic resources.
Xo-LF-3	primarily Late Formative	northeastern Lake Xochimilco	small hamlet
Xo-Cl-5	Classic	northwestern Lake Xochimilco	small hamlet
Xo-ET-1	Epiclassic	northeastern Lake Xochimilco	small hamlet
Xo-ET-2	Epiclassic	northern Lake Xochimilco	small hamlet
Xo-ET-8	Epiclassic	northwestern Lake Xochimilco	hamlet
Xo-ET-9	Epiclassic	northwestern Lake Xochimilco	small nucleated village
Xo-LT-1	Early Postclassic	northeastern Lake Xochimilco	hamlet
Chalco Region			
Ch-MF-11	Middle Formative	eastern Lake Chalco	hamlet
Ch-LF-49	Late Formative	river delta near eastern shore of Lake Chalco	small hamlet
Ch-LF-51	Late Formative	eastern Lake Chalco	hamlet
Ch-TF-57	Terminal Formative	river delta near eastern shore of Lake Chalco.	small hamlet
Ch-Cl-46	Classic	river delta near eastern shore of Lake Chalco	small dispersed village (?)
Ch-Cl-47	Classic	river delta near eastern shore of Lake Chalco	small hamlet
Ch-Cl-48	Classic	river delta near eastern shore of Lake Chalco	small hamlet
Ch-Cl-49	Classic	river delta near eastern shore of Lake Chalco	hamlet
Ch-ET-23	Epiclassic	river delta near eastern shore of Lake Chalco	hamlet
Ch-ET-24	Epiclassic	river delta near eastern shore of Lake Chalco	local center
Ch-ET-25	Epiclassic	River delta near eastern shore of Lake Chalco	hamlet
Ch-ET-26	Epiclassic	river delta near eastern shore of Lake Chalco	hamlet
Ch-ET-27	Epiclassic	river delta near eastern shore of Lake Chalco	hamlet
Ch-LT-63	Early Postclassic	river delta near eastern shore of Lake Chalco	small hamlet
Ch-LT-65	Early Postclassic	river delta near eastern shore of Lake Chalco	hamlet

Table 7.20 cont.

Ch-LT-66	Early Postclassic	river delta near eastern shore of Lake Chalco	small hamlet
Ch-LT-67	Early Postclassic	river delta near eastern shore of Lake Chalco	small hamlet
Ch-LT-68	Early Postclassic	eastern lakeshore of Lake Chalco	hamlet
Ch-LT-69	Early Postclassic	eastern lakeshore of Lake Chalco	small hamlet
Ch-LT-71	Early Postclassic	eastern Lake Chalco	small hamlet
Ch-LT-76	Early Postclassic	southeastern Lake Chalco	small hamlet
Ch-LT-77	Early Postclassic	southeastern Lake Chalco	small hamlet
Ch-LT-78	Early Postclassic	southeastern Lake Chalco	small hamlet
Ch-LT-79	Early Postclassic	southeastern Lake Chalco	small hamlet
Ch-LT-80	Early Postclassic	southeastern Lake Chalco	hamlet
Ch-LT-90	Early Postclassic	central Lake Chalco	small hamlet

Ixtapalapa Peninsula Region (almost all known sites on this peninsula are less than 1 km from good agricultural land)

Ix-A-70	Middle and Late Postclassic	southwestern Lake Texcoco	local center

Texcoco Region

Tx-LF-13	Late Formative	eastern Lake Texcoco	hamlet
Tx-LF-14	Late Formative	eastern Lake Texcoco	small nucleated village, excavated by Frederick and Morett (Frederick, pers. comm. 1999)
Tx-LF-15	Late Formative	eastern Lake Texcoco	hamlet
Tx-LF-26	Late Formative	southeastern Lake Texcoco	hamlet
Tx-TF-28	Terminal Formative	eastern Lake Texcoco	hamlet
Tx-TF-29	Terminal Formative	eastern Lake Texcoco	hamlet
Tx-TF-44	Terminal Formative	southeastern Lake Texcoco	small nucleated village, maybe a saltmaking locus
Tx-TF-45	Terminal Formative	southeastern Lake Texcoco	hamlet, maybe a saltmaking locus
Tx-TF-46 "El Tepalcate"	Terminal Formative	southeastern Lake Texcoco	large nucleated village, maybe a saltmaking locus
Tx-EC-1	Classic	eastern Lake Texcoco	hamlet
Tx-EC-33 Tx-LC-19	Classic	southeastern Lake Texcoco	hamlet
Tx-ET-1	Epiclassic	eastern Lake Texcoco	hamlet
Tx-ET-15	Epiclassic	eastern Lake Texcoco, lakeshore	small dispersed village
Tx-ET-16	Epiclassic	eastern Lake Texcoco	camp?
Tx-LT-1	Early Postclassic	eastern Lake Texcoco, on small island	hamlet
Tx-LT-2	Early Postclassic	eastern Lake Texcoco, near small island	hamlet
Tx-LT-3	Early Postclassic	eastern Lake Texcoco	small hamlet
Tx-LT-4	Early Postclassic	eastern Lake Texcoco	hamlet
Tx-LT-5	Early Postclassic	eastern Lake Texcoco, shoreline	hamlet, maybe saltmaking
Tx-LT-6	Early Postclassic	eastern Lake Texcoco, shoreline	hamlet

Table 7.20 cont.

Tx-LT-7	Early Postclassic	eastern Lake Texcoco, shoreline	hamlet
Tx-LT-32	Early Postclassic	eastern Lake Texcoco	hamlet
Tx-LT-33	Early Postclassic	eastern Lake Texcoco	hamlet
Tx-LT-34	Early Postclassic	eastern Lake Texcoco	hamlet
Tx-LT-35	Early Postclassic	eastern Lake Texcoco	small dispersed village
Tx-LT-36	Early Postclassic	eastern Lake Texcoco	small hamlet
Tx-LT-37	Early Postclassic	eastern Lake Texcoco	camp?
Tx-LT-38	Early Postclassic	eastern Lake Texcoco	hamlet
Tx-LT-39	Early Postclassic	eastern Lake Texcoco	hamlet
Tx-LT-40	Early Postclassic	eastern Lake Texcoco, shoreline	small hamlet?
Tx-LT-41	Early Postclassic	eastern Lake Texcoco, shoreline	small hamlet
Tx-LT-49	Early Postclassic	eastern Lake Texcoco, shoreline	small hamlet
Tx-A-1	Middle and Late Postclassic	eastern Lake Texcoco, on small island	hamlet
Tx-A-4	Late Postclassic	eastern Lake Texcoco	small hamlet
Tx-A-7	Late Postclassic	eastern Lake Texcoco	small hamlet
Tx-A-8	Late Postclassic	eastern Lake Texcoco	small hamlet
Tx-A-11	Late Postclassic	eastern Lake Texcoco, shoreline	small dispersed village
Tx-A-12	Middle and Late Postclassic	eastern Lake Texcoco, shoreline	hamlet
Tx-A-42	Late Postclassic	eastern Lake Texcoco	camp?
Tx-A-43	Late Postclassic	eastern Lake Texcoco	camp?
Tx-A-44	Middle and Late Postclassic	eastern Lake Texcoco	small hamlet
Tx-A-45	Late Postclassic	eastern Lake Texcoco	hamlet
Tx-A-46	Late Postclassic	eastern Lake Texcoco	small dispersed village
Tx-A-47	Late Postclassic	eastern Lake Texcoco	hamlet
Tx-A-48	Late Postclassic	eastern Lake Texcoco	small hamlet
Tx-A-52	Late Postclassic	eastern Lake Texcoco, shoreline	hamlet
Tx-A-53	Middle and Late Postclassic	eastern Lake Texcoco, shoreline	small dispersed village
Tx-A-54	Late Postclassic	eastern Lake Texcoco, shoreline	hamlet
Tx-A-110	Middle and Late Postclassic	southeastern Lake Texcoco	small dispersed village

(Adapted from Blanton 1972; Parsons 1971; Parsons et al. 1982, 1983)
*Sites are listed in order: Lake Xochimilco, Lake Chalco, Lake Texcoco. This listing does not include the two lakebed sites reported by Litvak (1962, 1964) in unsurveyed portions of Lake Texcoco.

Postclassic, and earlier periods as well, lack ceramics analogous to the distinctive Texcoco Fabric Marked pottery that is associated with saltmaking during the Middle and Late Postclassic. Therefore, some of these Early Postclassic (and earlier) sites along the shorelines of Lake Texcoco that are included in these tables may have been primarily places where salt was made.

Table 7.23 shows the percentages of different lakebed-lakeshore sites, across all time periods, for all three lakes and for Lake Texcoco alone.

Table 7.21. Lakebed-lakeshore site types by period (Lakes Xochimilco, Chalco, and Texcoco).

Site Type	Early Form.	Middle Form.	Late Form.	Term. Form.	Classic	Epi.	Early Post.	Mid/ Late Post	Totals
camp						1	1	2	4
small hamlet	1	1	3	1	3	2	15	5	31
hamlet	1	1	4	3	3	6	15	6	39
small dispersed village					1	1	1	4	7
large dispersed village									0
small nucleated village			1	1		1			3
large nucleated village									0
local center						1		1	2
Totals	2	2	8	5	7	12	32	18	86

Table 7.22. Lakebed-lakeshore site types by period (Lake Texcoco only).

Site Type	Early Form.	Middle Form.	Late Form.	Term. Form.	Classic	Epi.	Early Post.	Mid/ Late Post	Totals
camp						1	1	2	4
small hamlet							5	5	10
hamlet			3	3	2	1	11	6	26
small dispersed village						1	1	4	6
large dispersed village									0
small nucleated village			1	1					2
large nucleated village									0
local center								1	1
Totals	0	0	4	4	2	3	18	18	49

Table 7.23. Percentages of lakebed-lakeshore sites in different site categories, all time periods.

Site Type	Camp	Small Hamlet	Hamlet	Small Dispersed Village	Large Dispersed Village	Small Nucleated Village	Large Nucleated Village	Local Center
all lakes	4.7	36.0	45.3	8.1	0	3.5	0	2.3
Lake Texcoco only	8.2	20.4	53.1	12.2	0	4.1	0	2.0

Summary and Conclusions

The data considered in this section reveal several obvious patterns.

(1) There is very little known occupation of the "remote" lakebed or "remote" lake-shore of Lake Texcoco prior to the Late Formative. This contrasts with freshwater Lake Chalco-Xochimilco, where such occupation extends back into the Early Formative and beyond.

(2) There is a very substantial increase in "remote" lakebed-lakeshore occupation be-ginning in Early Postclassic times and extending through the Middle and Late Postclassic. Part of this increase around Lake Texcoco undoubtedly relates to a significant expansion in saltmaking (Middle and Late Postclassic saltmaking sites can be readily identified as such, and do not appear in Tables 7.20-7.23). Similarly, in Lake Chalco-Xochimilco there is a great increase in the Middle and Late Postclassic in the numbers of lakebed sites that appear to be associated with chinampa cultivation.

(3) Most of the "remote" lakebed-lakeshore occupation is in the form of small sites, most of which we classified as "small hamlets" or "hamlets." This is especially the case for Lake Texcoco. A few of these small sites on Lake Chalco-Xochimilco have been excavated (Parsons et al. 1985), and these appear to be places of permanent residence of chinampa farmers. Such farmers, of course, might well have also engaged in occasional hunting, fishing, and collecting of aquatic resources, just as they have done in historic times. Except for Tx-LF-14 and Tx-TF-46, none of the Lake Texcoco lakebed-lakeshore sites have been excavated, but all those listed in Tables 7.20-7.23, except for those we called "camps," appear to have functioned as permanent domestic residences. This con-trasts notably with the lakebed of central Lake Texcoco where few, if any, sites can be considered anything more substantial than temporary camps (see next section).

Archaeological Survey in Central Lake Texcoco, 2003[1]

Although the non-urbanized remnant of the former bed of Lake Texcoco is still a comparatively large and intact landscape, there were no systematic archaeological sur-

---

[1]This section is a modified English-language version of a portion of an article in Spanish by Parsons and Morett (2005).

Plate 7.4. Example of a lakebed archaeological site in eastern Lake Texcoco, May 1969.

veys in this area prior to 2003. Surveys along the former lakebed's eastern, southern, and northwestern margins in the 1960s and 1970s (Parsons 1971, 1974; Blanton 1972; Sanders 1976; Sanders et al. 1979), and several casual walk-abouts in more recent years, revealed surficial archaeological remains. These remains are typically small sherd and lithic scatters on the order of 5-50 m in diameter (Plate 7.4). The surface pottery I have seen at such places ranges in age from Late Formative (ca. 400 B.C.) to Late Postclassic, with a predominance of Middle and Late Postclassic materials. Remarkably, in 1972 the remains of a mammoth were discovered at and immediately beneath the lakebed surface a few kilometers north of Chimalhuacán, with no overlying alluvial deposit and no clear signs of aeolian deflation (Mirambell 1972). This find, together with a subsequent geomorphological study of this part of the lakebed (Cordova 1997:412-40), indicates that parts of the lakebed have had no significant alluvial or aeolian deposition for several millennia: an ideal natural laboratory for the study of archaeological surface remains, especially since portions of the old lakebed remain comparatively undisturbed.

There have been only two kinds of major man-made disturbance to the central lakebed of Lake Texcoco. The first, over several decades in the early twentieth century, occurred when commercial *tequesquite* production was undertaken over large sections of the northern lakebed (Flores 1918) (tequesquite is an impure saline product, once commonly

Plate 7.5. Early twentieth-century plowed "fields" for tequesquite production somewhere in northern Lake Texcoco. From Flores (1918: Foto 4, reproduced as Plate 3.1 in Parsons 2001:171).

used for feeding animals). This included shallow "plowing" or furrowing over large tracts of the dried-up lakebed in order to increase the evaporation surface area (Plate 7.5). We could still discern the traces of this activity in many parts of our 2003 survey area in central Lake Texcoco. The second major disturbance occurred during the late 1970s and early 1980s when sizable areas, including some of our 2003 survey area, were plowed in large, widely spaced furrows, apparently with large machines, to facilitate the planting of grass and trees in order to increase the amount of "green space" on the desiccated former lakebed near Mexico City. By 2003 a thick cover of grass and trees had taken root in several areas.

During May 20-Aug. 1, 2003, archaeologists from the University of Michigan and the Universidad Autónoma de Chapingo carried out intensive archaeological surface surveys on the former lakebed of central Lake Texcoco (Parsons and Morett 2004a, 2004b, 2005). Working in a team of 5-8 people spaced at intervals of 10 m, we walked systematically over an area of approximately 22 km². In this fashion we recorded over 1100 "off-site" locations with archaeological remains (Fig. 7.8). The contents of these locations ranged from single artifacts (usually stone tools or debitage, or potsherds) up to sherd and lithic scatters containing several dozen artifacts distributed over areas roughly 100 m in diameter. The analyses of these materials are ongoing, and only the highlights of our preliminary studies are presented here.

Our preliminary observations indicate that several types of artifacts are particularly numerous:

(1) Single chert "saw" tools (Plate 7.6), at about 250 locations. Possibly originally hafted on wooden handles, these serrated tools may have been used to cut through tough

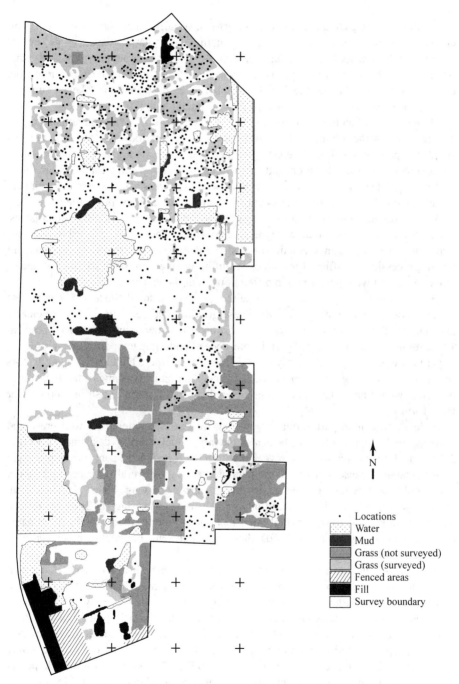

Figure 7.8. Area of 2003 surface survey in central Lake Texcoco, showing locations (n = 1143) with archaeological materials (adapted from Parsons and Morett 2004a, 2004b). Figure 2.2 shows location of this survey area within Lake Texcoco and the Valley of Mexico.

reed stalks or perhaps to butcher fish or waterfowl. We also found numerous small chert chips, sometimes near the saw tools and sometimes in isolation. These chips suggest re-touch of the saw tools in the course of their use. As far as I can determine, these distinctive chert saw tools are unique to the lakebed area, and have not been reported from other parts of the Valley of Mexico. Their apparent restriction to the lakebed suggests that they were associated with functions that were unique to this setting.

(2) Single obsidian blades, usually green in color (Plate 7.7), but sometimes gray, at 110 locations. Although these blades were probably cutting tools, we do not yet understand their precise functions. Interestingly, chert and obsidian implements co-occur only infrequently at the same location, and green and gray obsidian artifacts are seldom found together. The obsidian blades may have functioned to process fish or waterfowl, or to cut aquatic plants. Most gray obsidian occurs in the form of scrapers, projectile points, and backed-knives, and almost certainly many of these tools were used for different purposes, and in different localities, than were the green obsidian blades. These distributional patterns suggest that certain specialized tasks (perhaps associated with the procurement and/or processing of different resources, or different stages in the processing of one or more resources) were performed in different parts of the lakebed.

(3) Individual *molcajetes* or *comales*, either alone or in small clusters of several vessels, at about 50 locations (Plate 7.8). These grinding and cooking vessels are clearly associated with food preparation, as are the ground stone manos and metates we noted at 14 locations. These artifacts suggest the presence of enduring, temporary encampments, or perhaps some type of seasonally occupied residence where hunters/fishers/collectors prepared meals at intervals over periods of time. Alternatively, some of the *molcajetes* or manos would have functioned to grind seeds, insects, or small fish into powder or paste form.

In the north-central part of our survey area, we also encountered the well-preserved remains of what appears to have been a single large ritual offering (designated Location 210). A shallow excavation here revealed within the top 20 cm a concentration of over 20 long-handled censers, a very large ceramic basin and several large ceramic jars, a number of jadeite beads, and one remarkable greenstone carving (Plate 7.9). These Late Postclassic artifacts had been placed upon a platform (measuring ca. 2 × 2 m) resting atop wooden support posts. Several other locations in the lakebed contained remnants of censer handles and/or jadeite beads; these may represent comparable, much less well preserved offerings.

Projectile points, mainly gray obsidian but a few of green obsidian and chert, occur at only 15 locations. Most of these are large, tanged implements (Plate 7.10) that may have functioned to spear large fish. However, the largest of these are generally so finely made that I suspect they may have had ritual, not utilitarian, functions (the point shown in Plate 7.10 is an excellent example of such a finely made artifact). We found no fired-clay pellets of the type reported for hunting birds with blow-guns in inland sectors of the Valley of Mexico during the sixteenth century (Linne 1937). This paucity of projectile points and apparent absence of clay pellets may indicate that most hunting and fishing on Lake Texcoco was done with nets, although we can still say little about fishhooks.

Also interesting is the presence of worked stone blocks at several locations. These typically measure 25-30 cm long × 20-25 cm wide × 6-8 cm thick (Plate 7.11). These may represent some sort of formal territorial markers, perhaps originally in the form of constructions with masonry foundations—analogous to historic period practices in the marshlands around Lake Titicaca (Levieil and Orlove 1990). These features could represent the remains of lakebed shrines, dedicated to water-related deities, that may have marked divisions between local communities, as suggested by Broda (1991) (see discussion in Chap. 3).

We also found numerous clusters (not marked on Fig. 7.8) of unworked rocks roughly the size of grapefruits (Plate 7.12). These rock clusters are generally 3-5 m in diameter. They do not appear to be fire-cracked. They may represent portions of house foundations, or hearths, or perhaps the remnants of duck decoys (Plate 5.53).

We also found a half dozen notched sherds, which are almost certainly net-sinkers (Plate 7.13). All these are made from Classic-period Thin Orange sherds, the only definite examples of Classic-period pottery we have so far identified in the entire 2003 survey. Thin Orange is a particularly thin-walled and light ceramic. It is possible that Postclassic netters deliberately sought out old fragments of this pottery for its unique qualities—perhaps it was somewhat naturally buoyant, and thus prevented submerged nets from sinking too deeply below the water surface when harvesting fish or insects that were most abundant in the upper levels. Alternatively, these artifacts may have been used by Classic-period netters on their infrequent forays into the lake that apparently left few, if any, other detectable archaeological traces.

The chronology of this lakebed occupation is not always clear because most locations lack datable ceramics. However, some 50 locations contain Aztec III Black/Orange and other distinctive types of Late Postclassic ceramics, by far the dominant type of datable pottery. Diagnostic Middle Postclassic (Aztec II and II-III B/O) pottery occurs at 16 locations. Datable Early Postclassic (Mazapan phase) pottery occurs at 11 locations, while recognizable Epiclassic (Coyotlatelco phase) pottery is found at only 6 locations. Aside from the Thin Orange notched sherds noted above, we found virtually no Classic (ca. A.D. 100-650) or Formative (pre-A.D. 100) pottery. We also found one probable Archaic projectile point.

Thus, a systematic surface survey in 2003 over some 22 km² in north-central Lake Texcoco reveals a diffuse scatter of ceramic and lithic artifacts and clusters of unworked rocks at over 1100 localities. Chert "saws," obsidian knives, scrapers, and blades, and ceramic grinding and cooking vessels are the most abundant and recognizable artifacts; obsidian (and a few chert) projectile points also occur, but in decidedly low frequency, as do several ground stone manos and metates. A fair quantity of lithic debitage (both chert and obsidian) also occurs, presumably reflecting tool maintenance while in use. No definite permanent settlements were identified, although there is abundant evidence of what appear to represent short-term encampments where food was prepared. Most localities appear to represent places where several different kinds of specific tasks were performed. One exceptionally well preserved formal ritual shrine reflects the cosmological importance of the lakebed setting.

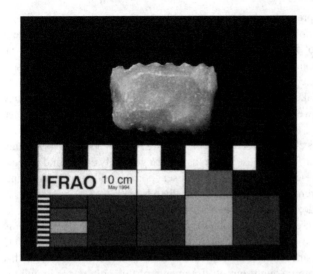

Plate 7.6. Chert saw tool found on Lake Texcoco survey.

Plate 7.7. Green obsidian blade found on Lake Texcoco survey.

Plate 7.8. Late Postclassic *molcajete* found on surface of eastern Lake Texcoco, 1967 survey. Vessel measures ca. 25 cm in diameter.

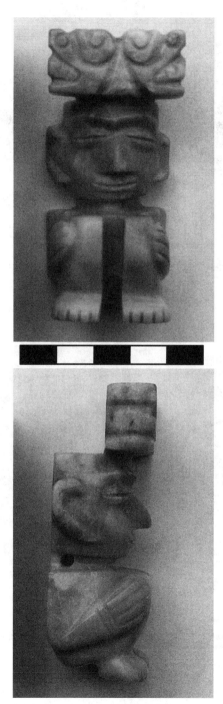

Plate 7.9. Greenstone figurine from excavation at Location 210, northern Lake Texcoco. Scale in cm.

Plate 7.10. Example of large obsidian projectile point found on Lake Texcoco survey.

Plate 7.11. Example of a worked stone block found on Lake Texcoco survey.

Plate 7.12. Cluster of unworked stones found on Lake Texcoco survey.

Plate 7.13. Notched ceramic sherd, probably a net-sinker, found on Lake Texcoco survey.

Overall Summary and Conclusions

The major points considered in this chapter can be briefly summarized as follows:

(1) The archaeological record in wetland environments is greatly affected by post-depositional forces, both natural and cultural in origin. Consequently, unusual care is required in interpreting the meaning of ancient material remains in these settings.

(2) Traditional wetland societies worldwide share a significant number of commonalities in terms of (a) natural setting, (b) resources exploited, (c) essential infrastructural tasks, (c) technologies associated with procurement, processing, and storage of aquatic resources, and (d) regional settlement patterning. Consequently, we might expect a certain general level of similarity in the material remains associated with these commonalities.

(3) Archaeological and ethnographical-historical studies in the U.S. Great Basin provide an unusually sound foundation for developing expectations about how aquatic resources were traditionally exploited in a particular wetland setting. With care, these expectations from the Great Basin might be projected into other, less completely well studied settings, such as the Valley of Mexico.

(4) The known archaeological record in the Valley of Mexico speaks primarily to the consumption of aquatic resources: it is clear that waterfowl, fish, and reeds have been important for millennia in this region. Although insights into the production, processing, storage, and distributional mechanisms of these resources are less abundant, there are clear indications from both excavation and regional survey data that, at least from Epiclassic times onward, the marshlands and open-water zones of Lake Texcoco were intensively utilized for both utilitarian and ceremonial purposes.

(5) The available settlement pattern data suggest that the central sector of Lake Texcoco was exploited primarily by people who resided in permanent settlements around the lake margins, and who made extended forays into the more remote lakes and marshlands primarily in the form of temporary encampments where food was prepared and where there may have been stays of a few days.

(6) At this stage of research in the Valley of Mexico, there are few, if any, definitive archaeological artifact "signatures" that can confidently be associated with the procurement and processing, or even with the consumption, of aquatic resources—aside from the physical presence of the actual animals and plants themselves in domestic middens. At this point, the best possible candidate for such a "signature" may be the distinctive chert "saw" tools that are so abundant in central Lake Texcoco, but which appear to be virtually absent at lakeshore or inland sites elsewhere in the Valley of Mexico.

– 8 –

Overall Conclusions

I began this study as a narrowly focused effort to describe the remnants of a vanishing aquatic economy at Chimalhuacán on the southeastern shore of ex-Lake Texcoco in the central Valley of Mexico, and to consider the archaeological implications of my findings. After completing my fieldwork at Chimalhuacán in 1992, I expanded the scope of my library research as I came to realize that my original objectives might be better served by broadening my understanding of traditional aquatic economies in other parts of the world. As a consequence, this monograph is more broadly comparative than I had originally envisioned. I conclude by summarizing the most important points I have considered and by offering suggestions for some directions that future archaeological research in and around ex-Lake Texcoco might take.

Consequences of the Absence of Pastoralism in Ancient Mesoamerica

Alone among the primary civilizations of the ancient world, prehispanic Mesoamerica lacked domestic grazing animals analogous to llamas and alpacas in Andean South America, and to sheep, goats, and cattle in much of the Old World. This absence of pastoralism meant that ancient Mesoamericans lacked access to the vast stores of energy bound up in vegetation that they could not consume directly, but that could be appropriated indirectly in the form of meat, milk, hides, fiber, and manure, as accessed by the human masters of domesticated herbivores in other parts of the world. And yet, we know that the ancient Mesoamericans attained levels of organizational complexity and population size and density on par with those that characterized ancient Andean, African, Near Eastern, Asian, and European societies. How are we to reconcile this *apparent* inequity in ancient Mesoamerica between organizational complexity and high population density, on the one hand, and a seemingly "impoverished" resource base, on the other?

It is also the case that within prehispanic Mesoamerica, and especially in Postclassic times after approximately A.D. 1000, the most highly centralized and most expansive polities, the largest populations and the highest population densities, and the largest urban centers all seem to have developed in and around the Valley of Mexico and across the *tierra fría* of highland central Mexico, from Tlaxcala on the east to Michoacán and Jalisco on the west. This region is, of course, the broad axis characterized by Pleistocene volcanism that had impounded drainage and produced many lakes and marshlands. The agricultural potential of these wetlands, where marshes were transformed into gardens through large-scale drainage in later prehispanic times, has been comparatively well studied, and the importance of the water-borne transportation and communication provided by large bodies of water has often been recognized. However, although some attention has been paid to the significance of aquatic fauna and flora, these resources have usually been mistakenly relegated to secondary or tertiary status relative to agricultural production.

In this monograph I argue that the "domestication" of wetland resources was one way in which ancient Mesoamericans developed a component of their economy that was fully complementary to agriculture in much the same way as was pastoralism in other parts of the ancient world where complex societies and high population densities existed.

The Domestication of Wetlands in the Valley of Mexico

The available data—archaeological, historical, and ethnographic—indicate that the notion of the domestication of a nonagricultural, aquatic landscape can be usefully applied to the Lake Texcoco wetlands during prehispanic and historic times, especially during the period after approximately A.D. 1000. The exploitation of a full range of extraordinarily productive aquatic resources (Table 8.1) was comprehensive, specialized, and established on the basis of an impressive level of technological expertise and a thorough understanding of the specific qualities of many different plants and animals. This specialization is graphically indicated by the 1550 map (Fig. 3.17), which depicts two sectors of Lake Texcoco, separated by a substantial reed barrier, within which different kinds of aquatic vegetation and different kinds of activities are shown. Such intensity of aquatic resource utilization was unparalleled in complex societies in other parts of the ancient world where aquatic resources, while often important, tended to be much more secondary and supplementary relative to agriculture and pastoralism. Across the lakes and marshlands of highland central Mesoamerica where prehispanic pastoralism did not exist, aquatic resources were primary and complementary.

Table 8.1 might be expanded to include the importance of aquatic plants as sources of household fuel and as green fertilizer in plant cultivation (the latter is documented historically, although the former is not). Similarly, aquatic insects were often important as agricultural fertilizer. The significance of wetlands in the Valley of Mexico is also reflected in their importance in prehispanic cosmology: numerous religious ceremonies and ritual performances dedicated to major and minor water-related deities were conducted within the borders of the lakes and marshes. Such cosmological importance is also attached to bodies and sources of water in many other parts of the ancient world, of course, but I know of no other region where lakes and marshes have been endowed with more (or even as much) spiritual significance than they were in the precolumbian Valley of Mexico.

Table 8.1. Summary of the aquatic resources of Lake Texcoco.

Fauna		Flora		Inorganic
Primary Importance	insects waterfowl fish	"reeds"	construction and utensils food	salt
		algae	food	
Secondary Importance	frogs salamanders turtles	miscellaneous	food and medicine	
Tertiary Importance	molluscs crustaceans			

The Control, Distribution, and Exchange of Aquatic Resources

Historical and ethnographic sources clearly indicate that in the Valley of Mexico, aquatic resources were formerly regarded in much the same way as was agricultural land. Places of productive and predictable fishing, reed-collecting, and perhaps algae- and insect-collecting were often closely controlled by individuals or by specific local communities. There are good indications that the productive potential of such aquatic territories equaled that of agricultural lands in terms of energy and nutrition. Aquatic resources were often procured and processed by specialists, who did little agriculture, and who exchanged their aquatic products through markets or other forms of redistribution. Aquatic specialists would have required agricultural foodstuffs and a wide variety of craft goods, including very large quantities of maguey fiber (*ixtle*), in either raw or spun form, for making nets and lines. This specialization and exchange were greatly facilitated by water-borne transportation and communication throughout the Valley of Mexico heartland. One of the important and very obvious conclusions of this monograph is that we must incorporate the aquatic landscape, as well as the agricultural landscape, into our thinking about prehispanic "carrying capacity" and demographic potential in the Valley of Mexico (and probably elsewhere across highland Central Mexico).

The Archaeological Implications

Archaeological research has only begun to make significant contributions to the understanding of the prehispanic aquatic economy in the Valley of Mexico. We know more about the consumption of aquatic resources (primarily fauna) than we do about how they were produced, processed, and distributed through exchange networks. Some historically documented aspects of the aquatic economy are likely to be virtually invisible archaeologically (e.g., the production and processing of insects and algae). The broadly comparative perspective I have aimed to achieve in this monograph suggests that we may expect to find the archaeological remains of permanent and/or temporary occupations both within and around the margins of marshes and lakes. These occupations may have once included floating or anchored natural islands of compacted aquatic vegetation that may have been expanded and secured by the addition of masses of reed mats and bundles, or even of earth-rock fill from nearby areas of higher ground.

With post-depositional drainage and desiccation, as we have in the Valley of Mexico, we would probably expect such "island" occupations to simply have settled down onto the dried-up lakebed surface, with only the ceramic and lithic materials preserved, and with little or no vertical depth (unless covered by subsequent alluvial or aeolian deposition). The discovery of substantial ancient occupation within and around the former lakebed need not necessarily mean that water levels were unusually low in the past; conversely, the absence of such occupation need not imply an unusually high water level.

Clusters of unworked stones in this stoneless setting might have been associated with the foundations of living surfaces and/or with cooking hearths in domestic structures built largely, or entirely, of reeds. We might also expect that much of this occupation would be quite diverse, ephemeral, wide-ranging, and diffuse—deriving from a variety of specific activities carried out afoot or in boats over large wetland areas, or from temporary encampments with a very limited range of domestic and/or processing functions.

Our 2003 pilot survey in central Lake Texcoco revealed small concentrations of numerous classes of artifacts that we believe represent many different kinds of production and processing and ritual activities, including shrines where offerings of greenstone and incense were made, and temporary encampments where food was prepared and consumed. We found no clear signs of any permanent, domestic residence for which the labels "hamlet" or "village" would seem appropriate. Occupation of this latter type may be found in still-unsurveyed areas to the east of our 2003 survey area, in bands several kilometers wide, closer to the former lakeshores but still well below the elevations surveyed in earlier regional studies.

I am still unable to identify an "aquatic tool kit," an assemblage of ceramic and/or lithic or bone artifacts that can be confidently linked to specific activities associated with the production or processing of aquatic resources. Most of the artifact classes found in our 2003 lakebed survey, for example, also occur in sites at higher elevations throughout the Valley of Mexico that are well inland from the wetlands. The only exceptions presently known to me are the numerous and very distinctive chert "saw" tools (Plate 7.6) that, as far as I can determine, occur only within the lakebed zone.

As archaeological investigation intensifies and expands in and around Lake Texcoco, we must be prepared to find multiple functions reflected in the artifacts that may occur at any particular locale. Such functional overlap is likely to occur because of the potential for relatively rapid changes in the distribution of aquatic plants and animals in specific wetland settings caused by seasonal, inter-annual, and longer-term variability in water levels and geochemical composition.

Regional surveys, including our 2003 study of central Lake Texcoco, clearly indicate that there was a major expansion and intensification of wetland resource exploitation during the Postclassic period. The Classic-period economy, dominated by Teotihuacan, appears to have been even less focused on the resources of Lake Texcoco than were earlier Formative-era communities. The location of urban Teotihuacan well inland from the lakeshore also contrasts notably with the lakeshore (or even lakebed) setting of most major Late Postclassic centers. This inland setting would seem to reflect the secondary importance in Classic-period economy not only of wetland resources but also of the water-borne transportation-communication networks that were so vital in Postclassic times. The underlying causes of this fundamental Classic-to-Postclassic shift remain to be defined and investigated. Climate change may have been involved, but I suspect that we will have to go well beyond purely environmental factors to reach a satisfactory explanation.

Future Research Directions

The following are my specific suggestions for future archaeological investigations in and around ex-Lake Texcoco.

(1) Extend the 2003 lakebed survey area eastward toward the former lakeshore. This should make it possible to determine whether the diffuse artifact scatters located in the 2003 survey extend shoreward, or whether there were larger, more enduring hamlets or villages closer to the former shoreline.

(2) Undertake test excavations at several dozen key points identified in the 2003 lakebed as possible encampments on natural/artificial islands. These excavations should help clarify the nature of long-term alluvial or aeolian deposition (seasonal, inter-annual, and longer term), the impact of post-depositional flooding, and the possible existence of buried occupations of the Classic and Formative periods that may lie hidden well below the modern ground surface of the former lakebed.

(3) Undertake extensive excavations at 6-8 representative sites identified as probable encampments in the 2003 lakebed survey, and at promising locations suggestive of more permanent occupation that might be discovered in new surveys farther east, in order to clarify occupational chronology, territoriality, the range of functions represented over time and space, and exchange relationships with agricultural settlements situated at higher elevations inland from the lakeshore.

(4) Develop a detailed typology of lithic and ceramic artifacts in lakebed contexts. Subject these artifacts, especially the lithics, to detailed microscopic study to clarify use, function, and provenance. Such studies may help to define an "aquatic tool kit."

(5) The absence of naturally derived stone in Lake Texcoco means that subsurface probes using magnetometer, resistivity, sonic, or ground-penetrating radar techniques should be unusually useful and productive, since virtually all stone will be cultural in origin. Such probes should be implemented widely over the former lakebed to clarify the subsurface nature of surface remains, and to discover buried occupation that may be invisible at the modern ground surface.

There is a distinct note of urgency for any future systematic archaeological study of ex-Lake Texcoco. The only relatively undisturbed, non-urbanized area of the former lakebed/lakeshore lies around and immediately east of the 2003 survey area. Parts of this area lie within the federally protected region in which our 2003 survey was carried out. However, most of this surviving band of still-open terrain is within agricultural and grazing lands controlled by local communities and private owners—all subject to rapid and unpredictable development, either through urban sprawl or through the further mechanization of agriculture, a tremendously destructive force in terms of the archaeological record. Even the federally protected zone in central Lake Texcoco can easily be expropriated by higher-priority modern development undertakings, as the recent airport expansion project aptly demonstrated. Although this airport project was abandoned amidst great controversy in 2002, there continues to be tremendous pressure to develop this landscape and its surroundings, and it may not endure for much longer in its present form.

Bibliography

Acuña, R. (editor)
1985 [1579, 1580] *Relaciones Geográficas del Siglo XVI: Mexico, Tomo I*. México, D.F.: Universidad Nacional Autónoma de México.
1986a [1579, 1580] *Relaciones Geográficas del Siglo XVI: Mexico, Tomo II*. México, D.F.: Universidad Nacional Autónoma de México.
1986b [1579, 1580] *Relaciones Geográficas del Siglo XVI: Mexico, Tomo III*. México, D.F.: Universidad Nacional Autónoma de México.

Aguilera, C.
2001 Algunos aspectos de la cultura del Lago de Zumpango. *Expresión Antropológica*, nueva época, 12:71-83. Toluca: Colegio Mexiquense.

Aguirre, G.
1955 *Programas de Salud en la Situación Intercultural*. México, D.F.: Instituto Indigenista Interamericano.

Aguirre, J., and M. García
1994 *El Modo de Vida Lacustre en la Cuenca del Alto Lerma: Un Estudio Etnoarqueológico*. Tesis de Licenciatura en Arqueología, Escuela Nacional de Antropología e História, México, D.F.

Ajofrín, Francisco de
1986 [1763-1767] Diario del Viaje a la Nueva España. In *Viajeros Extranjeros en el Estado de México*, edited by M. García and J. Iturriaga, pp. 157-62. México, D.F.: Universidad Autónoma del Estado de México.

Albores, B.A.
1995 *Tules y Sirenas – El Impacto Ecológico y Cultural de la Industrialización en el Alto Lerma*. El Colegio Mexiquense y Secretaria de Ecología, Gobierno del Estado de México, Toluca.

Alcocer, J., and W.D. Williams
1993   Lagos salinos mexicanos: importancia, valor y amenazas. In *Biodiversidad Marina y Costera de México*, edited by S.I. Salazar-Vallejo and N.E. Gonzalez, pp. 849-65. México, D.F.: Comisión Nacional de Biodiversidad.

Alcocer-Durand, J., and E. Escobar-Briones
1992   The aquatic biota of the now extinct lacustrine complex of the Mexico Basin. *Freshwater Forum* 2(3):171-83.

Aldrich, J.M.
1912a The biology of some western species of the Dipterous genus Ephydra. *Journal of the New York Entomological Society* 20:77-99.
1912b Flies of the leptid genus Atherix used as food by the California Indians. *Entomological News* 23:159-63.

Allanson, B.R. (editor)
1979   *Lake Sibaya*. Dordrecht, Germany: Kluwer Academic Publishers.

Allen, H.
1974   The Bagundji of the Darling Basin: cereal gatherers in an uncertain environment. *World Archaeology* 5(3):309-22.

Altamiro, F. (editor)
1895   *Estudios Referentes a la Desecación del Lago de Texcoco, Año de 1895*. Secretaría de Fomento, Instituto Médico Nacional, México.

Alvarez del Castillo, C.
1982[?] *Dos Estudios Paleobotánicos en la Cuenca de México*. Cuadernos de Trabajo No. 20, Depto. de Prehistória, Instituto Nacional de Antropología e História, México, D.F.

Alvarez del Villar, J., and L. Navarro
1957   *Los Peces del Valle de México*. México, D.F.: Comisión para el Fomento de la Piscicultura Rural.

Alzate, J.A.
1831   *Gacetas de Literatura de México*. 4 vols. Puebla, Mexico: Hospital de San Pedro.

Ancona, L.
1933   El ahuautle de Texcoco. *Anales del Instituto de Biología* 4:51-69. México, D.F.

Apenes, O.
1939   Sitios arcaicos en el Lago de Texcoco. *Actas, 27 Congreso Internacional de Americanistas* 2:64-68. México, D.F.
1943   The pond in our backyard. *Mexican Life* March 1943:15-18. México, D.F.
1947   *Mapas Antiguas del Valle de México*. Pub. No. 4, Instituto de História, Universidad Nacional Autónoma de México, México, D.F.

Aréchiga, E.
2004   El desagüe del Valle de México, siglos XVI-XXI. *Arqueología Mexicana* 12(68):60-65.

Argueta, A.
2005 *Los saberes P'urhépecha. Los animales y el diálogo con la naturaleza.* Paper presented to the Seminario del Grupo Kw'anískuyarhani de Estudios del Pueblo P'urhépecha, Pátzcuaro, Michoacán, México, May 28, 2005.

Armillas, P.
1971 Gardens on swamps. *Science* 174(4010):653-61.

Arnold, P.
1999 *Eating Landscape: Aztec and European Occupation of Tlalocan.* Boulder: University Press of Colorado.

Attema, P.
1993 *An Archaeological Survey in the Pontine Region: A Contribution to the Early Settlement History of South Lazio [Italy].* PhD dissertation, Groningen University, Groningen, The Netherlands.
1996 Inside and outside the landscape: perceptions of the Pontine Region in central Italy. *Archaeological Dialogues* 3(2):176-95.

Aveni, A.
1991 Mapping the ritual landscape: debt payment to Tlaloc during the month of Atlcahualco. In *To Change Place: Aztec Ceremonial Landscapes*, edited by D. Carrasco, pp. 58-73. Niwot: University Press of Colorado.

Avila, P.
1999 El valle Morelia-Queréndaro y su deterio ambiental. In *Frutos del Campo Michoacano*, edited by E. Barragán, pp. 172-92. Zamora: El Colegio de Michoacán.

Ávila, R.
1991 *Las Chinampas de Ixtapalapa, D.F.* México, D.F.: Instituto Nacional de Antropología e História.

Baicich, P.J., and C.J. Harrison
1997 *A Guide to the Nests, Eggs, and Nestlings of North American Birds*, 2nd ed. New York: Academic Press.

Bancroft, H.H.
1875 *The Native Races of the Pacific States of North America. Vol. 2: Civilized Nations.* New York: Appleton.

Baños, E., and M. Sanchez
1998 La industria salinera prehispánica en la Cuenca de México. In *Sal en México, II*, coordinated by J. Reyes, pp. 65-83. Colima, Mexico: Universidad de Colima.

Barlow, R.H.
1949 *The Extent of the Empire of the Culhua Mexica.* Ibero-Americana No. 28. Berkeley and Los Angeles: University of California Press.

Barrett, S.A.
1910   *The Material Culture of the Klamath and Modoc Indians of Northeastern California and Southern Oregon.* University of California Publications in American Archaeology and Ethnology 5(4):230-92. Berkeley.

Basadre, Modesto
1884   *Riquezas peruanas. Colección de artículos descriptivos para 'La Tribuna.'* Lima. [Cited in Crequi-Montfort and Rivet 1927.]
1894-95   Los indios Urus. *Boletín de la Sociedad Geográfica de Lima* 4:190-99. [Cited in Crequi-Montfort and Rivet 1927.]

Bastien, J.
1978   *Mountain of the Condor: Metaphor and Ritual in an Andean Ayllu.* St. Paul: West Publishing Co.

Bellin, J.
1754   *Carte des Environs de la Ville de Mexico.* Paris. Clements Rare Book Library, University of Michigan. Ann Arbor.

Beltran, E.
1958   *El Hombre y su Ambiente: Ensayo sobre el Valle de México.* México, D.F.: Fondo de Cultura Económica.

Bernal, I. (editor)
1957   Relación de Tequixquiac, Citlaltepec, y Xilocingo. *Tlalocan* 3(4):289-309. México, D.F.

Bernick, K. (editor)
1998   *Hidden Dimensions: The Cultural Significance of Wetland Archaeology.* Vancouver: UBC Press.

Berres, T.E.
2000   Climate change and lacustrine resources at the period of initial Aztec development. *Ancient Mesoamerica* 11:27-38.

Beyer, H.
1969 [c. 1920]   La tiradera (atlatl), todavia en uso en el Valle de México. In *El México Antiguo: Homenaje Para Honrar la Memória del Ilustre Antropólogo Hermann Beyer*, C. Cook de Leonard, coordinadora, 11:421-25. México, D.F.: Sociedad Alemana Mexicanista.

Bishop, W.H.
1883   *Old Mexico and Her Lost Provinces.* New York: Harper & Brothers.

Blache, J., and F. Miton
1963   *Première Contribution a la Connaissance de la Pêche dans le Bassin Hydrographique Logone-Chari Lac Tchad.* Paris: Office de la Recherche Scientifique Technique Outre-Mer.

Blake, M., B. Chisholm, J. Clark, B. Voohies, and M. Love
1992   Prehistoric subsistence in the Soconusco region. *Current Anthropology* 33:83-94.

Blanton, R.
1972 *Prehispanic Settlement Patterns in the Ixtapalapa Peninsula Region, Mexico.* Occasional Papers in Anthropology No. 6, Dept. of Anthropology, Pennsylvania State University. University Park, PA.

Blanton, R., S. Kowalewski, G. Feinman, and J. Appel
1981 *Ancient Mesoamerica.* Cambridge: Cambridge University Press.

Bodenheimer, F.S.
1951 *Insects as Human Food: A Chapter in the Ecology of Man.* The Hague: W. Junk Publishers.

Boyd, C.E.
1968 Freshwater plants: a potential source of protein. *Economic Botany* 22:359-68.
1974 Utilization of aquatic plants. In *Aquatic Vegetation and its Use and Control*, edited by D.S. Mitchell, pp. 107-15. Paris: UNESCO.

Boyd, C.E., and P. McGinty
1981 Percentage digestible dry matter and crude protein in dried aquatic weeds. *Economic Botany* 35:296-99.

Bradbury, J.
1975 Paleolimnology of Lake Texcoco, Mexico: evidence from diatoms. *Limnology and Oceanography* 16:180-200.
1986 Paleolimnología del Lago de Chalco, México: el medio ambiente litoral. In *Tlapacoya: 35,000 Años de História del Lago de Chalco*, edited by J. Lorenzo and L. Mirambell, pp. 167-72. México, D.F.: Insituto Nacional de Antropología e História.
1989 Late quaternary lacustrine paleoenvironments in the Cuenca de México. *Quaternary Science Reviews* 8:75-100.
2000 Limnologic history of Lago de Patzcuaro, Michoacán, Mexico for the past 48,000 years: impacts of climate and man. *Palaeogeography, Palaeoclimatology, Palaeoecology* 163:69-95.

Breunig, P., K. Neumann, and W. VanNeer
1996 New research on the Holocene settlement and environment of the Chad Basin in Nigeria. *African Archaeological Review* 13:111-46.

Bridgewater, N., T. Heaton, and S. O'Hara
1999 A late Holocene paleolimnological record from central Mexico, based on faunal and stable-isotope analysis of ostracod shells. *Journal of Paleolimnology* 22:383-97.

Broda, J.
1971 Las fiestas aztecas de los dioses de la lluvia. *Revista Española de Antropología Americana* 6:245-327.
1991 The sacred landscape of Aztec calendar festivals: myth, nature, and society. In *To Change Place: Aztec Ceremonial Landscapes*, edited by D. Carrasco, pp. 74-120. Niwot: University Press of Colorado.

Browman, D.
1981   Prehistoric nutrition and medicine in the Lake Titicaca Basin. In *Health in the Andes*, edited by J.W. Bastien and J.M. Donohue, pp. 102-18. American Anthropological Association Special Publication No. 12.
1989   Chenopod cultivation, lacustrine resources, and fuel use at Chiripa, Bolivia. *Missouri Archaeologist* 47:137-72.

Brumfiel, E.
1987   *Aztec Xaltocan: Regional Articulation in the Late Postclassic Valley of Mexico.* Report to the H. John Heinz III Charitable Trust, Dept. of Anthropology and Sociology, Albion College.
1990   *Postclassic Xaltocan: Archaeological Research in the Northern Valley of Mexico: 1990 Annual Report.* Dept. of Anthropology and Sociology, Albion College.
1996   *El hombre y el lago en Xaltocan postclásico.* Paper presented at the XXIV Mesa Redonda, Sociedad Mexicana de Antropología, Tepic, Nayarit, Mexico.
1997   *Unidades Domesticas en Xaltocan Postclásico: Informe Annual de 1997.* Report submitted to Instituto Nacional de Antropología e História, México, D.F.

Brumfiel, E., and C. Frederick
1992   Xaltocán: Centro regional de la Cuenca de México. *Boletín del Consejo de Arqueología, 1991*, pp. 24-30. México, D.F.: Instituto Nacional de Antropología e História.

Bruton, M.N.
1979   The utilization and conservation of Lake Sibaya. In *Lake Sibaya*, edited by B. Allanson, pp. 286-312. Monographiae Biologicae, vol. 36. The Hague: W. Junk Publishers.

Buel, J.W.
1890   *Heroes of the Dark Continent.* Boston: Eastern Publishing Co.

Burns, J.
2003   The killing of Iraq's ancient marsh culture. *New York Times* Jan. 26, 2003, p. 14.

Butler, V.L.
1996   Tui chub taphonomy and the importance of marsh resources in the western Great Basin of North America. *American Antiquity* 61:699-717.

Bye, R.A.
1981   Quelites: ethnoecology of edible greens – past, present, and future. *Journal of Ethnobiology* 1:109-23.

Caballero, M., and B. Ortega
1998   Lake levels since about 40,000 years ago at Lake Chalco, near Mexico City. *Quaternary Research* 50:69-79.

Caballero, M., S. Lozano, B. Ortega, J. Urrutia, and J. Macías
1999   Environmental characteristics of Lake Tecocomulco, northern Basin of Mexico, for the last 50,000 years. *Journal of Paleolimnology* 22(4):399-411.

Calta, M.
1992   Bug seasoning – when insect experts go in search of six-legged hors d'oeuvres. *Eating Well* Nov./Dec. 1992, pp. 22-25.

Camacho, J.M.
1943   Urus, Changos y Atacamas. *Boletín de la Sociedad Geográfica de La Paz* 66:9-35.

Capriles, J.
2003   *Entre el valle y la peninsula: Variabilidad en la utilización de recursos faunísticos durante Tiwanaku (400-1000 D.C.) en el sitio Iwawi, Bolivia.* Tesis de Licenciatura, Carrera de Arqueología, Facultad de Ciencias Sociales, Universidad Mayor de San Andrés, La Paz.

Carballal, M., and M. Flores
1993   *El Peñon de los Baños (Tepetzingo) y sus alrededores: interpretaciones paleoambientales y culturales de la porción noroccidental de Lago de Texcoco.* Tesis de Licenciatura, Escuela Nacional de Antropología e História, México, D.F.
2004   Elementos hidráulicos en el Lago de México-Texcoco en el Posclásico. *Arqueología Mexicana* 12(68):28-33.

Carmouze, J., J.R. Durand, and C. Lévêque (editors)
1983   *Lake Chad: Ecology and Productivity of a Shallow Tropical Ecosystem.* The Hague: W. Junk Publishers

Carmouze, J., and J. Lemoalle
1983   The lacustrine environment. In *Lake Chad: Ecology and Productivity of a Shallow Tropical Ecosystem*, edited by J. Carmouze, J. Durand, and C. Lévêque, pp. 125-43. The Hague: W. Junk Publishers.

Carrasco, D. (editor)
1991   *To Change Place: Aztec Ceremonial Landscapes.* Niwot: University Press of Colorado.

Casaverde Rojas, J.
1977   El trueque en la economía pastoral. In *Pastores de Puna*, edited by J.A. Flores, pp. 171-91. Lima: Instituto de Estudios Peruanos.

Castillo, M.
1994   *Xochimilco Prehispánico: La Vida Cotidiana durante el Postclásico Tardío.* Tesis de Licenciatura, Escuela Nacional de Antropología e História, México, D.F.

Cervantes de Salazar, Francisco
1914 [1580s] *Crónica de la Nueva España.* Madrid: The Hispanic Society of America.

Charlton, T.
1969   Texcoco fabric-marked pottery, tlateles, and salt making. *American Antiquity* 34:73-76.
1971   Texcoco fabric-marked pottery and salt making: a further note. *American Antiquity* 36:217-18.

Chavez, S.
1999   *Historical, Ethnographic, and Ecological Data regarding Zea Mays (Tonqo) Cultivation at High Altitudes: Implications for the Archaeology of the Titicaca Basin.* Manuscript on file, Museum of Anthropology, University of Michigan. Ann Arbor.

Chavez, S., and D. Jorgenson
1980   Further inquiries into the case of the Apapa-Thunderbolt. *Ñawpa Pacha* 18:73-80. Berkeley.

Ciudad Real, Antonio de
1976 [1580s] *Tratado Curioso y Docto de las Grandezas de la Nueva España*. México, D.F.: Universidad Nacional Autónoma de México.

Clark, J.D.
1971 A re-examination of the evidence for agricultural origins in the Nile Valley. *Proceedings of the Prehistoric Society* 37(1):34-77.

Clavijero, F.J.
1964 [1780] *História Antigua de México*, edited by R.P. Mariano. México, D.F.: Editorial Porrua, S.A.

Cline, S.L, and M. Leon-Portilla (editors)
1984 *The Testaments of Culhuacán*. Latin American Center Publications, Special Studies Vol. 2, Nahuatl Series No. 1, University of California at Los Angeles. Los Angeles.

Cobo, Bernabé
1890 [1580s] *História del Nuevo Mundo*. Sevilla: E. Rasco.

Coe, M.
1964 The chinampas of Mexico. *Scientific American* 260:90-96.

Coles, J.
1998 Prologue: wetland worlds and the past preserved. In *Hidden Dimensions: The Cultural Significance of Wetland Archaeology*, edited by K. Bernick, pp. 3-23. Vancouver: UBC Press.

Conconi, J.R.E., J. Moreno, C. Mayadon, F. Valdez, M. Perez, E. Prado, and H. Rodriguez
1984 Protein content of some edible insects in Mexico. *Journal of Ethnobiology* 4(1):61-72.

Connah, G.
1981 *Three Thousand Years in Africa: Man and His Environment in the Lake Chad Region of Nigeria*. Cambridge: Cambridge University Press.

Cook, S., and W. Borah
1979 *Essays in Population History: Vol. 3, Mexico and California*. Berkeley: University of California Press.

Corbet, F.M.
1958 Lunar periodicity of aquatic insects in Lake Victoria. *Nature* 182:330-31.

Cordova, C.
1997 *Landscape Transformation in Aztec and Spanish Colonial Texcoco, Mexico*. PhD dissertation, University of Texas at Austin. University Microfilms, Ann Arbor.

Cornell Lab of Ornithology
2005 *The Birds of North America Online*. American Ornithologists Union.

Corona, J. (editor)
1964 *Antigüedades de Méxi, ʔ, Basadas en la Recopilación de Lord Kingsborough*. 2 vols. México, D.F.: Secretaría ʔe Hacienda y Crédito Público.

Cortés, Hernán
1963 [1519-1522] *Cartas y Documentos*. México, D.F.: Editorial Porrua.

Cowan, F.
1865 *Curious Facts in the History of Insects*. Philadelphia: J.B. Lippincott.

Créqui-Montfort, G. de, and P. Rivet
1927 La langue Uru ou Pukina. Appendice V: Estraits des Auteurs Anciens et Modernes sur les Uru, les Çipaya et les Cango. *Journal de la Socièté des Americanistes de Paris* 19:96-116.

Darby, W.J., P. Ghalioungui, and L. Grivetti
1977 *Food: The Gift of Osiris*. 2 vols. New York: Academic Press.

Darch, J.P. (editor)
1983 *Drained Field Agriculture in Central and South America*. B.A.R. International Series No. 189, Oxford.

Dávalos, H.
1954 La alimentación entre los Mexicas. *Revista Mexicana de Estudios Antropológicos* 15:103-18.

Davies, S., S. Metcalfe, A. MacKenzie, A. Newton, G. Endfield, and J. Farmer
2004 Environmental changes in the Zirahuén Basin, Michoacán, Mexico during the last 1000 years. *Journal of Paleolimnology* 31(1):77-98.

Décima, E., and D. Dincauze
1998 The Boston Back Bay fish weirs. In *Hidden Dimensions: The Cultural Significance of Wetland Archaeology*, edited by K. Bernick, pp. 157-79. Vancouver: UBC Press.

Dedenbach-Salazar, S.
1990 *Inka Pachaq Llamanpa Willaynin: Uso y Crianza de los Camelidos en la Época Incaica*. Bonner Amerikanistische Studien 16, Bonn.

Deevey, E.S.
1957 Limnological studies in Middle America, with a chapter on Aztec limnology. *Transactions, Connecticut Academy of Arts and Sciences* 39:213-28.

DeFoliart, G.
1990 Insects as food in indigenous populations. *Proceedings of the First International Congress of Ethnobiology* 1:145-50. Belem, Brazil.

Dejoux, C.
1976 *Synecologie des Chironomides du Lac Tchad: Dipteres, Nematoceres*. Paris: Recherche cientifique et Technique d'Outre-Mer.
1991 *El Lago Titicaca: Sintesis del Conocimiento Limnológico Actual*. La Paz: ORSTOM.

Dejoux, C., and A. Iltis (editors)
1992   *Lake Titicaca: A Synthesis of Limnological Knowledge.* Monographiae Biologicae, vol. 68. Dordrecht: Kluwer Academic Publishers.

DeLong, D.
1960   Man in a world of insects. *The Ohio Journal of Science* 60(4):193-206.

DeLucia, K., and E. Brumfiel (editors)
2004   *Space and Social Organization at Postclassic Xaltocan, Mexico.* 2003 Annual Report submitted to Instituto Nacional de Antropología e História, México, D.F.

Diaz del Castillo, Bernal
1908 [1582] *The True History of the Conquest of New Spain*, translated by A.P. Maudsley. London: The Hakluyt Society.
1956 [1582] *Discovery and Conquest of Mexico.* New York: Farrar, Straus, and Cudahy.
1960 [1582] *História Verdadera de la Conquista de la Nueva España.* México, D.F.: Editorial Porrúa.

Dilke, O., and M. Dilke
1961   Terracina and the Pomptine marshes. *Greece and Rome*, second series, 8(2):172-78.

Dillon, J.C., and P.A. Phan
1993   Spirulina as a source of proteins in human nutrition. In *Spiruline, Algue de Vie/Spirulina, Algae of Life*, edited by F. Doumenge et al., pp. 103-7. Bulletin del Institut Oceanographique, Número Special 12, Musée Oceanographique, Monaco.

Dortch, C.
1997   New perceptions of the chronology and development of aboriginal fishing in southwestern Australia. *World Archaeology* 29(1):15-35.

Doumenge, F., H. Durand-Chastel, and A. Toulemont (editors)
1993   *Spiruline, Algue de Vie/Spirulina, Algae of Life.* Bulletin del Institut Oceanographique, Número Special 12, Musée Oceanographique, Monaco.

Dourojeanni, M., R. Hofmann, R. García, J. Mlleaux, and A. Tovar
1968   Observaciones preliminares para el manejo de las aves acuáticas del Lago Junín, Perú. *Revista Forestal del Peru* 2(2):3-52. Instituto de Investigaciones Forestales, Universidad Agraria La Molina, Lima.

Dufour, D.
1987   Insects as food: a case study from the northwest Amazon. *American Anthropologist* 89:383-97.

Duges, A.
1888   Batracios del Valle de México. *La Naturaleza*, 2a serie, 1:136-46. México.

Dunn, F.
1965   On the antiquity of malaria in the Western Hemisphere. *Human Biology* 37:385-93.

Dunning, J.B., Jr.
1984 *Body Weights of 686 Species of North American Birds.* Western Bird Banding Assoc.,
Monograph No. 1. Cave Creek, Arizona: Eldon Publishing Co.

Duran, Fray Diego
1971 [1581] *Book of the Gods and Rites and the Ancient Calendar,* translated and edited by F.
Horcasitas and D. Heyden. Norman: University of Oklahoma Press.

Durand-Chastel, H.
1980 Production and use of Spirulina in Mexico. In *Algae Biomass,* edited by G. Shelef and
C.J. Soeder, pp. 51-64. New York: Elsevier.

Durand, J.R.
1983 The exploitation of fish stocks in the Lake Chad region. In *Lake Chad: Ecology and
Productivity of a Shallow Tropical Ecosystem,* edited by J.P. Carmouze, J.R. Durand, and
C. Lévêque, pp. 425-81. The Hague: W. Junk Publishers.

Duviols, P.
1976 Une petite chronique retrouvées: errores, ritos, supersticiones y ceremonias de los yndios
de la provincia de Chinchaycocha y otras del Piru. *Journal de la Socièté des Americanistes* 63:275-97. Paris.

Ebeling, W.
1986 *Handbook of Indian Foods and Fibers of Arid America.* Berkeley: University of California Press.

Enfield, G., and S. O'Hara
1999 Degradation, drought, and dissent: an environmental history of colonial Michoacan, west
central Mexico. *Annals of the Association of American Geographers* 89(3):402-19.

Ensminger, A., M. Ensminger, J. Konlande, and J. Robson
1995 *The Concise Encyclopedia of Foods and Nutrition.* Boca Raton: CRC Press.

Erickson, C.
1988 *An Archaeological Investigation of Raised Field Agriculture in the Lake Titicaca Basin
of Peru.* PhD dissertation, Dept. of Anthropology, University of Illinois. Urbana.

Erlandson, J.M.
2001 The archaeology of aquatic adaptations: paradigms for a new millennium. *Journal of
Archaeological Research* 9(4):287-350.

Essig, E.O.
1934 The value of insects to the California Indians. *Scientific Monthly* 38(2):181-86.

Estioko-Griffin, A.A., and P. Bion Griffin
1981 The beginnings of cultivation among Agta hunter-gatherers in northeastern Luzon. In
Adaptive Strategies and Change in Philippine Swidden-Based Societies, edited by Harold
Olofson, pp. 55-72. Laguna, Philippines: Forest Research Institute College.

Etkin, N.L. (editor)
1994   *Eating on the Wild Side: The Pharmalogic, Ecologic, and Social Implications of Using Non Cultigens.* Tucson: University of Arizona Press.

Evans, S.
1980   *A Settlement Systems Analysis of the Teotihuacan Region, Mexico, A.D. 1350-1520.* PhD dissertation, Pennsylvania State University, University Park. University Microfilms, Ann Arbor.

Evans, S., and P. Gould
1982   Settlement models in archaeology. *Journal of Anthropological Archaeology* 1:275-304.

Fabiola, A., O. Palaco, and H. Pollard
2001   Ofrendas de peces asociadas a entierros del Clásico-Epiclásico en Urichu, Michoacán, México. *Archaeofauna* 10:149-62.

Fain, C.
1955   The People of the Lake. *Antiquity and Survival* 1:303-14.

Farrar, W.V.
1966   Tecuitlatl: a glimpse of Aztec food technology. *Nature* 211(5047):341-42.

Fisher, C., H. Pollard, I. Israde-Alcántara, V. Garduño, and S. Banerjee
2003   A re-examination of human-induced environmental change within the Lake Patzcuaro Basin, Michoacán, Mexico. *Proceedings of the National Academy of Sciences* 100(8):4957-62.

Fisher, C., H. Pollard, and C. Frederick
1999   Intensive agriculture and socio-political development in the Lake Patzcuaro Basin, Mexico. *Antiquity* 73:642-49.

Fjeldså, J., and N. Krabbe
1990   *Birds of the High Andes.* Zoological Museum, University of Copenhagen. Svendborg, Denmark: Apollo Books.

Flores, T.
1918   *El Tequesquite del Lago de Texcoco.* Anales del Instituto Geológico de México, no. 5, México, D.F.

Forbes, D.
1870   On the Aymara Indians of Bolivia and Peru. *Journal of the Ethnological Society of London* 2:193-305.

Foster, G.
1948   *Empire's Children: The People of Tzintzuntzan.* Institute of Social Anthropology, Publication No. 6. Washington, D.C.: Smithsonian Institution.

Fowler, C.S.
1982   Settlement patterns and subsistence systems in the Great Basin: the ethnographic record. In *Man and Environment in the Great Basin,* edited by D.B. Madsen and J.F. O'Connell, pp. 121-38. Society for American Archaeology Papers No. 2.

1990a *Tule Technology: Northern Paiute Uses of Marsh Resources in Western Nevada.* Smithsonian Folklore Studies No. 6. Washington, D.C.: Smithsonian Institution Press.
1990b Ethnographic perspectives on marsh-based cultures in western Nevada. In *Wetland Adaptations in the Great Basin,* edited by J. Janetski and D. Madsen, pp. 17-31. Museum of Peoples and Cultures, Occasional Papers No. 1, Brigham Young University. Provo.
1992 *In the Shadow of Fox Peak: An Ethnography of the Cattail-Eater Northern Paiute People of Stillwater Marsh.* Cultural Resources Series No. 5, U.S. Fish and Wildlife Service. Portland, Oregon.

Fowler, C.S. (compiler and editor)
1989 *Willard Z. Park's Ethnographic Notes on the Northern Nevada Paiute of Western Nevada, 1933-1934, Vol. 1.* Anthropological Papers No. 114, University of Utah. Salt Lake City.

Fowler, C.S., and J.E. Bath
1981 Pyramid Lake Northern Paiute fishing: the ethnographic record. *Journal of California and Great Basin Anthropology* 3(2):176-86.

Fowler, C.S., and N.P. Walter
1985 Harvesting pandora moth larvae with the Owens Valley Paiute. *Journal of California and Great Basin Anthropology* 7:155-65.

Frederick, C.
1995 *Fluvial Responses to Late Quaternary Climatic Change and Land Use in Central Mexico.* PhD dissertation, Dept. of Geography, University of Texas, Austin. University Microfilms, Ann Arbor.

Frederick, C., B. Winsborough, and V. Popper
2005 Geoarchaeological investigations in the Northern Basin of Mexico. In *Production and Power at Postclassic Xaltocan,* edited by E. Brumfiel, pp. 71-116. Memoirs in Latin American Archaeology, University of Pittsburgh Press.

Fulford, M., T. Champion, and A. Long (editors)
1997 *England's Coastal Heritage: A Survey for English Heritage and the RCHME.* English Heritage Archaeological Report No. 15, London.

Furst, J.L.
1995 *The Natural History of the Soul in Ancient Mexico.* New Haven: Yale University Press.

Furst, P.
1978 Spirulina. *Human Nature* 1(3):60-65.

Gadow, H.
1908 *Through Southern Mexico: Being an Account of the Travels of a Naturalist.* London: Witherby and Co.

Gallegos, A.J.
1993 The past, present, and future of algae in Mexico. In *Spiruline, Algue de Vie/Spirulina, Algae of Life,* edited by F. Doumenge et al., pp. 133-39. Bulletin del Institut Oceanographique, Numero Especial 12, Musée Oceanographique, Monaco.

Garay, Francisco de
1888   *El Valle de México. Apuntes Históricos sobre su Hidrografía*. México: Secretaría de Fomento.

García Mora, C.
1979   Nota para la antropología de la subcuenca Chalca del Valle de México. *Biótica* 4(1):13-32. México, D.F.

García Quintana, J., and J.R. Romero
1978   *México-Tenochtitlán y su Problematica Lacustre*. Instituto de Investigaciones Históricas, Cuaderno No. 21, Serie Histórica, Universidad Nacional Autónoma de México, México, D.F.

García Sanchez, M.A.
1998   *El Comercio de Productos Lacustres: Relaciones de Pervivencia Cultural entre los Valles de Toluca y México, 1880-1970*. Tesis de Maestro en Antropología Social, Centro de Investigaciones y Estudios Superiores en Antropología Social, Instituto Nacional de Antropología e História, México, D.F.

García y Cubas, A.
1858   Valle de Mexico, Carta XVII. In *Atlas Mexicano*. Imprenta Litografica de H. Iriarte y Cia., México. Clements Rare Book Library, University of Michigan. Ann Arbor.

García-Cook, A.
1982   *Análisis Tipológico de Artefactos*. México, D.F.: Instituto Nacional de Antropología e História.

Gardiner, C.H.
1956   *Naval Power in the Conquest of Mexico*. Austin: University of Texas Press.

Gibson, C.
1964   *The Aztecs Under Spanish Rule: A History of the Indians of the Valley of Mexico 1519-1810*. Stanford: Stanford University Press.

Gilmore, H.W.
1953   Hunting habits of the early Nevada Paiutes. *American Anthropologist* 55:148-53.

Gómara, Francisco Lopez de
1987 [1552] *La Conquista de México*. História 16, Información y Revistas, Madrid.

Gonzalez, Luis, et al.
1902   *Memoria Histórica, Técnica y Administrativa de las Obras del Desagüe del Valle de México, 1449-1900*. 2 vols. México: Tipografía de la Oficina Impresora de Estampillas.

Gorenflo, L.
1996   Regional efficiency in prehispanic central Mexico: insight from geographical studies of archaeological settlement patterns. In *Arqueología Mesoamericana: Homenaje a William T. Sanders*, edited by G. Mastache, J. Parsons, M. Serra, and R. Santley, pp. 135-60. México, D.F.: Instituto Nacional de Antropología e História.

Gorenflo, L., and N. Gale
1986 Population and productivity in the Teotihuacan Valley: changing patterns of spatial association in prehispanic central Mexico. *Journal of Anthropological Archaeology* 5:199-228.

Gosling, Cecil
1916 *An Account of a Visit to Angwaki, a Village of the Uros Indians on the River Desaguadero in Bolivia.* Gothenburg, Sweden. [Cited by Crequi-Montfort and Rivet 1927.]

Griffin, P. Bion
1981 Northern Luzon Agta subsistence and settlement. *Filipinas* 2:26-42.

Gronenborn, D.
1998 Archaeological and ethnohistorical investigations along the southern fringes of Lake Chad, 1993-1996. *African Archaeological Review* 15:225-60.

Grove, A.T.
1970 Rise and fall of Lake Chad. *The Geographical Journal* 42:432-39.

Guérin-Méneville, F.E.
1857 Mémoire sur trois espèces d'insectes hémiptères dont les oeufs servent à faire une sorte de pain nommé Huqutlé au Mexique. *Bull. Soc. Imp. Zool. d'Acclimat* 4:578-81. Paris.

Gurría, J.
1978 *El Desagüe del Valle de México durante la Época Novohispana.* Instituto de Investigaciones Históricas, Cuaderno Serie Histórica No. 19, Universidad Nacional Autónoma de México, México, D.F.

Guzmán, A., O. Polaco, and H. Pollard
2001 Ofrendas de peces asociadas a entierros del Clásico-Epiclásico en Urichu, Michoacán, Mexico. *Archaeofauna* 10:149-62.

Haggard, J.V.
1941 *Handbook for Translators of Spanish Historical Documents.* Archives and Collections, University of Texas. Austin.

Harner, M.
1977 The ecological basis for Aztec sacrifice. *American Ethnologist* 4:117-35.

Harrington, M.R.
1927 Some lake-bed camp sites in Nevada. *Indian Notes* 4(1):40-47. Museum of the American Indian, Heye Foundation. New York.
1933 A cat-tail eater. *Masterkey* 7:147-49.

Harris, M.
1978 *Cannibals and Kings.* New York: Random House.
1979 *Cultural Materialism: The Struggle for a Science of Culture.* New York: Random House.

Harrison, P.
1978   Bajos revisited: visual evidence for one system of agriculture. In *Prehispanic Maya Agriculture*, edited by P. Harrison and B. Turner, pp. 247-54. Albuquerque: University of New Mexico Press.

Hassig, R.
1981   The famine of one rabbit: ecological causes and social consequences of a pre-columbian calamity. *Journal of Anthropological Research* 37:171-81.
1986   Famine and scarcity in the Valley of Mexico. *Research in Economic Anthropology, Supplement 2*, pp. 303-17. New York: JAI Press.

Hay, G.
1870   Apuntes geográficos, estadísticos, e históricos del distrito de Texcoco. *Boletín de la Sociedad Mexicana de Geografía y Estadística*, 2a epoca, 2:541-55. México: Imprenta del Gobierno en Palacio.

Hayden, B.
1990   Nimrods, piscators, pluckers, and planters: the emergence of food production. *Journal of Anthropological Archaeology* 9(1):31-69.

Heiser, C.
1978   The totora (Scirpus californicus) in Ecuador and Peru. *Economic Botany* 32:222-36.

Heizer, R.
1949   Fish poisons. In *Handbook of South American Indians*, 5:277-81, edited by J. Steward. Smithsonian Institution, Bureau of American Ethnology Bulletin No. 143, Washington, D.C.
1950   Kutsavi, a Great Basin Indian food. *Kroeber Anthropology Society Papers* 2:35-41.

Heizer, R., and L. Napton
1970   *Archaeology and the Prehistoric Great Basin Lacustrine Subsistence Regime as seen from Lovelock Cave, Nevada.* Contributions of the University of California Archaeological Research Facility No. 10. Berkeley.

Hernández, Francisco
1942 [1570s]   *História de las Plantas de Nueva España.* 3 vols. México, D.F.: Imprenta Universitaria.
1959a [1570s] *Obras Completas, Tomo II: História Natural de Nueva España, Volumen I.* México, D.F.: Universidad Nacional Autónoma de México.
1959b [1570s] *Obras Completas, Tomo III: História Natural de Nueva España, Volumen II.* México, D.F.: Universidad Nacional Autónoma de México.

Herrera, Alfonso
1888   Apuntes de ornitología. La migración en el Valle de México: Apuntes para el catálogo de las aves inmigrantes y sedentarias del Valle de México. *La Naturaleza*, 2a serie, 1:165-69, México.
1895   Fauna del Lago de Texcoco: Notas acerca de la zoología del Lago de Texcoco y sus alrededores. In *Estudios Referentes a la Desecación del Lago de Texcoco, Año 1895*, edited by F. Altamiro, pp. 41-62. Instituto México Nacional, Secretaría de Fomento, México.

Herrera, Antonio
1726   "An Hydrographical Draught of Mexico as it Lies in its Lakes." In *History of the Vast Continent* . . . , vol. 3, plate 104, pp. 194-95. Clements Rare Book Library, University of Michigan. Ann Arbor.

Hitchcock, S.W.
1962   Insects and Indians of the Americas. *Bulletin, Entomological Society of America* 8(4):181-87.

Home, Everard
1824   An account of the organs of generation of the Mexican Proteus, called by the natives axolotl. *Philosophical Transactions of the Royal Society of London* 114:419-23.

Horn, D.D.
1984   *Marsh Resources and the Ethnoarchaeology of the Uru-Muratos of Highland Bolivia.* PhD dissertation, Department of Anthropology, Washington University, St. Louis. University Microfilms, Ann Arbor.

Humboldt, Alejandro de
1870   El axolote o proteus mexicanus. *Boletín de la Sociedad Geográfica y Estadística de la República Mexicana*, 2a época, 2:77-91. México.

Humboldt, Alexander von
1984 [1822]   *Ensayo Político sobre el Reino de la Nueva España.* México, D.F.: Editorial Porrúa.

Hungerford, H.B.
1948   The Corixidae of the Western Hemisphere. *University of Kansas Science Bulletin* 32:1-827.

Ibarra, D.E.
1962   Los desconocidos Urus del Poopó. *Zeitschrift für Ethnologie* 87:77-92. Berlin: Braunschweig.
1985   *Pueblos Indígenos de Bolivia.* La Paz: Librería Editorial Juventud.

Iltis, A., and J. Lemoalle
1983   The aquatic vegetation of Lake Chad. In *Lake Chad: Ecology and Productivity of a Shallow Tropical Ecosystem*, edited by J.P. Carmouze, J.R. Durand, and C. Lévêque, pp. 125-43. The Hague: W. Junk Publishers.

Israde-Alcántara, V. Garduño-Monroy, C. Fisher, H. Pollard, and M. Rodríguez-Pascua
2005   Lake level change, climate, and the impact of natural events: the role of seismic and volcanic events in the formation of the Lake Patzcuaro Basin, Michoacan, Mexico. *Quaternary International* 135(1):35-46.

Ivanhoe, F.
1978   Diet and demography in Texcoco on the eve of the Spanish Conquest: a semiquantitative reconstruction from selected ethnohistorical texts. *Revista Mexicana de Estudios Antropológicos* 24(2):137-46.

Janetski, J.C., and D. Madsen (editors)
1990   *Wetland Adaptations in the Great Basin.* Occasional Papers No. 1, Museum of Peoples and Cultures, Brigham Young University. Provo.

Jones, T., G. Brown, L. Raab, J. McVicker, W. Spaulding, D. Kennett, A. York, and P. Walker
1999   Environmental imperatives reconsidered: demographic crises in western North America during the Medieval Climatic Anomaly. *Current Anthropology* 40(2):137-70.

Kelly, R.
1988   Archaeological context. In *Preliminary Investigations in Stillwater Marsh: Human Prehistory and Geoarchaeology,* edited by C. Raven and R. Elston, pp. 5-20. Silver City, Nevada: Intermountain Research Reports.
2001   *Prehistory of the Carson Desert and Stillwater Mountains.* University of Utah Anthropological Papers No. 123. Salt Lake City: University of Utah Press.

Kennedy, D.
1998   *My Mexico: A Culinary Odyssey with More Than 300 Recipes.* New York: Clarkson Pottery.

Kent, A., T. Webber, and D. Steadman
1999   Distribution, relative abundance, and prehistory of birds on the Taraco Peninsula, Bolivian altiplano. *Ornitologia Neotropical* 10:151-78.

King, F.H.
1911   *Farmers of Forty Centuries, or Permanent Agriculture in China, Korea, and Japan.* Reprint. Emmaus, PA: Rosedale Press.

Kolata, A.
1993   *The Tiwanaku: Portrait of an Andean Civilization.* Cambridge and Oxford: Blackwell Publishers.

Kolata, A. (editor)
1996   *Tiwanaku and its Hinterland: Archaeology and Paleoecology of an Andean Civilization.* Washington, D.C.: Smithsonian Institution Press.

Korstanje, M.A.
2001   *The Role of Wild Resources in Productive Societies: The Cases of Northwestern Argentina's Rock Shelters.* Paper presented at a symposium, "The Call of the Wild: Critiquing the Wild Resources/Domestic Staple Dichotomy," Annual Meeting Society for American Archaeology. New Orleans.

Kroeber, A., and S. Barrett
1960   *Fishing Among the Indians of Northwestern California.* Anthropological Records Vol. 21, No. 1. Berkeley and Los Angeles: University of California Press.

LaBarre, W.
1941   The Uru of the Rio Desaguadero. *American Anthropologist* 43:493-522.
1946   The Uru-Chipaya. In *Handbook of South American Indians, Vol. 2: The Andean Civilizations,* edited by Julian Steward, pp. 575-85. Bulletin 143, Smithsonian Institution Bureau of American Ethnology. Washington, D.C.

1948   *The Aymara Indians of the Lake Titicaca Plateau, Bolivia.* Memoir 68, American Anthropological Association.
1951   Aymara biologicals and other medicines. *Journal of American Folklore* 64:171-78.

Latta, F.
1949   *Handbook of Yokuts Indians.* Oildale, California: Bear State Books.

Lemoine, E.
1978   *El Desagüe del Valle de México durante la Época Independiente.* Cuaderno, Serie Histórico No. 20, Instituto de Investigaciones Históricas, Universidad Nacional Autónoma de México, México, D.F.

Leonard, J.
1966   The 1964-65 Belgian trans-Saharan expedition. *Nature* 209(5019):126-28.

Leopold, A.S.
1959   *Wildlife of Mexico: The Game Birds and Mammals.* Berkeley and Los Angeles: University of California Press.
1985   *Fauna Silvestre de México.* México, D.F.: Ediciones del Instituto Mexicano de Recursos Naturales Renovables.

Levieil, D., Q. Cutipa, C. Goyzueta, and F. Paz
1989   The socio-economic importance of macrophyte extraction in Puno Bay. In *Pollution in Lake Titicaca, Peru: Training, Research, and Management*, edited by T. Northcote, P. Morales, D. Levy, and M. Greaven, pp. 155-75. Westwater Research Centre, University of British Columbia, Canada, and Instituto de Aguas Alto Andins, Universidad del Altiplano. Puno, Peru.

Levieil, D., and B. Orlove
1990   Local control of aquatic resources: community and ecology in Lake Titicaca, Peru. *American Anthropologist* 92:362-82.
1992   The socio-economic importance of macrophytes. In *Lake Titicaca: A Synthesis of Limnological Knowledge*, edited by C. Dejoux and A. Altis, pp. 505-11. Dordrecht, The Netherlands: Kluwer Academic Publishers.

Linne, S.
1937   Hunting and fishing in the Valley of Mexico in the middle of the 16th century. *Ethnos* 2:56-64.
1940   Bird-nets of Lake Texcoco, Mexico Valley. *Ethnos* 5:122-30.
1948   *El Valle y la Ciudad de México en 1550.* The Ethnographic Museum of Sweden, new series, Publication No. 9, Stockholm.

Litvak, J.
1962   Un monticulo excavado en Culhuacán, 1960. *Tlatoani*, 2a epoca, 16:24-31. México, D.F.
1964   *Estrategrafía Cultural y Natural en un Tlatel en el Lago de Texcoco.* México, D.F.: Instituto Nacional de Antropología e História.

Livingston, S.D.
1986   Archaeology of the Humboldt Lake site. *Journal of California and Great Basin Anthropology* 8(1):99-115.

Lizot, J.
1977   Population, resources, and warfare among the Yanomami. *Man* 12(3-4):497-517.

Lorenzo, J.L.
1986   Conclusiones. In *Tlapacoya: 35,000 Años de História del Lago de Chalco*, edited by
        J. Lorenzo and L. Mirambell, pp. 225-88. Colección Científica, Instituto Nacional de
        Anthropología e História, México, D.F.

Loud, L., and M. Harrington
1929   Lovelock Cave. *University of California Publications in American Archaeology and
        Ethnology*, 25(1):1-183. Berkeley.

Lozano-García, M., and B. Ortega-Guerrero
1994   Palynological and magnetic susceptibility records of Lake Chalco, central Mexico. *Pal-
        aeogeography, Palaeoclimatology, Palaeoecology* 109:177-81.
1998   Late Quaternary environmental changes of the central part of the Basin of Mexico: cor-
        relation between Texcoco and Chalco Basins. *Review of Palaeobotany and Palynology*
        99:77-93.

Lozano-García, M., B. Ortega, M. Caballero, and J. Urrutia
1993   Late Pleistocene and Holocene paleoenvironments of Chalco Lake, central Mexico.
        Quaternary Research 40:332-42.

Lozano-García, M., and M. Xelhauntzi
1997   Some problems in the late Quaternary pollen records of central Mexico: the Basin of
        Mexico and Zacapu. *Quaternary International* 43/44:117-23.

MacGregor, L.R.
1975   Los insectos y las antiguas culturas Mexicanas, un ensayo etnoentomológico. *Revista de
        la Universidad de México* 29(6-7):8-13.

Madsen, D.
1982   Get it where the gettin's good: a variable model of Great Basin subsistence and settle-
        ment based on data from the eastern Great Basin. In *Man and Environment in the Great
        Basin*, edited by D. Madsen and J. O'Connell, pp. 207-26. Society for American Archae-
        ology Papers No. 2.
1988   The prehistoric use of Great Basin marshes. In *Preliminary Investigations in Stillwa-
        ter Marsh: Human Prehistory and Geoarchaeology*, vol. 2, edited by C. Raven and R.
        Elston, pp. 414-26. Silver City, Nevada: Intermountain Research Reports.

Madsen, D. and J. Kirkman
1988   Hunting hoppers. *American Antiquity* 53:593-604.

Madsen, D., and J. O'Connell (editors)
1982   *Man and the Environment in the Great Basin*. Society for American Archaeology Papers
        No. 2.

Madsen, David, and D. Schmitt
1998   Mass collecting and diet breadth model: a Great Basin example. *Journal of Archaeologi-
        cal Science* 25(5):445-55.

Manelis de Klein, H.E.
1973   Los Urus: El extraño pueblo del altiplano. *Estudios Andinos* 7:129-50. Cuzco.

Martin del Campo, R.
1955   Productos biológicos del Valle de México. *Revista Mexicana de Estudios Antropológicos* 14(1):53-77.

Maudsley, A.P.
1916   The Valley of Mexico. *The Geographical Journal* 48(1):11-26.

Maxwell, G.
1957   *People of the Reeds*. New York: Harper & Brothers Publishers.

Mayer, Brantz
1844   *Mexico As It Was and As It Is*. New York: J. Winchester New World Press.
1850   *Mexico, Aztec, Spanish and Republican*. 2 vols. Hartford: S. Drake & Co.

Mayer-Oakes, W.
1959   *A Stratigraphic Excavation at El Risco, Mexico*. Proceedings of the American Philosophical Society, vol. 103, no. 3. Philadelphia.

McBride, G.M.
1921   *The Agrarian Indian Communities of Highland Bolivia*. Research Series No. 5, American Geographic Society. New York.

McBride, H.
1974   *Formative Ceramics and Prehistoric Settlement Patterns in the Cuauhtitlan Region, Mexico*. PhD dissertation, Dept. of Anthropology, University of California at Los Angeles. Los Angeles.

McClung de Tapia, E.
1987   Patrones de subsistencia urbana en Teotihuacan. In *Teotihuacan: Nuevos Datos, Nuevos Sínteses, Nuevos Problemas*, edited by E. McClung de Tapia and E. Rattray, pp. 57-74. Instituto de Investigaciones Antropológicas, Universidad Nacional Autónoma de México, México, D.F.

McClung de Tapia, E., and B. Aguilar
2001   Vegetation and plant use in postclassic Otumba. *Ancient Mesoamerica* 12:113-26.

McClung de Tapia, E., M. Serra, and A. Limón
1986   Formative lacustrine adaptation: botanical remains from Terremote-Tlaltenco, D.F., México. *Journal of Field Archaeology* 13:99-113.

Meek, S.E.
1903   Distribution of the fresh-water fishes of Mexico. *The American Naturalist* 37(443):771-84.
1904   *The Fresh-Water Fishes of Mexico North of the Isthmus of Tehuantepec*. Publications of the Field Columbian Museum, Zoological Series No. 5. Chicago.

Melville, E.
1994   *A Plague of Sheep: Environmental Consequences of the Conquest of Mexico.* Cambridge: Cambridge University Press.

Messer, E.
1972   Patterns of "wild" plant consumption in Oaxaca, Mexico. *Ecology of Food and Nutrition* 1:325-32.

Metcalfe, S., S. O'Hara, M. Caballero, and S. Davies
2000   Records of Late Pleistocene-Holocene climatic change in Mexico – a review. *Quaternary Science Review* 19:699-721.

Metcalfe, S., F. Street-Perrott, R. Brown, P. Hales, R. Perrott, and F. Steininger
1989   Late Holocene human impact on lake basins in central Mexico. *Geoarchaeology* 4:119-41.

Metraux, A.
1935   Contribution a l'ethnographie et a la linguistique des indiens Uro d'Ancoaqui (Bolivie). *Journal de la Société des Americanistes de Paris* 27:75-110.

Minc, L.
1999   *The Aztec Salt Trade: Insights from INAA of Texcoco Fabric-Marked Pottery.* Paper presented at the 64th Annual Meeting of the Society for American Archaeology. Chicago.

Mirambell, L.
1972   Una osamenta fósil en el ex-Lago de Texcoco. *Boletín, Instituto Nacional de Antropología e História,* Época II, 2:9-16. México, D.F.

Montúfar, A., and N. Maldonado
1998   Estudio arqueobiológico de los sedimentos del subsuelo en el edificio Real Seminario de Minas, 1772, México. *D.F. Arqueología,* 2a epoca, 20:97-113.

Moore, K., D. Steadman, and S. DeFrance
1999   Herds, fish, and fowl in the domestic and ritual economy of formative Chiripa. In *Early Settlement at Chiripa, Bolivia: Research of the Taraco Archaeological Project,* edited by C. Hastorf, pp. 105-16. Contribution No. 57, University of California Archaeological Research Facility, University of California. Berkeley.

Moreno, R.
1969   El axolotl. *Estudios de Cultura Nahuatl* 8:157-73.

Morton, J.
1975   Cattails (Typha spp.): weed problem or potential crop? *Economic Botany* 29:7-29.

Moseley, M.
1975   *The Maritime Foundations of Andean Civilization.* Menlo Park: Cummings.

Motolinia, Fray Toribio de
1903 [c. 1560]   *Memoriales de Fray Toribio de Motolinia,* edited by L. García. Casa del Editor, México. Reprinted 1999. Charlestown, MA: Acme Bookbinding.
1967   *Memoriales de Fray Toribio de Motolinía.* Edición Facsimilar, edited by E. Arviña. Guadalajara, Mexico.

1971 [1541] *Memoriales o Libro de las Cosas de la Nueva España y de los Naturales de Ella*, edited by E. O'Gorman. México, D.F.: Universidad Nacional Autónoma de México.

Muller, F.
1952 Recursos naturales del lago de Xochimilco del siglo X al XVI. *Boletín de la Sociedad Mexicana de Geografía y Estadística* 73:7-16.

Murra, J.
1965 Herds and herders in the Inca State. In *Man, Culture, and Animals*, edited by A. Leeds and A. Vayda, pp. 185-215. Publication 78, American Association for the Advancement of Science. Washington, D.C.

Murray, M.A.
2000 Fruits, vegetables, pulses and condiments. In *Ancient Egyptian Materials and Technology*, edited by Paul T. Nicholson and Ian Shaw, pp. 609-55. Cambridge: Cambridge University Press.

Musset, A.
1991 *El Agua en el Valle de México, Siglos XVI-XVIII*. México, D.F.: CEMCA.

Muzzolini, A.
1993 The emergence of a food-producing economy in the Sahara. In *The Archaeology of Africa: Foods, Metals, and Towns*, edited by T. Shaw, P. Sinclair, B. Andah, and A. Okpoko, pp. 227-39. London: Routledge.

Napton, L.K.
1969 The lacustrine subsistence pattern in the desert west. *Kroeber Anthropological Society, Special Publication No. 2*, pp. 28-69. Berkeley: University of California.

National Geographic Society
1999 *National Geographic Field Guide to the Birds of North America*. Washington, D.C.: National Geographic Society.

Newman, M.T.
1976 Aboriginal New World epidemiology and medical care and the impact of Old World disease imports. *American Journal of Physical Anthropology* 45:667-72.

New York Times
1951 Mexican airliner downed. Pilot puts craft into mud of Lake Texcoco – passengers saved. *New York Times* Sept. 2, 1951, p. 19. New York.

Nichols, D., and C. Frederick
1993 Irrigation canals and chinampas: recent research in the Northern Basin of Mexico. *Research in Economic Anthropology, Supplement 7*, pp. 123-59. New York: JAI Press.

Nicholson, H.
1971 Religion in pre-hispanic central Mexico. In *Archaeology of Northern Mesoamerica, Part One*, edited by G. Ekholm and I. Bernal, pp. 395-446. *Handbook of Middle American Indians, Volume 10*, R. Wauchope, general editor. Austin: University of Texas Press.

Niederberger, C.
1976   *Zohapilco: Cinco Milenios de Ocupación Humana en un Sitio Lacustre de la Cuenca de México*. México, D.F.: Instituto Nacional de Antropología e História.
1979   Early sedentary economy in the Basin of Mexico. *Science* 203(4376):131-42.
1987   *Paleopaysages et Archeologie Pre-Urbaine du Bassin de Mexico*. 2 vols. Collection Etudes Mesoamericaines I-II, Centre d'Etudes Mexicanines et Centramericaines, México, D.F.

Noguera, E.
1943   Excavaciones en El Tepalcate, Mexico. *American Antiquity* 9:33-43.

Northcote, T., P. Morales, D. Levy, and M. Greaven (editors)
1989   *Pollution in Lake Titicaca, Peru: Training, Research, and Management*. Vancouever, B.C., Canada: Westwater Research Centre.

Nuñez Ortega, A.
1878   Los navegantes indígenas en la época de la Conquista. *Boletín de la Sociedad Mexicana de Geografía y Estadística*, 3a época, 4:47-57.

Nuttall, Z.
1891   The atlatl or spear-thrower of the ancient Mexicans. *Archaeological and Ethnographical Papers of the Peabody Museum* 1(3):171-204.

Ober, F.A.
1884   *Travels in Mexico and Life Among the Mexicans*. Boston: Estes and Lauriat.

Odum, E.P.
1975   *Ecology: The Link between the Natural and the Social Sciences*, 2nd ed. New York: Holt, Rinehart, and Winston.

Offner, J.
1980   Archival reports of poor crop yields in the early post-conquest Texcocan heartland and their implications for studies of Aztec period population. *American Antiquity* 45:848-56.

Ogilvie, A.G.
1922   *Geography of the Central Andes*. Publication No. 1, American Geographic Society of New York. New York.

O'Hara, S., and S. Metcalfe
1997   The climate of Mexico since the Aztec period. *Quaternary International* 43/44:25-31.

O'Hara, S., S. Metcalfe, and F. Street-Perrott
1994   On the arid margin: the relationship between climate, humans, and the environment: a review of evidence from the highlands of central Mexico. *Chemosphere* 29(5):965-81.

O'Hara, S., F. Street-Perrott, and T. Burt
1993   Accelerated soil erosion around a Mexican highland lake caused by prehispanic agriculture. *Nature* 362:48-51.

O'Neill, G.
1962   *Postclassic Ceramic Stratigraphy at Chalco in the Valley of Mexico*. PhD dissertation, Columbia University, New York. University Microfilms, Ann Arbor.

Orlove, B.
2002 *Lines in the Water: Nature and Culture at Lake Titicaca*. Berkeley: University of California Press.

Orme, A.R.
1990 Wetland morphology, hydrodynamics and sedimentation. In *Wetlands, A Threatened Landscape*, edited by M. Williams, pp. 42-94. Oxford, U.K.: Basil Blackwell.

Orozco y Berra, M.
1864 *Memoria para la cartografía hidrográfica del Valle de México*. Mexico: Sociedad Mexicana de Geografía y Estadística.

Ortega, M.
1972 Study of the edible algae of the Valley of Mexico. *Botanica Marina* 15:162-66.

Ortiz de Montellano, B.
1978 Aztec cannibalism: an ecological necessity? *Science* 200:611-17.
1990 *Aztec Medicine, Health, and Nutrition*. New Brunswick and London: Rutgers University Press.

O'Shea, J.M.
1989 The role of wild resources in small-scale agricultural systems: tales from the lakes and the plains. In *Bad-Year Economics: Cultural Responses to Risk and Uncertainty*, edited by P. Halstead and J. O'Shea, pp. 57-67. Cambridge: Cambridge University Press.

O'Sullivan, A.
2003 Place, memory and identity among estuarine fishing communities: interpreting the archaeology of early medieval fish weirs. *World Archaeology* 35(3):449-68.

Palavecino, E.
1949 Los indios Uru de Iruito. *Runa* 2:59-88. Buenos Aires.

Palerm, A.
1973 *Obras Hidráulicas Prehispánicas en el Sistema Lacustre del Valle de México*. México, D.F.: Instituto Nacional de Antropología e História.

Park, J.E.
2001 *Food from the Heartland: The Iwawi Site and Tiwanaku Political Economy from a Faunal Perspective*. Master's thesis, Dept. of Archaeology, Simon Fraser University, Calgary.

Parsons, J.R.
1971 *Prehistoric Settlement Patterns in the Texcoco Region, Mexico*. Memoirs, no. 3. Museum of Anthropology, University of Michigan. Ann Arbor.
1974 *Patrones de Asentamiento Prehispánico en el Noroeste del Valle de México, Región de Zumpango. Temporada de 1973*. Informe presented to the Instituto Nacional de Antropología e História, México, D.F.
1976 The role of chinampa agriculture in the food supply of Aztec Tenochtitlan. In *Cultural Change and Continuity: Essays in Honor of James B. Griffin*, edited by C. Cleland, pp. 233-57. New York: Academic Press.

1991   Political implications of prehispanic chinampa agriculture in the Valley of Mexico. In *Land and Politics in the Valley of Mexico: A Two Thousand Year Perspective*, edited by H.R. Harvey, pp. 17-42. Albuquerque: University of New Mexico Press.

1996   Tequesquite and ahuauhtle: rethinking the prehispanic productivity of Lake Texcoco-Xaltocán-Zumpango. In *Arqueología Mesoamericana: Homenaje a William T. Sanders*, edited by A.G. Mastache, J. Parsons, R. Santley, and M. Serra, pp. 439-60. México, D.F.: Instituto Nacional de Antropología e História.

2001   *The Last Saltmakers of Nexquipayac, Mexico: An Archaeological Ethnography*. Anthropological Papers, no. 92. Museum of Anthropology, University of Michigan. Ann Arbor.

Parsons, J.R., E. Brumfiel, M. Parsons, and D. Wilson
1982   *Prehispanic Settlement Patterns in the Southern Valley of Mexico: The Chalco-Xochimilco Region*. Memoirs, no. 14. Museum of Anthropology, University of Michigan. Ann Arbor.

Parsons, J.R., K. Kintigh, and S. Gregg
1983   *Archaeological Settlement Pattern Data for the Chalco, Xochimilco, Ixtapalapa, Texcoco, and Zumpango Regions, Mexico*. Technical Reports, no. 14. Museum of Anthropology, University of Michigan. Ann Arbor.

Parsons, J., and L. Morett
2004a   Recursos aquáticos en la subsistencia Azteca: cazadores, pescadores, y recolectores. *Arqueología Mexicana* 12(68):38-43.

2004b   *Reconocimiento Arqueológico del Lago Texcoco, Cuenca de Mexico: Informe Preliminar de la Temporada de 2003 (20 de mayo-1 de agosto)*. Report submitted to Instituto Nacional de Antropología e História, México, D.F.

2005   La economía aquática en el Valle de México: Perspectivas arqueológicas, históricas, y etnográficas. In *Etnoarqueología en Mesoamérica: El contexto dinánuca de la cultura material a través del tiempo*, edited by E. Williams, pp. 127-63. Colegio de Michoacan, Zamora, Michoacán, Mexico.

Parsons, J., and M. Parsons
1990   *Maguey Utilization in Highland Central Mexico: An Archaeological Ethnography*. Anthropological Papers, no. 82. Museum of Anthropology, University of Michigan. Ann Arbor.

Parsons, J., M. Parsons, V. Popper, and M. Taft
1985   Chinampa agriculture and Aztec urbanization in the Valley of Mexico. In *Prehistoric Intensive Agriculture in the Tropics*, edited by I. Farrington, pp. 49-96. B.A.R. International Series No. 232, Oxford.

Paso y Troncoso, F. del
1905   *Papeles de la Nueva Espana*. 6 vols. Madrid: Estudio Tipográfico Sucesores de Rivadeneira.

Pauly, A.F.
1956   *Paulys Realencyclopädie der Classischen Altertumsvissenschaft. Supplementband VIII*. Stuttgart: Alfred Druckenmüller Verlag.

Payno, M.
1870 Bosques y arbolados. *Boletín de la Sociedad de Geografía y Estadística de la República Mexicana*, segunda época, 2:77-91. México.

Pellicer, Carlos (editor)
1970 *José María Velasco: Pinturas Dibujos Acuarelas.* México, D.F.: Fondo Editorial de la Plástica Mexicana.

Pennington, J.
1998 *Bowes and Church's Food Values of Portions Commonly Used*, 17th ed. Philadelphia: Lippincott, Williams, and Wilkins.

Peñafiel, A.
1884 *Memoria sobre las Aguas Potables de la Capital de México.* México: Oficina Tipográfica de la Secretaría de Fomento.

Pérez, J.
1985 La pesca en el medio lacustre y chinampero de San Luis Tlaxialtemalco. *Cuadernos de la Casa Chata* 116:113-29. México, D.F.: Museo Nacional de Culturas Populares.

Peterson, J.T.
1981 Game, farming, and interethnic relations in northeastern Luzon, Philippines. *Human Ecology* 9:1-22.

Phillips, C.A.
2002 *Neglected Artifacts: A Study of Re-Worked Ceramic Sherds from the Lake Patzcuaro Basin, Mexico.* Master's thesis, Dept. of Anthropology, Michigan State University. East Lansing.

Pick, J., and E. Butler
2000 *Mexico Megacity.* Boulder: Westview Press.

Pomar, Juan de
1891 [1582] Relación de Texcoco. In *Nueva Colección de Documentos para la História de México*, edited by J. García Icazbalceta, pp. 1-64. México: Editorial Salvador Chavez Hayhoe.

Posey, D.A.
1978 Ethnoentomological survey of Amerind groups in lowland Latin America. *Florida Entomologist* 61:225-29.

Posnansky, A.
1932 Los Urus o Uchumi. In *Actas y Trabajos del XXV Congreso Internacional de Americanistas* 1:235-300. La Plata, Argentina.

Pourmaréde, D.J.
1859 Desagüe del Valle de México. *Boletín de la Sociedad Mexicana de Geografía y Estadística* 7(1):463-89. México: A. Boix.

Price, B.
1978   Demystification, enriddlement, and Aztec cannibalism: a materialist rejoinder to Harner. *American Ethnologist* 5:98-115.

Puleston, D.
1968   *Brosimum alicastrum as a Subsistence Alternative for the Classic Maya of the Central Southern Lowlands.* Master's thesis, Dept. of Anthropology, University of Pennsylvania. Philadelphia.
1973   *Ancient Maya Settlement Patterns and Environment at Tikal, Guatemala: Implications for Subsistence Models.* PhD dissertation, Dept. of Anthropology, University of Pennsylvania, Philadelphia. University Microfilms, Ann Arbor.
1978   Terracing, raised fields, and tree cropping in the Maya Lowlands: a new perspective of the geography of power. In *Prehistoric Maya Agriculture*, edited by P. Harrison and B. Turner, pp. 225-46. Albuquerque: University of New Mexico Press.

Purdy, B. (editor)
2001   *Enduring Records: The Environmental and Cultural Heritage of Wetlands.* Oxford, U.K.: Oxbow Books.

Ramírez, Balthazar
1906 [1597]   Descripción del reino del Perú. In *Exposición de la Republica del Peru presentada al excmo. gobierno argentino en el juicio de límites con la Republica de Bolivia*, edited by Victor M. Martua, tomo 1, pp. 116-18. Barcelona: Impr. de Henrich y Comp.

Ramírez, J.F.
1976 [c. 1867]   *Memória acerca de las obras e inundaciones en la Cd. de México.* México, D.F.: Instituto Nacional de Antropología e História.
1902   Flora del Valle de México. *La Naturaleza*, segunda serie, tomo 3, nos. 9-10, pp. 696-706. México: Sociedad Mexicana de História Natural.

Ramos-Elorduy de Conconi, J.
1987   *Los Insectos como Fuente de Proteínas en el Futuro*, segunda edición. México, D.F.: Editorial Limusa.
1999   El consumo de insectos como un hábito ancestral. In *Chalchihuite: Homenaje a Doris Heyden*, edited by M. Rodriguez-Shadow and B. Barba de Piña Chan, pp. 275-305. México, D.F.: Instituto Nacional de Antropología e História.

Ramos-Elorduy, J., H. Bourges, and J. Pino
1982   Valor nutritivo y calidad de la proteína de algunos insectos comestibles de México. *Folia Entomológica Mexicana* 53:111-18. México, D.F.

Ramos-Elorduy, J., and J. Pino
1989   *Los Insectos Comestibles en el México Antiguo: Estudio Etnoentomológico.* México, D.F.: A.G.T. Editor.
1990   Contenido calórico de algunos insectos comestibles de México. *Revista de la Sociedad Química de México* 34(2):56-68.
1996   El consumo de insectos entre los aztecas. In *Conquista y Comida: Consequencias del Encuentro de dos Mundos*, edited by Janet Long, pp. 89-101. México, D.F.: Universidad Nacional Autónoma de México.

Raven, C., and R.G. Elston
1988   *Preliminary Investigations in Stillwater Marsh: Human Prehistory and Geo-Archaeology*, vols. 1 and 2. U.S. Fish and Wildlife Service, Region 1, Cultural Resource Series No. 1. Portland, Oregon.

Raven, C., R. Elston, and K. Katzer
1988   Site descriptions, stratigraphy, and cultural features. In *Preliminary Investigations in Stillwater Marsh: Human Prehistory and Geo-Archaeology*, vols. 1 and 2, edited by C. Raven and R. Elston, pp. 42-154. U.S. Fish and Wildlife Service, Region 1, Cultural Resource Series No. 1. Portland, Oregon.

Raymond, A.W., and Virginia M. Parks
1990   Archaeological sites exposed by recent flooding of Stillwater Marsh, Carson Desert, Churchill County, Nevada. In *Wetlands Adaptations in the Great Basin*, edited by J. Janetski and D. Madsen, pp. 33-61. Occasional Papers No. 1, Museum of Peoples and Cultures, Brigham Young University. Provo, Utah.

Reseau Mega-Tchad
1991   *L'Homme et le Milieu dans le Bassin du Lac Tchad.* Paris: ORSTOM.

Reyes, Vicente
1878   La ley de periodicidad de la lluvia en el valle de México. *Boletín de la Sociedad Mexicana de Geografía y Estadística*, 3a época, 4:314-19. México, D.F.

Richardson, M.
1979   Primary productivity values in freshwater wetlands. In *Wetland Functions and Values: The State of our Understanding*, edited by P. Greeson, J.R. Clark, and J.E. Clark, pp. 131-45. Minneapolis: American Water Resources Association.

Robb, J., and D. Van Hove
2003   Gardening, foraging, and herding: neolithic land use and social territories in southern Italy. *Antiquity* 77(296):241-54.

Rodríguez, A.B.
1944   *Guía Para Conocer las Plantas más Comúnes en el Bosque de Chapultepec.* Instituto de Biología, Folletos de Divulgación Científica No. 39, Universidad Nacional Autónoma de México, México, D.F.

Rojas Rabiela, T.
1985   *La Cosecha del Agua en la Cuenca de México.* Centro de Investigaciones y Estudios Superiores en Antropología Social, Cuadernos de la Casa Chata No. 116, Museo Nacional de Culturas Populares, México, D.F.
1991   Ecological and agricultural changes in the chinampas of Xochimilco-Chalco. In *Land and Politics in the Valley of Mexico: A Two Thousand Year Perspective*, edited by H.R. Harvey, pp. 17-42. Albuquerque: University of New Mexico Press.
2004   Las cuencas lacustres del altiplano central. *Arqueología Mexicana* 12(68):20-27.

Rojas Rabiela, T. (editor)
1983   *La Agricultura Chinampera: Compilación Histórica.* Texcoco, Mexico: Universidad Autónoma de Chapingo.

Rojas Rabiela, T., A. Rafael, K. Strauss, and J. Lameiras
1974   *Nuevas Noticias sobre las Obras Hidraúlicas Prehispánicas y Coloniales en el Valle de México.* México, D.F.: Instituto Nacional de Antropología e História.

Rojas Rabiela, T., E. Rea, and C. Medina (editors)
1999   *Vidas y Bienes Olvidados: Testamentos Indígenas Novohispanos. Vol. 1: Testamentos en Castellano del Siglo XVI y en Nahuatl y Castellano de Ocotelulco de los Siglos XVI y XVII.* México, D.F.: Centro de Investigaciones y Estudios Superiores en Antropología Social y Consejo Nacional de Ciencias y Tecnología.

Ronzio, R.A.
1997   *The Encyclopedia of Nutrition and Good Health.* New York: Facts on File.

Roush, Laura
2005   Xaltocán fish in the twentieth century: an ethnoarchaeological study. In *Production and Power at Postclassic Xaltocan*, edited by E.M. Brumfiel, pp. 247-53. Mexico City: Instituto Nacional de Antropología e História; Pittsburgh: University of Pittsburgh.

Rowe, J.
1980   An account of the shrines of ancient Cuzco. *Ñawpa Pacha* 17:2-80. Berkeley.

Ruddle, K.
1973   The human use of insects: examples from the Yukpa. *Biotropica* 5(2):94-101.

Rzedowski, J.
1957   Algunas asociaciones vegetales de los terrenos del Lago de Texcoco. *Boletín de la Sociedad Botánica de México* 21:19-33. México, D.F.
1988   *Vegetación de México.* México, D.F.: Editorial Limusa.

Saenz, C., and R. Posadas del Río
1978   Extracción y aprovechamiento del ahuahutle (Hemiptera: Corixidae) del Lago de Texcoco. *Folia Entomología Mexicana* 39-40:129-30. México, D.F.

Sahagun, Fray Bernardino de
1963   *Florentine Codex: General History of the Things of New Spain. Book 11: Earthly Things*, translated and edited by C.E. Dibble and A.J. Anderson. Monographs of the School of American Research and the Museum of New Mexico, Santa Fe. Salt Lake City: University of Utah Press.
1969   *História General de las Cosas de Nueva España.* 4 vols. México, D.F.: Editorial Porrua.
1970   *Florentine Codex: General History of the Things of New Spain. Book 1: The Gods*, translated and edited by C.E. Dibble and A.J. Anderson. Monographs of the School of American Research and the Museum of New Mexico, Santa Fe. Salt Lake City: University of Utah Press.
1979   *Florentine Codex: General History of the Things of New Spain. Book 8: Kings and Lords*, translated and edited by C.E. Dibble and A.J. Anderson. Monographs of the School of American Research and the Museum of New Mexico, Santa Fe. Salt Lake City: University of Utah Press.
1981   *Florentine Codex: General History of the Things of New Spain. Book 2: The Ceremonies*, translated and edited by C.E. Dibble and A.J. Anderson. Monographs of the School of

American Research and the Museum of New Mexico, Santa Fe. Salt Lake City: University of Utah Press.
1982 *História General de las Cosas de Nueva España.* 3 vols. México, D.F.: Editorial Robredo.

Salim, Shakir Mustafa
1962 *Marsh Dwellers of the Euphrates Delta.* London School of Economics, Monographs on Social Anthropology, No. 23. London: The Athlone Press.

Sámano, A.
1934 Contribución al conocimiento de las algas verdes de los lagos del Valle de México. *Anales del Instituto de Biología, Universidad Nacional Autónoma de México* 5:149-60. México, D.F.
1940 Algas del Valle de México, Parte II. *Anales del Instituto de Biología, Universidad Nacional Autónoma de México* 11:41-50. México, D.F.

Sanchez, O.
1968 *La Flora del Valle de México.* México, D.F.: Editorial Herrero.

Sanders, W.
1957 *Tierra y Agua (Land and Water): A Study of the Ecological Processes in the Development of Civilization.* PhD dissertation, Dept. of Anthropology, Harvard University, Cambridge.
1976 *Final Field Report: Cuauhtitlan-Temascalapa Survey Project.* Report to Instituto Nacional de Antropología e História, México, D.F. Dept. of Anthropology, Pennsylvania State University. University Park, PA.

Sanders, W., J. Parsons, and R. Santley
1979 *The Basin of Mexico: Ecological Processes in the Evolution of a Civilization.* New York: Academic Press.

Santamaría, M.
1993 [1912] Las chinampas del Districto Federal. In *La Agricultura Chinampera, Compilación Histórica,* edited by T. Rojas, pp. 43-76. Texcoco, Mexico: Universidad Autónoma de Chapingo.

Santley, R.
1977 *Intra-Site Settlement Patterns at Loma Torremote and their Relationship to Formative Prehistory in the Cuauhtitlan Region, State of Mexico.* PhD dissertation, Pennsylvania State University, University Park. University Microfilms, Ann Arbor.

Santley, R., and E. Rose
1979 Diet, nutrition, and population dynamics in the Basin of Mexico. *World Archaeology* 11:185-207.

Sauer, C.
1962 Seashore – primitive home of man? *Proceedings of the American Philosophical Society* 106(1):41-47. Reprinted 1963 in *Land and Life: A Selection from the Writings of C.O. Sauer,* edited by J. Leighly, pp. 300-312. Berkeley and Los Angeles: University of California Press.

Schilling, E.
1983 [1938] Los 'jardines flotantes' de Xochimilco. In *La Agricultura Chinampera: Compi-lación Histórica*, edited by T. Rojas, pp. 71-98. Texcoco, Mexico: Universidad Autóno-ma de Chapingo.

Schmidt, D.N.
1988   Some observations on vertebrate taxonomy and site formational processes in Stillwater Marsh. In *Preliminary Investigations in Stillwater Marsh: Human Prehistory and Geo-archaeology*, edited by C. Raven and R. Elston, vol. 2, pp. 359-71. Silver City, Nevada: Intermontane Research Reports.

Schoeninger, M.
1995   Chapter 7: Dietary reconstruction in the prehistoric Carson Desert: stable carbon and ni-trogen isotopic analysis. In *Bioarchaeology of the Stillwater Marsh: Prehistoric Human Adaptation in the Western Great Basin*, edited by C. Larson and R. Kelly, pp. 96-106. Anthropological Papers of the American Museum of Natural History, no. 77. New York.

Schull, W.J.
1990   *The Aymara: Strategies in Human Adaptation to a Rigorous Environment*. Dordrecht, The Netherlands.

Serra, M.C.
1980   La unidad habitacional en Terremote Tlaltenco, D.F.: un analisis de distribución espacial para definir áreas de actividad, primera parte. *Anales de Antropología* 17(1):167-86.
1982   Un análisis de distribución espacial para definir áreas de actividad. La cerámica. Segunda parte. *Anales de Antropología* 19:9-20. México, D.F.
1988   *Los Recursos Lacustres de la Cuenca de México durante el Formativo*. Instituto de In-vestigaciones Antropológicas, Universidad Nacional Autónoma de México, México, D.F.

Serra, M., and M. Civera
1982   Entierros en un sitio Formativo del sur de la Cuenca de México. *Anales de Antropología* 19:55-91. México, D.F.

Serra, M., and R. Valadez
1985   Fauna de la localidad de Terremote, Tlaltenco, D.F. *Anales de Antropología* 22:159-213.

Seurat, L.G.
1900   Sobre la fauna de los lagos y lagunas del Valle de México. *La Naturaleza*, segunda serie, tomo 3, nos. 5-6, pp. 403-6. México: Sociedad Mexicana de História Natural.

Sherbondy, J.
1982   El regadio, los lagos y los mitos de origen. *Allpanchis* 20(17):3-32. Cuzco.

Siemens, A.
1998   *A Favored Place: San Juan River Wetlands, Central Veracruz, A.D. 500 to the Present*. Austin: University of Texas Press.

Siemens, A., and D. Puleston
1972   Ridged fields and associated features in southern Campeche: new perspectives on the Lowland Maya. *American Antiquity* 37(2):228-39.

Simmonds, P.
2001 [1859] *The Curiosities of Food, or the Dainties and Delicacies of Different Nations Obtained from the Animal Kingdom*. Berkeley: Ten Speed Press.

Simms, S.R.
1984 *Aboriginal Great Basin Foraging Strategies: An Evolutionary Analysis*. PhD dissertation, University of Utah, Salt Lake City. University Microfilms, Ann Arbor.
1985 Acquisition cost and nutritional data on Great Basin resources. *Journal of California and Great Basin Anthropology* 7:117-25.

Sluyter, A.
1994 Intensive wetland agriculture in Mesoamerica: space, time and form. *Annals of the Association of American Geographers* 84(4):557-84.

Smith, C.E., and P. Tolstoy
1981 Vegetation and man in the Basin of Mexico. *Economic Botany* 35:415-33.

Smith, H., and R. Smith
1971 *Synopsis of the Herpetofauna of Mexico. Vol. 1: Analysis of the Literature on the Mexican Axolotl*. Augusta, West Virginia: Eric Lundberg.

Solis, Antonio de
1704 *História de la Conquista de México*. Brussels: Francisco Foppens.

Southwood, T.
1977 Entomology and mankind. *American Scientist* 65:30-39.

Squier, G.E.
1877 *Peru – Incidents of Travel and Exploration in the Land of the Incas*. New York: Harper & Brothers.

Starbuck, D.
1987 Faunal evidence for the Teotihuacan subsistence base. In *Teotihuacan: Nuevos Datos, Nuevas Síntesis, Nuevas Problemas*, edited by E. McClung de Tapia and E. Rattray, pp. 75-90. Instituto de Investigaciones Antropológicas, Universidad Nacional Autónoma de México, México, D.F.

Starr, F.
1900 *Notes Upon the Ethnography of Southern Mexico, Part 1*. Proceedings of the Davenport Academy of Sciences, vol. 8. Davenport.

Steward, J.H.
1933 *Ethnography of the Owens Valley Paiute*. University of California Publications in American Archaeology and Ethnology, vol. 33, no. 3. Berkeley.

Sugiura, Y.
1990 *El Epicásico y el Valle de Toluca: Un Estudio de Patrón de Asentamiento*. Tesis de doctorado, Universidad Nacional Autónoma de México, México, D.F.
1998 *La Caza, la Pesca, y la Recolección: Etnoarqueología del Modo de Subsistencia Lacustre en las Ciénegas del Alto Lerma*. Instituto de Investigaciones Antropológicas,

Universidad Nacional Autónoma de México, México, D.F.
2000   Cultura lacustre y sociedad del Valle de Toluca. *Arqueología Mexicana* 8(43):32-37.

Sugiura, Y., and E. McClung de Tapia
1988   Algunas consideraciones sobre el uso de recursos vegetales en la cuenca del Alto Lerma. *Anales de Antropología* 15:111-26. Instituto de Investigaciones Antropológicas, Universidad Nacional Autónoma de México, México, D.F.

Sugiura, Y., and M. Serra
1983   Notas sobre el modo de subsistencia lacustre: la laguna de Santa Cruz Atizapan, Estado de México. *Anales de Antropología* 10:9-25. Instituto de Investigaciones Antropológicas, Universidad Nacional Autónoma de México, México, D.F.

Sullivan, A.P.
1983   Storage, nonedible resource processing, and the interpretation of sherd and lithic scatters in the Sonoran Desert lowlands. *Journal of Field Archaeology* 10:309-23.

Sutton, J.E.
1974   The aquatic civilization of middle Africa. *Journal of African History* 15:527-46.

Sutton, M.Q.
1985   The California salmon fruit fly as a food resource in northeastern California. *Journal of California and Great Basin Anthropology* 7:176-82.
1988   *Insects as Food: Aboriginal Entomophagy in the Great Basin*. Ballena Press Anthropological Papers No. 33. Novato, California: Ballena Press.
1995   Archaeological aspects of insect use. *Journal of Archaeological Method and Theory* 2:253-98.

Taylor, R.L.
1975   *Butterflies in My Stomach: Insects in Human Evolution*. Santa Barbara, California: Woodbridge.

Terrell, J., J. Hart, S. Barut, N. Cellinese, A. Curet, T. Denham, C. Kusimba, K. Latinis, R. Oka, J. Pallka, M. Pohl, K. Pope, P. Williams, H. Haines, and J. Staller
2003   Domesticated landscapes: the subsistence ecology of plant and animal domestication. *Journal of Archaeological Method and Theory* 10(4):323-68.

Tesch, M., and R. Abascal
1974   Azadas. *Comunicaciones* 11:37-40. Puebla, México: Fundación Alemana para la Investigación Científica.

Tezozómoc, H.A.
1944 [c. 1598]   *Crónica Mexicana*. México, D.F.: Editorial Leyenda.

Thesiger, W.
1964   *The Marsh Arabs*. New York: E.P. Dutton & Co.
1979   *Desert, Mountain and Marsh: The World of a Nomad*. London: Collins.

Tichy, F.
1983   El patron de asentamiento con system radial en la meseta central de México: 'sistemas ceque.' *Jahrbuch für Geschichte von Staat, Wirtschaft und Gessellschaft Lateinamerikas* 20:61-84. Cologne.

Tolstoy, P.
1971   Utilitarian artifacts in central Mexico. In *Archaeology of Northern Mesoamerica, Pt. 1*, edited by G. Ekholm and I. Bernal, pp. 270-96. *Handbook of Middle American Indians, Vol. 10*, R. Wauchope, general editor. Austin: University of Texas Press.
1975   Settlement and population trends in the Basin of Mexico (Ixtapalapa and Zacatenco phases). *Journal of Field Archaeology* 2:331-49.

Tolstoy, P., S. Fish, M. Bokenbaum, and K. Vaughn
1977   Early sedentary communities of the Basin of Mexico. *Journal of Field Archaeology* 4:91-106.

Tolstoy, P., and L. Paradis
1970   Early and Middle Preclassic culture in the Basin of Mexico. *Science* 167:344-51.

Tortolero, A.
1993   Haciendas, pueblos y gobierno porfirista: los conflictos por el agua en la región de Chalco. In *Entre lagos y volcanes: Chalco-Amecameca, pasado y presente, Vol. 1.* Toluca: El Colegio Mexiquense.

Tricart, J.
1985   *Pro-Lagos: Los Lagos del Eje Neovolcánico de México.* Instituto de Geografía, Universidad Nacional Autónoma de México, México, D.F.

Tschopik, H.
1946   The Aymara. In *Handbook of South American Indians. Vol. 2: The Andean Civilizations*, edited by J. Steward, pp. 501-74. Smithsonian Institution, Bureau of American Ethnology Bulletin 143. Washington, D.C.

Tuohy, D.R.
1990   Pyramid Lake fishing: the archaeological record. In *Wetland Adaptations in the Great Basin*, edited by J. Janetski and D. Madsen, pp. 121-58. Occasional Papers No. 1, Museum of Peoples and Cultures, Brigham Young University. Provo, Utah.

Tveskov, M., and J. Erlandson
2003   The Haynes Inlet weirs: estuarine fishing and archaeological site visibility on the southern Cascadian coast. *Journal of Archaeological Science* 30:1023-35.

Tylor, E.B.
1861   *Anahuac: or, Mexico and the Mexicans, Ancient and Modern.* London: Longman, Green & Roberts.

United States Department of Agriculture (USDA)
2004   Natural Resources Conservation Service, U.S. Dept. of Agriculture, Washington, D.C. [http://plants.usda.gov/].

Urbina, M.
1904   Plantas comestibles de los antiguos Mexicanos. *Anales del Museo Nacional*, segunda época, 1:503-91, México.

Vacher, J., E. Brasier de Thuy, and M. Liberman
1992   Influence of the lake on littoral agriculture. In *Lake Titicaca: A Synthesis of Limnological Knowledge*, edited by C. Dejoux and A. Iltis, pp. 511-22. Dordrecht, The Netherlands: Kluwer Academic Publishers.

Vaillant, G.
1930   *Excavations at Zacatenco.* Anthropological Papers Vol. 32, No. 1, American Museum of Natural History. New York.
1931   *Excavations at Ticoman.* Anthropological Papers Vol. 32, No. 2, American Museum of Natural History. New York.
1935   *Excavations at El Arbolillo.* Anthropological Papers Vol. 35, No. 2, American Museum of Natural History. New York.

Velázquez de la Cadena, M., E. Gray, J. Iribas, I. Navarro, and R. Nelson
1993   *Inglés Sín Barreras: El Gran Diccionario Velázquez Español-Inglés.* Los Angeles: Lexicon School of Languages.

Vellard, J.
1952   Peuples pecheurs du Titicaca: Les Urus et leurs voisins. *Les Cahiers D'Outre-Mer* 5(18):135-48. Paris.
1992   Former lake fisheries and fish fauna of the lake. In *Lake Titicaca: A Synthesis of Limnological Knowledge*, edited by C. Dejoux and A. Iltis, pp. 495-99. Dordrecht, The Netherlands: Kluwer Academic Publishers.

Vetancurt, Fr. Agustin de
1971 [1698] *Teatro Mexicano: Descripción Breve de los Sucesos Ejemplares, Históricos y Religiosos del Nuevo Mundo de las Indias*, pp. 3-66. México, D.F.: Editorial Porrua.

Vierra, Juan de
1952 [1777] *Compendiosa Narración de la Ciudad de México*, edited by G. Obregón. México, D.F.: Editorial Guaranda.

Wachtel, N.
1986   Men of the water: the Uru problem (sixteenth and seventeenth centuries). In *Anthropological History of Andean Polities*, edited by J. Murra, N. Wachtel, and J. Revel, pp. 283-310. Cambridge: Cambridge University Press.

Ward, H.G.
1981 [1828] *Mexico en 1827*, translated by R. Haas. México, D.F.: Fondo de Cultura Económica.

Watts, W., and J. Bradbury
1982   Paleoecological studies at Lake Patzcuaro on the west-central Mexican Plateau and at Chalco in the Basin of Mexico. *Quaternary Research* 17:56-70.

Webster, A.
1993   *The Role of the Camelid in the Development of the Tiwanaku State.* PhD dissertation, University of Chicago. University Microfilms, Ann Arbor.

Webster, A., and J. Janusek
2003   Tiwanaku camelids: subsistence, sacrifice, and social reproduction. In *Tiwanaku and Its Hinterland: Archaeology and Paleoecology of an Andean Civilization*, vol. 2, edited by A. Kolata, pp. 343-62. Washington, D.C.: Smithsonian Institution Press.

Weller, M.W.
1981   *Freshwater Marshes: Ecology and Wildlife Management*. Minneapolis: University of Minnesota Press.

Went, A.
1946   Irish fishing weirs, I: notes on some ancient examples fished in tidal waters. *Journal of the Royal Society of Antiquaries of Ireland* 76:176-94.

West, R.C.
1948   *Cultural Geography of the Modern Tarascan Area*. Smithsonian Institution, Institute of Social Anthropology, Publication No. 7. Washington, D.C.

West, R., and P. Armillas
1950   Las chinampas de México: Poesía y realidad de los 'jardines flotantes.' *Cuadernos Americanos* 2(50):165-82.

Wetterstrom, W.
1993   Foraging and farming in Egypt: the transition from hunting and gathering in the Nile Valley. In *The Archaeology of Africa: Foods, Metals, and Towns*, edited by T. Shaw, P. Sinclair, B. Andah, and A. Okpoko, pp. 165-226. London: Routledge.

Wheat, M.M.
1959   *Notes on Paviotso Material Culture*. Anthropological Papers No. 1, Nevada State Museum. Carson City.
1967   *Survival Arts of the Primitive Paiutes*. Reno: University of Nevada Press.

Whitmore, T., and B. Turner II
2002   *Cultivated Landscapes of Middle America on the Eve of Conquest*. Oxford: Oxford University Press.

Whitmore, T., and B. Williams
1998   Famine vulnerability in the contact-era Basin of Mexico. *Ancient Mesoamerica* 9:83-98.

Wilke, P.J.
1978   *Late Prehistoric Human Ecology at Lake Cahuilla, Coachella Valley, California*. Contributions of the University of California Archaeological Research Facility, no. 38. Berkeley.

Wilke, P.J., and H.W. Lawton
1976   *The Expedition of Captain J.W. Davidson from Fort Tejon to the Owens Valley in 1859*. Ballena Press Publications in Archaeology, Ethnology, and History, no. 8. Novato, California.

Wilken, G.
1970   The ecology of gathering in a Mexican farming region. *Economic Botany* 24(3):286-95.

Williams, B.
1989   Contact period rural over-population in the Basin of Mexico: carrying-capacity models tested with documentary data. *American Antiquity* 54:715-32.

Williams, E.
2005   La pesca, la caza y la recolección en el Lago de Cuitzeo, Michoacán: rescate etnográfico e implicaciones arqueológicas. In *Etnoarqueología en Mesoaméric: El contexto dinánuca de la cultura material a través del tiempo*, edited by E. Williams, pp. 127-63. Colegio de Michoacan, Zamora, Michoacán, Mexico.

Williams, M.
1990   Understanding wetlands. In *Wetlands, A Threatened Landscape*, edited by M. Williams, pp. 1-41. Oxford: Basil Blackwell.

Wise, K.
1993   Late Intermediate Period architecture of Lukurmata. In *Domestic Architecture, Ethnicity, and Complementarity in the South-Central Andes*, edited by M. Aldenderfer, pp. 103-13. Iowa City: University of Iowa Press.

Worthington, E.B.
1933   Primitive craft of the central African lakes. *The Mariner's Mirror* 19:146-63.

Author Index